BEHIND THE MESSAGE

Information Strategies
for Communicators

KATHLEEN A. HANSEN
University of Minnesota

NORA PAUL
University of Minnesota

PEARSON

Boston ■ New York ■ San Francisco
Mexico City ■ Montreal ■ Toronto ■ London ■ Madrid ■ Munich ■ Paris
Hong Kong ■ Singapore ■ Tokyo ■ Cape Town ■ Sydney

Series Editor: *Molly Taylor*
Series Editorial Assistant: *Michael Kish*
Marketing Manager: *Mandee Eckersley*
Editorial Production Administrator: *Anna Socrates*
Editorial-Production Service: *Omegatype Typography, Inc.*
Manufacturing Buyer: *JoAnne Sweeney*
Composition and Prepress Buyer: *Linda Cox*
Cover Administrator: *Kristina Mose-Libon*
Electronic Composition: *Omegatype Typography, Inc.*

For related titles and support materials, visit our online catalog at www.ablongman.com.

Between the time Website information is gathered and then published, it is not unusual for some sites to have closed. Also, the transcription of URLs can result in typographical errors. The publisher would appreciate notification where these errors occur so that they may be corrected in subsequent editions.

Library of Congress Cataloging-in-Publication Data

Hansen, Kathleen A.
    Behind the message : information strategies for communicators / Kathleen A. Hansen, Nora Paul.
        p.   cm.
    ISBN 0-205-38680-6 (alk. paper)
      1. Mass media—Research—Methodology.   2. Communication—Research—Methodology.
    I. Paul, Nora.   II. Title.

P91.3.H365 2004
302.23'07'2—dc21

                                                                    2003041901

Printed in the United States of America

10   9   8   7   6   5   4   3   2   1   [HAM]   08   07   06   05   04   03

To my students over the years
from whom I've learned so much
  —Kathy

To my boys, always
  —Nora

CONTENTS

CHAPTER ELEVEN
Evaluating and Selecting the Information You've Gathered   233

CHAPTER TWELVE
Synthesizing Information   259

CHAPTER THIRTEEN
Law and Ethics of Gathering and Using Information   270

PREFACE

We are pleased to introduce what we are calling the "successor edition" to the three editions of *Search Strategies in Mass Communication* by Jean Ward and Kathleen A. Hansen. Since 1987, when the first edition of *Search Strategies* appeared, there has been a revolution in the information gathering landscape where mass communication professionals live. This revolution was reflected in the three editions of *Search Strategies* and was equally reflected in the curriculum and teaching methods employed by schools of journalism and mass communication to help students master the information process in their respective fields of professional focus. Professional communicators also found the information process outlined in *Search Strategies* of great value in their day-to-day work.

Jean Ward has retired from the University of Minnesota, but her legacy of curriculum innovation and intellectual leadership continues to influence educators and students through the wide adoption of information gathering courses and approaches in journalism schools across the country. We are deeply indebted to Jean's creativity, foresight and amazing energy, and fully acknowledge her influence on this new work.

This new book retains the conceptual framework of the information gathering and evaluation process from *Search Strategies*, but updates and refines the model and reorganizes much of the content. In addition, this new book reflects the most current thinking about the means and methods of information gathering and analysis for all sorts of messages. Between the two of us, we have more than fifty years of accumulated expertise and experience in professionally practicing, researching, and writing about the information process as it applies to mass communication work. This book incorporates our best thinking on the subject.

The new subtitle reflects a subtle but important shift in our approach, as well. The book no longer treats just the search strategy, but places the overall model into an **information strategy** framework. Searching continues to be an important part of the process, but there are many other methods of information gathering; the processes of message analysis and information selection, evaluation, and synthesis are also acknowledged with the new subtitle.

In this age of "media convergence," the original book's strategy of treating the information needs of all mass communicators from a common perspective now seems so obvious as to be cliché. However, it has never been so clear that this "generic" approach to communicators' information strategies is the right way to address the topic. Hence, this book continues to argue that students and professional communicators in various media industries may use information in many ways, but a common information strategy process allows all of them to proceed securely in developing an information gathering and evaluation strategy. For example, a news reporter, an advertising copywriter, and a public relations specialist may require the same census figure on the percentage of the American population over 50 years of age. The subsequent use of this information by these media professionals will vary, but the process for getting the information is the same. The model also applies to the search process for academic and scholarly work.

This book introduces several new features and content. Chapter 1 introduces the information universe that communicators now face, and incorporates new material that helps readers understand the types of media messages and types of message delivery formats that affect the information strategy in the journalism and strategic communications industries.

Chapter 2 highlights the information strategy model that forms the conceptual framework for the book as a whole. Those familiar with the *Search Strategies* books will recognize that the model has been revised to reflect the new focus on information strategies rather than simply on the search process. The process of analyzing both the context and the content of the message assignment is reflected in the "message analysis" step of the model, treated in Chapter 3. The contributors to the information strategy process are handled in several ways. Chapter 4 introduces four sources of information for communicators (informal, institutional, scholarly, and journalistic sources). Chapter 4 also introduces the concept that information may be available from people, paper, or digital contributors. Chapter 5 introduces the three major methods for gathering information: monitoring, searching, and interviewing. The crucial role that the library plays in any information strategy is reflected in the fact that Chapter 6 is devoted entirely to a discussion of the library as an information source.

Chapters 7 through 10 use a common organization scheme. Informal, institutional, scholarly, and journalistic sources are described in depth, and the major means for tapping into these contributors are discussed. Each of these contributor chapters also includes a discussion of the cautions for communicators in using materials from these sources. A significant feature of each of the contributor chapters is a case study example that provides readers with practical insight into the ways that communicators have used information from these sources. The case example in Chapter 7 reflects an advertising perspective. The Chapter 8 case example reflects a newspaper journalism focus. Chapter 9 includes a magazine journalism case example. The case example for Chapter 10 focuses on a public relations issue.

Chapter 11 discusses the critical thinking and information evaluation skills that are necessary for any message creator in the current age. Means for evaluating statistical claims and survey data, and strategies for evaluating information from online sources, are covered in depth. The difficult process of synthesizing information and deciding what it all means is the focus of Chapter 12. The final chapter reviews the social responsibility context within which information gathering and evaluation takes place.

Another major feature of the book is the focus of the appendix case study, which follows the information strategy process from beginning to end. The case study reproduces the entire text of a major, page-one news story, identifies the sources of information that contributed to every paragraph, and suggests several access points a reporter might use to locate those sources. The case study was a significant feature of the third edition of *Search Strategies* and proved to be such a valuable teaching tool that we have retained it for this new book. However, because the exemplar story was researched and written before wide adoption of the Internet as a reporting tool, the case study outlines the ways this real-world example might have played out differently if the reporter had access to the sorts of materials now easily accessible through the World Wide Web. In addition, we have provided a guide for readers with a strategic communications focus to understand how the information process outlined in the case study relates to their work as well.

This book continues to offer the "Topical Tool Index" and the "General Index" features that allow communicators to use the book as a desk reference for help with solutions to information problems. Many communications professionals have told us how valuable the *Search Strategies* books were for their day-to-day work and we have designed the indexes in this new book to meet that need.

Readers will also find extensive sidebars and examples throughout each chapter. These materials illustrate concepts or practices introduced by the information strategy model, or provide examples of the types of sources, tools, or resources that are most valuable for journalism and strategic communications practitioners.

The process approach to finding and evaluating information for mass communication has been tested as a teaching strategy for twenty years at the University of Minnesota. Thousands of students have learned to follow the information strategy process and have successfully applied these principles in their academic and mass communication work. We are grateful to them, and for the enthusiasm of faculty colleagues from around the country who recognized the importance of information studies in the mass communication curriculum and developed new courses for their programs. Their feedback and suggestions for ways to improve and update the approach and the model have been most helpful. We would like to thank the reviewers of this book: Rebecca J. Johnson, Marshall University; Stephen Ponder, University of Oregon; Bruce Renfro, Southwest Texas State University; and Leonard F. Strazewski, Columbia College Chicago.

Among many other debts of gratitude, one of the most significant for this new book is to University of Minnesota graduate student Betsy Neibergall, who served as the research assistant for the project and as a major resource for many of the strategic communications examples in the book. Betsy's work is most significantly represented in the appendix case example revision to incorporate Internet materials, but her suggestions and comments on all the drafts of the book as it took shape have helped ensure that we have treated the strategic communications aspects of the topic in full measure.

We are also grateful to Allyn and Bacon editor Molly Taylor and editorial assistant Michael Kish, and to production manager Amelia Bowen at Omegatype. It is always daunting to consider making huge changes in something that has worked for years. The Allyn and Bacon staff understood what we were proposing to do and encouraged us to take chances in accomplishing our goal. We are confident that this new approach retains the best of the "old," while significantly enhancing and expanding the coverage and treatment of this crucial process for mass communication scholarly and professional practice.

K. A. H.
N. P.

CHAPTER ONE

INFORMATION UNIVERSE—
INTRODUCTION

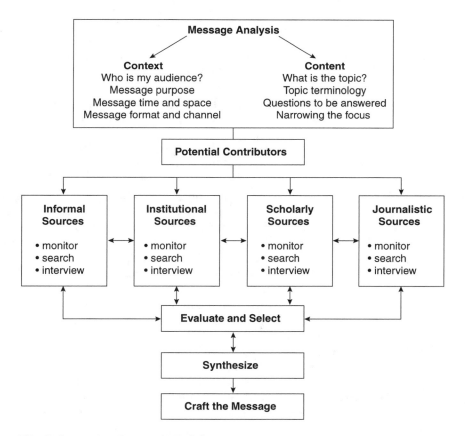

The Information Strategy Model

We live in a world of information riches and communications access unimaginable even a decade ago. We can instantly contact a friend half way around the world. We can find articles from magazines long missing from the library's shelves. We can read the opinions of columnists in newspapers outside our circulation area. We can hear songs long absent from radio playlists. Annual reports of businesses, minutes of meetings, documents from government agencies, short stories by high schoolers, recipes from chefs, sports scores from obscure matches, catalogs from distant stores, weather forecasts, economic trends, health statistics, movie reviews—all are only as far away as our keyboards. It is this information universe, vast and complicated, that we intend to guide you through.

As a communicator, you must also know how to use the non-digital information that pre-existed the digital and now co-exists with it. Paper documents, non-Internet accessible databases, human sources, polls and surveys, original research reports, and printed books are all essential sources to the communications researcher. We will describe their importance and use relative to online information to give you a holistic picture of the current world of information. We will focus on navigating the information universe for the purposes of communications message creation, but the information you find in this book will help you in all your information seeking needs.

Everyone has heard of the Big Bang theory of the creation of the universe, which posits that "10 to 20 billion years ago a highly concentrated mass of gaseous matter at a single point in space underwent a gigantic explosion (the big bang). The universe then began to expand away from this point of explosion."[1]

In the world of information, the Big Bang was the introduction of the hypertext transfer protocol (http) and the World Wide Web. The Internet, the vast network of networks that is the distribution means for transferring information from one computer to another, had existed for decades but was exclusively available to academics and government researchers and scientists. When access to the Internet became publicly available and the protocol for easy creation of documents to transfer through the network was created, the universe of information began to expand away from this point of explosion. The World Wide Web made it possible to access information in computer files around the world

Before the Big Bang that created the information universe we currently inhabit, there were islands of information that had to be navigated separately. Information was found in libraries and databases, in press releases and market research reports, in file cabinets and in people's heads. There had been electronic information sources; bibliographic and full-text databases had been around for decades, but they were in separate collections for which access had to be individually negotiated. There were the beginnings of networked communications and file access with the development of electronic bulletin board services and gopher which indexed individual files on networked computers.

The introduction of the World Wide Web simplified access to collections of articles, documents, and data that had previously been sitting in computerized information outposts all over the world. The development of browser software that could decipher hypertext documents and facilitate file transfers from one computer server to another created an explosion of information access for anyone with a computer, a modem, and a way to get on the Web. A study in 2000 ("How Much Information") by researchers at the University of California at Berkeley in the School of Information Management and Systems reported the size of both the "surface" Web and the "deep" Web. They estimate the surface Web consists of approximately 2.5 billion documents and grows at a rate of 7.3 million pages a day, and the deep Web has 550 billion documents. Truly this represents an information explosion that continues to accelerate.[2] Figure 1.1 shows the growth graphically.

Since 1995, the World Wide Web, the Internet, and networked communications have changed the way researchers do their work. It is one of those "good news/bad news" situations with which life is fraught. The good news is that there is better, faster, more comprehensive access to information than at any time in the history of the world. This access has moved us from the Industrial Age to the Information Age and from a manufacturing economy to an information economy. The bad news is that there is better, faster, more comprehensive access to information than at any time in the history of the world—and it can be overwhelming. What can be worse than not enough choices? Too many choices! And that is what communications researchers and messages creators are dealing with—an abundance of information options.

When a simple Google (www.google.com) search will list dozens of places where you can get statistics about cancer mortality—how do you select which one to use? When a search on a word that the old library catalog would have led to seven books now leads to thousands of resources—how do you begin to sort through them? The skills of question formation and source evaluation have never been more important.

Despite much change, information remains the foundation for expression. Messages consist of information and expression. *Expression* is the arrangement of words

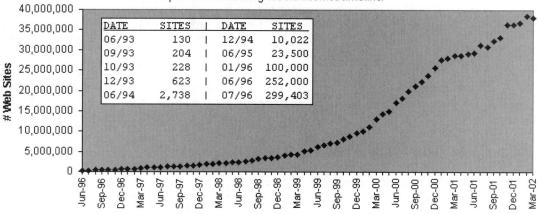

FIGURE 1.1 Growth of the Internet.

Source: Robert H Zakon. Reprinted by permission.

and images that sends the information to the audience, whereas *information* consists of the facts and ideas on which the expression rests. Figure 1.2 provides a good example of the difference.

Obviously, a message is no better than the information in it. Becoming a savvy information consumer is an increasingly critical skill. This book will help you hone your ability to frame and pose interesting questions as the starting point for message creation. The information strategy outlined in this book will also help you develop your selection and evaluation abilities.

EXPANDING/FRAGMENTING UNIVERSE

As the proliferation of information delivery options continues—wireless handheld information appliances, wired cars, personalized information/entertainment capture machines, shaving mirrors that have a scrolling bar with news headlines displayed—communicators will become more stuck in the information morass. This ubiquitous information environment will also be a good news/bad news situation. Although access to what you want and what you need in terms of information becomes increasingly customizable, it also becomes more fragmented. The Internet and the World Wide Web can be seen as the big shopping carts of information, but as the number of dispensaries and information repositories increases, it will become more challenging to manage and maintain your information stockpile. This is indicative of the move away from the notion of mass media and mass audience to a world of niche information and specialized interest groups.

So, another skill that will be essential to information seekers and users (along with question formation and source evaluation skills) will be information management. A key management task is knowing when to use particular sources and methods to meet the audience's need for information. The old sources of information—libraries, archives, public records, microfilms, human beings—are still there and still need to be used, in some cases. But the pace of technological change and the vast number of choices to meet a specific information need call for new skills and new conceptual approaches to message making.

To fully understand how messages and information are inextricably linked in this new information environment, we need to review some of the basis characteristics of mass communication messages and mass media audiences.

TYPES OF MEDIA MESSAGES

Messages may inform, educate, entertain, persuade—or all of these. Let's examine the types of media messages for which information is selected and evaluated. You, as a communicator, may be responsible for crafting different types of messages; it is important for you to understand the different information needs of different kinds of messages.

FIGURE 1.2 This institutional advertisement is a good example of *information* and *expression*. The informational components used are the nutritional facts about papaya and the effects of viruses on Hawaiian farming. The way these facts are conveyed, using a compelling photo, copy fonts, arrangement, and logo, represents the "expression" component of the ad.

Courtesy of the Council for Biotechnology Information.

News

The story goes something like this: The young journalist asks the old hand for the definition of *news*. The old hand replies, "I can't define it, but I know it when I see it." Textbooks include the usual list of definitions: news is unusual, news is change, news has impact, news is interesting, news is timely, news is nearby, news is information, news is conflict, news is about people, news is surprising. This will do for our purposes. But there are many types of news stories, and they have different standards for the information they contain and the information that you would need in order to craft that message.

1. *Straight, hard news.* This is sometimes also called the objective report. The story consists of a timely account of an event, with a tight focus and limited demand on the communicator's information skills. Reporters show up, use their senses to cover the event, go back to the newsroom, and prepare the report of what happened.

2. *Depth report.* This is a step beyond straight news. For a depth report, the communicator collects and includes additional information that is independent of the event but related to it. For instance, in a story about the announcement of a new device for purifying water in developing countries, the reporter would include background information about the device's manufacturer and the countries where the device might be most useful. The communicator is transmitting information, not opinion. The depth report consists of verifiable fact, just as in straight news.

3. *Analysis or interpretive report.* The focus here is on an issue, problem, or controversy. The substance of the interpretive report is still verifiable fact, not opinion. But instead of presenting facts as in straight news or a depth report and hoping the facts speak for themselves, the interpretive reporter clarifies, explains, analyzes. The report usually focuses on *why* something has happened or not happened. The information requirements are greater for the interpretive report, due to the need to clarify and explain rather than simply narrate.

4. *Investigative report.* The goal of the investigative report is opening closed doors and closed mouths. The focus is on problems, issues, controversies. The effort is on unearthing hidden or previously unorganized information in order to clarify, explain, and analyze something. For example, a news organization might search a government database that lists aircraft license holders and another database that lists convictions for drunk driving in that community. By comparing information in the two databases, the investigative reporter might uncover instances of aircraft pilots who have lost their driving privileges yet who continue to fly. The investigative report requires the communicator to have a high level of information sophistication, and the ability to convey complex information in a straightforward way for the audience.

5. *Feature.* The feature primarily differs from the other types of news reports in intent. The four types we've discussed so far seek to inform the audience. Features are designed to capture audience interest. The feature story depends on style, grace, and humor as much as the information it contains. There are several types of features:

- *News.* A story about a man who used cardiopulmonary resuscitation (CPR) to revive a pet dog rescued from the bottom of a pool might be reported as a news feature. It is based on an event, but covered as a feature, with more emphasis on the drama of the event than on the information about how to do CPR on a dog.

- *Personality sketch or profile.* A story about the accomplishments, attitudes, and characteristics of an individual seeks to capture the essence of a person. Personality features are usually accompanied by photos. The communicator needs a well-honed skill for noticing details and focusing on what makes the person interesting.
- *Informative.* A sidebar to accompany a main news story might be written as an informative feature. For example, a space flight story might be accompanied by an informative feature that describes how astronauts prepare food while in weightless conditions. The reporter has to have a good command of (sometimes) technical information to convey the story to the audience.
- *Historical.* Holidays are usually the spur for this type of piece, with focus on the history of the Christmas tree, the first Thanksgiving dinner, and so on. Features about the anniversary of the founding of an important local business or the celebration of statehood could also be created from background information generated by the curious communicator. Such reports obviously require extensive historical information.
- *Descriptive.* Many features are about places people can visit, or events they can take part in or enjoy. Tourist spots, historical sites, recreational areas, and festivals all generate reams of feature story copy, pictures, and video. Much of the background information in descriptive features is generated by public relations specialists. The challenge is to find a fresh way of providing the information to the audience.
- *How-To.* Some features are created to provide information such as how to improve your golf game, become a power shopper, or install your own shower tile. The communicator needs a solid grasp of the subject matter to do a respectable job with this type of piece. The information in how-to features must be descriptive, specific, and very clearly communicated.
- *Advertising features.* This form is becoming more common. Many magazines carry inserts that look like a feature piece but are actually generated by an advertiser or a public relations firm. For example, in a newsweekly magazine you might find an insert about living a healthy lifestyle, with articles and photographs, sponsored by a pharmaceutical company. *The New York Times* regularly carries advertising features sponsored by countries seeking to improve their image and generate business contacts and investment.

6. *Opinion writing.* This category includes editorials, columns, and reviews. Opinion pieces are characterized by the presentation of facts and opinion to entertain and influence the audience. Nonetheless, they still require correlation and analysis of information. Because their purpose is persuasion, opinion pieces must contain clear, detailed information and make logical and understandable arguments in support of the point of view being espoused.

- *Editorials.* The editorial is a reflection of management's attitude rather than a reporter's or editor's personal view. Most editorials are unsigned and run on a specific page of the newspaper or during a particular time of the broadcast. Editorials usually seek to do one of three things: commend or condemn an act, persuade the audience to a particular point of view, or entertain and amuse the audience. The information in an editorial must be stated as evidence for the position that is being taken.

- *Columns.* A column includes the personal opinions of the writer on the state of the community and the world. Many columns are written by syndicated, national writers, but local commentators and columnists also have a following in their communities. Columnists use information selectively, based on their point of view and the argument they are making.
- *Reviews.* Reviewers make informed judgments about the content and quality of something presented to the public—books, films, theater, television programs, concerts, recorded music, art exhibits, restaurants. A reviewer's responsibility is to report and evaluate on behalf of the audience. The information must be descriptive as well as evaluative. The reviewer describes the concert and then evaluates the quality of the performance.

All of these types of news reports share the common characteristics of accuracy, verifiability, clarity of writing, and solid presentation of information. However, the specific information requirements and the ultimate intent for each type of report shape the process by which each message is created.

Advertising

Advertising is defined as a paid form of nonpersonal communication from an identified sponsor using mass media to persuade or influence an audience.[3] Because there are so many diverse advertisers attempting to reach different types of audiences with their persuasive messages, many forms of advertising have developed. We will discuss eight types.

1. *Brand or national consumer advertising.* This advertising emphasizes brand identity and image. Brand advertising is actually a limited and unrepresentative part of the U.S. advertising industry, but it is very visible and thus highly influential. Examples of this type of advertising are the well-known campaigns for products such as Coca-Cola, Nike, Budweiser, American Express, and other national brands of products and services. Brand advertising seeks to generate demand for a product or service and then convince the audience that a *specific* brand is the one they want. For example, Nike ads seek to generate demand for expensive athletic shoes, and to convince purchasers that they want Nikes rather than Reeboks. The information component of brand campaigns is extensive, but usually does not actually appear in the content of the ads. Rather, information influences the development of the advertising campaign strategy and the choice of media for ad placement.

2. *Retail.* Advertising that is local and focuses on the store where products and services can be purchased is called retail advertising. The messages emphasize price, availability, location, and hours of operation. The advertising placed in the newspaper by your local grocery store or department store is a form of retail advertising. The goal of retail ads is to inform the audience that a specific store carries a variety of products, rather than to generate demand for any one category of products. In our Nike example, you may see many retail ad inserts in the Sunday newspaper informing you that lots of stores carry Nikes at a particular price, along with information about the availability and price of many other brands. The retail ad inserts try to entice you to go to one store rather than another to buy your Nikes. The information content of retail ads is usually high, in keeping with the purpose of the advertisements.

3. *Directory.* Ads that help you learn where to buy a product or service are directory ads. The yellow pages are the most common form of directory ads, but many other directories perform the same function. The classified advertising in the local newspaper is a form of directory advertising. If you were seeking information about where to purchase athletic shoes, the yellow pages ads would help you learn where the nearest athletic shoe store is. Directory ads are almost purely information based.

4. *Political.* Ads designed to persuade people to vote for a politician are familiar fixtures on the media landscape every political season. Information for political ads includes background research about the opposition candidate as well as material about the candidate sponsoring the ad, the latest polls of likely voters, public attitudes about the issues, and other facts that inform the strategy for the copy and placement of the ad.

5. *Direct-Response.* These ads can appear in any medium. A direct-response ad tries to stimulate a sale directly. The consumer can respond by phone, mail, or electronically; the product is delivered directly to the consumer by mail or some other carrier. Examples include the many program-length ads (infomercials) for hair-care products, exercise equipment, or kitchen gear that are now seen on broadcast and cable stations, along with the huge variety of direct-mail ads and catalogs that pile into mailboxes all around the country. These ads have a high information component. The message-makers can assume the audience is already interested in or curious about the goods or services, because watching an infomercial or reading a catalog is a voluntary activity. The direct-response piece includes lots of information about the products. The goal is to make the sale.

6. *Business-to-Business.* Messages directed at retailers, wholesalers, distributors, industrial purchasers, and professionals such as lawyers and physicians comprise business-to-business (or "B-2-B") advertising. These ads are concentrated in business and professional publications. For example, banks advertise to small business owners; equipment manufacturers advertise to factory managers, hospital administrators, restaurant owners, and others who might purchase their equipment; software training companies advertise to office managers. Unless you do the type of work that makes you an audience member for these kinds of messages, you aren't likely to see very many business-to-business ads. The background information needed to produce these ads has to be highly detailed, because they are directed toward a specialist audience with specific needs for products or services tailored for that particular industry. Figure 1.3 is an example of a business-to-business ad.

Careful. Other stations might get jealous.
Speed. Quality. Flexible workflow. From acquisition to air, you can have it all with Avid. Of course, your competition might not be too happy about it. For more info, visit www. avid.com or call 800 949 2843.

Avid
make manage move | media

FIGURE 1.3   Business-to-Business Ad.   This ad for a company that provides digital video editing hardware and software demonstrates the specialized target audience and ad placement characteristic of this type of advertising. The ad appeared in a trade publication read by broadcast and cable professionals. It uses terminology and concepts familiar to television practitioners.

Source: Avid. Reprinted by permission.

7. *Institutional.* Institutional advertising is sometimes also called *corporate* advertising. The focus of the message is on establishing a corporate identity or winning the public over to the organization's point of view. Rather than outlining the product or service offered by the institution, the ad attempts to create an image or reinforce an attitude about the company as a whole. Or the ad may attempt to influence policy making by advocating a particular position on a national issue that affects the interests of the sponsoring institution. Examples of institutional ads can be seen during Sunday morning television news programs with sponsors such as Archer Daniels Midland or Merrill Lynch. The information component of an institutional ad usually consists of extensive background research about the attitudes and psychologies of the intended audience, who typically are powerful people in a position to affect the institution's well-being.

8. *Public service.* This type of ad communicates a message on behalf of a good cause, such as stopping drunk driving or preventing AIDS. Unlike the other types of advertising, these ads are created for free by advertising professionals, and time or space are donated by media. Public service ads typically include information that emphasizes the nature of the problem or the cause to induce the audience to take the problem seriously.

Unlike in news, it is much harder for the average media observer to decipher the information process that informs advertising production. Much of the information that is used in the creation of advertising never actually appears in the copy of the ad or in the visuals that are produced. Instead, that extensive research helps the advertising professionals understand the product or service, identify the intended audience and the competitors' advantages and disadvantages, decide how much should be spent on the campaign, and determine where the ads should appear.

Public Relations

Many people do not realize how much of what we see in the media began as a message created by public relations (PR) specialists. Public relations is a major source of news. This is not a slander against news professionals. A significant routine for news professionals is to monitor and use news releases generated by PR specialists, attend news conferences organized by PR professionals, cover events sponsored by PR strategists, and use material from the media kits that PR firms create for their clients. The collaboration between PR specialists and news professionals to generate information of interest to the public is simply one way that a complex and disorganized information environment is made more manageable by message creators. Every news professional understands that PR specialists are trying to present their firm or client in the best light, and that a news release or media kit may not tell the whole story. Therefore, PR-generated messages are always checked, edited, and perhaps supplemented by information independently gathered by news professionals.

Much PR appears in the mass media, but most PR is produced for specialized media such as trade, association, and employee publications and audiovisual productions. These types of media are not usually highly visible to the general public. Just as there are various forms of news and advertising, there are a number of forms of public relations messages.

1. *Internal PR.* This includes corporate newsletters, crisis management plans (how to deal with a crisis such as the product-tampering incident that hit Tylenol), corporate intelligence reports, and other forms of communication that are intended for the internal audience of employees and officers of a company. Also included here are the annual reports prepared for stockholders in publicly held firms. Internal public relations pieces are information-rich and require extensive understanding of the company, the issues and problems the company faces, the finances of the firm, and any other factors that employees and stockholders would have an interest in knowing about.

2. *News releases.* News releases are sent to media outlets by PR specialists who want to generate interest for their client or company. A news release might be prepared as a simple *announcement* story (IBM's third-quarter profits rose or fell), an *advance* story (Barnum and Bailey's circus will be unloading the animals for their three-day stay in town at such-and-such a place and time), as *followup* after an event (Ground was broken for a new nursing home at a ceremony yesterday), or in *response* to a trend or current event (Interest rates are at an all-time low, so ABC Mortgage is offering the following tips to consumers about refinancing). The best news releases are produced to have the look and feel of a news story that might have been produced by news professionals. They therefore share many of the same information characteristics as news reports. The one big difference, as we have already stated, is that PR specialists are not obligated to tell all sides of the story.

3. *Broadcast news releases.* A video news release (VNR) is a news release in the form of a broadcast news story delivered via satellite to any broadcast or cable station that wishes to use the material. The video and voice-over are designed to look like a piece that you would see on any television news program. *B-roll footage,* or video images sent to the media via tape or satellite feed, is closely related to a VNR. The difference is that b-roll does not include a narrated voice-over and is not edited as a ready-to-go news package. Reporters use b-roll footage from companies to enhance their own stories. For example, for an upcoming Norah Jones concert, a music promotion company may send out b-roll footage of the singer in concert to all cities where she will be appearing on tour. A local television station may also send out a reporter to film the crowds who have gathered to camp out for tickets, and then use this footage with the b-roll of Jones in concert to create a final news story.

An audio news release is designed to be played on the radio. The audio clip might be a *voicer,* a news story recorded by a PR professional in the style of a radio announcer; or the clip might be an *actuality,* the actual voice of a newsmaker or news source speaking.

Broadcast news releases are usually accompanied by a print news release or an announcement to alert news professionals that the VNR or audio report is available. Once again, these PR announcements are produced to have the look and sound of reports produced by news professionals, but with a different standard for completeness of information. PR news releases rarely include information representing all sides of the issue.

4. *Media kits.* The media kit consists of a fact sheet about the client or event, biographic sketches of major people involved, a straight news story, news-column material, a news feature, a brochure, photographs, and—for kits delivered via videotape, CD-ROM, or the Internet—moving images, sound, and action. Often, these materials

■ ■ ■ ■ ■

BOX 1.1
A HAPPY "BIRTHDAY" AWARD FOR 3M POST-IT NOTES CAMPAIGN

Brodeur's work with 3M was awarded a Bell Ringer for Best Video News Release, was a Bronze Anvil "Award of Commendation" winner and earned an Honorable Mention at the PRWeek Awards. Following are highlights from the program:

SITUATION ANALYSIS
The 3M Office Supplies Division markets an extensive range of products for the office and home, including the ubiquitous line of paper and electronic Post-it Products. However, because of new communication tools and low-end competitors entering into its market, the Post-it brand needed an awareness boost and decided to use the product's 20th birthday to re-energize the brand. 3M charged Brodeur Worldwide with building and executing an informal yet creative program to modernize and build renewed awareness for the brand. With limited planning time, a media relations program with a focus on broadcast was developed in order for the campaign to be nimble, yet also effective.

The biggest obstacle Brodeur Worldwide faced was convincing the media to cover a ubiquitous product that people have been using for 20 years. 3M initially wanted its executives to tell the history of the Post-it Note from a corporate perspective in the VNR. But Brodeur advised 3M that this angle would not be compelling enough to compete with hard news and interest national broadcast media.

In support of the 20th birthday, Brodeur Worldwide's graphic design department created and produced a "storybook" that presented the media with information about the product and its birthday in a fun and lighthearted way. Additionally Brodeur brokered a birthday-related sponsorship for the Post-it brand with the National Foundation for Advancement in the Arts (NFAA). But the key element to the program, which was going to capture the attention of the broadcast news arena, was a soft news-style VNR created and distributed by Brodeur Worldwide.

STATEMENT OF OBJECTIVES
3M wanted to generate as much widespread national broadcast coverage as possible in order to create excitement for the 20th birthday of the Post-it Note. 3M wanted to increase general consumer awareness of the Post-it brand and launch the redesigned Post-it brand mark without advertising support. 3M also hoped that the campaign would provide an internal morale boost to employees.

The 3M/Brodeur team agreed that success for the VNR would consist of securing several placements that would generate buzz and also encourage print and online coverage.

PROGRAM PLANNING AND STRATEGY
Brodeur used its own in-house broadcast producer, Tom Merluzzi, who has over 25 years of national broadcast experience, to facilitate and produce the VNR. With an in-house expert, Brodeur was able to deliver a broadcast news quality piece, provide an objective perspective from a former producer and work more efficiently as opposed to using an outside contractor. Merluzzi was the director, producer, and creative editor for the VNR. He hired and supervised the freelance filming crews and contracted with Finish, an editing house in Boston, to piece together the final film.

Prior to filming the VNR, Brodeur spent hours brainstorming numerous ideas on how to tell the history of the Post-it Note while creating a VNR that would interest the media and reach the general consumer. Keeping in mind that 3M wanted to celebrate the Post-it Note's birthday in a sincere yet creative manner, Brodeur recommended the company tell the history in an amusing and lighthearted way by incorporating "man-on-the street" sound bites into the VNR. The two Post-it Note inventors, Art Fry and Spencer Silver, would be the "historians" and talk about the product's invention. And the inventors' historical content would be interspersed with amusing sound bites from a diverse

(continued)

BOX 1.1   CONTINUED

cross-section of people right off the street, describing their favorite uses of Post-it Notes. This would position the Post-it Note as a product of 3M innovation but also as an endearing icon of popular culture.

Next Brodeur focused on choosing appropriate locations for the VNR shoots. As opposed to using 3M's corporate office, Brodeur suggested that the homes of Fry and Silver would be more appropriate to accent the informal nature of the brand. For the interviews with the general public, Brodeur selected Santa Monica, CA, New York, NY, and Miami, FL, because these locations are populated with a diverse group of people. And finally, the Brodeur Worldwide team devised a set of open-ended questions to ask that would elicit fun, lighthearted and creative responses.

Once the locations were chosen and the interview style and questions determined, Brodeur had to work out a timeline for filming and deadlines. This was an important part in the planning process because of the various locations and interviews taking place. It was important to have the VNR completed on time because you can't push back a birthday.

The editing process of the VNR required a great degree of creativity, as many sound bites were needed to keep up the pace of the story. To accomplish this, particular attention was given to the opening sequence. It employs a series of sound bites that state the obvious but segue into the invention story: "Post-it Notes are…yellow …little pieces of paper…that you can post anywhere…when you have to leave a message or leave a bookmark or something… Two guys invented that? What a great idea!"

Brodeur recognized that this story could be difficult to pitch, especially to the national media, so they needed to find an angle that would attract the producers. The strategy behind using a VNR in this campaign was to have it reach the large spectrum of Post-it Note product users through broadcast coverage. From the office worker, to the college student, to the housewife, Brodeur wanted to show that the Post-it Note was used by all, thus the 20th birthday should be celebrated by all.

Believing that national broadcast coverage would spark regional broadcast and print and online coverage, Brodeur Worldwide decided to pre-pitch the national broadcast media to create an early buzz. Several major broadcast programs and stations were given the VNR along with supporting materials and a creative pitch in advance to achieve pre-birthday coverage.

Two days prior to the birthday, the team distributed a media advisory alert and made the VNR accessible to all media via satellite. The Brodeur team continued to pitch the story up until the day of the celebration. On the day of the celebration, Brodeur went to New York City with Art Fry and Spencer Silver. The group met with CNN for a live interview and conducted a variety of phone interviews as well. Brodeur also rented the "JumboTron" in New York's Times Square and ran the VNR for the general public to view.

RESULTS DOCUMENTATION

To date, Brodeur has generated more than 119 million impressions for the Post-it Notes' 20th Birthday. The VNR was picked up by over 100 broadcast outlets, exceeding both 3M's and Brodeur's expectations. The goals of the VNR were met entirely. As anticipated, Brodeur successfully placed the story on a weekly program, "CBS Sunday Morning," the Sunday before the birthday, sparking interest in the VNR and story before a media alert or release had even been distributed. The team wanted coverage on at least one morning program, and in reality they received two—"Good Morning America," and "CBS Early Show." They wanted a hit on one business program, and instead got two— CNNfn and "CNN Headline News." In addition, the broadcast coverage led to coverage in radio, print and online publications, including: "Nightly Business Report," National Public Radio, Washington Post, Los Angeles Times, Baltimore Sun, Associated Press, People.com (People Online Daily), MSNBC.com, USAToday.com and CBSMarketwatch.com.

Many members of the media commented on the professional quality of the VNR. In fact a producer at CBS stated "we almost never use company footage, but yours was so well done we were comfortable using it as is." The vice president of 3M's Office Supplies Division was so impressed with the VNR, he chose to use it at the annual stockholders meeting. The 20th Birthday of the Post-it Note VNR was not just a success with the media on the day of the event but continued to interest the media in the days and weeks following the birthday.

Source: BrodeurNews. Thursday, June 28, 2001, Volume 1, Issue 2. Reprinted by permission.

are packaged in a folder or other unique format that is professionally designed and printed (see Figure 1.4). Media kits are intended to provide story ideas for news professionals and to generate interest and attention for the client. Media kits are often prepared to generate impact as part of a major campaign or new product launch, as well as to provide information about ongoing programs, products, or services that require detailed explanation or regularly receive widespread interest from media. For

FIGURE 1.4   Media Kit Example.

Source: Big Fish Communications, Web site beabigfish.com. Reprinted by permission.

example, the Salvation Army might update its Kettle Bell Ringing media kit before the holiday season begins each November. Gateway might prepare a media kit for a trade show that details the specifications of a popular line of computers, then also use that media kit to meet requests for media throughout the year. With all the different components that go into a media kit, you can understand that the information needs for these types of messages are very great.

5. *Backgrounder or briefing session.* PR specialists provide in-depth information about an issue or event for reporters in backgrounders or briefing sessions. Handouts (information sheets or reports) are offered and the principal news source makes a presentation. In contrast to a news conference, there is little give and take between reporters and the person running the session. Backgrounders and briefing sessions are used to explain a policy or situation rather than to announce something. The National Transportation Safety Board, for example, might hold a briefing session following an airplane crash. The handouts prepared for these sessions are sometimes quite extensive, requiring solid information preparation by the PR specialists working on them.

6. *News conferences.* There are two categories of news conferences: information or personality. The information news conference usually has a single motive—someone wants media attention for an announcement, for an update on a breaking event, for followup about an investigation, or some other specific item of interest to news professionals. There is give and take as reporters ask questions of the person at the podium. The personality news conference is designed to provide news professionals with access to someone famous, about-to-be-famous, or otherwise in the public spotlight. For example, when a professional sports team signs a major college star, there is usually a personality news conference where the individual appears (usually in uniform) and answers questions. Information for a news conference must be prepared by PR specialists: an opening statement must be crafted, perhaps a briefing paper for the person at the podium is generated that anticipates reporters' questions, and there may be a handout outlining the major points made in the announcement. Again, PR specialists must understand what makes news and prepare their news conference information to meet those requirements.

7. *Media tour.* As in a briefing or background session, the purpose of a media tour is to provide in-depth information to reporters. However, the format of the meetings that take place on the media tour is often highly interactive, with one-on-one between a reporter and company official (and public relations specialist). The tour may include legs to different cities (New York, Boston, and San Francisco), where the PR specialists generally book several appointments per day with different media. The information provided as part of a media tour is generally slightly less timely than that in a news backgrounder or briefing. A media tour might be arranged so reporters can try a new high-tech product while a company representative walks them through the features, or for food editors to taste-test a new bread mix that company officials bake in special portable ovens to ensure that it rises correctly.

8. *Special events.* PR specialists may plan special events (sometimes disparagingly labeled *pseudo-events*) for clients who want media attention for a cause or issue. There may be a jump-rope-a-thon for cancer research, or a grain company may sponsor a food lift for famine victims. To have news value, special events must be planned. The information that announces them and entices coverage by news professionals must have all the same characteristics that we have already mentioned. Coverage of special events is usually framed as a feature.

9. *Responses to media inquiries.* There are cases when a company may not proactively send out a news release or hold a press conference, but may receive requests from the media for comment. Examples may range from the local television morning show producer who calls a clothing boutique requesting ideas for an upcoming segment on fall fashions, to a national newsmagazine reporter who calls a major corporation for reaction to allegations of wrongdoing brought by a former employee. In these cases, the public relations practitioner needs to act quickly to help meet the journalist's deadline, which often involves gathering additional background information about the situation and arranging a meeting or conference call with company management to discuss how best to respond. Often, companies have prepared *talking points* in advance for recurring issues, crises, or other situations where media calls are anticipated. Getting back to a reporter in a timely manner is key to maintaining good relationships with the media, even if the response is that your company will not be able to provide the requested statement or information at that particular time. Keeping the reporter informed is always a better approach than stonewalling.

Public relations specialists know the story preferences of various types of media and they understand how to prepare information to meet the needs of news professionals. It is sometimes difficult to detect when something has been generated as a result of public relations work. However, it is fair to say that a significant proportion of the stories you find in the business section of the newspaper have been generated by news releases or media kits prepared by public relations professionals. Many of the feature segments you see on local television news programs have arrived via a VNR.

For example, a local television news program ran a story about the anniversary of the invention of the Tootsie Roll, complete with video of the Tootsie Roll manufacturing process, happy Tootsie Roll eaters, and proud corporate officers extolling the virtues and longevity of the Tootsie Roll. There is no doubt whatsoever that the piece was a VNR that came into the local station and found a place on the newscast for its feature interest. The public relations specialists working for the Tootsie Roll parent company knew they had a story that would appeal to audiences all over the country.

MEDIA MESSAGE DELIVERY FORMATS AND CONVERGENCE

For communication professionals and for audiences, there are important differences among types of message delivery formats. A broadcast news report handles information differently than does a report that runs on the front page of a newspaper. Information for that report is handled differently still when it is prepared to appear on a computer screen or on a hand-held, text-based device such as a personal digital assistant (PDA).

To further complicate matters, many of these media formats are converging. The traditional distinctions between media delivery channels are disappearing. Communication careers are evolving in response. Communicators must know how to tell stories using words, pictures, sound, moving images, and vast stores of background information—in many cases for the same organization that is delivering messages to audiences in multiple forms. This brief overview of message formats serves as a starting point for our discussion of the information strategies used to create messages for each format.

Print

Print media include words, pictures, and graphic images on paper. Researchers know that reading requires a conscious effort on the part of the reader. The audience involvement level for print media is high. In addition, print creates a concrete and permanent record of a message. The message can be re-read, saved, and referred to later.

Newspapers are a ubiquitous form of print media. There are daily or weekly newspapers that seek to inform a general audience about the news and interesting events in the community. There are specialized newspapers that focus on one particular area of interest (the weekly labor paper in a factory town, the daily business papers that serve a corporate audience). Some newspapers seek a local audience, others strive to have a national impact. Newspapers may have an upscale reputation (the *New York Times*) or downscale appeal (the *New York Post*). All of these characteristics influence the type of information that is needed for generating content on a routine basis. Much content in newspapers is generated by wire services, the most important of which in the United States is the Associated Press. Newspapers carry retail, directory, business-to-business, corporate, and public service advertising, providing a venue for many of the forms of advertising messages we have already discussed.

Magazines are another print format. Unlike newspapers, most magazines are highly niche-oriented. This means that they focus on one particular topic for a highly specialized audience. There are magazines to appeal to those interested in yachting or in dirt motorcycling. There are magazines that run articles meant to entertain (*People*), to influence political debate (*The Nation*), to titillate (*Playboy*), to inform (*Gourmet*), and to accomplish many other purposes. Again, all of these factors influence the information routines that must be followed in creating messages for these media. Magazines carry much brand advertising, along with other forms that are directed toward highly specialized audiences.

There is an enormous newsletter publishing industry. Organizations use newsletters to convey news and information to a specific constituency. Individuals publish newsletters to inform an audience about stock picks, new technology developments, industry trends, and many other purposes. A significant number of newsletters are desktop publishing ventures, with just a handful of people responsible for reporting, writing, editing, and designing the articles, as well as selling ads to appear in the publication. Many newsletters carry hefty subscription prices and reach a limited but well-heeled audience. Obviously, anyone writing for such publications needs specialist information credentials.

Other forms of print media include posters and brochures, books and pamphlets, and other highly niched forms of communication. Print media allow for the presentation of lengthy information, the analysis and development of a linear argument, and the creation of messages that have reference value. An analysis piece on the future of U.S.–Russian relationships can be written for print media. An ad that describes the features and key advantages of a particular brand of stereo speakers is tailored for print formats.

Broadcast

Broadcast media include over-the-air and cable television and radio. Broadcast information is fleeting—in one ear or eye and out the other. Unless the broadcast organization also supports a Web site, you can't go back and re-hear a radio report the way you can re-read a newspaper or magazine report. You can watch a television news report over again if you've taped it, but that usually doesn't happen. Broadcast media require little involvement from the audience member. They are passive media. The audience member cannot select which reports come first in the newscast the way a newspaper reader can read the sports section first. However, broadcast media enable the conveyance of action, sound, movement, and emotional impact. The entire script for a typical half-hour television broadcast news program would take up no more than two-thirds of the front page of any daily newspaper. But the information experience of the broadcast is encoded at least as much in the pictures and sounds as it is in the words that are read.

Broadcast formats deliver messages to mass audiences, but any particular broadcast station or program may have a small, niche appeal, just as with magazines. In radio, there are formats for every interest. Radio stations may have an all-news format, or an all-talk format, or a country music, classical music, or R&B music format, or a combination that appeals to a segment of a community. There are national radio networks that provide affiliate stations with news and information. It is relatively inexpensive to create radio ads and purchase time on many radio stations, which provides small, local retailers a venue for their messages.

Television in the United States was once the supreme domain of the three over-the-air networks: ABC, NBC, and CBS. However, their share of the television audience at any particular moment has fallen precipitously in the past decade, as cable television and digital media have made inroads into the viewing audience's loyalties. Cable now offers several all-news formats, along with every conceivable type of niche format (cooking channel, sports channel, science fiction channel, history channel). Broadcast networks have found that nightly network news operations are costly to run, and have scaled back their commitments to news bureaus and personnel. At the same time, broadcast news magazine programs (*60 Minutes, Dateline, 20/20*) cost less to produce than an equivalent hour of fictional entertainment programming, so viewers find many examples of broadcast news magazines available any night of the week. Most national television advertising is brand advertising, thus providing national advertisers with a visible and influential platform for their image-building messages.

Local broadcast stations, both those affiliated with a network and those that operate as independents, offer local news and information programming, albeit in a breathless, if-it-bleeds-it-leads style that many viewers find offensive. Unlike the network news operations, local news programs actually generate money for most local stations, because the stations sell most of the advertising spots themselves and keep the revenue. Local news programs include weather and sports segments, which means that news professionals must tailor their reports to short, punchy tidbits that will fit in the first 10 minutes of the newscast. Local stations run many retail ads, along with messages sponsored by political candidates (during election cycles), direct-response merchants, and public service groups.

Broadcast media are visceral, providing an emotionally surrounding set of stimuli that may or may not convey information. But a very large number of citizens claim that they get most of their news and information about the world from broadcast media, so communicators must learn how to best use these formats to inform and entertain.

Converged Media

We cannot talk about media formats without talking about the hybrid combination of print and broadcast that has developed for delivery via digital devices. These are *immersive* media. They may be delivered over the Internet, over an interactive hand-held device, or in some other digital form. They combine printed words, pictures, sound, and in some cases, three-dimensional environments. The difference between digital media and print or broadcast is the interactivity level. Converged media formats can be highly interactive. The audience member can take part in the story, control the pace and direction of the story, and influence how a message is delivered. In addition, every message *taker* can also be a message *maker*. Electronic newspaper readers can interact with each other and the reporters by posting their own messages in the forum portion of the electronic publication. Advertisers create sites where visitors can interact with information on the screen, with each other, with company officials, and with product spokespersons.

The information component in messages created for these media is an interesting blend of print and broadcast. A digital document can connect the reader to many layers of print information, but can also provide an audiovisual experience. Converged media message delivery can be very rich in information.

NEW FORMS BRING NEW
INFORMATION CHALLENGES

It is not really correct to refer to most digital formats as mass media just yet. In fact, the very nature of media is moving away from a *mass* model to one where individual interests can be easily met. Media organizations have been attempting to reinvent themselves and their media models for decades.

Early experiments with digital publishing were costly and largely unsuccessful. Projects such as Knight-Ridder's Viewtron service in the 1980s required users simultaneously to use both their phone and television; there were few subscribers. The next level of media experimentation saw media companies align with emerging proprietary online information services such as Prodigy and CompuServe. These partnerships were fee-based ways to deliver electronic versions of news. Then along came the World Wide Web and its mantra, "Information wants to be free!" Publishers of news and information for which you had to pay a price in the past put their new, experimental online publications out on the Web for free. Magazine publishers put selected stories online, hoping to tease people to buy the whole issue in print. Services providing access to archives of articles, such as Northern Light and Electric Library, offered bargain basement pricing for what had been expensive access in the past. The new information world was a buyer's and browser's market.

But there is a swing back to the days of fee-based information access. As publishers of information realize they can't subsidize the high cost of production of online publications with the traditional business models (primarily advertising), they are trying to devise ways to ensure they get money for providing their information, either through subscription services or "per article" access fees. Totally free access to information for online versions of traditional publications may be coming to an end.

The good news is that organizations that want their information to be widely distributed and accessible are using the Internet to enhance services to information seekers. Companies, associations, and government agencies have become rich resources for background, statistics, images, and data. Access through the Internet has actually reduced the cost of retrieving this information—it is just a keystroke, not a long-distance phone call away.

This access is another advantage of the wired world. In the past, people who were close to the key sources of information had a distinct advantage. They could go to the State House or to the association headquarters and ask for what they needed. The Internet has, in many cases, leveled the playing field. This is particularly true for communicators in small towns, who were believed to be at a disadvantage compared to their colleagues in metropolitan areas. With government records, reports, and databases being made available online, people in different locations now have equal access to information.

However, as easy as it is to put something online, it is even easier to take it off. By no means should you feel that you have unlimited access to information from any source online. Nothing made this as clear as the actions of some government agencies in the wake of the September 11, 2001, terrorist attacks in New York and Washington, D.C. Information from a number of government Web sites was removed in the interest of national security—but to the concern of advocates of open records and government access.

That is why it is essential for you to understand the limits to the scope of the Internet-accessible resources of a government agency, association, or publisher. For the most part, creators of Internet sites started with current information and moved forward. They rarely converted pre-Internet reports and data to make them available online. This is why it is important for you to cultivate the tried and true methods of information collection beyond just knowing how to use a search engine on the Web. If you need information prior to 1995, you will probably need to tap into it using old

■ ■ ■ ■ ■

BOX 1.2
**EXAMPLES OF DOCUMENTS REMOVED FROM FEDERAL AND STATE
WEB SITES SINCE SEPTEMBER 11, 2001**

- The Department of Energy's Office of Defense Programs page was removed from the National Nuclear Security Administration's site on November 1, 2001. The Office of Defense Programs page states "The Defense Programs (DP) Website is unavailable until further notice."
- The International Nuclear Safety Center removed interactive maps from its site. These maps allowed users to click on a location of a nuclear power plant to learn more about it.
- Most of the Geographic Information Services at the Bureau of Transportation Sta-

tistics have been removed from the Web site www.bts.gov/gis/. The site is a national resource for transportation spatial data and GIS in transportation information.
- According to the Project on Government Oversight (POGO), the Department of Energy removed from its Web site (at POGO's request) detailed maps and descriptions of all ten nuclear facilities with weapons-grade plutonium and highly enriched uranium.

Source: OMB WATCH, ombwatch.org. Reprinted by permission.

techniques such as phone calls, in-person interviews, and trolling through paper records.

In addition, understand that the report on the Internet may be the latest, completed compilation of information from that agency, but it might not represent the latest information the agency has. There may well be more current figures available, just waiting to be compiled.

As awesome as the scope of information available online might be, for the most part it is only an accumulation of information since the start of the World Wide Web—there are decades of history and records and information that will never be online.

In this book we explain different sources of information, different techniques for tapping into those sources, and the ways you can effectively determine the best source and technique for your specific information task. In the next chapter, we describe the information-seeking model on which this book is based. It will supply you with a critical thinking path to follow so you won't get lost in the vastness of the information universe.

SELECTED ADDITIONAL READINGS

Brown, John Seely and Paul Duguid. *The Social Life of Information*. Boston: Harvard Business School Press, 2000.
Fidler, Roger F. *Mediamorphosis: Understanding New Media*. Thousand Oaks, CA: Pine Forge Press, 1997.

Follman, Jeanne M. *Getting the Web: Understanding the Nature & Meaning of the Internet.* Duomo Press, 2001.

Gleick, James. *What Just Happened: A Chronicle from the Information Frontier.* New York: Pantheon Books, 2002.

Swiss, Thomas. *Unspun: Key Concepts for Understanding the World Wide Web.* New York: New York University Press, 2001.

NOTES

1. "Big Bang," *Academic Press Dictionary of Science and Technology,* www.academicpress.com/inscight/06081998/big-ban3.htm.

2. "How Much Information," www.sims.berkeley.edu/research/projects/how-much-info/internet.html#3.

3. William Wells, John Burnett, and Sandra Moriarty, *Advertising: Principles and Practices,* 3rd edition (Englewood Cliffs, NJ: Prentice-Hall, 1995), 12–13.

CHAPTER TWO

THE MESSAGE ANALYSIS/ INFORMATION-GATHERING MODEL

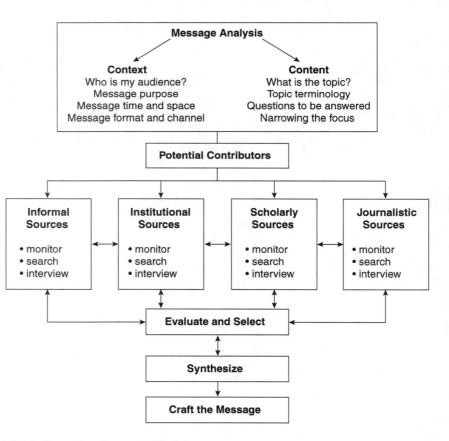

Message Analysis

Context
Who is my audience?
Message purpose
Message time and space
Message format and channel

Content
What is the topic?
Topic terminology
Questions to be answered
Narrowing the focus

Potential Contributors

Informal Sources	Institutional Sources	Scholarly Sources	Journalistic Sources
• monitor • search • interview	• monitor • search • interview	• monitor • search • interview	• monitor • search • interview

Evaluate and Select

Synthesize

Craft the Message

The Information Strategy Model

Communicators perform two basic tasks: they gather and evaluate information, and they tell stories. These two tasks are fundamental to every type of message. The way the information is crafted into a story differs depending on whether the story is told as a straight news piece in a newspaper or on a Web site, a brand ad on television, or a news release prepared for a radio program. The storytelling techniques you use have to account for the media format in which the information is delivered and the audience expectations for the message.

STORYTELLING AND THE MEDIA

You need to understand some of the general characteristics of storytelling, and some of the components of storytelling that influence media messages in order to understand how storytelling and information gathering are related. Storytelling has a long history. Early humans made elaborate cave paintings long before writing or printing were invented. Archaeologists think these paintings had several purposes—to catch and hold attention, to shock and frighten, to imprint information in memory. The cave paintings provided a method of socialization in early society. Later, pre-industrial societies had stories that were rich in symbolic content. Nomadic and agrarian societies used their stories for ritual, entertainment, socialization, and informational purposes.

"Enough storyboarding. Let's shoot something."

Modern societies rely on stories told in a variety of media to explain how the world works, why the established order prevails, and why things are the way they are. The overwhelming bulk of storytelling received by modern audiences is in the mode of fiction, through television, movies, computer and video games, and entertainment media. On average, individuals in the industrialized world devote three hours a day to television viewing—fully half of their leisure time, and more than any single activity save work and sleep.[1] Most prime-time television, video, film, and game content is devoted to fiction.

The word *story* does not apply just to fiction, however. The distinction between fiction and nonfiction stories is an absolutely critical one for you to grasp. It affects every decision that you make about the selection and evaluation of information for messages. Most adults understand that there are different kinds of truth. A fictional story about a young person's journey to adulthood can capture the truth of adolescence even though it is a fictional account. But communicators working in the news industry cannot invent a fictional character and present that person as the subject of a nonfiction story even if the dramatic and storytelling appeal of doing so may seem irresistible. *Washington Post* reporter Janet Cooke and *New Republic* reporter Stephen Glass are two famous cases of journalists being fired for fabricating characters and anecdotes in their news reports.[2]

Likewise, an advertisement about the engine characteristics of a brand of automobile is distinct from an ad that seeks to associate that same brand of automobile with virility, freedom, or sex appeal. Both ads may present some sort of truth in their stories about the appeal of that automobile to certain types of drivers, but the line between fact and fiction has to be bright and clearly drawn. Public relations messages, while usually created to "put the best foot forward," nonetheless must be grounded in fact. Any public relations practitioner who invents convenient fictions and passes them along as fact will soon be discovered and discredited.

Nonfiction stories have a much higher standard for truth and verifiability than do fiction stories. Messages with a large, anonymous audience need higher information truth and verifiability standards than do messages prepared for an acquaintance. You cannot simply say whatever you want, or make up whatever is convenient, in mass media stories without sacrificing standards of accuracy. Opinions are not all equal, information is not all of the same quality, evidence is not all at the same level of acceptability and appropriateness.

Stories, whether they are fiction or nonfiction, have common elements. They must convey drama, with a beginning, middle, and end, and a sense of resolution of a problem or dilemma. Stories must create a sense of setting: Where is this action taking place? Can we feel, hear, see, smell the locations and environs? Stories have characters we can identify with or who take us into an entirely different world. Stories should include character development, so that we have empathy for the person with whom we are supposed to identify: admiration, sympathy, support. Stories create suspense in order to keep our interest—will the defendant be convicted, will the toothpaste help the guy win the girl? Stories usually have to include background information, and occasionally statistics, to provide the evidence needed to demonstrate the truth of the narrative. Even the simplest straight news story or 30-second television ad (as Figure 2.1 demonstrates) contains these basic story elements.

Garfield's AdReview

BY BOB GARFIELD

Secret of Secret's success: 'to be continued' workhorse

REMEMBER THE TASTER'S Choice campaign?

Of course you do. There's no forgetting the coy, smirking relationship between the coquettish woman and her downstairs neighbor, who used insipid banter ostensibly about instant coffee as a freeze-dried flirtation dance. Some viewers rooted for romance. We rooted for an outbreak of non-life-threatening but painful and embarrassing sores.

The insufferable couple didn't put Starbucks out of business. It did, however, briefly capture America's attention. So it's surprising that few have attempted to exploit the natural intrigue of the "to be continued" genre. Turns out, the gimmick can work when not manufactured by clods.

The evidence: a new series of 30-second spots for Secret antiperspirant from Leo Burnett USA, Chicago, and master storyteller Joe Pytka.

Antiperspirant, as you know, is a chemical applied to the armpits to inhibit sweat and the associated stench—not an obvious linchpin for sustained drama. On the other hand, underarm perspiration is linked to emotional upset, suggesting any number of dramatic possibilities. This campaign engagingly explores some.

The central figures are Jack and Shirley, husband and wife facing life's little nerve-wracking moments—the kind of moments wherein, if your deodorant is gentle enough for a woman, but not strong enough for a man, you might stain your blouse and surround yourself in a cloud of putrid musk.

In the first spot, Shirley is a wreck about asking the boss for a raise. Between Jack's support and large quantities of eccrine-gland-inhibiting aluminum zirconium trichlorohydrex, she marches coolly to the office. When she returns, she announces she has quit to go back to art school. Now Jack, who has to make the nut

SECRET
Leo Burnett USA, Chicago
Ad Review Rating:
★★★☆

for their gorgeous apartment on one salary, is sweating.

The plot thickens in the second spot when Shirley, played marvelously by Anne Stedman, sits in a figure-study class and encounters the nude model—her ex-boyfriend.

"Shirley?" he says.

"Teddy?!" she replies. Her nervous smile is perfection. And, oh, yes: to be continued.

In the third of the three initial spots, the figure class has miraculously yielded an exhibition of very good student oil paintings, featuring a Michelangelo-esque one by Shirley herself. The exhibition scene begins marvelously with a closeup of Jack, checking out her work, cocking his head quizzically from side to side as he focuses his attention pretty much on Teddy's ground zero. When he and Teddy meet, the plot thickens.

Shakespeare it ain't, but between the sitcom-ishness and Pytka impeccable timing, the story holds your attention. And unlike the Taster's Choice inanity, these vignettes are to the point. Though we are never bludgeoned with silly product talk, the downside of the endocrine system is never lost on the viewer.

At no point in the narrative is Shirley not under some sort of emotional stress, yet her sweat glands at least remain poised. Her life may be veering out of control, but her underarms apparently are fresh as a daisy.

The only glaring flaw is the absence of the Secret theme line: "Strong enough for a man," etc. It is one of the great USPs in advertising history, and it should be in there somewhere. Otherwise, the lesson is clear: Serialized advertising can be a powerful weapon, especially if you...

... arm Pytka.

★ See the spots on **AdReview.com**

FIGURE 2.1 Storytelling in Advertisements.

Source: Advertising Age's AdReview. Reprinted with permission from the July 22, 2002 issue of *Advertising Age.* Copyright, Crain Communications Inc. 2002.

Storytelling can serve different kinds of goals. Determining the intention or purpose of the story or message is an important first step in crafting the message. Messages can *inform* or *enlighten* people about current events or issues or about the availability of products or services. They can provide *background* and *context* to a discussion of ideas. Stories can be written to *persuade* people to make certain purchases or hold certain views. News, advertising, and public relations messages perform some or all of these functions, while employing different storytelling techniques and formats to communicate with audiences in the most effective way.

This review of storytelling goals and techniques to reach different audiences suggests that information for messages is not randomly selected or haphazardly put together. Every message has an intended purpose and specific audience. The information that will meet one purpose and influence one type of audience member is not the same as that needed for another. Communicators at work in this message environment need a conceptual tool, a road map of the information universe, that can help them learn how best to reach their audiences with the most appropriate information. That is the goal of the information strategy model outlined and developed in this book.

ROLES AND USES OF MODELS

Models help describe and decipher complex systems or events, help users learn complex skills, and provide the framework for doing experiments and testing theories. Despite some obvious disadvantages (overgeneralization, untested accuracy, incorrect relationship between variables), models are helpful in many situations. Most students of mass communication recognize a model that identifies a message sender, a channel of delivery, a message, a receiver, an effect of the message, and the purpose for sending and receiving the message. Represented in graphic form, the model of message delivery, receipt, and effects can illustrate relationships that are essentially abstract.

Library and information science specialists have long studied the process of searching for information. The term *search strategy* comes from the work done in this field. A search strategy is a systematic means of acquiring and appraising information that illuminates a subject. People in everyday settings use search strategies for a variety of ordinary tasks—seeking a telephone number, checking the reputation of a physician or dentist, learning how to eliminate aphids from house plants. Mass communicators must be more inventive and persistent than most people in their information search strategies. We use search strategy techniques, along with the skills of monitoring and interviewing, as part of an overall information strategy designed specifically for communicators. The model outlined here recognizes that in an information-rich environment, it is impossible to remember thousands of specific information-finding tools capable of locating specific facts or answering specific questions. Instead, the information strategy model presents a process or method that offers a map of the information universe and suggests a systematic course to follow for any message type or any search topic.

For mass communicators, the strengths of the information strategy process are as follows:

1. It helps you think through the message's purpose, context, audience, and key topics

2. It guides your identification and selection of a manageable portion of the topics which need to be examined
3. It provides a method for in-depth examination of the segment of the topic selected
4. It helps you identify appropriate sources and select effective techniques for researching the topic
5. It provides a context for creating a unified, coherent, and focused message
6. It gives you a vocabulary for discussing your message analysis, information gathering, and selection processes with others
7. It saves time by helping you avoid wading through masses of information that may be interesting, but in the end, not very useful for the message task

THE INFORMATION STRATEGY MODEL FOR COMMUNICATORS

Figure 2.2 presents the information strategy model for mass communicators. The model identifies the steps in the information strategy process and indicates the paths between the steps. As the two-way arrows indicate, the process may include some backtracking in the course of verifying information or raising additional questions. As a graphic representation of both the steps to take in the process and the sources that meet a particular information need, the model serves as an outline of your entire information-gathering process.

The information strategy model for mass communicators applies to any type of message task and any topic that you may be working on. The process applies to an information search for news, advertising, public relations, or any other type of messages. The information strategy process can facilitate the search for information on any topic that forms the subject of a mass communication message.

There are five specific elements that affect the information requirements for mass communication messages. Communicators, unlike other creators of stories, need to concern themselves with finding locally relevant, timely, and accurate data. They need to be aware of different viewpoints on an issue for their audience. And they need to take care in the attribution of sources. Let's look at each of these.

Maxim of Relevance

1. *Locally relevant information.* You need to speak to your audience. In the case of news in particular, this means finding sources that can provide the local angle and relevance your audience seeks. Putting events or issues in a local context might require finding relevant local statistics, interviewing people in the community, or discovering similar incidents from the past. When creating advertising messages that will appear in a local market, you need to know how local audience members will respond to your tactics and strategy and how best to reach them with your messages.

2. *Timely information.* Media professionals generally require *timely* information, material that is up-to-date and reflective of the most current thinking or understanding of the topic or issue. An advertising or public relations message must also reflect the most current information about the product or service.

Quantity

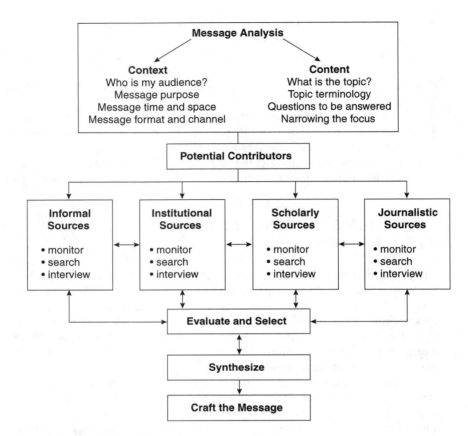

FIGURE 2.2   The Information Strategy Model

3. *Accurate information.* You are frequently confronted with situations where experts or documentary sources disagree on facts or where biases in opinion must be revealed. It is your responsibility to resolve inconsistencies in fact and figures, and to expose bias and incompleteness in your information.

4. *Variety of viewpoints.* There is rarely one truth. Effective communicators know that there are a range of viewpoints, opinions, and perspectives on any issue. Determining those different viewpoints is an important step in providing accurate and relevant messages.

5. *Attribution of information.* This is standard practice in news reports, and is also apparent in many advertising and public relations messages. Audience members need to know where the information in a message came from if they are to believe what they are being told. Therefore, communicators go to great lengths to gather information from sources (people, documents, observations, etc.) that can be named and identified in the message.

The information strategy outlined in this book helps you to identify your message task, locate sources for the local, timely, accurate information you need, identify the variety of viewpoints, and ensure that the information you find is credible, recognizable, and verifiable.

There is one other major consideration for most communicators: They work under severe *time constraints*. This fact is taken into account by the information strategy process. Speed and efficiency in message analysis and information gathering are useful for anyone, but they are crucial for those who produce mass media messages. The process is not reserved only for those who work on long-term projects or months-long campaigns. Every communicator working on a deadline can follow the process profitably and with sound results, no matter how little time is available.

Manner

Message Analysis

The information process begins with an analysis of both the *context* and the *content* required for the message. *Context analysis* involves determining the intended audience of the message and the purposes or intentions for the message to be created. *Content analysis* refers to specifying the message topic's scope and focus. This part of the process sets the stage for every step of the process that follows, and is therefore one of the most important and challenging parts of your work.

A fundamental question that every communicator asks is "Who is my audience?" You cannot proceed until this question is examined and some preliminary decisions are made. Understanding the audience is the key to selecting and evaluating information and to creating and delivering the message. For a message to be effective, someone (the *right* someone) must receive it and react the way the communicator intended.

The start of the information process also includes some preliminary decisions about the purpose of the message. It goes without saying that the purpose of the message influences the type of information that is needed and the way the story is told. Whether the message is intended to inform, to provide depth, context, and discussion, or to persuade will affect every subsequent decision in the process. In addition, it is important to do some initial thinking about the size or length of the message, the format for the message, and the channel(s) by which the message will be delivered.

We have already briefly discussed some of the storytelling traditions and requirements that influence how the message is constructed and delivered. The characteristics of specific media formats also help define who will receive the message and how the story will be told. A message that will appear on a printed page has different information requirements than one that will appear on a computer screen. A message with visual elements requires different information strategies than one that will be heard on the radio.

You must also think about the content and topic of the message at this point in the strategy. You try to determine the scope of the topic, the terminology relevant to the topic, the questions that must be answered in the course of the search, and the focus for the message.

Inexperienced information gatherers often begin with a topic that is much too broad and undefined. Advertising and public relations professionals do not need to know how computers are manufactured in order to produce an integrated marketing campaign for a personal computer. However, background information about trends in the computer marketplace, the jargon used by computer specialists to describe their machines, data on who buys computers, examples of other computer ads, clips of previous news articles that have been written about personal computers, and ideas about where ads and public relations story ideas may be placed are necessary parts of the creation of that campaign. Similarly, a reporter does not have to learn how to build a house in order to write a series of stories about housing codes. But solid information about housing laws, code violators and the types of problems they cause, and the kinds of actions taken to ensure safe housing are appropriate topics for the information strategy. Chapter 3 discusses analyzing the message assignment in more detail.

Potential Contributors of Information

Once the nature of the audience, message, and topic are determined, it is time to identify the potential contributors to the information strategy. The model proposes four contributors of information valuable to a mass communication message: informal sources, institutional sources, scholarly sources, and journalistic sources. You may begin the process with any one of these sources, or may investigate two or three types simultaneously.

The information generated from each of these four contributors has distinct and inherent biases that must be kept in mind. These biases are connected to the motivation that lies behind the generation of information from each of these types of contributors.

Informal sources generally refer to individuals and their ideas, opinions, and perspectives. The information from these sources will be impressionistic and fragmentary. It will represent a perspective that is personal, limited in scope, and unlikely to carry an official point of view.

Institutional sources range in size and importance from the neighborhood block association, the school PTA, or the local shoe store, to the federal government of the United States, the American Medical Association, or the General Motors Corporation. Institutional sources collect, organize, and disseminate information for a variety of purposes, one of which is to provide information for mass communication professionals.

Scholarly sources include work produced by subject experts in academic institutions and research organizations. Scholarly work is peer-reviewed and is usually produced to advance new knowledge or understanding of a topic or issue rather than influence policy or pursue a political agenda, as some institutionally generated information might be.

Journalistic sources include mass media content that is produced to inform, educate, or persuade and is intended for a mass audience with a general background in the subjects explored. Information from journalistic sources is valuable for its timeliness and relevance for the audience.

Each of these contributors of information provides material in three formats: through people, paper, or digital means. In Chapter 4, we discuss in more detail the characteristics of these three formats in which information can be found.

The model also proposes three means of locating information from each of the contributors. Communicators regularly *monitor* these sources as a part of their information routine, they *search* for specific information when faced with a particular message task, and they *interview* people or data that provide perspectives representative of that type of information source. In chapter 5, we talk about these techniques in more detail. The library as an information resource is discussed in Chapter 6. The four contributors are discussed in more detail in Chapters 7 through 10.

Information Evaluation and Selection

Once the communicator has gathered information from all of the appropriate contributors, the complex task of evaluating and selecting the best materials begins. Again, you must keep the audience in mind. If the intended audience member is information-rich (that is, the audience member already knows a great deal about the topic of the message), then you must apply one set of evaluation and selection criteria. If the audience member is information-poor, a different set of criteria apply.

However, all of the information gathered for a message can be evaluated using standard metrics for evaluation, which include credibility, accuracy, timeliness, authority, statistical validity, and reputation. At this stage, you seek to eliminate erroneous materials, update facts, identify differences in viewpoints, and put information in context.

Selecting information for messages involves applying standards to compare the quality of information, and choosing the information that is most relevant and appropriate for the audience and the message goal.

Information selection also includes relevancy testing, which involves asking if the information intended for the message is necessary and on target. Much more material than can ever be included in the message will come to your attention if the information strategy has been successful. That means that a stringent relevancy test should be applied to ensure that only the most important and useful information is included in the final product.

You also try to assess the agenda of the information provider. All information comes with a point of view. This is inevitable, because all information is created by human beings with perspectives, expertise, biases, and experiential differences. You cannot do your work without using information from all of the sources we have identified, but a downside of that reality is that some time and effort must be spent at this point in the search process to fully expose and understand the strengths and weaknesses of each piece of material that might possibly be used in a message. The evaluation and selection process is discussed in more detail in Chapter 11.

Synthesizing Information

The final step of the information strategy process before you produce the message is to synthesize the information. This is the point when you try to answer the question, What does all of this information *mean*? This process is particularly hard to describe, because so much of it takes place inside the minds of creative communicators. However, an important element of this step includes reviewing the purpose for the message (to inform, persuade, entertain, alert, to add depth or context, etc.). You also must review what you have learned about the audience through your search for information. With these elements reinforced, you then try to reach some conclusions about the topic of the message and the most effective way to reach the audience. The synthesis process is discussed in more detail in Chapter 12.

The Legal, Ethical, and Social Environment

Communicators are constantly aware of the legal, ethical, and social context in which messages are received. The information strategy model is employed in an environment that requires you to adhere to legal requirements concerning privacy and libel, regulatory constraints, and verifiability of information. The advertising substantiation rule, for instance, requires an advertiser to have evidence to substantiate any claim that an ad makes about a product or a service. News reporters take into consideration individuals' right to privacy as spelled out in a myriad of federal and state laws and regulations as they collect information for use in their stories.

Ethical constraints also enter the picture for information gatherers. Some information may be regarded as useful, even essential, for you to produce a message, but may not be obtainable by ethical means. Rifling through files in an unattended office, electronically monitoring private conversations, or misrepresenting your identity or purpose to gain information are considered unethical means of gathering information. Other material may be obtained through legal and ethical means, but the *use* of that information in a message may be unethical. Revealing information from the proceedings of juvenile courts, publishing the names of sexual assault victims, and printing or broadcasting the name of someone arrested but not yet charged with a crime usually fall into this category. When ethical constraints prevail, use your information strategy skills to locate alternative material that can be used without violating ethical standards.

The way communicators do their work is recognized as a concern for society as a whole. Communicators are among the most significant information brokers in society. They process ideas, facts, opinions, and fantasies into messages received by millions. They hold great power to focus the public's attention in some directions rather than others. They provide the public with some scenes and plots and shine a spotlight on some facts, while leaving others in the dark. For this reason, media performance in our society comes under great scrutiny and frequent attack. Communicators who use flawed, incomplete, inaccurate, or biased information are rightly exposed for their failure to meet the audience's need for information. You have an obligation to employ sound search practices and to use the best information available for your messages.

The legal, ethical, and social climates within which the information strategy is employed are discussed in more detail in Chapter 13.

CONCLUSION

Information strategy is not a magic method to cure all the ills of which mass communicators have been accused. It treats the information component of mass media messages, recognizing that responsibility for the expressive component is equally significant. Information strategy can help communicators be responsible professionals, but it must be employed by those who have the motivation to be responsible. Information strategy can help communicators work rapidly and efficiently, but the rapidity with which information can be collected should not be an excuse to take shabby shortcuts. To the contrary, the very abundance of information requires that you exercise discretion, caution, and judgment in gathering information for your messages. The model for locating and evaluating information is designed to assist you in meeting the growing demands you face. It is a conceptual tool to be applied to all information-gathering tasks.

One of the most challenging steps in the information process is that of figuring out exactly what a message should consist of and why it is being created. Chapter 3 examines the process of analyzing the message assignment, a task which sets you on the path of defining the information needs intrinsic to a message. That is where we turn our attention next.

SELECTED ADDITIONAL READINGS

Basch, Reva and Mary Ellen Bates. *Researching Online for Dummies.* 2nd edition. Hoboken, NJ: John Wiley & Sons, 2000.

Berkman, Robert I. *Find It Fast: How to Uncover Expert Information on Any Subject Online or in Print.* 5th edition, New York, NY: HarperResource, 2000.

Booth, Wayne C., Gregory G. Colomb, and Joseph M. Williams. *The Craft of Research* (Chicago Guides to Writing, Editing, and Publishing). Chicago, IL: University of Chicago Press, 1995.

Reddick, Randy and Elliot King. *The Online Journalist: Using the Internet and Other Electronic Resources.* 3rd edition. Belmont, CA: Wadsworth, 2000.

Rubin, Rebecca B., Alan M. Rubin, and Linda J. Piele. *Communication Research: Strategies and Sources.* 5th edition. Belmont, CA: Wadsworth, 1999.

NOTES

1. Robert Kubey and Mihaly Csikszentmihalyi, "Television Addiction Is No Mere Metaphor," www.sciam.com/2002/0202issue/0202kubey.html.

2. Robin Pogrebin, "Magazine inquiry on a writer finds much fabricated work," *New York Times,* 12 June, 1998, 1A.

CHAPTER THREE

ANALYZING THE MESSAGE ASSIGNMENT

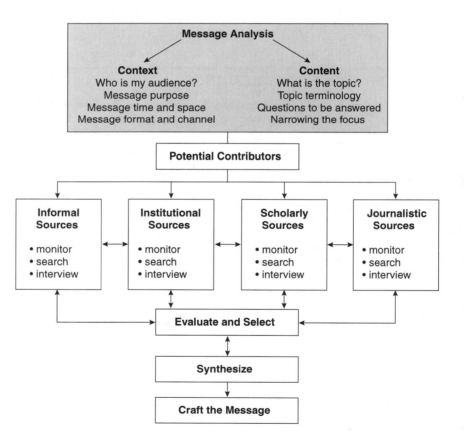

The Information Strategy Model

Where do ideas for messages come from? How does the newspaper fill its newshole—the space available for news stories—everyday? How does the copywriter come up with the attention-grabbing words and visuals that break through the advertising clutter? How does a PR professional begin writing a news release about a new product? Anyone who works in mass communication quickly learns that the very first steps in the information strategy are perhaps the most important of all. The message analysis stage of the process sets the foundation for all of the work that follows.

IDEA GENERATION

Let's start with idea generation. While it is true that many tasks in your day are assigned by others, the actual creative work of crafting a message still rests on the skill and imagination of the individual doing the information searching and writing (that's you!). One important skill that good communicators develop early in their careers is the ability to understand *what it is possible to ask about.* Any idea is fair game. Because solid information strategy skills allow you to find answers to just about anything, you are not limited to only those questions that can be answered easily and quickly. Advanced answer-finding skills free you up to ask unusual, different, perhaps difficult questions.

A variety of techniques help you generate ideas for messages. Brainstorming, making idea maps and point-of-view diagrams, keeping a journal or daybook for scribbling notes, and reading everything you can get your hands on all provide grist for the idea mill. A well-developed sense of curiosity and a studied naiveté keep you open to new ways of looking at the world around you. Common sense and healthy skepticism (not cynicism) keep you grounded.

Donald Murray, in *Writing to Deadline*, describes the idea-generation techniques of idea mapping and creating point-of-view diagrams for communication professionals.[1] Idea mapping, he explains, is a more creative way of exploring a subject than using traditional subject outlines. The subject or topic is drawn in a circle on the middle of a page. All the ideas that occur to you are drawn out along lines that emerge from the center circle. The technique is not intended to serve as a definitive method of topic outlining, but as a quick and intuitive first step in thinking about a message task. You may need to spend no more than five minutes making a map. A sample idea map is shown in Figure 3.1.

A point-of-view diagram uses a similar technique. A subject or topic is again drawn in a circle in the middle of a page. Draw as many arrows pointing toward the center as you can imagine. The arrows represent the points of view from which the subject or topic can be seen. By diagramming the topic in this way, you can generate a variety of perspectives on that idea and even begin to identify possible audiences or interviewees for the message. A sample point-of-view diagram is shown in Figure 3.2.

It is easy in the idea generation stage to fall into overuse of clichés and stereotypes. It is a challenge finding a fresh perspective on the message on which you are working. A way to avoid clichés and maintain a fresh perspective is to be sure you truly understand all angles of the message task. This process can be broken down into two parts: analyzing the context for the message and analyzing the content of the message.

FIGURE 3.1   Idea Map.

Source: Donald Murray, *Writing to Deadline—The Journalist at Work.* Reprinted by permission.

FIGURE 3.2   Point-of-View Diagram.

Source: Donald Murray, *Writing to Deadline—The Journalist at Work.* Reprinted by permission.

THE CONTEXT FOR THE MESSAGE

The context for your message includes audience, message purpose, message time and space, and message format and channels.

Audience

One of the most basic pieces of advice given to any novice communicator is to "Know your audience." Knowing your audience is key to how information is selected and evaluated, and how messages are created and delivered. Those who work in mass communication want their work to have impact, and that requires a solid understanding of the intended audience for the message.

It is easy to fall into the trap of thinking that the only audience you must be concerned with is the anonymous audience member at the end of the message-delivery process—the person reading the newspaper, watching the newscast, seeing the ad, or viewing the video news release clip on the local news station. But that is a mistake. There are actually many audiences for any type of message, some of whom have the power to decide whether a message ever reaches the anonymous audience member at all.

Gatekeeper Audience.   The first of the important audiences that influence message making is the gatekeeper audience. The word *gatekeeper* refers to those within the organization who have the power to decide which messages are produced, by whom, where they will appear, and with what characteristics. For example, one important set of gatekeepers within a newspaper organization is the assistant managing editors who decide daily which stories to assign to which reporters. A similar function is performed by producers and assignment editors in a local television news station. An infinite variety of events, places, people, or ideas form the basis of a news story on any given day. Editors or producers in a news organization attempt to create order out of chaos by limiting what gets defined as news in the first place. Hard news is most often based on prescheduled events (meetings, trials) or on unscheduled events (fires, tornadoes). Communicators who want to be assured of regularly having a story in the newspaper or on the newscast understand that their best bet is to work on a beat that generates hard news on a routine basis. That way, they are more likely to get assigned to cover things that their editors (the gatekeeper audience members) have already defined as newsworthy.

Another function of gatekeepers is to maintain the standards and the "voice" that define the specific organization for which they are keeping the gates. Within a newspaper organization, the assistant managing editor who assigns stories to various reporters on a beat has the responsibility to decide whether the reporters' stories are acceptable before they are sent along to the next step in the process of getting printed in the newspaper. Reporters quickly internalize the story qualities that their editors (the gatekeeper audience members) want. One editor may respond positively every time a reporter writes a story that includes a quote from a particular source. That reporter will try to include that source in her stories as often as possible. In a television news operation, the program producer might respond well every time a reporter and photographer team does a story that is accompanied by particular types of videotape images. Again, that team will try as often as possible to select that type of video to please the producer and thus assure a spot on the newscast.

In an advertising agency, a similar gatekeeper function is performed by the account management professionals. They are responsible for contact with the client who is paying to have the ads created. If the account manager is unhappy with the advertising campaign the other ad professionals have created, it may not get passed along for client approval. Communicators learn to adjust their efforts and create ads that are most likely to be defined by account managers as acceptable and ready for client review. The client is another gatekeeper, who makes the final decision about whether and when the ads in a campaign are ready for public consumption.

These internal gatekeepers comprise some of the most important audiences that communicators deal with. If the message doesn't get past the gatekeeper audience, it will never get to the anonymous audience "out there." As you can imagine, the standards that gatekeeper audiences demand may not always be the same as those that would be demanded by the general public. But the first eyes to see a message are those of the internal gatekeeper who decides whether or not the message moves to the next step. It is a fact of human nature that we want to be effective in what we do, and you learn to create messages that are acceptable to all of the internal gatekeepers within the organization in order to be effective.

Colleague and Professional Audience.   Another audience for communicators' messages is the colleague and professional audience. Once again, this is not the general public of anonymous audience members we usually associate with the word audience. Instead, you select information and create messages that will be influential with, or impress, your colleagues and the other professionals with whom you interact. For example, public relations professionals quickly learn to produce news releases that fit the formula sought by the media organizations they are trying to influence. The only way to be effective with a news release is to have a news organization pick it up or run a story based on it. Thus, effective PR specialists are those who can mimic the news style of the local media market and tailor their news releases so that they get the maximum exposure. Similarly, reporters might be tempted to write their stories in a way that they know (consciously or unconsciously) will avoid offending their most important sources (the professionals from whom they have to seek information on a regular basis). Some advertising copywriters and art directors create ads with the hope that they will get nominated for the advertising award shows that help boost careers and increase salaries. The award shows are almost always judged by fellow advertising professionals.

These colleague or professional audience members exert an enormous influence on the way communicators in all media industries do their work. Communicators rely heavily on each other for ideas, and the rewards in most areas of communication work are measured by professional reputation and recognition rather than by high salaries. It is not surprising that communicators seek to create messages that will garner attention and recognition from peers in the industry. Also, many communicators, especially those who work in news, are heavily reliant on information that is provided by others (government officials, industry sources, etc.), so there might be a reluctance to do anything that will cause someone to turn off the information flow. That is one of the reasons news organizations may rotate journalists off a specific beat—they don't want reporters to get too close to their sources. So messages are created with the colleague or professional audience members in mind.

Anonymous Audience.   After the gatekeeper and colleague/professional audience members are considered, then you must think about the *anonymous* audience. This is the audience that most people think of when they hear the word. But all audience members are not identical. Therefore, communication researchers have devised many ways to categorize the anonymous audience.

The anonymous audience in the United States is defined primarily by advertisers. The business of mass communication is to sell the attention of audiences to advertisers. In an advertising-supported media environment, it is advertisers who underwrite the creation and distribution of news and entertainment messages. No matter what kind of message is being produced, content and programming decisions are made to entice the consumers that advertisers want to reach. Advertisers want to reach those most likely to be interested in purchasing their products or services. That means they pay attention to the media habits of their potential customers, and tailor their messages and purchase advertising space and time in places where their audience is most likely to be found. For example, advertisers understand that you reach teens through MTV or *Tiger Beat* rather than the History Channel or *Gourmet.*

News professionals also pay attention to the market for their messages. A magazine story about the latest tour of a rock band is more likely to run in *Rolling Stone* than in *The Atlantic.* The freelance magazine writer knows where to "shop" an article depending on the audience for that magazine. A news story may emphasize different factors depending on the audience, as well. A story about the federal budget that runs in the college newspaper will focus on changes in the student loan program, whereas a story on the same general topic that runs in the magazine sponsored by the American Association of Retired Persons (AARP) will emphasize the budget's implications on Medicare or Social Security. It is impossible to escape the audience definitions established by advertisers. They influence what is published, by whom, where, and how successful any message is deemed to be.

Segmented Audiences.   Advertisers and those who generate news and information for audiences segment the anonymous audience into markets by *demographic, geographic,* and *psychographic* categories.

Demographic Factors.   These are social and economic characteristics that influence how someone behaves as an individual. Standard demographic variables include a person's age, gender, family status, education, occupation, income, race, and ethnicity. Each of these variables or characteristics can provide clues about how a person responds to messages. Advertisers are clearly interested in knowing, for instance, how age influences a person's need for goods and services. Think about the kinds of items teenagers purchase, the programs they watch on TV, and the magazines they read. Compare those to the products their parents purchase, the programs they watch, and the magazines they read.

The influence of an audience member's age is also a factor in the types of news messages that appeal to one group versus another. Younger people (teens, young adults) generally do not watch the national evening news on television or read a daily newspaper, for example. The news stories on those programs or in the newspaper reflect the knowledge that the audience is more mature, settled, and concerned about different topics and issues than are the younger members of the household. Each of the other demographic variables mentioned can be examined for their influence on messages and how they are tailored to meet specific audience characteristics.

Geographic Categories.   Geographic factors also help define the anonymous audience. We all understand geographically defined political jurisdictions such as cities, counties, and states. These are important geographic audience categories for politicians and for news stories or ads about politics and elections. Also, local retail advertisers want to reach audiences who are in the reading or listening range of the local newspaper or radio station and within traveling distance of their stores. The audience for a newspaper is generally defined as those within a specific metropolitan area—stories and ads are written to appeal to the residents of a well-defined locality. Local television stations tailor their messages to the audience reached by their broadcast signal.

Larger, more abstract geographic definitions help define the audience for national advertisers and those creating news or public relations messages for a regional or national audience. *Washington Post* reporter Joel Garreau argued that regional differences in North America (Canada, the United States, and Mexico) are important markers for understanding differences in populations that span a continent. He invented nine nonpolitical regions whose boundaries don't correspond to any current political jurisdictions. They are New England, The Foundry, Dixie, The Islands, MexAmerica, Breadbasket, Ecotopia, The Empty Quarter, and Quebec. For one example, Garreau examined three major cities in Texas. By political considerations, the three are all part of one jurisdiction: the state of Texas. But to Garreau, Fort Worth is actually part of the Breadbasket because of its strong cattle-town heritage; San Antonio, with its large, urban Spanish-speaking community, fits into MexAmerica; and Dallas is part of Dixie, with dramatic social change and economic growth. These distinctions may be irrelevant to those who draw political boundaries, but if Garreau's characterizations are right, the cultural implications are crucial for those who create messages.[2] Audience members for some types of messages in San Antonio cannot be characterized as Texans or even Southerners if one of their main cultural and regional identifiers is their close affiliation with other inhabitants of MexAmerica.

Another geographic definition segments audiences into rural, urban, suburban, and edge communities (the office parks that have sprung up on the outskirts of many urban communities). These geographic categories help define rifts between regions on issues such as transportation, education, taxes, housing, and land use. Politicians have long understood that voters can be defined using these types of categories. Those who create media messages pay attention to these categories as well. Newspaper publishers in metropolitan areas, for example, have long struggled with how to maintain their focus on the central city that defines the newspaper, while also attracting and keeping readers who live in the suburbs and work in an edge community high-rise office building.

Demographic and geographic audience characteristics are gathered from many sources, including the U.S. Census and thousands of individual studies and research services conducted by media industry professionals. Many of the tools and sources discussed in later chapters of this book provide access to this crucial information for communicators.

Psychographic Categories.   The anonymous audience is also defined according to psychographic categories. *Psychographics* refer to all of the psychological variables that combine to form a person's inner self. Even if two people share the same demographic or geographic characteristics, they may still hold entirely different ideas and values that define them personally and socially. Some of these differences are explained by looking at the psychographic characteristics that define them. Some psychographic variables are described here:

1. *Motives.* This is an internal force that stimulates someone to behave in a particular manner. A person has media consumption motives and buying motives. A motive for watching television may be to escape; a motive for choosing to watch a situation comedy rather than a police drama may be the audience member's need to laugh rather than feel suspense and anxiety.

2. *Attitudes.* This is a learned predisposition or a feeling held toward an object, person, or idea that leads to a particular behavior. Attitudes are enduring; they are positive or negative, affecting likes and dislikes. A strong positive attitude can make someone very loyal to a brand (one person likes Peter Jennings so she always watches ABC national news; someone likes the politics of Ben & Jerry's ice cream's owners so he buys that brand instead of Häagen-Dazs). A strong negative attitude can turn an audience member away from a message or product (a reader doesn't like the editorial position of her local newspaper so she buys *USA Today* instead; someone is offended by the advertising created for GUESS? jeans and decides not to buy any products made by that firm).

3. *Personalities.* This is a collection of traits that make a person distinctive. Personalities influence how people look at the world, how they perceive and interpret what is happening around them, how they respond intellectually and emotionally, how they form opinions and attitudes.

4. *Lifestyles.* These factors form the mainstay of psychographic research. Lifestyle research studies the way people allocate time, energy, and money. One of the best-known lifestyle models is the Values and Lifestyles System (VALS) devised by SRI Consulting Business Intelligence, a research firm. The model categorizes people according to their psychological characteristics and their resources, and is used by advertisers to determine what kind of products and advertising appeals will best work with an anonymous audience member who falls into one of the eight categories in the VALS model. For example, someone who falls into the Striver category is said to be seeking self-definition, motivation, and approval and is lacking economic, social, and psychological resources. The Actualizer group is made up of successful people with high self-esteem and high income, with a wide range of interests and a taste for finer things. These categories are most useful for advertisers, but they also help other message creators understand why advertisers support the types of media they do and why some types of messages are created while others are not. Figure 3.3 shows the psychographic breakdown for a particular zip code area in Florida.

All of these demographic, geographic, and psychographic categories help define the anonymous audience member. In the first steps of the information strategy process, you must think about the intended audience for the message and begin to identify the message format and types of information that will most effectively reach that audience member. Before any work can start in earnest on message production, you must have a clear idea about who is intended to receive the message and what characteristics they might have that could influence the rest of the search process.

Message Purpose

As we have already discussed, messages fulfill seven functions:

1. They provide information about the availability of products and services (advertising and publicity)

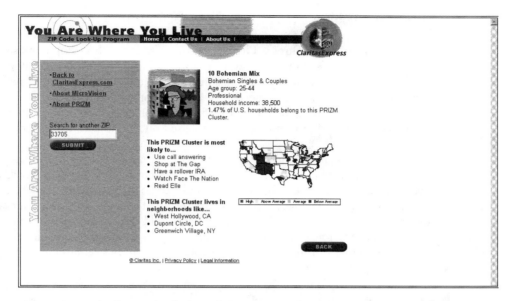

FIGURE 3.3 Audience Analysis.   Companies are developing increasingly sophisticated lifestyle segmentation systems. This example shows how geographic and demographic information has been combined to describe characteristics of most residents living in a ZIP code in St. Petersburg, Florida.

Source: Claritas Inc. Reprinted by permission.

2. They entertain (special features, advertising)
3. They inform (basic news, advertising, publicity)
4. They provide a forum for ideas (editorials, interpretive stories, documentaries, commentaries)
5. They educate (depth stories, self-help stories and columns, and informative pieces)
6. They serve as a watchdog of government (investigative pieces and straight coverage of trials and other public events)
7. They persuade (advertising, publicity, editorials, and commentaries)[3]

Communicators pay attention to these expectations as they seek information for messages. For a message to have audience appeal, it must meet the audience's expectations in purpose and form. Analyzing the context for a message includes the task of clearly understanding the purpose of the message. All of the subsequent information-gathering steps are affected by this basic requirement.

Message Time and Space

Messages must be tailored to meet the time and space constraints imposed by the context within which the message is being created. You cannot explore all information available for every message on every occasion. Deadlines and costs involved in collecting some information force you to make choices about particular angles and information sources. A long, interpretive news story on which a reporter might work for days must use many information sources. That stands in contrast to a breaking news story about a local fire that occurs an hour before deadline. The advertising campaign that will run over many months and include ads in several media is likely to rest on a large information base. But one ad placed in a local newspaper by the neighborhood shoe store does not require such an extensive information search. You make choices about the management of both time and money based on the time and space constraints of your message task.

Time factors in broadcast news, for example, may be the major information constraints. If you have just 1 minute and 20 seconds to tell a story with words and pictures, the information strategy must be tailored to help identify the most efficient sources for telling that story. Space factors may be the major information constraints for a message that will be delivered on a hand-held information device such as a cell phone or a PDA. The efficient information search is essential to the audience's expectation of effective storytelling and the media organization's requirement for economy in producing a message.

Message Formats and Channels

Different media formats reach different audiences. The characteristics of specific media formats define who will receive the message and how the story must be told.

Print Media.   Print media deliver messages that have lasting value because they can be saved, reread, and passed along to others. A reader takes in print messages one sentence at a time, one topic at a time, in a linear fashion. Audience credibility is very high for print media, although print works better for some types of audiences than for others. Obviously, a print message requires an attention level that is beyond some audience members. Messages with text require literacy skills. The storytelling constraints of print messages include lack of moving images and sound. Words must convey both pictures and sound.

Because print media rely so heavily on language, messages usually maintain a higher level of formality (the writer uses a more formal voice in word selection and sentence structure) than is used in broadcast. The audience makes a conscious decision to read a particular story or ad, so communicators can be confident that the audience expects the message to convey more detail and specific information. Print media allow the audience member to exert control over how messages are received; the reader chooses which stories to read, which ads to pay attention to, which section of the newspaper or magazine to read first.

Newspapers.   The frequency of newspaper publication means audiences receive recent information in a daily paper. The sheer size of most papers allows for a huge variety of messages, with something for nearly everybody. One reader can enjoy the national news reports and columnists, while another spends the most time with the sports pages, and yet another works the crosswords and reads the comics. Most papers have a regional and local audience, so the stories and ads can be geographically specific in their content focus. The stories in newspapers are usually relatively short (compared to magazine stories, for instance), which means they have to be tightly written and well organized so the audience can grasp the important facts quickly and skim through the extensive content of the newspaper.

Newspaper management measures their audience for the benefit of advertisers who want to know the circulation and readership characteristics. Newspapers offer advertisers extensive market coverage (the ability to reach a large number of people in a local market), with ad rates set according to the type of advertisement (brand, retail, classified) and the demographics of the audience. Newspaper readership increases with age and educational attainment. A benefit of newspaper advertising messages is that they can help consumers comparison shop.

Magazines. Most magazines are published weekly or monthly. Magazines can target audiences very specifically for both editorial and advertising content. Magazines cover regions of the country (*Mpls./St. Paul Magazine*), demographic groups (*Modern Maturity*), and types of editorial content (*Forbes, House Beautiful, Sports Illustrated*). Audiences give high marks to magazine articles and advertising for credibility and authority. Magazines have visual quality, and many people collect magazines (*National Geographic*) for the photographs as much as for the writing. People read an issue of a magazine over several days, so the stories can be longer, the ad copy can be more extensive. Advertising rates for magazines are based on the circulation size, readership, and demographics of the audience. Large advertisers create different versions of ads to run in various magazines so they can reach different audience members with specifically tailored ads. Figure 3.4 shows some of the features of a media directory.

Broadcast Media. Broadcast messages transmit sounds and/or images along with the words. Over-the-air and cable television and radio are different media than print, with different storytelling constraints and audience expectations. Messages tap into different human senses; sight and sound are at least as important as words. Broadcasting offers messages that affect viewers' emotions for a few seconds and then disappear. Unlike print, broadcast messages do not allow audience members time to digest information and images at their leisure. Some people who write for broadcast say they try to imagine that they have to tell their story to someone who is at a bus stop waiting to board an approaching bus that is already visible halfway down the block. The time constraints mean that audiences do not expect much detail in broadcast stories, but they do expect immediacy and impact. When news is breaking, most people know that they can turn to television or radio for the latest reports, and even live reports from the scene of an event.

Broadcasting uses images and sound to set the tone for the writing. A sound or image that would take several paragraphs to explain in print can be conveyed immediately in a broadcast. Most broadcast messages use a less formal tone than print messages. Words are not supposed to get in the way of the sounds and images. Broadcast messages emphasize information over explanation and people over concepts. Broadcast messages are intrusive; audiences have no control over the pace at which messages

FORBES ASAP (12A-990)   T
555 Airport Blvd 5th Fl   **(650) 558-4800**
Burlingame, CA 94010-2002   Fax: (650) 558-4995
                                E-Mail: stories@forbesasap.com
                                Home Page: www.forbesasap.com
Circ: 900,000; **Freq:** Quarterly; **Pub:** Forbes, Inc.
Uses: Industry News, Staff Written Articles, Color Photos; **Editorial Calendar:** Available.
Ad Rate: $52,880; **Trim Size:** 8 x 10.5 Col: 2.
Lead Times: Advertising - 1 month prior.
Profile: Written for an audience of corporate managers, entrepreneurs and other innovators who want to succeed in the digital world. Enhances Forbes' editorial coverage for the high-tech sector, providing readers with the essential tools and practical strategies for succeeding in the digital age. Editorial spotlights emerging technologies, the latest business opportunities, and leading innovators and start-up companies. Offers expert analysis of industry trends and developments that drive the next generation Internet and its infrastructure.
News Executives/Editors:
Editor In Chief . . . . Steve Forbes
                                    Phone: (212) 620-2282
                                            sforbes@forbes.com
    Contact Notes: - Based at the New York, NY bureau -
Editor . . . . Patrick Dillon
                                            pdillon@forbes.com
Managing Editor . . . . Lee Patterson
                                            leep@forbes.com
Editorial Director . . . . Tina Russo McCarthy
                                    Phone: (212) 367-3373
                                        trussomccarthy@forbes.com
    Contact Notes: - Based at the New York, NY bureau -
Section Editor . . . . Matthew Schifrin
                                    Phone: (212) 367-3377
                                            mschifrin@forbes.com
    Contact Notes: - Based at the New York, NY bureau - He oversees the "Best of the Web" section. All editorial inquiries and information for this section should be directed to the New York bureau address.
Senior Editor . . . . Carol Pogash
                                            cpogash@forbes.com
    Contact Notes: *Preferred order:* E-Mail. Send pitches via e-mail only; do NOT call. She accepts pitches from all industries, but there must be a tech element. Their lead time is long because of their frequency, so she cannot use timely or breaking news pitches. She likes stories that are quick, interesting and different; spicy in her readers; and are serious but slightly humorous at the same time. Anecdotes are good because they have human appeal. She wants more coverage of sports-related stories that include a technology angle. She oversees the "Uplink" section and responds best to those who refer to a previous story in her section and can then explain how their pitch would fit that section. The "Uplink" section appears in the front of the book and contains short, punchy pieces. Only pitch groundbreaking technological advancements, not just incremental developments. She is interested in innovative business players and new ideas in the tech industry.
Editor at Large . . . . Michael Malone
                                            mmalone@forbes.com
Contributing Editor . . . . Edward Clendaniel
                                            eclendaniel@forbes.com
Consulting Editor . . . . Owen Edwards
                                            oedwards@forbes.com
General Columnist
    "Editor's Letter" . . . . Patrick Dillon
                                            pdillon@forbes.com
Reporter . . . . Michael Boland
                                            mboland@forbes.com

Selected Editorial Offices/Bureaus

FORBES ASAP (12A-990A)
28 W 23rd St Fl 10   **(212) 620-2200**
New York, NY 10010-5254   Fax: (212) 367-3371
Editor In Chief . . . . Steve Forbes (212) 620-2282
                                            sforbes@forbes.com
    Mailing Address: 60 5th Ave
                    New York, NY 10011-8802
Editorial Director . . . . Tina Russo McCarthy (212) 367-3373
                                        trussomccarthy@forbes.com
    Contact Notes: She oversees the "Best of the Web" section which appears on a quarterly basis. The section rates consumer and B2B Web sites according to such categories as content, ease of navigation, and design.
Section Editor . . . . Matthew Schifrin (212) 367-3377
                                            mschifrin@forbes.com
    Contact Notes: *Preferred order:* E-Mail. Contact all "Best of the Web" editors via e-mail only. He oversees the "Best of the Web" section which appears on a quarterly basis. The section rates consumer and B2B Web sites according to such categories as content, ease of navigation, and design. He is always looking for new categories; please refer to their list of current categories and sites at www.forbesbest.com for further details. Pitches should be concise and use bullets to highlight your site's most important features. The best way to pitch about whether or not your site has been previously included in their list. If it has, send him a brief rundown of new Web site features. If your site is new to their database, it is very important to state which category you are pitching and the reasons

your site should be chosen. Focus on the innovative of your site relating to the categories listed on their Web site. The section also evaluates several products and tech devices (both portable and B2B applications), and selects one Web application to test for its "Web Lab" exclusive. He is open to relevant product pitches for these assessments and also for the newsletters he publishes for the company.
Senior Editor . . . . Nikhil Hutheesing (212) 367-3376
                                            nhutheesing@forbes.com
    Contact Notes: *Preferred order:* E-Mail. He accepts inquiries for the "Best of the Web" section via e-mail only.
Senior Editor . . . . Missy Sullivan (212) 367-3375
                                            msullivan@forbes.com
    Contact Notes: *Preferred order:* E-Mail. She accepts inquiries for the "Best of the Web" section via e-mail only.
Associate Editor . . . . Dolly Setton (212) 367-3374
                                            dsetton@forbes.com
Senior Reporter . . . . Ben Berentson (212) 367-3379
                                            bberentson@forbes.com
    Contact Notes: Special Coverage: Online investing.
Automotive Senior Reporter . . . . Ben Berentson (212) 367-3379
                                            bberentson@forbes.com
    (See above for contact notes)
Investments Senior Reporter . . . . Ben Berentson (212) 367-3379
                                            bberentson@forbes.com
    (See above for contact notes)
Sports Business Senior Reporter   Ben Berentson (212) 367-3379
                                            bberentson@forbes.com
    (See above for contact notes)
Reporter . . . . Jennifer McCullam (212) 367-3372
                                            jmccullam@forbes.com
Advertising Sales Director . . . . Kevin Gentzel (212) 620-2309
                                            kgentzel@forbes.com
    Mailing Address: 60 5th Ave
                    New York, NY 10011-8802

FORTUNE (12A-1000)   T
1271 Avenue Of The Americas   **(212) 522-1212**
New York, NY 10020-1300   Fax: (212) 522-0810
                                E-Mail: letters@fortune.com
                                Home Page: www.fortune.com
Circ: 875,520; **Audited By:** ABC-Audit Bureau of Circulations; **Freq:** Bi-Weekly; **Issued:** Mon; **Pub:** Time, Inc.
Uses: New Products, Industry News, By-lined Articles, Staff Written Articles, Letters, No Photos; **Editorial Calendar:** Available; **Publication Available Online.**
Sub Rate: $59.95; **Ad Rate:** $73,400; **Trim Size:** 8 x 10.875 Col: 3.
Lead Times: Features, News & Advertising - 1 month prior.
Profile: Edited primarily for high-demographic business people. It reports in-depth on hard-to-access executives and personalities, offers foresight and forecasts, and provides actionable business-building solutions and ideas. Specializes in big stories about companies, business personalities, technology, managing, Wall Street, media, marketing, personal finance, politics, policy and important corporate trends.
News Executives/Editors:
Group Publisher . . . . Michael Federle (212) 522-2728
                                            michael_federle@timeinc.com
Editor In Chief . . . . Norman Pearlstine (212) 522-4440
                                            norman_pearlstine@timeinc.com
    Contact Notes: Do NOT contact him with any editorial inquiries. You must call the editorial assistant before faxing anything. They can provide you with the most appropriate fax number for your inquiry. Know the magazine and the kinds of things they cover before you pitch anyone. All pitches should be sent to the main e-mail address. In addition to his editorial duties, he is responsible for Time, Inc.'s new media, international and television activities.
Executive Editor . . . . Peter Petre (212) 522-2077
                                            peter_petre@fortunemail.com
    Contact Notes: Mon-Fri, *Preferred order:* U.S. Mail, Fax. Do not call. Contact beat reporters first, but he is willing to look at material sent via mail or fax. He oversees the "Technology" section, as well as the annual "Technology Buyer's Guide" issue. They do get overloaded with info on the science and technology arena so please be very selective when sending materials.
Executive Editor . . . . Joseph Nocera (212) 522-1012
                                    Fax: (212) 522-2352
                                            jnocera@fortunemail.com
    Contact Notes: He is coordinating a book project on the Enron bankruptcy scandal being written by senior writers Peter Elkind and Bethany McLean.
Managing Editor . . . . Rik Kirkland (212) 522-4706
                                            richard_kirkland@fortunemail.com
    Contact Notes: Mon, Tue, Between 11am and 5pm, *Preferred order:* Fax, U.S. Mail.
Editorial Director . . . . John Huey (212) 522-3613
                                    Fax: (212) 522-7205
                                            john_huey@timeinc.com
    Contact Notes: He is not a PR contact.
Editorial Director . . . . Geoffrey Colvin (212) 522-4361
                                    Fax: (212) 467-4392
                                            gcolvin@fortunemail.com

FIGURE 3.4 Bacon's Magazine Directory. Bacon's Media Directories provide circulation information and a description of the audience segment(s) the publication aims to reach, in addition to media contact information.

Source: Bacon's Information, Inc. Reprinted by permission.

are received or the subject matter of messages within any particular broadcast. Unless people switch stations, use the mute button on the remote control, or tape messages and then fast-forward through the ones that are not interesting, they have no way to pick and choose which messages to receive from a broadcast.

Television Messages. Television messages convey drama better than abstract ideas. Pictures of a house fire make the local news, even though there may be no lasting public affairs implications to the story; a story about a city council vote to change the fire code is less likely to make the news, even though the lasting implications of that story are much greater. Television messages are very short (some ads are just 15 seconds long; most television news stories run no more than 1 minute 45 seconds to 2 minutes).

The audience for television is measured in many ways, especially for advertising purposes. Advertisers want to know who is watching which programs at what times, because advertising costs are set according to the size and characteristics of the viewing audience. Television advertising messages are placed within entertainment or news programming based on the characteristics of the audiences for those programs, and the ads are tailored to appeal to, and have impact with, those target audience members.

Radio Messages. Radio messages use only words and sounds to convey visually descriptive images. Some people argue that radio is a better broadcast medium for news than television, because the pictures in television overwhelm the words, whereas the radio story enables the audience to focus on the words and information without the distraction of visual input. With radio, the listeners' imaginations play a role in constructing the meaning of a message, which enables listeners to create their own picture of what is happening. Radio messages can be very creative and engaging for the audience, who actively create mental pictures of what is happening. Radio reports must be written for the ear, not the eye. Sentence structure and word choice must reflect the simplicity that the delivery format requires.

Radio provides audiences with news summaries and updates, usually on the hour or half-hour, so information can be updated continually. Virtually every household in the United States has a radio, and the radio market is highly segmented with many program formats. Radio audiences are measured for advertisers by geographic areas and demographic characteristics. Advertisers know radio messages can reach highly targeted audiences with relatively low cost. Audience inattentiveness and message clutter are some of the drawbacks of radio as a medium to reach audiences.

Digital Media. The digital media messages delivered via computer, cell phone, PDA, and unimagined new devices combine the characteristics of print and broadcast. For the computer, messages must be designed to appeal to the visual senses but must look good on a computer screen and sound good through the relatively simple speakers most multimedia computers employ. Messages can contain moving images and sound, but also usually convey information in print format. The virtually unlimited storage capacity of computer networks allows for extensive background information to be loaded and available for audiences to tap into if they wish, so these media messages can be more complete than those delivered in any other format. Yet, this information is often written in short chunks rather than lengthy paragraphs; chunks have quickly become a convention of the medium.

Audiences *choose* to receive messages, and actively *seek* messages via this medium. Audiences expect interactivity; they interact with content, choose stories at their own pace and in the order they prefer. Message content cannot simply be transferred from print or broadcast media and dumped onto computer screens unchanged. Messages must be designed so that audience members can interact with the content *and* with other audience members. This medium allows you to create hypertext links within a message to related information. Therefore, you have to understand what kinds of related materials audience members might want.

Writing styles and visual/audio encoding strategies are still developing for messages delivered via these new media. No one yet knows which format and style will most appeal to audiences and which message providers will be successful in the long term, so you can be creative and exercise your storytelling skills as you generate messages.

All of these message context issues, then, must be analyzed at the start of an information search. As you begin to define the nature of the audience, the purpose of the message, and the time, space, format, and channel characteristics of the message, a more clearly outlined information process starts to emerge. The rest of the information strategy is highly dependent on the decisions that you make about the message task in this very first step.

THE CONTENT OF THE MESSAGE

The other part of the message analysis step requires you to start to define the actual *content* areas that the message must incorporate. Originality, or at least a fresh slant, is a prerequisite for much media work. We have already discussed some of the techniques that communicators use to generate interesting ideas. This becomes especially important as the message content is defined.

What Is the Topic?

You usually start a message task with an assigned topic or an idea for an enterprise project you intend to work on. This assignment sets the initial boundaries for the information search. For example, the advertising team knows their client and has a general familiarity with the product or service that the advertising will promote. The public relations professional knows that the CEO will be delivering a speech about a specific topic to the company shareholders. The news professional knows that the story is supposed to be about the new parking policy downtown. But beyond those broad outlines, you have enormous leeway in defining the specifics of the message.

For reasons of time savings, you often concentrate on obvious or simple approaches to a message. But this may lead to a message that does nothing more than convey the conventional wisdom in an area, failing to provide the audience with a more creative and original approach. The information strategy process provides you with a method for identifying fresh angles or new twists on a topic. One of the advantages of using idea-mapping and point-of-view diagrams is that they help you identify what you *think* you know about a topic. It is then easier to find an original or fresh approach to the topic.

How do you get beyond the conventional wisdom in a particular field? The media are accused of being trapped by conventional wisdom. There is even a column about it in *Newsweek* magazine, which publishes a tongue-in-cheek "Conventional Wisdom Watch" every week (see Figure 3.5), with up or down arrows assigned to individuals or events. The arrows represent the conventional wisdom opinion among media pundits, many of whom are often proved wrong later on.

To get beyond the conventional wisdom in a field, you must first understand what it is. Conventional wisdom usually contains a grain of truth. It is different than faith, blind prejudice, or stereotypes. The essential elements of conventional wisdom about any topic can usually be demonstrated in some manner. For example, conventional wisdom says that cats are difficult to train, Midwestern universities have good hockey teams, and women are good listeners. Each of these is based on some socially-arrived-at assumptions about reality.

Conventional wisdom abounds in every field and for every topic. Advertisers and marketers operated under the assumption that women generally were not big purchasers and users of technology, until a national study done for a women's magazine showed that 65 percent of the women surveyed had purchased a personal computer for home use in the previous two years. Fifty-three percent of the women surveyed said that advertising for computer-related products did not appeal to them because it was aimed at men.[4] Advertisers trapped by the conventional wisdom about who purchases products and services lose opportunities to create messages with a fresh, effective appeal.

One source of conventional wisdom is easy to trace. Media professionals are beholden to many people, organizations, institutions, and routines that influence how and where information for messages comes from. These individuals and groups provide information subsidies in the form of news releases, media kits, sound-bite-ready interviewees, briefing papers, privately funded research studies, and thousands of other sources of facts, figures, and interpretations. The savvy communicator understands that information subsidies are a necessary part of the information routine of every busy mass media professional. However, a solid information strategy helps minimize the influence these information subsidies have on the perspective and tone of messages. Although it is impossible to avoid using information subsidies, you use the information process to independently uncover additional material and points of view on the topic.

For example, news professionals have regular contact with hundreds of information subsidizers in their everyday routines. The city hall reporter has contacts with the mayor's office, each city councilmember's office, lobbyists trying to generate favorable decisions for their clients, city employee union representatives, contractors doing work for the city, citizens and neighborhood groups seeking to affect public policy, and many others. Most of these individuals and groups provide the reporter with news releases, pamphlets outlining their goals and accomplishments, suggestions for interviewees, and exhortations to see the world from their point of view.

CONVENTIONALWISDOM

WISHFUL THINKING EDITION

While soft targets are hit abroad and the clock ticks in Iraq, Americans seek escape with James Bond and mall invasions. Hold your breath.

	C.W.	
Kissinger	▲	Back in the saddle as chair of "independent" commission re: 9-11. Will Dr. Secrecy expose the truth?
Air safety	◀▶	New TSA airport teams seem on the case. But now we have to worry about surface-to-air missiles.
U.N.	▲	Inspectors' shakedown cruise goes smoothly. But wait until they arrive unannounced at a "palace."
Red Sox	▲	New owners hire hip 28-year-old GM and stats whiz Bill James to fight The Curse with brains. Good luck.
Cruises	▼	Old: Have fun but don't forget sunscreen. New: Have fun but don't forget biohazard suit.
Lisa Marie	▼	Jacko's ex splits with Nicolas Cage after less than four months. Listen to daddy: Only fools rush in.

FIGURE 3.5 **Newsweek's "Conventional Wisdom Watch" Column.** This regular column underscores the prevalence of conventional wisdom use in the media.

Source: From Newsweek 12/9/02 © 2002 Newsweek, Inc. All rights reserved. Reprinted by permission.

Good city hall reporters pay attention to these sources of information, but they also develop their own methods and routines for locating information that can help put all of the competing sources of information in context. For instance, the mayor's office may send out an impressive study indicating overall crime is down. The neighborhood watch groups may issue their own report claiming that their volunteer efforts have meant the difference in lowering property crime rates, rather than improvements in policing. The police department may provide their own data indicating that their budget has been cut and they need more funding to stem the rise in the one category of crime that went up, assault with a weapon. The city hall reporter would ask, "What do each of these groups have to gain or lose from the release of this information in this form? Who is trying to influence me, and with what kinds of evidence? What else can I do and where else can I seek information that will put these information subsidies in perspective?"

Strategic communicators deal with their own forms of information subsidy. Advertising agency staff maintain regular contact with the clients for whom they create messages. The client is the most important information subsidy provider for ideas and data about the products or services being advertised. However, agency team members supplement the client information with material about audiences, media outlets, and competitor companies from many other sources. If a client asks their public relations agency to write a news release announcing that the client's company is the first to introduce a new type of snack, the PR agency would do well to check other sources to verify that a similar product is not already on the market. Media planners (those who decide where to place ads) and media buyers (those who purchase ad time and space) are inundated with media kits trying to prove that an ad placed in such-and-such a magazine is a better buy than one placed in another title, for instance. These media kits are compiled by the publishers of those magazines who want the ad dollars for their publications. Skilled media planners and buyers supplement these information subsidies by using the many specialized information tools in the advertising field to make their own comparisons about which publication does the best job reaching the target audience. So the task of defining the specific topic includes an assessment of the relative value of the information subsidies that are likely to be available about that topic.

Another major aspect of topic definition involves drawing the boundaries for the information strategy. It is never possible to examine an idea in its entirety. You have to carve out a manageable portion of an idea if you are going to make your deadline and do a credible job with the message. When drawing these boundaries for the strategy, it helps to think about how and where information is produced. For this, you need to identify the *disciplines* of knowledge-production in a subject area.

Information does not exist in the environment like some kind of raw material. It is produced by individuals who work within a broad field of knowledge, a stream of previous accomplishments, a method of generating new information. Disciplines are systems for producing and disseminating knowledge. Looking through a college course catalog gives clues to discipline structure. Fields such as political science, biology, history, and mathematics are unique disciplines with their own logic for how and where new knowledge is introduced and made accessible.

You must become comfortable with identifying the disciplines that might contribute information to any strategy. You must learn how to move seamlessly from one discipline to another during your strategy, and how to compare and evaluate information that comes from a variety of perspectives and knowledge systems. The way people talk about the topic within a discipline conforms to the conventions and ways of thinking that have developed in that particular field over a (usually) long period of time.

For example, think about the disciplines that might contribute information to a search on the topic of the role of sports in society. Try to anticipate the perspective each discipline might have on the topic. In other words, what is important to the people in that discipline about the topic? What is the most likely focus of their study about the topic? What "take" are they likely to have on the topic?

We might identify three disciplines that have something to say about the role of sports in society: medicine, sociology, and economics. The medical scientists will obviously be interested in how sports affect individuals' health and well-being. Sports injuries, physical conditioning for those who take part in sports, life expectancy for those who regularly exercise, and other similar perspectives are likely to be represented in the information generated by this discipline.

The sociologists are likely to be interested in the topic as it affects social relationships. How does a society treat its sports heroes? How are young people socialized into the ideal of team cooperation? What differences are there between boys and girls and their participation in organized sports? The discipline of sociology is likely to generate information on all of these questions, and more.

The economists are interested in the financial aspects of sports. What kind of economic contribution does a major league sports franchise make to a city? Should public financing be used in building new sports facilities when a team threatens to leave? What kind of management–labor relations are represented by negotiations in major league sports contracts? The discipline of economics clearly has its own perspective on the topic, which is quite different from the medical scientists or the sociologists.

So we see that a single topic can be approached from many different perspectives, depending on how the disciplinary boundaries are drawn and how the topic is framed. The message analysis step of the information strategy model requires you to make some decisions early on, to focus the topic on a manageable and appropriate scope for the rest of the strategy.

Topic Terminology

People in different disciplines have their own jargon and terminology for discussing their field and the ideas they work with. You must know how to decode this language in order to be able to talk to experts, understand what they are writing, and make the material clear for the nonspecialist audience that will see the final message. The language of a topic is the key that opens the door to discussion of most subjects. Language is the access code through which formal collections of information in libraries and databases are indexed and organized. In addition, terminology shifts over time as new words are added and as some language falls out of use and is replaced. When the former Soviet Union collapsed, millions of records in library catalogs and electronic databases suddenly no longer corresponded to any existing political entity!

Political perspectives also play a role in decoding language. A body of water in the Middle East is called the Persian Gulf by some and the Arabian Gulf by others, depending on their political perspective. Think about the different connotations of the terms *pro-choice* and *pro-abortion; right-to-life* and *anti-choice*. You must understand how the audience will react to language and terminology choices. During your information search you must use appropriate terminology to locate relevant information.

For example, a news reporter working on a story about health care costs will encounter terms such as *HMO*, *fee for service*, *cost sharing*, *primary care networks*, *third-party payers*, *preferred provider organizations* and many others. An advertising professional working on an ad campaign for a health insurer must have a grasp of the same terminology. Without a clear understanding of these terms and the way they are used by specialists in that field, the communicator is bound to miss important information and perhaps make mistakes in any message that is generated for an audience. By first understanding the jargon and terminology in that subject area, the communicator can be more accurate and save much time in the next steps of the information strategy.

Questions to Be Answered

Good ideas for messages come from asking a variety of questions.

News Questions. For news, journalists systematically ask a set of questions that have become routine:

- *Who.* Who is important in this story? Who has information about this topic? Who is my audience?
- *What.* What events or activities are important? What kind of report are we doing? What kind of information will be useful? What information do we have already? What do we need to say about this?
- *Where.* Where did the action take place? Where have we already sought information? Where will the story appear?
- *When.* When did the activity take place? When is the information needed? When will the story appear? When should we do a follow-up story?
- *Why.* Why did this activity take place? Why should we tell a story about it? Why does the audience care?
- *How.* How can we explain the meaning of the event? How much information do we need? How will the information be used? How will we attribute the information? How can we get help with the project? How will the audience react to this report?

Advertising Questions. Advertising professionals have also developed a standard set of questions that they ask at the start of a message task:

- What should our advertising accomplish?
- To whom should we advertise?
- What should we say?
- How should we say it?
- Where should we say it?
- How much should we spend?
- After the campaign, did we accomplish our advertising goals?

Public Relations Questions. Public relations professionals ask a similar set of questions when they are doing their strategic planning research:

- *Defining the problem.* Monitor knowledge, opinions, attitudes, and behaviors to answer the question, "What is happening now?"
- *Planning and programming.* Use the information gathered to determine, "What should we do and why?"
- *Taking action and communicating.* Design a message or program to meet specific objectives by determining, "How do we do it and say it?"
- *Evaluating the program.* Assess the first three steps by asking, "How did we do?"[5]

Narrowing the Focus

In addition to asking about the disciplines that might contribute and the terminology of the field, you can pose several other questions at the start of the search. These include decisions about the complexity of the topic, geographic limits, time period limits, depth of treatment, and the type of message that will be produced. For example, if the broad question is, "What are the causes of the growing rate of homelessness in the United States?" the formula for narrowing the question might work this way:

- Which disciplines contribute information to this topic? Sociology, political science, economics, banking and finance, and urban affairs are places to start.

- What factors make this topic complex? Academics, politicians, social workers, activists, and advocates for the homeless have entirely different ways of approaching the issue and defining the problem. The social and political climate affects lawmakers and policy officials in subtle and frequently unknown ways. Reliable statistics on the prevalence of the problem are difficult to come by.

- What are the geographic limits of the topic? Although homelessness exists throughout the United States, how the condition is understood and approached varies from community to community and from state to state. The geographic area in which the message will be distributed may be important in establishing geographic boundaries for the topic. On the other hand, some policies and programs emanate from the federal government and apply nationally.

- What time period factors can be used to limit the topic? Much of mass communication work emphasizes recency. Therefore, the newest information is likely to be stressed. However, trends in homelessness over time (particularly the last decade or so) will surely help put the problem into an historical context. Some types of messages would benefit from an overview of how homelessness has been handled throughout many decades, because this is a problem that has been with us for a very long time.

- How in-depth will the message be? You and your organization may make major research efforts for some projects, while others are deadline-driven and perfunctory. A major magazine article on homelessness requires extensive research, using varied print, electronic, and interview sources. A short news story concerning the take-over of vacant houses by advocates for the homeless, produced on a short deadline, may allow just a cursory background search. Message analysis helps you specify the detail and depth required in the strategy.

■ What is the nature of the audience? We've already outlined extensive means for analyzing the audience for your message. This is a crucial part of the process.

■ What kind of message will be produced? This has also been discussed in depth. As we've said, the standards for evidence and documentation vary from one type of message to another. The purpose of the message and the format of message delivery have a profound influence on the decisions you make about your information strategy.

Once all of these angles have been examined, you are in a position to focus selectively on some aspects of the larger question and develop an exacting standard for raising questions and seeking information to address your information needs. Going through this routine frequently allows you to revise or refine the question, making your information-seeking tasks much more manageable.

Even with a well-defined message analysis process you might find yourself at a dead end. If your original hypothesis doesn't seem to be panning out in your initial investigation of the topic, it might be time to rethink, refocus, or even broaden your question.

CONCLUSION

In this step of the information strategy, you work through the tasks in the message-analysis box: You identify the context for your message and begin to identify the content that will be important to your message. The investment of time and resources in developing a media message is considerable. Message analysis, as an integral part of information strategy, allows you to identify your audience and the nature of your message, move among disciplines and subject areas, and focus the major questions sharply. Message analysis has the capacity to help you stay on track and avoid getting lost in the many subtopics that can be found in a larger topic. In Chapter 4 we discuss the potential contributors to your information strategy.

SELECTED ADDITIONAL READINGS

Avery, Jim. *Advertising Campaign Planning*, 2nd ed. Chicago: The Copy Workshop, 1997.

Browne, M. Neil and Stuart Keeley. *Asking the Right Questions: A Guide to Critical Thinking*, 6th edition. Upper Saddle River, NJ: Prentice Hall, 2001.

Murray, Donald. *Writing for Your Readers*, 2nd edition. Chester, CT: Globe Pequot Press, 1992.

Yopp, Jan Johnson and Katherine C. McAdams. *Reaching Audiences: A Guide to Media Writing*, 2nd edition. Boston: Allyn & Bacon, 1998.

NOTES

1. Donald Murray. *Writing to Deadline: The Journalist at Work.* Portsmouth, NH: Heinemann, 2000, 40–49.

2. Joel Garreau. *The Nine Nations of North America.* New York: Avon Books, 1989.

3. Doug Newsom and James A. Wollert. *Media Writing: Preparing Information for the Mass Media,* 2nd edition. Belmont, CA: Wadsworth, 1988, 18–19.

4. Stuart Elliott. "Put down your rotary-dial phone and listen up: Women are big buyers of high-tech products." *New York Times,* 30 July 1996, C5.

5. Scott Cutlip, Allen Center, and Glen Broom. *Effective Public Relations,* 8th edition. Upper Saddle River, NJ: Prentice Hall, 2000, 341.

CHAPTER FOUR

UNDERSTANDING POTENTIAL CONTRIBUTORS

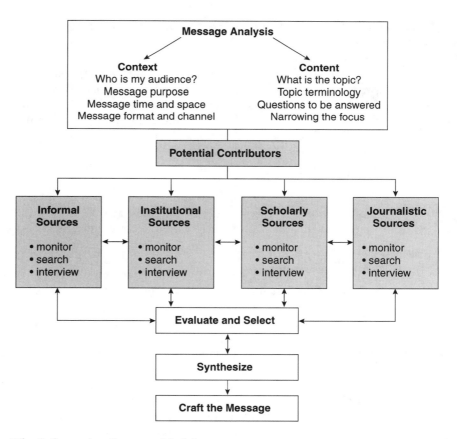

The Information Strategy Model

You've done your analysis of the message task before you. You know the type of message you will be creating and the reason it is being created. You've determined the context of the story (where it will be delivered, how much time you have to prepare it, who the audience is) and you've started the content analysis (what terms are relevant). Now you need to begin scanning the information landscape for resources that will help you develop the message itself.

The information strategy model in this book has *Potential Contributors* as the step after *Message Analysis*. In this chapter we provide an overview of the four categories of contributors, and the types of information—people, paper, and digital—that can be found through each contributor type. We compare and contrast the forms of information and data that come from different contributors.

UNDERSTANDING POTENTIAL CONTRIBUTORS

Communicators rely on four types of contributors for information, inspiration, and insights. Whether you are seeking a specific fact, a good anecdote to illustrate your story, background information about the product or service you are advertising, or promotional or persuasive literature to understand different points of view, you need to know how to find, and use, the information provided by informal sources, institutional sources, scholarly sources, and journalistic sources.

Informal Sources

Informal sources include observations about audiences, messages, and the environment in which the communicator operates, as well as networks of supervisors, colleagues, clients, neighbors, and friends the communicator deals with every day.

Monitoring.   Monitoring online forums, chat rooms, and listservs has become a routine part of a communicator's everyday function. A public relations specialist working for an automobile tire company regularly scans the electronic message boards and online forums where people discuss tire safety controversies and other issues. A beat reporter who covers the large plastics factory in the community regularly monitors the electronic business forums that summarize news and information about the plastics industry. An advertising account executive working on a fast food restaurant account monitors the chat rooms where teenagers discuss their favorite foods and restaurant hang-outs.

Likewise, communicators regularly scan mass communication outlets for information about the topics and issues that they cover or the clients for whom they are creating messages. In many media organizations, staff members are assigned to monitor CNN, CNBC, Fox News, or C-SPAN throughout the day for news tips or public relations opportunities or challenges. Communicators create personal clip files of items they find online or in their casual reading of newspapers and magazines that relate to the area in which they work.

Bus stop posters, bumper stickers, billboard copy, T-shirt messages, and other informal messages visible in every community can also trigger ideas or perspectives for the more formal part of the information strategy. Communicators actually pay attention to the junk mail they receive because it is a form of monitoring what is going on and observing what companies, people, and organizations are doing and saying about themselves.

Searching. Communicators search for information from informal sources when they have a specific information task. A news professional who has just been assigned to do a story about changes in airport security screening processes is likely to spend some time searching for information from electronic listservs, chat rooms, and online forums where passengers and airline workers discuss the changes. The reporter is also likely to go to the local airport to observe how the changes are affecting the movement of people and cargo through the facility. The reporter also may search his or her own memory about travel before the changes, and make comparisons to the current situation.

Interviewing. Communicators interview informal sources to understand the goals of a client, to better define the nature of the message assignment, or to learn about people's opinions, attitudes, concerns, and interests. People frequently talk about new projects with coworkers and get examples or leads to additional information. Informal discussions with neighbors, friends, or interesting people in the community help you generate innovative ideas and new approaches for messages.

Even at their best, however, informal sources provide just a portion of the information that is needed for a message. Informal sources may be incomplete, outdated, self-serving, or contain errors of fact or interpretation. These informal sources are best used as stimulators—the first words on the subject rather than the last. Informal sources are discussed in more detail in Chapter 7.

Institutional Sources

The second major category of information sources is institutions, which produce a huge variety and amount of information essential to the functioning of society. Institutions in both the public sector (governments at all levels) and the private sector (businesses, political organizations, trade and industry associations, foundations, religious organizations, unions, and professional associations) generate information for a number of purposes. They produce information to ensure their own survival and well-being, to promote their point of view, to gain public acceptance or understanding, to raise money or enroll new members, to communicate with their members and supporters, and to communicate with the public at large. Much of the information institutions develop to serve these purposes is also extremely valuable for mass communicators seeking information for messages.

Monitoring. Again, communicators monitor institutional sources as a routine part of their work. The beat reporter who covers the local school board regularly attends school board meetings and gets him or herself on the mailing list for meeting notices, minutes, and announcements. The advertising account executive who works on the campaign for a soft drink company routinely scans the company's annual report and the industry newsletters and trade association publications for information about trends in the soft drink industry and changes in consumer preferences and attitudes. The public relations specialist working for the state Department of Tourism monitors announcements from the union representing state workers as the new contract negotiations proceed, to stay alert to any likely interruptions of service or staffing for state parks and other tourist facilities in the event of a strike.

Searching.   Communicators search for institutional sources of information in every facet of their work. The federal government of the United States generates an enormous quantity of information that is crucial to communicators' daily routines. For instance, advertisers working for an overnight delivery service might use Federal census data to decide whether a community has enough of the small businesses that make up the bulk of the company's clients to warrant running an aggressive ad campaign there. A reporter working on a story about the effects of new legislation to regulate hand guns will certainly search for information about hand gun use and criminal activity from the Federal Bureau of Investigation, the Justice Department, and the Bureau of Alcohol, Tobacco and Firearms, along with information from Congress.

Interviewing.   Institutional sources also provide thousands of interviewees for communicators in their message production work. Government officials, corporate spokespersons, trade association presidents, and rank-and-file members of hobby organizations such as the Poodle Club of America provide communicators with their institution's point of view. Public officials and business leaders may hold news conferences and conduct press briefings. Institutional representatives may participate in online forums to respond to consumer, voter, media, or general public questions and concerns.

Just as with informal sources, you must recognize that information is developed by institutions for their own purposes and may be disclosed to you selectively and with a specific purpose in mind. Organizations as different from one another as the U.S. Department of Defense and the Women's International League for Peace and Freedom share this characteristic. Institutional sources are discussed in more detail in Chapter 8.

Scholarly Sources

The third major category of information sources is scholarly information produced by subject experts working in academic institutions, research centers, and scholarly organizations. Scholars generate information that advances our knowledge and understanding of the world. The research they do creates new opportunities for inventions, practical applications, and new approaches to solving problems.

Scholars introduce their discoveries to the world in a formal system of information dissemination that has developed over many decades. Much of the work that scholars produce is collected and archived by libraries, which organize the information according to the structure of information for each particular field of study. Scientists and humanists use different research methods and study different phenomena. They publish their findings in forms that are characteristic of their disciplines and make these documents accessible through a variety of indexes, abstracts, and electronic sites that are specific to their fields.

Monitoring.   Communicators monitor scholarly sources to stay abreast of the most current research being done in a field. For instance, an advertising account executive who works with a manufacturer of medical devices will subscribe to electronic services that distribute information about the latest research in that field. That advertising professional may also regularly check in with the independent bioengineering researchers at the local university, to stay current with the major developments and ongoing work in that subject area. A reporter working on the cops and crime beat may meet the criminal justice researcher at the local university once a month for coffee, to talk about the latest trends and research in the field of crime prevention.

Searching.   Communicators search for scholarly information to get the most sophisticated background information and complete grounding in the subject areas of their messages. For example, a reporter working on a story about a new variety of apples developed by researchers at the local university will search for scholarly background information about how new strains of fruit are produced, the success rate of new varieties, and similar types of experiments done elsewhere. A public relations practitioner preparing a speech for the CEO of a chemical company that is introducing a new herbicide product will search for relevant scholarly articles and information about the testing, safety, and effects of that herbicide that have been done independently from the company's own research (which might be seen as biased).

Thousands of formal search tools (print and electronic indexes, abstracts, bibliographies, resource guides) help communicators locate scholarly information on any topic imaginable. Because scholarly research undergoes a process of *peer review* before being published (meaning that other experts review the work and pass judgment about whether it is worthy of publication), you can be assured that the information you find in your search for scholarly sources has met the standards for accuracy, credibility, and validity in that field.

Interviewing.   Communicators interview scholarly sources to provide depth, background, and credibility to their messages. Audiences usually accord respect to scholars who have independence, long experience, and expert knowledge of a subject area. For this reason, communicators like to be able to attribute information in messages to scholars, to lend credibility and credence to their messages. Interviews with scholars are essential so you can update the information you find in their published work, which usually suffers from a time lag between creation and publication because of the peer review process. Scholarly sources are discussed in more detail in Chapter 9.

Journalistic Sources

The fourth major category of information sources is journalistic materials produced for a general audience and distributed through the popular media (newspapers, magazines, radio, television, Web sites). Journalistic sources also include industry-specific news sources such as *PRWeek, Advertising Age,* or *Editor & Publisher* magazine. Much of the work that communicators do relies on the previous journalistic work in that area. The basic rule to "check the clips" before starting on any information task applies to newsrooms of all types. Advertising libraries maintain *tear sheet* files of ad examples from magazines and newspapers in a myriad of product and service categories so ad professionals have some idea about how a particular item has been advertised before they start to develop a new campaign. And because public relations professionals are judged, in part, by the coverage their clients receive in the popular media, they therefore use a variety of means to document coverage.

Monitoring. Communicators monitor journalistic sources routinely. Newspaper, broadcast, and Web site professionals read, watch, and listen to their own organization's news output and monitor their competitors. The morning news huddle at most newspaper offices includes a critique of that day's paper, along with an analysis of competitors' news decisions. Advertising professionals pay close attention to the ads that appear everywhere in the public arena to garner ideas and understand competitors' strategies. Public relations professionals monitor the stories that appear about their clients and respond if necessary with news releases, statements, news conferences, and other types of communications.

Searching. Communicators search for journalistic sources to be sure that messages are consistent with past efforts within a media organization, and to find additional information and ideas for the messages they are creating. Many of the print and electronic tools for searching information allow you to quickly locate content from the popular media for background, context, comparison, and to advance a story or expand or refine a campaign. For instance, a local reporter working on a story about urban sprawl in her community would search for news stories from media outlets in communities that have similar problems, to put the local story in context. An advertising professional working on a campaign for a brand of computers would scour journalistic sources for information about the company and the product category, and for insights into computer buyers.

Interviewing. Communicators interview journalistic sources to gain additional background information from colleagues (provided there is no competitive issue at stake) and to share ideas, techniques, and strategies for producing messages. Despite fierce competition among media outlets, individual media professionals are generally collegial and willing to set aside competitive instincts to advance their mutual interests, better the practice of their craft, or more competently serve the audience's need for information. Journalistic sources are discussed in more detail in Chapter 10.

UNDERSTANDING THE WAYS INFORMATION FROM POTENTIAL CONTRIBUTORS IS AVAILABLE

The information that is valuable and accessible to communicators crafting messages, as we've just discussed, comes from four types of contributors. From each of these four contributors, information is available in three formats: through people, through paper, or in digital form.

These three forms can exist individually, as distinct units within a potential contributor's area. An institutional contributor will, for example, have people you can talk to, a publication you can subscribe to, and a Web site you can access. There are also collections that hold valuable resources in *all* of these information types—libraries, for example, which are discussed in Chapter 6. (These library collections may be internal to an organization, or may be more publicly accessible.) But now, let's look at the forms in which individual contributors might present the information they have.

People as Sources

People are primary sources. The information they know, the opinions they hold, the perspectives they have on the issue you might be interested in—these are unfiltered, unedited. For each of the four types of contributors of information, there will be people in various positions and with various motives for providing information.

People as Informal Contributors.   For informal contributors, you need to locate people who have an opinion on, interest in, or personal experience with the topic you are researching. People as informal contributors can be found everywhere, but finding the right people can be a challenge. People as a source of information can be insightful but unreliable—what they tell you will be what they, as individuals, know or believe. The same person who might be used as an informal contributor might, in another setting and for another set of questions, be an institutional contributor. For example, if you were working on an ad campaign to get drivers to slow down on neighborhood streets, the lawyer who lives down the block might provide an informal opinion as a resident of that neighborhood, but if you talked to her about the legalities of police enforcement of speed limits, she would be talking to you as an institutional contributor.

People as Institutional Contributors.   People are the employees of the business, the government officials in agencies, the information officers of organizations, and the leaders and members of associations. The kinds of information you get and the motivation the person has for giving it depend on the person's position within the institution. For example, you'll get a different take on the working conditions at an automobile factory if you talk to people on the line than if you talk to the public relations officer for the company or to the union steward in the shop. People within institutions provide information within the context of their work, what they are responsible for in the institution, and the constraints of the institution toward contributing information. Financial officers at publicly held companies have a legal responsibility to widely disseminate financial information, whereas financial officers at privately held companies do not. It is important to know, when talking to people from institutions, whether they are speaking as an institutional source or as an informal source—is it their personal opinion they are giving or the party line? Some people from institutions are responsible for presenting the institutional view on an issue, but talking with a "regular" employee might give you a more personal view of what is going on inside the organization.

Tapping into individuals is not the only way to use people sources in institutions. Advertisers or public relations campaign developers might want to survey or canvass the members of an entire association. Reporters might want to send a message to all of the people at a governmental agency to get information. Whether individually or collectively, people are primary sources for communicators needing to tap into institutional information.

People as Scholarly Contributors.   In the realm of scholarly contributors, the scholars, researchers, or students themselves are the people sources. Scholars as contributors may reveal very different information than you find in scholarly *paper* sources. Speaking directly to the scholar allows you to tap into a broader pool of knowledge and interest, and may reveal those nuggets of research or insight that did not make their way into the scholarly publication. Discovering the interests of the scholar beyond what is represented in the publication might lead you into new information avenues to explore.

People as Journalistic Contributors.   People-based information from journalistic contributors will come in the form of the reporter, the station manager, the news researcher. Depending on the context of the information request you present, you get different kinds of information from journalists. If the media organization itself is the focus of the research, the information you will get is likely to be the party line of the organization acting as an institution. If you are tapping one of the employees of a media organization about a story she has written, you are likely to get a more personal view of what went on in the crafting of that message. If you are seen as a competitor, you are unlikely to get any information at all. The products of journalistic organizations are messages, and if the journalist believes you are going after the same sort of message, that reporter won't be a very willing contributor.

Paper Sources

Information from all four types of potential contributors can be found in paper form. This form for information production and distribution has been king for centuries, but is being challenged by the notion of the paperless society. Paper is still a dominant form, although we talk about digital distribution later in this chapter.

As an information form, paper has some distinct advantages: portability, ease of use, the lack of need for technical equipment to access. But it has disadvantages: Paper can easily be misplaced or destroyed. A paper document misfiled within a large filing system is as good as lost. Also, the relative permanence of paper-based records makes it difficult to keep such information updated or to easily append updated information to the original. Finding specific information within a large paper-based document can be tedious, because there is usually little or no indexing (except in the paper-based documents known as books). We talk more about locating paper-based documents in Chapter 6, when we discuss library collections.

Informal Contributors on Paper.   Information from people unaffiliated in the other categories of contributors might come in the form of paper. Someone who has lost a cat can put up a flyer; an individual who is anxious to sway the opinion of neighbors on an issue he or she feels strongly about might send around a newsletter or petition; bumper sticker messages can give information about a person's world view; posters on public bulletin boards can reveal political or social views of residents in the area. These are all examples of paper-based information from informal contributors. Communicators need to keep their eyes open to these informal contributions of paper-based information. They can provide clues about rising public opinion, lifestyles, and attitudes in an area—signaling emerging trends. The trouble with paper-based information from these sources is that it is truly ephemeral—after a good rain, the messages on that outdoor bulletin board will be ruined. The messages are transient and there is generally no central collection. Paper-based information from informal contributors can generate excellent ideas but can rarely be relied on as a definitive source of information.

Institutional Contributors on Paper.   Reports, minutes of meetings, newsletters, journals, arrest records, property filings, driver's licenses, subdivision plan maps, advertising in magazines and newspapers or on billboards, stockholder prospectuses, membership directories, court verdicts, environmental impact statements—all of these are examples of the kinds of paper-based information that institutional contributors create, distribute, and use. Information in paper form is created for different purposes by these institutions. Some paper-based information is required by law. Some paper-based information is created to sell a message about the organization. Some information satisfies the organizational mission to tell people about an issue or topic. Some information supports the network of members of the organization.

Paper-based information might be created and distributed on a routine basis, as with periodicals or journals coming from an association, annual reports for businesses, or quarterly releases of statistical information from a government agency. Some paper-based information comes out on an as-needed basis—alerts, recall notices, or news releases.

It is important to consider the purpose that is served by the paper publication. The monthly newsletter distributed to employees in a company contains different information for a different purpose than the annual report sent to stockholders or the advertising brochure sent to potential clients. The minutes of meetings held by an association governing body contain different information for a different reason than the journal distributed to members that informs them about issues of interest.

Some of the paper-based information is made widely available and other information is proprietary. A "white paper," for example, detailing the current state of affairs and possible avenues for addressing a particular issue within a company or an industry might be made available to the public, or it might have been written only for the eyes of those who commissioned the study. Even determining the existence of proprietary information within an organization can be difficult. In the case of government information, the public might have access to a particular report but portions of the report might be *redacted*—blacked out—if it is considered vital to national security or somehow "privileged."

Some paper publications stand alone, others are cumulatively collected. Releases of statistical data from different government agencies, for example, are issued periodically and then compiled into an annual survey or census of information.

Libraries, which are discussed in Chapter 6, are a communicator's most important source of paper-based information from institutional contributors.

Scholarly Contributors on Paper.   Academics, researchers, and students at universities make their contributions to scholarly knowledge available in paper form. Masters' theses, doctoral dissertations, academic reports, scholarly journals, and books all serve the purpose of publishing and distributing the new knowledge gleaned from the research efforts of these scholars.

Journals that publish scholarly contributions are different than the journals that might be published by an institution or by a media organization. Scholarly journals usually have a board of editors and a panel of peer reviewers who determine whether the submitted material has sufficient merit to be published.

Paper-based material from scholarly sources is usually found most readily in the sponsoring institution's library. For example, a dissertation written by a University of Texas student would be available at the University of Texas library. However, many books by professors reach a much wider distribution and can be readily bought, or found in various libraries. There is more discussion about how to locate and use the materials in different types of libraries in Chapter 6.

Journalistic Contributors on Paper.   Until the mid- to late 1980s, virtually all the information held by newspaper media contributors was in paper form. Walking into any newsroom, you would see a fire inspector's nightmare—piles of papers, files, reporters' notebooks, clippings of news stories, stacks of faxes, and heaps of news releases. The institutional history of the organization and its publications was paper-based (with some microfilm of the past newspaper editions thrown in). News stories were clipped and filed from each day's publication and were the essential resource for reporters and editors. By the mid-1980s, most major newspapers began to replace paper-based archiving of past stories with digital archiving. This made sense as newspapers moved away from hot type production methods to cold type—using the computer as an editing, page layout, and production system.

Newspapers also publish books of collections of photos, columns, or historical front pages. These paper-based resources can be extremely useful to communicators who are looking at community issues, events, and coverage.

Magazines are, of course, also paper-based versions of information coming from journalistic contributors. These are generally more popular in nature—trying to reach the informal audience in contrast to the publications coming from institutional or scholarly contributors.

Specialized industry news sources, such as *Advertising Age* and *PRWeek*, are of special interest to strategic communicators. These are journalistic treatments of the industry and should not be confused with institutional or trade publications that advance a particular industry's agenda. Strategic communicators monitor the trends in their own field through these journalistic sources.

In some cases, the biggest value of general-interest journalistic paper publications to strategic communicators is not the journalistic information found in them but the advertising, from institutional sources, that is packaged with the news.

Digital Sources

As we discussed in Chapter 1, the information age has been spurred, in part, by the phenomenal growth of digital information resources. This growth began in the 1980s with electronic bulletin board services. Then, compact disc distribution of publications came along. By the early 1990s, e-mail and the World Wide Web completely changed the information landscape. But we must consider more than the communication and publication aspects of the digital medium; the computational aspects of digital information, in the form of databases, give communicators access to rich stores of material. Databases hold digital versions of newspaper and magazine articles, broadcast programs, research reports, and journals. Databases of public records, such as property values or arrest reports, hold years of statistics that can be retrieved and analyzed. Digital collections of advertising campaigns can inspire an ad team.

Digital information, then, can represent electronic communications, publications, and compilations of articles or statistics in a database. Here is how the four contributor types provide digital information.

Informal Digital Sources.   The rise of digital communications is the biggest boon to communicators seeking informal information. *Newsgroups* are electronic message boards where people can post a message on any topic and get responses from others who have used that board to get information or state an opinion. Although the nature of these informal sources makes it difficult to get an accurate count, there may be more than 80,000 newsgroups at the time of this writing.[1]

Individuals are also part of the tremendous growth in *Weblogs*. These are electronic columns or newsletters where people can post ideas and links to things they find interesting, and other people contribute to the collection. Like newsgroups, Weblogs are often very specifically focused on a particular subject.

Individuals also can publish their own Web pages—personal-interest sites where people compile and share information on topics they are interested in or knowledgeable about. In the past, people with a particular obsession—Siamese cats, or collecting model trains, or flower arranging—had no easy way to share the information they had accumulated. But now, with a Web page, they can. Many families, for example, are creating their own home pages that let different family members post information about what is happening in their lives. Genealogical research has blossomed on the Web, as people share information.

People can distribute electronic newsletters through e-mail to individuals or to groups of people who have signed up for a distribution list. You will need to judge these personal publications with a grain of salt—as with all informal contributors' information. These are good sources as the first step in an information strategy, but rarely will you want to use them as definitive or unconditionally reliable sources.

Institutional Digital Sources.   Web publication of information by and about various institutions is the primary way these organizations spread the word about their groups and activities. Government Web sites have databases of statistics that can be searched, links to reports and publications, and contact lists of individuals in the agency. Company Web sites can be used both for public relations purposes, providing information of interest to stockholders and others who want to know about the company's makeup and organization, and for e-commerce purposes, by making product information and purchasing available online. Associations put material on Web sites to support the goals of the organization, to inform members of benefits, and to provide promotional material to attract new members.

Institutions also use digital means to distribute online newsletters and e-mail updates to people interested in staying in touch with the latest material coming out of those companies, associations, or government agencies. The people who work within these institutions and the people who have had experiences with these institutions use newsgroups as a way to share news and views. Newsgroups can be an interesting way to get both informal and institutional contributions about a company, association, or agency.

Databases, available either through Web sites or on CD, are rich sources of information, particularly databases compiled by government agencies whose job is to make this information available to its employers—the public. Although some government databases were made unavailable for security reasons after the attacks on September 11, 2001 (such as the locations and construction details of bridges around the country), there are still thousands of stashes of statistics available to the communicator. In fact, the material in databases available on the Web is part of the vast information netherland known as the "invisible Web."

Also included in the invisible Web, that portion of the Web that search engines can't index, are pages behind registration screens, pages created with Flash software, most PDF (Portable Document Format) documents, and archives of journalistic content. Experts estimate the invisible Web may represent more than 80 percent of the Web's content.

Scholarly Digital Sources.   Remember that the original purpose for creating the Internet was to facilitate and ensure the exchange of information and research between scholars and researchers. It is ironic, then, that most scholarly publications have not migrated to the digital space, and that the use of Web pages for posting information about the research and publications of individual scholars is so inconsistent. In many university settings, getting professors to contribute rich content to their faculty pages is a frustrating mission. But this is beginning to change.

Research projects and papers of numerous professors, doctoral students, and researchers can be found on university Web sites. Also, now there are some online-only publications that uphold the same rigorous peer review and high academic standards as their printed predecessors. An example is the *Journal of Interactive Advertising*: www.jiad.org. In some cases, institutional sources—such as associations—make compilations of papers available, such as the Association for Education in Journalism and Mass Communication's database of AEJMC conference papers: www.aejmc.org.

The supporting datasets used to analyze scholarly research are rarely available online, but the clever communicator knows that the database must exist and that the scholar will be the "people source" to use to find out about it.

Journalistic Digital Sources.   As we discussed in the section on paper-based information, news media moved to digital production of their newsprint products some twenty years ago. And in the past half-decade, they have made a further leap to digital information forms with the growth of online news publications. News organizations, with rare exception, now have digital versions of their print, television, or radio counterpart available on the Web. What this means for the communicator is unprecedented access to news coverage from news media organizations around the world.

Many new Web sites give access not only to current stories, but to the archive of previously published stories. Sometimes free, sometimes for a fee, these archives are important resources to communicators needing background on a topic or event. Also of great value are the directory services many sites compile. Community publishing has been a feature of many major news sites. They provide a space where local organizations can post information about themselves—a great service for communicators looking for local institutional sources. The forum areas on news sites can help you tap into the informal sources in the community because this is where you find "just folks" talking about issues of interest. Often, news sites make available the databases of statistics they have used to report a story. The "computability" of digital information allows the user of a news database to find crime statistics or school test scores, for example, for a specific locale. Some journalistic organizations are making facsimiles of their publications available online so you can see all the articles and ads as they appeared in the print publication. This is particularly of interest to strategic communicators, who need to track the placement and play of stories and ads.

CONCLUSION

At this point in the information strategy, your task is to understand potential contributors, and in what forms—people, paper, and digital—this information can be found for each contributor type. This requires you to recognize the nature, characteristics, and limitations of information that is available from these contributors. When you begin an information strategy it may appear to be chaotic, so at this point you are trying to consciously think about who is likely to be creating the type of information you need. In the next chapter, we talk about specific techniques for tapping into the information these contributors have to offer—monitoring, searching, and interviewing.

NOTES

1. "FAQ Materials: Where Do I Find a Complete List of Usenet Newsgroups?" From the home page of Professor Timo Salmi. Department of Accounting and Finance. *University of Vaasa, Finland.* www.uwasa.fi/~ts/http/newsgrps.html.

CHAPTER FIVE

INFORMATION GATHERING
Monitoring, Searching, and Interviewing

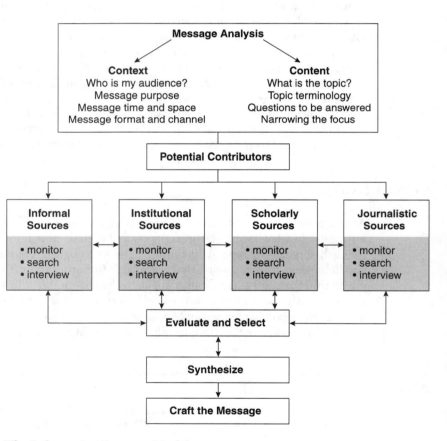

The Information Strategy Model

Think about the ways you learn things in your daily life.

- You observe what is going on around you: the dark clouds mean it will probably rain, the long line at the restaurant means it must be very popular (or it has inefficient service), the peeling paint on your house tells you it might be time for some fix-up work.
- You look things up: phone numbers, word definitions, reviews of movies you plan to see, locations of places on a map.
- You talk to people: ask a friend who saw the movie how it was, call some painting contractors to find out how they work and how much they cost, consult the doctor about the bad cold you got after getting caught in the rain.

These three techniques you use everyday for personal information seeking will serve you well with the formal information gathering you need to do as a communicator. Observing (monitoring), looking things up (searching), and talking to people (interviewing) are the core skills for the information worker. But the way you apply these techniques changes according to the source you are tapping for the information (informal, institutional, scholarly, and journalistic) and the form in which you find the information (from a person, on paper, or in digital form—as discussed in Chapter 4). In this chapter we discuss the general modes and objectives of each of these three information-seeking techniques. In Chapters 7–10 we go into detail about how to apply these techniques for the specific information you can find from each type of contributor.

These techniques will rarely be used in isolation. A search for one piece of information might lead you to the name of someone you will need to interview to actually get the information. Monitoring the "informationscape" might give you a lead to something you'll need to do a search on for more information later. Though there will be some cases in which a single technique is used, for the most part, these techniques will be used in combination—with one being used in one phase of the message creation process, and another in a different phase of the work. Monitoring, searching, or interviewing might be used at different times to tap into the same source of information, to elicit a new depth or a different take on the information.

Let's say you're a reporter in Buffalo and the city leaders have decided to crack down on raves because of reported drug use and "kids out late on the streets." As the reporter assigned to the story, you might monitor postings to the *alt.rave* newsgroup or the *buffalo raves* listserv to find out where these parties are being held and which musicians will be playing. These would be informal sources of information. You might then search the database of news stories to get background on raves in the area, a journalistic information source. One of the articles quotes a scholarly source, Douglas Rushkoff, a New York University professor of media culture who specializes in youth culture. You then do a Web search to get some background on Rushkoff and find his Web page (digital information). You find his e-mail address and interview him via e-mail on his views of the role of raves in a teenager's life. You might go back to the alt.rave newsgroup and post a message asking for anyone interested in talking with you about raves to call you at the office.

Circling through information sources, types of information, and information-seeking techniques is part of the ability to dance through data and information that must become part of a communicator's repertoire.

Let's look at each of these techniques, how and when they should be applied, what kinds of information tasks you will use them for, and how you might use the information you find.

MONITORING

Monitoring refers to surveillance of the information environment in order to stay up to date on a topic, to get a feel for the lay of the land, to get early warning about new or interesting developments, or to discover the current prevailing opinion on a subject. Monitoring is generally more informal and random than either searching or interviewing. Monitoring is about listening and observing, it is serendipitous rather than targeted like a search or a formal interview would be. With monitoring you might have an idea of what you hope to find, but you never really know what you will find.

Clyde Bentley, a journalism professor at the University of Missouri, wrote a message about playing with Webcams for reporting that describes well the more random nature of monitoring as opposed to searching and interviewing:

> We've been kicking around ideas here on what we could do if a Webcam was part of the toolbox of a photojournalist. I'm curious about the possibilities of portable (cellular?) and temporarily placed cams—say at fires or sporting events. Sending a reporter/photographer out on assignment is akin to hunting, but a journalistic Webcam is more like fishing with bait and a bobber—you wait for the news to happen. In that sense, we would get the ultimate immediacy by being there before the news happens.

That is one of the goals of careful monitoring, to get there before the news happens.

Another goal of monitoring and observing is to generate creative ideas, to get the feeling for a place. The advertising professional newly assigned to a fast food account would do well to go to one of the restaurants and listen to what people are saying as they stand in line, and as they leave the restaurant. Getting a sense of the mood of people as they move through the restaurant can provide insight into a theme for the ad campaign.

Monitoring what people are saying can give reporters angles on stories they might be covering. When a drug is withdrawn by the Food and Drug Administration (FDA), the reporter can scan the comments posted to a message board for users of that type of medication. Is the reaction relief, anger, fear—what sorts of concerns are being expressed? From FDA officials, an institutional source, the reporter will get the institutionally sanctioned information, but monitoring the postings on a newsgroup, an informal source, will give a sense of the people's feelings.

Monitoring can be used to stay on top of an ongoing research interest. The public relations officer who is in charge of an auto insurance company's messages to the public can set up her computer to capture news related to the auto industry and insurance. This use of the bait and bobber might snag an interesting story that she needs to know to stay smart about her account.

There are two key components in the information-gathering technique of monitoring. One is observation—personally witnessing something. The other is tracking—setting up techniques to capture random information that might be of interest.

Observation

Fundamentally, all the content of mass communication originates with observation. In news reporting throughout most of the nineteenth century, a high percentage of the information originated with the reporter as the observer. Today, reporters and other mass communicators rely on others—often specialists in various fields—as their observers for much more of the information that is transmitted.

When three tardy whales became stranded in the fall ice off the coast of Alaska, journalists from around the world converged on the area to cover the story. They described, taped, and photographed what they saw. But for additional sources, they used local villagers, marine biologists, state historians, engineers who knew about equipment to keep ice from forming, ice-breaking-ship experts, meteorologists, and economists who could talk about the effect of so many visitors on the local economy. Together, these varied and expert observers undoubtedly gave a more complete and accurate account of the stranded whale situation than reporters could have done by merely using their own powers of observation.

Nevertheless, the major difficulties with observation are scarcely eliminated simply because the number and expertise of the observers have increased. Observation takes place within a context. Observers often see what they expect to see, or are prepared to see, and fail to perceive equally visible elements that are not part of what they expect. Another factor is that observers have limits in their own sense organs—someone with an acute sense of smell may detect a natural gas leak that others might not notice; one person may see a boat sinking across the lake while others see nothing.

Observation seems inseparably linked with inference. The observer at the scene of the stranded whales might infer that this was an unusual situation. However, local villagers might tell the observer that every fall a few tardy whales are trapped by ice and die or are killed by hunters. The villager might add that any whale so unwary as to stay too long in waters that freeze should not be freed to propagate its defective genes. The possibility of faulty inference is a problem for both the mass communicator as an observer and other observers on whom communicators rely.

Faulty inference can happen anywhere, as this story illustrates. Friends were walking on a college campus; there were not many other people around. They rounded a corner and saw a young woman lying on the grass, thrashing around and making loud noises. A young man appeared to be struggling with her. One of them rushed to this scene and began to pull the man off the woman, thinking that an assault was going on. The man said, "She's having an epileptic fit, I'm trying to help her so she doesn't hurt herself." Clearly, faulty inference and quick assumption led the observers to the wrong reaction to the situation.

Bias on the part of the observer invariably affects the observation process. Professional communicators try to be aware of bias in themselves and in others upon whom they rely. They are aware that all individuals have assumptions about the world—beliefs about what is ordinary and normal, as well as convictions about what "ought" to be. These convictions influence what is perceived and how the perceptions are interpreted. Recognizing the role of bias in the observation, communicators hope to limit the effect of bias by developing better techniques for observation and monitoring and by sharing the responsibility with other observers.

The effect of the observer on the scene is an additional factor to be considered. The presence of observers can change the event being observed. This is most clearly seen in confrontations that take place specifically for the purpose of attracting media attention. Even in so mundane an event as a parade, the bands make sure they are playing when they pass the television cameras. When an observer visits a classroom, even kindergarteners adapt their behavior to the presence of the stranger. A most striking example of an institution that has changed as a result of observation is the U.S. presidential nominating convention. After fifty years of broadcasting coverage, the conventions bear no resemblance to the nineteenth- and early-twentieth-century negotiations that took place in smoke-filled rooms. Party managers learned to arrange the conventions to take account of—and advantage of—television coverage. The institution that broadcasters found so significant and fascinating gradually changed, in large measure because of the attention that broadcasters were directing its way.

For some kinds of observation, observers may have a reasonable hope that their presence can be, in part, neutralized as an effect. For example, the observer in the kindergarten might devise methods to counteract the intrusion. However, at the institutional level, such as the nominating conventions, individuals and media organizations are powerless to counteract their effect. They are inextricably intertwined with the event itself. The best they can do is recognize that they, the observers, are part of the activity.

Observation, then, is affected by the inherent perceptual limitations of the observer, expectations, inference, bias, and the effect of the observer on the action. The mass communicator as an observer may be more or less affected by these factors than are others who supply information to the communicator. Skill, experience, and awareness of the problems in accurately observing events can help to counteract the inevitable difficulties of observation.

Types of Observation.   Communicators rely on three kinds of observation: routine, participant, and unobtrusive.

Routine Observation.   The most frequently used type of observation is so routine as to be habitual. It involves simply going to the scene of the action. Professionals in all fields of mass communication perform routine observations. Advertising specialists attend the unveiling of new auto models. Public relations practitioners go to events they have sponsored as attention getters, to observe the effect of the event. News reporters go to meetings, conventions, accidents and disasters, parades, fairs, speeches, and countless other kinds of events.

Being on the scene of a dramatic event helps the communicator give a credible report. Although, as we have noted, an observer's accuracy and interpretations may be flawed, no one questions that the observer can be more accurate in most emergencies than a nonobserver. For example, a story about the terrorist attacks in New York City on

September 11, 2001, turns into a dramatic first-person account with the use of routine observation skills and clear writing. First-person style is generally against the rules for a standard news story, but it can be a powerful form of storytelling when the reporter relates, first-hand, the experience of a news event. A first-person account of the attack on the World Trade Center, such as the one reported in the *Montana Kaimin* by a former University of Montana student in Box 5.1, brings a different angle to the day's events.

Conferences, meetings, and government activities at all levels usually are covered with observation as a prominent technique. Before conferences, public relations staff prepare advance material to assist those who cover the sessions. The staff provides press credentials and assists with facilities for transmitting the reports. Reporters receive packets of background material to help them with routine aspects of their work. The lead of even a straight news story usually reflects some details that can be accurately gathered only by an observer. The Associated Press account of the opening of a United Nations conference illustrates this convention:

> Nairobi, Kenya (AP)—Singing "We are the Women of the World," some 11,000 delegates opened a series of workshops Wednesday to mark the end of the United Nations Women's Decade.
>
> Dame Nita Barrow of Barbados convened the delegates, warning that the session was their "last chance" to press the United Nations to set up a permanent women's forum and to "recognize us as an asset and not a liability."[1]

Observation can give human interest to an otherwise routine story about proposed policy changes in services and facilities affecting the public. Malcolm Gladwell of the *Washington Post* filed this story about proposed congressional changes in the Medicaid program, which includes observations designed to interest the reader:

> Bronx, N.Y.–In the corner of the recreation room of the Hebrew Home for the Aged, here, a nurse is playing "God Bless America" on the piano. Two other nurses are walking through the room singing, and round them are 30 white-haired women in wheelchairs, some nodding or clapping along, some staring blandly into space.
>
> This is music time on the Hebrew Home's Alzheimer's floor, one of a series of planned activities that fill up the days of the hundreds of residents here suffering from dementia. A decade ago these women would have been strapped into their wheelchairs and parked in front of a television. But over the past few years, Hebrew Home and other nursing homes around the country have increasingly devoted extra time and resources to "special care" programs of light exercise, arts and crafts and recreation designed to treat those suffering from Alzheimer's more like human beings.
>
> The catch, of course, is that special care programs cost money. In a place like Hebrew Home—where more than 90 percent of the residents have their bills paid by Medicaid—that means public money. And with Congress about to cut tens of billions of dollars in federal aid to nursing homes, the fate of programs like music time is suddenly up in the air.[2]

The subsequent paragraphs gave routine information about the costs of special care program and the effects of those programs on short-term and long-term prospects for patients. The story incorporated findings from a number of scholarly studies and

BOX 5.1
PERSONAL OBSERVATIONS ON SEPTEMBER 11, 2001

Nate Schweber, a former *Kaimin* reporter and current intern at *Rolling Stone* magazine, dispatched this eye-witness account late Tuesday afternoon from the magazine's office in Manhattan.

UM ALUMNUS RECOUNTS
TUESDAY'S TRAGEDY
Column by Nate Schweber

All of the people who witnessed the "apparent terrorist attacks" in New York and Washington D.C. have their own story to tell. Mine is certainly not the most dramatic, nor relevant, but this is what I saw:

At 9:15 a.m. I was waiting for a late subway at a station on 72nd Street. A conductor bellowed the news above the screech of passing trains.

"Subway service is delayed because two planes crashed into the World Trade Center."

A pale-faced man in a yellow tie told a huddled crowd about the footage he'd just seen on TV. Soon all the subway passengers—who normally keep to themselves—started asking each other what happened. Each new person who walked into the subway station told about the last thing they saw on TV before dashing out the door.

In the subway car the patrons passed the news—"one of the planes was hijacked from Boston," "police estimate 40,000 people work in the Twin Towers"—like firemen passing buckets of water. Runners zipped between subway cars so the information could pass from the last car, to the lead car, and back again.

When I got off the subway and looked south down 6th Avenue, I could see smoke billowing from one of the towers.

Thousands of people seeped from the bottom of the skyscraper canyon, cell phones at ear, and gaped at the wreckage. We were about 60 blocks away.

The burning tower seemed to shake, then a half second later it crumbled from the top to the bottom. The building seemed to pour outward as it fell, like someone split it by jabbing a shovel down the middle. I think I felt people gasp, I know I saw them cry. All I heard were sirens.

I ran down to the street and headed south against the flow of foot traffic.

The streets were jammed curb to curb with pedestrians who parted for the onslaught of emergency vehicles. Crowds huddled around storefront televisions and black BMWs with sub-woofers blaring the news on WOR.

I followed the smoke, which stretched halfway up the sky to the noontime sun, about 60 blocks south to Canal Street in Chinatown. There NYC police set up a blockade to herd people north. I tried to bust through with a wind sprint only to be manhandled back by three of NYC's finest.

I watched hundreds of folks walk out of the dust cloud with surgical masks over their noses and mouths. I saw one disheveled man in a black suit covered in gray soot from top to toe. His jacket was torn, his briefcase was slashed, one shoe was missing and he had soot caked onto all his exposed skin. Every time he moved, puffs of soot rose from his clothes.

I watched the smoke, sirens and survivors for about an hour, then I turned around and joined the exodus north. I was surprised at how calm and kind people were. I saw people trip and fall only to be helped up by those around them. Churches set up sidewalk stands to give away water, milk, apple juice and plums. I saw people weeping, walking and embracing.

Now, seven hours since the attack, I see F-16 fighter jets circling the Empire State Building. The streets and sidewalks are mostly empty, though I still hear a surround sound of sirens. Some subways are running and since Mayor Rudolph Giuliani called for everyone to vacate Manhattan, New York is looking more like a ghost town than it probably ever has before.

And as I look down the Avenue of the Americas I can still see the smoke from where the two tallest buildings in America's most famous city once stood.

Source: Montana Kaimin, Wednesday, Sept. 12, 2001. Reprinted by permission.

other types of technical information. But the human-interest lead and reporter observations make the difference between a routine, bureaucratic story about budget issues and an engaging interpretation of the effects of policy decisions.

Participant Observation.   Nellie Bly, the trail-blazing female journalist, epitomized participant observation when, in 1887, she spent ten days in an asylum pretending to be insane so she could expose the horrible conditions. Participant observation involves joining or living with a group and becoming a part of the action.

Members of the group being observed—for instance, prison inmates—may not know the observer's true identity, but he or she is seen as being part of the group. This method of observation is common in sociological and anthropological research, as well as in communication research. It allows the information gatherer to get direct experience and to reduce reliance on the expertise or testimony of others. In becoming part of the scene the observer begins to understand it as an insider, to decode the various systems at work, and to interact casually with members of the group.

Participant observation is an expensive technique, requiring a substantial amount of time in the field. It is also fraught with ethical and legal issues. When members of ABC News' *Prime Time Live* got jobs in several Food Lion supermarkets in order to place hidden cameras and capture video of old meat being redated and, in some cases, repackaged, the report caused a drop in the company's stock price and a lawsuit against ABC.[3]

For that reason, among others, participant observation is less frequently used in mass communication than is the routine observation of single events. However, when a community problem is very pressing or perplexing or when a publication has the resources to devote to the topic, participant observation may be a major technique.

Participant observation generally begins only after you have made a thorough study of the event or group to be observed. The observation will, of course, include interviewing other group members. As well as being costly, participant observation can be dangerous. Solid preparation helps you prepare for the situation to be faced. It prepares you intellectually to interact on the scene while maintaining sufficient social and emotional distance so that an independent perspective remains.

Reporter Tony Horowitz has some advice for those who use participant observation methods. His front-page story for the *Wall Street Journal* exposed the horrific conditions in a poultry production plant in Morton, Mississippi, and raised concerns about conditions in similar plants all across the south. His editors instructed him to tell no lies, so on his poultry plant job application form he listed Dow Jones & Company, publisher of the Wall Street Journal, as his previous employer and he accurately detailed his university education. He disclosed his identity as a reporter to the workers he visited and interviewed in their homes, and carefully protected the identities of the sources who expressed criticisms. His advice: participant observation is something that must be worked out with editors; journalists must decide ahead of time how to handle the ethical problems of misrepresenting themselves; and they must determine how much information they are prepared to divulge about themselves so that they can avoid a lot of questions without being dishonest. Horowitz claims that participant observers have to be prepared for the exhaustion of maintaining a double identity.[4]

Even excellent preparation may not prevent every false move, as one Wisconsin high-school student learned. With help from a corrections official and a social worker, he posed as an offender in a boys' correctional institution, an experience he reported in his high-school newspaper. However, when his first meal tray was placed before him, he forgot his new identity and politely said, "Thank you" for the tray. This lapse immediately marked him as an outsider; the noisy room fell silent, and other inmates stared suspiciously. The student had reason to worry that his experiment was seriously undermined. He did, however, manage to complete his 24 hours in the institution, and his story won a high-school press award.[5]

Unobtrusive Observation.   In some circumstances, unobstrusive observation may be more effective than participant observation, especially if the observer's presence will change the situation being observed.

Everette E. Dennis has presented a series of *touchstones* through which communicators can keep tabs on community realities. Many of the methods he advocates require sensitive observation: learn how people live and work by observing housing standards, neighborhoods, and primary workplaces. Monitor such public gathering places as coin-op laundries, beauty parlors, restaurants, and bars. Use public transportation at various times during the day and night. Watch facilities such as emergency rooms, jails, and shelters for the homeless—action at these sites helps the observer understand the community's pressure points. Observe popular culture, from fast food to pop art. Note fads and trends that affect lifestyles and leisure time.[6]

Consider a team of reporters working on a series of articles about drunk drivers. People who drive while drunk cannot be expected to volunteer their testimony. Bartenders are unlikely to want to go on the record about the amount of drinking that may be done before patrons get into their cars. However, the reporters could station themselves in bars, and, as a team, carefully record what patrons drink and if they drive away from the bar. The observers would have to pay careful attention to the details: the time at which drinking begins, the number and kinds of drinks consumed, the approximate weight of each drinker, and so on. The observers would have to hear the actual drink orders, rather than assume they could identify the drinks by sight. Nonalcoholic beers look like alcoholic ones; ginger ale resembles some mixed drinks; and mineral water with a lime slice looks like gin and tonic. With these and other precautions, however, the observers could develop well-documented evidence for their series on drinking and driving. A table showing the level of intoxication for people of various weights consuming alcohol at specific rates per hour is available to assist in calculating driving impairment. The reporters could use such a table to illustrate the condition of the patrons being observed before they began driving their cars.

Unobtrusive observation has a place in public relations work, particularly in connection with special events and exhibits. Public relations staff frequently design and set up exhibits at conferences, tradeshows, and fairs. They observe the visitors' use of the exhibit, the attention the exhibit attracts, the public interest in handouts, and other evidence of success. They evaluate the usefulness of the exhibit to their overall strategy in public relations. To make such an evaluation, they may place themselves in positions where they can overhear candid remarks about the event, analyze the demand for materials distributed to passers-by, and observe the interaction of sales and public relations staff members with exhibit visitors.

When a company representative is giving a speech or a demonstration, public relations staff often assist with evaluating the response to the presentation. They may observe if the speaker can be heard easily, whether the audience is attentive and engaged, and if the audiovisual materials are effective. Often the public relations department has helped to draft the speech, arrange for the setting and the audiovisual materials, and analyze the potential audience. Thus, as informed observers they can view events in the light of planning and strategy and improve future performance in similar situations.

Unobtrusive observation techniques also are being adopted by advertising professionals. A very large Chicago agency has an ongoing research project in a town of 8,000 to 12,000 about 150 miles from Chicago. Advertising researchers visit the town on a regular basis and politely listen to conversations in coffee shops, churches, hairdressers' shops, and taverns. The agency professionals are trying to learn what is important to average folks, what occupies their hearts and minds. In the process, they think they will gain clues as to why people don't always follow cooking directions for frozen pizzas, or what they really think about prunes. The advertising professionals have learned to prepare themselves well for their visits. One advertising agency employee's too-hip hairdo marked her as an outsider, and another researcher learned to drive a pickup truck rather than his Audi to town.[7]

Developing Observation Techniques.   Skilled observers are trained, rather than born. With observation, as with all other skills, practice and preparation are required. Observation requires a total involvement of all your senses: seeing, hearing, smelling, touching, tasting. It also requires a finely tuned sense of intuition and interpretation. What mood are you sensing from the mass of people—are they getting ready to celebrate or to riot? Skilled observers have a checklist of things they consider as they prepare to observe an event or canvass a scene.

They think about what event it is they are going to be observing. What brought on the event—something happy, something traumatic? What emotions are likely to be at play? They consider who the participants will be, what kind of people they are likely to encounter during their observation: what are they going to be interested in, concerned about, how might they best be approached. They prepare for conditions they are likely to encounter on the scene—the weather, the physical space, the crowd. Being prepared allows you to focus more attention on what is happening than on having to figure out just where you are and who you are with.

Researching before observing is an essential step. For example, the student reporter who entered the juvenile detention center needed to be clear about what type of story he was going to write and who the audience for the story would be. He would be smart to also do some background research into the environment of detention centers—what kind of physical space he would be in, how are the staff organized, what types of kids are likely to be there, and what kinds of crimes have they committed. With that sort of preparation he would be able to concentrate on observing the physical conditions of the detention center, the behavior of inmates and staff toward one another, and inmates' concerns about their present and their future. He could go into observation mode with a firm foundation of understanding based on his previous research.

Observation in Virtual Spaces.   We've just walked through monitoring via observation in the real world, but there is a vast virtual world that can also be observed. Reading messages posted to forums or interest groups and observing the topics that spark the most interest and traffic can be an interesting indicator of current issues and trends. You have to be careful about how you use the information you find in these ways; the ethical and legal implications of these methods must be understood (see Chapter 13). You have to understand, too, that the cloak of anonymity that people wear online can make observation of their message behavior hard to decipher. The boastful or blustery messages that people send to newsgroups or out on e-mail lists must be likened to listening in on a conversation at a bar or overhearing the talk at a rally. You can't really know who the speaker is, what they know, how they know it, or why they are saying it. This kind of observation is good for scene setting and idea generation but is rarely useful for fact-finding.

The Webcams that are sprouting up all over the Internet can be interesting ways to remotely track activities in certain areas. Webcams (at least those that are not X-

"On the Internet, nobody knows you're a dog."

rated) are set up by a sponsor, often a news organization, so that people can go to the webcam site and look at the scene. Some webcams are live, but most simply provide a regular snapshot, refreshed every few minutes, of the area being cammed. Some allow you to actually move the camera or to zoom in on a part of the scene. This remote observation of places can be an interesting technique and a way to set the scene even if you can't be there. At the beginning of Vikings football training camp, the startribune.com news team set up a webcam so fans could get snapshots of the action at camp. In August 2001, Korey Stringer, an offensive lineman on the team, died of heat stroke. Even reporters and fans not on the scene were able to observe the activity and the trailer where Korey was treated because of the news Web site's webcam setup.

Observation, real or virtual, can be an effective way to monitor the activities, actions, and opinions of groups of people. It can be a way for you to get a sense of place and perspective about people or events you might be reporting on or developing a campaign for. Observation is an important technique for you to use when tapping into informal sources and can provide valuable insight into the workings of institutional sources.

Tracking

The other method for monitoring as an information-gathering technique is tracking. Tracking involves setting up routine surveillance methods for snagging items of interest from the data stream that flows through the Internet each day. Monitoring through tracking is useful for advertising account managers who have certain companies in their portfolio, for reporters who cover a specific beat, and for public relations officers who must keep up on industry happenings. The tracking technique employs either alert services or news filters to provide customized reports of recent news.

Alert services are generally found on specific Web sites. They can be called *watch lists, distribution lists,* or *current awareness services,* and are provided by the organization that created the Web site, to help people stay up-to-date on items of interest. When you sign up for an alert service you submit your e-mail information to the site and they put you on a distribution list of people interested in getting updates. Everyone who subscribes to an alert service gets the same information.

News filters, on the other hand, provide customization. They can be used to get news stories from wire services, or messages from newsgroups, that fit the subject profile you set up. You enroll in the service and provide keywords for the topics you want the filter to catch. The software stores your interest profile and uses it to check the stories or messages it filters. When it finds a story or message containing the keywords you have in your profile, the program snags that item and posts it to your e-mail box or puts it in an area on the service you can check. Some filters notify you when new information or changes have been made to a Web site you are interested in. Others automatically send new information directly to you.

For years, commercial online services like LexisNexis or Dow Jones have been providing alert and filter services, usually at a very high cost. The free alert services on the Internet are becoming viable alternatives.

A reporter for the *San Antonio Express-News* in the Laredo bureau uses the GAO (General Accounting Office) alert service. He said he used to have to wait for press releases from Washington to get a story and then he'd have to rely on the information that a Press Information Officer provided. With the alert he felt for the first time that he was on top of news because he received notes of released reports and those to come. Then he was able to link to the whole report rather than relying on the bits and pieces that were released from DC.

Using alerts and filters can be tricky. It is easy to get overwhelmed; you end up with the digital equivalent of an overflowing in-box, filled with news releases and reports you'll never get around to reading. Make sure you understand how the particular alert or filter service you will be using works. Some of them require you to choose from selected subject categories, others let you enter your own search terms for the topics you're interested in. If you create a profile using terms that are too broad you'll get irrelevant hits, but one that is too narrow will make you miss stories of possible interest. Some filters match, character by character, the word you put in (if you type in *labor* you won't get British articles with *labour* in them.)

There are some excellent services for finding alerts and filters. Bill Dedman's Alerts for Journalists page at powerreporting.com/category/Alerts_for_journalists provides information about alerts and filters in twelve different categories. Although it says it is for journalists, advertising and public relations professionals will also find it useful. Most sites related to business and the stock market have a service that lets you track a specific company and get alerts about news of interest, stock activity, and filings of information to the Securities and Exchange Commission. If you are responsible for covering a particular company, you would do well to explore some of these types of services.

A Weblog (also referred to as a "blog") is a Web site created by an individual who posts commentary on a routine basis about events in their lives or links to Web sites they find of interest. This is a sort of digital diary written by the site owner (also referred to as a "blogger") to which the people who read the site can make contributions or comments. The individuals who compile and maintain these Weblogs are your scouts on the net for news, interesting items, and new sites they think their audience would find useful or intriguing. Bloggers focus on topics ranging from robotics to digital poetry to social issues to fashion. As a monitoring tool, Weblogs provide an alternative take on your subject. They can also be efficiency tools for keeping up to date on a specific topic. For example, thousands of reporters start their days checking into Romanesko's Weblog on the Poynter Institute site—www.poynter.org. Jim Romanesko gets up early each morning and scans all the news about the news industry and puts together an invaluable column.

The first directory of Weblogs had twenty-three listed in 1999.[8] Now there are more Weblogs than can be tracked. A good place to find information about Weblogs is the Weblogs Compendium (www.lights.com/weblogs). There also is a directory (by no means comprehensive) at portal.eatonweb.com.

Monitoring both the virtual and the physical world through observation and tracking is one of the ways you will find, gather, and understand what is happening.

SEARCHING

The second information-gathering technique we need to discuss is searching. Looking up information in a book, tapping into a database of articles, using a search engine to find a Web site on the obscure topic you are researching—these are all examples of searching. The three forms that information comes in—people, paper, and digital—are searched in different ways and at different stages in the information-gathering process. Searching may be the required method for finding the information you need from one kind of source, while monitoring or interviewing might be a better method for another source.

Unlike the monitoring method, searching usually involves goal-directed and highly targeted information strategies using well-established sources of information found in many types of information spaces—libraries, databases, public records repositories, experts' experiences, and so forth.

Getting Started on Your Information Search

As we've discussed in Chapter 3, it is crucial for you to have a well-defined question in mind at the start of your search. You need to know whether you are looking for a quick fact, an in-depth analysis, a specific person's name, a particular public record, an overview of an industry, a demographic profile of your audience, a well-documented government statistic, and so on.

A number of obstacles confront you when you start your search. You may not know where to start. You may not know *how* to start. You may be asking a question that is too specific. You may be asking a question that is too broad. You may not have enough time or money. You may not understand the relevance of things you find as you search.

You can overcome all of these obstacles, however. First, think about the distinction between a search for primary sources and secondary sources. Primary sources are firsthand accounts, raw data, public documents, transcripts of speeches, and so on. They can be found in diaries, letters, public records, court filings, raw statistics, financial balance sheets, logs, family Bibles, individuals' Web pages, eyewitness news accounts of an event, and myriad other information sources.

Secondary sources are other people's analysis of primary data. Books, journal and magazine articles, demographic compilations, texts, encyclopedias, dictionaries, company information, industry overviews, news analyses of events or trends, and most of the materials found in library collections make up the majority of secondary sources.

These distinctions help you identify the appropriate contributor to your information strategy. We discuss specific information search strategies that apply to informal, institutional, scholarly and journalistic sources in Chapters 7–10. The main point here is to reinforce the notion that you can start every information search by asking where the information resides and who cares about your topic. For instance, if you are starting a process for locating information about an industry for which you will be preparing product advertising, you can identify the associations that are important for that industry, the trade journals that discuss the most recent news and trends for that field, the online sites where people talk about that industry and its products, the newspapers that write about it, the court records that document the legal status of competitors in the industry, the government records that document its regulation, the financial records that detail its economic health, the unions that represent the workers in that field, the demographic data that describe the customers for that industry's products and the audiences for its ads, the experts who can speak authoritatively for and about that industry, and so forth.

As a professional communicator, much of what you search for is found in the print and electronic files of libraries, physical or virtual. Types of libraries, the organization of tools in libraries, and their use for you as a communicator are discussed in Chapter 6. Our discussion of libraries here will focus on the conceptual search skills you need to successfully locate what you are looking for.

The key to searching libraries, or any collection of information, is to recognize that they attempt to organize the entire output of intellectual activity. They help users decode the structure of information for each new subject area. The tools and tactics used in this mammoth attempt sometimes are cumbersome, but, for the most part, they work. It is up to the efficient information searcher to unlock and decode these collections to make the best use of them.

You, as a searcher, can rely on some basic rules about how information is produced, published, organized, and made accessible. Every subject area has a structure that helps people organize and identify information about that topic. This structure of information is related to the way disciplines develop, as discussed in Chapter 3. A bibliographic chain of events can help explain how information is developed and organized. The four links in the chain correspond to the way knowledge creators develop new information. The structure of information also affects how materials relevant for that topic are arranged and made accessible to the searcher.

When a new set of ideas is introduced and worked on by a community of knowledge creators, the link in the bibliographic chain is loose and informal. Scholars talk to one another on the telephone, exchange e-mails and participate in listserv discussions, review first drafts of one another's papers, share progress reports and talk at conferences, publish informal newsletters, and create an in-group of people working on similar ideas. Libraries rarely penetrate into this realm of knowledge creation, but many of the directories and biographical guides found in libraries can help you identify who is working on a particular idea or in a particular discipline. A librarian may also help you find the informal electronic listservs and discussions groups that exist in a particular area so you can tap into these discussions directly.

The second link in the bibliographic chain consists of the first formally published results of new research or new ideas, including journals, magazines, books, recordings, Web sites, multimedia productions, and other materials that make up the bulk of library collections (discussed in Chapter 6). Also included are the proceedings of conferences, the papers delivered at conventions, and other formal presentations such as works of art or musical scores. Journalistic sources as well as scholarly works are included in this link of the chain. The important characteristic of this kind of information is that it has usually gone through some kind of review process. Experts in the field have examined the scholarly materials for errors, gaps, misinterpretations of data and other problems. Journalistic materials have been edited and scrutinized for obvious errors and inconsistencies. Another important characteristic of this link in the bibliographic chain is that this kind of material has been collected, organized, and cataloged by the librarians and archivists in charge of the library collections in which the material is found.

The third link in the bibliographic chain is comprised of the access tools for library information. Examples of tools in this category include print or electronic indexes to periodical and journal articles, abstracts of articles or books, bibliographies listing materials by subject or author, and the many other finding tools that libraries house, physically or virtually. Again, those materials have been created by people trained to organize and index materials, and in the orderly process of cataloging and characterizing work so that it is searchable in logical and efficient ways.

The final link in the bibliographic chain includes works that provide overviews or summaries that are useful when you are seeking basic information about a subject. Articles in encyclopedias, dictionaries, textbooks, handbooks, directories, and guidebooks fall into this category. These items are the most removed in time from the original ideas in the field and the cutting-edge thinking about that topic. For that reason, you should recognize that some of the information in these types of sources will need to be updated, but they are very useful as a starting point in your search.

Understanding this bibliographic chain can help you decode the structure of information in any discipline and the structure of knowledge to which libraries, database and Web site producers, and other information organizers have responded. In many cases, it makes sense for you to start with the fourth link and move backwards to the most recent material after gaining solid background knowledge in your subject.

Searching with Classification Schemes and Subject Headings

Librarians have developed several methods for categorizing the information housed in libraries into a system of identification and retrieval. These methods are called classification systems, and they determine how materials are described in catalogs and physically arranged on library shelves.

The Dewey Decimal Classification System is used most often in small libraries and public libraries. It works best for collections of materials that are not too large, that do not cover too many different subjects, or that do not have in-depth collections of a few specific topic areas. The system consists of ten major "classes" of knowledge such as philosophy, religion, social sciences, language, natural sciences and so forth. Dewey Decimal Classification numbers assigned to specific books or other items on the library shelf have three digits before the decimal point, and perhaps some further division after the decimal point. For instance, all books in a library collection that are categorized as American drama would be found under the main Dewey number 812. A book such as *Twenty-Five Best Plays of the Modern American Theater* might be given the Dewey number 812.503 in a library with a large American drama collection. The numbers after the decimal would indicate distinctions between, say, modern drama and colonial drama.

The other major classification system in libraries is the one developed by the Library of Congress (LC). This system is used in most academic libraries and in large libraries with very extensive collections on many different subjects. The LC system is more flexible than the Dewey system and allows for finer division between subjects and categories of knowledge. It is based on the alphabet and can be applied with great precision and descriptiveness to the books on the shelves. For instance, the book *The Elements of Journalism: What Newspeople Should Know and the Public Should Expect* is classified under the LC system as PN 4756.K67. The *P* category is for Language and Literature, *PN* is specifically about media, and the number *4756* is specifically for journalism ethics. The *K* in the number reflects the first author's surname, Kovach. The main point is that the system is very flexible and allows for collections of millions of items to be logically and efficiently organized on the shelves of huge libraries.

Why should any of this matter to you as an information searcher? For just one reason: the only way you can efficiently find things in any collection of information is to know how that material has been organized and classified for retrieval. You don't need to know that the LC classification for journalism ethics is PN 4756. You *do* need to know how to find those items on the library shelf if that is what you are looking for. Knowing that all the materials owned by that library on that topic are going to be shelved together using that classification number is the key to your success in locating what you need when you need it. Many Web sites also use a classification scheme when organizing their collections of information, to facilitate information retrieval.

Another major characteristic of information searching is the use of subject terms or headings. The major purpose of subject headings systems is to provide a standardized method of describing all information in the same general subject area, so that everything pertaining to a topic can be identified. When you are searching for information in print or digital format you are likely to have a general notion of the topic area you are researching, rather than a detailed list of authors or titles of materials you are seeking. For that reason, information catalogers and indexers have tagged records with subject headings to help people find them.

As with classification schemes, indexers spend enormous amounts of time developing subject headings that accurately reflect the structure of information in a subject area. These subject headings are used in many ways. They appear on the records in a library's catalog, they are used in the entries of indexes and the headings in abstracts, they may be used to organize material on Web sites. Information organizers may use the subject classification system created, again, by the Library of Congress, called the Library of Congress Subject Headings, which is particularly appropriate for very large collections. Smaller collections may use the Sears List of Subject Headings. Special collections may have their own subject headings, such as the Medical Subject Headings used, obviously, in medical collections. Once again, the point is not for you to know the intricacies of these systems. The point is that you can be a much more efficient information searcher if you know how to use the specific subject headings for your search.

Let's look at an example. Many online library catalogs allow you to search for information using keywords or subject headings. A keyword search in an online file retrieves records that contain that word or set of words anywhere in the record. A subject heading search retrieves only those records that have been assigned a specific subject heading by an information retrieval expert. If you search in the University of Minnesota Libraries online catalog using the keywords *drug abuse*, you retrieve 10,898 records. No communications professional working on a message about drug abuse will be able to make any sense of that kind of search result. However, if you search using the medical subject heading "drug abuse" in the very same online catalog, you retrieve ten highly specific, recent and relevant items that have been tagged by librarians with that subject heading.

You may never have to understand the intricacies of classification or subject headings schemes in any detail. However, because all collections, print and electronic, are categorized in these ways, it is helpful to have a general acquaintance with how they work and how they can help you. These systems allow you to decode the structure of information available in these vast collections and help you save time and energy in your information searches.

Specifics of Searching

> What good is a Web search engine that returns 324,909,188 matches to my keyword? That's like saying, "Good news! We've located the product you're looking for. It's on Earth."
> —*W. Bruce Cameron*

Just as you need to be aware of the different kinds of library classification schemes so you can efficiently search in library materials, you need to know a few principles of online searching so you can navigate the digital space. There are hundreds of books and Web sites devoted to the best techniques for Web searching. Online databases have manuals and training sessions to help people build expertise in locating materials in them. If you find yourself consistently using certain sources (either specific search engines on the Web or online databases), you would do well to invest some time in reading the user manual and learning the ins and outs of that particular search system. But the following general guidelines for searching will help you approach your online materials with a level of skill that avoids frustration, empty results, or overwhelming masses of data.

Basics of Searching on the Web. As we've discussed, the critical first step in searching is to focus your search. Have you got a clear sense of what you are trying to accomplish, what sources would be the most likely to help you, the key terms you'll want to search with? As with searching in library materials and documents, you need a solid understanding of the parameters of your information task or you can easily get lost in the vastness of the Web.

There are two levels of search on the Web. There are site-specific search engines that locate material contained within a Web site, and there are Web search engines that locate information widely across the Web. All search engines have the same sorts of functions. Where they differ is in how the database you are searching was created and how the searching within the database is conducted.

The first thing you should do when you go to an unfamiliar search site (or even one you've been using, but with some degree of frustration) is to find the search help file. Spending a few minutes with the help file will get you ready to do a thorough and effective search.

The most important distinction for you to understand about a Web search site is whether it is a *directory* or an *index*. A directory has hierarchically organized lists of subject categories, their databases are compiled and maintained by humans, and they allow users to browse by subject in search of relevant information. Examples of *directory*-type search sites are Yahoo, the Open Directory Project, and online library catalogs.

In contrast, *indexes* rely on software instead of humans to enter information about sites. This explanation of how *spider* (sometimes referred to as *robot*) software works comes from Danny Sullivan's *Search Engine Watch:*

> The spider visits a Web page, reads it, and then follows links to other pages within the site. This is what it means when someone refers to a site being "spidered" or "crawled." The spider returns to the site on a regular basis, such as every month or two, to look for changes. Everything the spider finds goes into the second part of a search engine, the index. The index, sometimes called the catalog, is like a giant book containing a copy of every Web page that the spider finds. If a Web page changes, then this book is updated with new information.
>
> Sometimes, it can take a while for new pages or changes that the spider finds to be added to the index. Thus, a Web page may have been "spidered" but not yet "indexed." Until it is indexed—added to the index—it is not available to those searching with the search engine.[9]

Examples of index sites are Google, Hotbot, and Altavista.

Search Logic, Also Known as Boolean Logic.   Underlying the use of either directories or indexes is the search logic. Knowing how the words you type into a search relate to each other is important, because the way you enter terms and the order in which terms are processed will greatly affect the results. *Boolean logic* (see Box 5.2) is the phrase used to describe the system that applies to electronic search logic.

Boolean Logic.   Boolean logic is a mathematical logic system that can be used to improve searching the Internet and World Wide Web. Boolean logic was invented and named after George Boole, who published his system in a thesis in 1854. It was of little interest to anyone at that time because it dealt with pure logic; it was mostly forgotten. Although Boolean logic had little practical use in the 19th century, it was ideal when applied to searching computerized databases. Boolean logic uses three logical *operators* to define what a search should find. These operators are *and, or,* and *not* (also referred to as *and not* or *but not*).

When using Boolean logic to search the Internet and World Wide Web, you may find it helpful to visualize what you are searching for in the terms of a Venn diagram. Try to avoid long, complex Boolean searches, because it is easy to get confused about exactly what results your search will get.

When you give search terms to some search engines, they automatically apply an *and* relationship to the terms. Other search engines automatically apply an *or* relationship. All search engines have a method by which you can designate the exact relationship you want—but you'll need to go to the help file to find out just how to do it.

This book is not intended to be a definitive guide to searching; there are some excellent ones listed at the end of this chapter. But just as with library classification schemes, it is important for you to have a fundamental understanding of how information gets into Web databases and how they interpret the search terms you enter.

BOX 5.2
BOOLEAN LOGIC DIAGRAMS

Boolean logic is most easily demonstrated by the use of Venn diagrams. The first operator, *and*, is used to narrow a search. This is unlike its use in spoken english, where it broadens terms when used. For example, if you were searching for pictures of cows and sheep together, then the search *Cows and Sheep* would result in only pictures of cows and sheep together being found. Pictures of only cows or only sheep would be excluded. The result of this search is shown in the following Venn diagram.

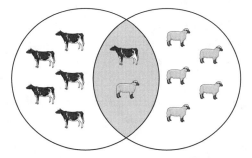

You can use the *and* operator with as many terms as you require. We can add another term to our original search, which will limit the result even further. The next diagram demonstrates the search *Cows and Sheep and Horses.*

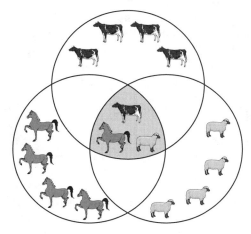

As you can see, the result is even smaller than *Cows and Sheep.* Only pictures that contain cows, sheep, and horses together will be found. Pictures that contain one or any two of the three animals will not be found.

The use of the operator *or* in a search has the effect of broadening a search. The search *Cows or Sheep* will produce results that contain cows only, sheep only, or cows and sheep together. This search result can be seen in the following diagram.

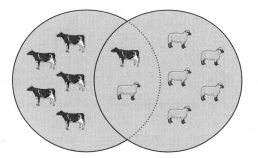

The final operator, *not*, completely eliminates one or more terms from the search. The search *Cows not Sheep* will obtain results that only have pictures of cows in them. Any pictures that contain sheep, even ones that also have cows in them, will be excluded.

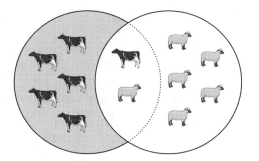

All three operators can be used in as long a search string as is required. However, the more operators you use, the more complicated

(continued)

BOX 5.2   CONTINUED

the search becomes. The search *Cows or Sheep not Horses* will produce the following result shown at the left. All pictures of only cows, only

sheep, and cows and sheep together will be found. Any picture at all that contains a horse will not be found.

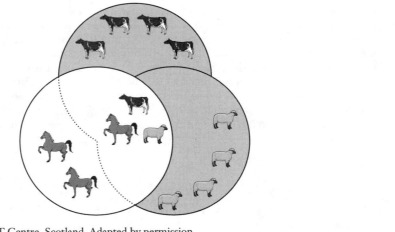

Source: Aberdeen College IT Centre, Scotland. Adapted by permission.

The Invisible Web.   There are more than 500 billion Web pages, but traditional search engines on the Web only cover approximately twenty percent of them. The other eighty percent has come to be known as *the invisible Web*. This invisible Web consists of material in databases on Web sites, Flash animations, and information behind registration screens. Knowing the scope of the material that you are searching for when you go to a Web search site is important—there may well be valuable information out there that requires a little more digging.

The InvisibleWeb.com site is a good resource (www.invisibleWeb.com) that points you to a list of database links and other resources internal to Web sites that you might need to search separately. If you need to do a thorough search on a topic, particularly one for which important information would be found in a database, directory, or chart, you will have to look into the hidden nooks and crannies of the Web to find what you need.

Popular, Scholarly, or Trade Materials

No matter how you conduct your search (using print resources or electronic means), you have one more conceptual skill to master before you can begin to make sense of what you find. Your search may lead you to materials that have been produced for publication (in print or online) in a *popular* source, a *scholarly* source, or a *trade* source. These three types of publications have vastly different audiences, purposes, and means for generating information. As an information searcher, you need to understand these distinctions and know what they mean for your information search. The information in Box 5.3 provides a brief overview of these three types of materials.

BOX 5.3
POPULAR, SCHOLARLY, OR TRADE?

POPULAR PERIODICALS
- Tend to have short articles (1–5 pages)
- Have the intent of informing or entertaining the readers
- Cover a variety of topic/subject areas (such as the newsweekly magazines like *Time* or *Newsweek*); *or* cover a single subject for the enthusiast (such as *Sports Illustrated* or *Audobon*)
- Have articles without footnotes, bibliographies, or cited references. This means you cannot check the author's information by tracking down the original information source.
- Are intended for a nonacademic, nonspecialist audience
- Use conventional or conversational language, as opposed to a specialized vocabulary
- Contain articles written by journalists rather than researchers or specialists in a given field
- Contain extensive commercial advertising
- Are issued frequently (weekly, biweekly, monthly)

SCHOLARLY PERIODICALS
- Often contain lengthy articles (five to fifty pages)
- Have the intent of advancing knowledge in a field or discipline
- Usually confine the subject matter to a single, very specific aspect of a subject (e.g., music theory, language development, film studies)
- Contain articles with footnotes, bibliographies, or cited reference pages. This means you can consult the same materials the author used in his or her research
- Are intended for an academic or scholarly audience
- Use technical or specialized vocabulary
- Publish articles written by academics, specialists, or researchers in the field (as opposed to articles written by journalists reporting on or synthesizing research)
- Publish articles that have gone through the *peer review* process (the articles have been read and approved by other scholars before being accepted for publication)
- Often publish reviews of the literature
- Often include articles with charts or tables
- Are often produced under the editorial supervision of a professional or scholarly association (e.g., the American Medical Association or the Association for Education in Journalism and Mass Communication), or by a scholarly press (such as Pergamon or Elsevier)
- Contain little or no advertising
- Are issued less frequently than popular sources (two to twelve times a year)

TRADE PUBLICATIONS
- Often contain regular columns of news and commentary, along with lengthier articles about current issues and trends of interest to the audience
- Have the intent of covering an industry or an area of professional activity (e.g., *The Cattleman Magazine*, *Retail Grocer*, *presstime* [the trade publication for the Newspaper Association of America], *American Advertising* [the trade publication for the American Advertising Federation])
- Confine the subject to a specific field or industry
- Are intended for a professional or specialist audience (managers, administrators, practitioners in an industry, etc.)
- Use a combination of conventional vocabulary and insider jargon
- Articles may be written by journalists or by specialists
- Contain business-to-business and general-interest advertising
- Are issued frequently (weekly or bi-weekly, many with updates online) to cover fast-breaking changes in products, technology or industry news

Source: Material adapted from "Popular or Scholarly," a handout produced by the staff of the University of Minnesota Libraries. Reprinted by permission. Available at wilson.lib.umn.edu/reference/popular.html.

If you are confused about the type of a particular publication you find in your search, look for a bibliography, or lack of one, at the end of the article. Also, look for a brief biography of the author, either at the beginning or end of the article, for information about the author's education and/or possible institutional affiliation. You can also look at the masthead of the publication for the name of the editor or the members of the editorial board to see if you recognize the perspective of those responsible for publishing the material. If you still have questions, check the reference tool *Magazines for Libraries* by Bill Katz and Linda Sternberg Katz for a description of more than 6,000 periodicals.

INTERVIEWING

Interviewing will be your bread and butter as a communicator. It is the means by which you elicit information from people, get new perspectives, and achieve new understandings. Tapping into people—primary sources—through interviewing is a skill honed over time. In this section we discuss the interviewing process, the types of interviews, and the ways that you can gather information not only from people but from data as well.

Interviewing is a technique that is incorporated at more than one point in the information-seeking process. The advertising researcher might use focus-group interviews to learn about issues to be examined more extensively through survey interviews later in the research process. (Focus-group and survey interviews are described later in this chapter.) News reporters do a preliminary set of interviews, along with background research in the news archive, to get themselves up to speed on the issues of the story they are covering. Public relations practitioners often interview sources such as company officials when writing news releases.

Interviews differ according to purpose, format, and medium. The techniques used for interviews also differ, depending on the goal you hope to reach through the interviewing process. Jane Pauley, former principal anchor of *Dateline NBC*, tells a story about an interviewing experience that suggests how much the art of the interview has changed since pencil and notebook customs began. Pauley describes sending a pre-interview e-mail message to the next day's interviewee, a note intended to put the interviewee at ease. Prior to the interview, when making a check on the interviewee's personal Web page, Pauley was surprised to find her own note posted there. The woman she planned to interview, whose husband was imprisoned in Iraq for violating the Iraqi border, had established a Web page with which to keep those interested advised of developments in the campaign to free her husband.

The anecdote suggests two important developments that have changed interviewing dynamics: electronic sources now play a direct and significant role in interviews and, further, interviewees have grown much more aware of technology and the ways digital technologies can help them to promote their own interests. Further, a veritable industry has developed to teach potential interviewees ways that they can negotiate with (and manipulate) interviewers. Like the woman with the Web site, some interviewees are developing skills that give them communication power and influence.

Each new communication technology affecting interviewing has been accompanied by methods of negotiating power in the use of the technology. Before telephone interviewing became prominent in news, you had to send letters or be physically present to seek and conduct interviews. Being able to reach a potential interviewee by phone changed the power relationship, because ignoring the reporter's request became more difficult and more personal. When interviewers began to use recorders to tape their interviews, many interviewees were too suspicious of recorders to permit their use. Later, interviewees had learned to record the interviews for themselves as a way to establish precisely what they and the interviewer had said during the exchange.

Currently, use of e-mail for requesting and conducting interviews draws different responses from the experts or celebrities from whom interviews are sought. Some experts resent getting e-mail messages from people they don't know and have a policy of ignoring interview requests unless they have signaled that they are open to an interview by providing their e-mail address to the interviewers. However, an advantage cited by e-mail enthusiasts is that there are some safeguards for accuracy in being able to examine the entire set of questions before starting to answer and being able to answer specific questions carefully and without interruption.

Electronic developments aside, the interview continues to be a powerful information-finding method. You learn much of what you know about the world from talking with others. Asking a knowledgeable person for information is such a common activity that you hardly think of it as an information-seeking act. In some cases, you take at face value what you hear from others. Informal conversation in the coffee shop or discussion about a course with classmates is usually accepted with little concern for checking the facts. But in your work as a communicator there is a higher level of reality-checking required before you accept as true what you hear in an interview or conversation.

Purposes of the Interview

Communicators share a number of goals in their information-seeking interviews—whether they work in news, advertising, or public relations positions. For example, a corporate official of a firm that manufactures street-sweeping equipment might be interviewed on a given day by a news reporter asking questions about unusual capabilities of a new piece of equipment being marketed, by a member of the firm's public relations staff who is working on an article for the employee magazine, or by a staff member in the agency that handles the advertising for the firm. Many of the questions they ask will be similar, but some will be distinctive, reflecting the differences in the ultimate use of the information. Their common goal is the gathering of factual and comprehensive material that will contribute to an appropriate and interesting message.

The goals of the interview itself, as stated in the example above, may vary. They may vary by the type of use the information will have (for advertising, public relations, or journalistic purposes) and by the type of story that is being told (business, human interest, civic issues). Here are some different types of interview goals and how they may fulfill different purposes.

Information Gathering.   Think about the street-sweeping equipment example. The interviewer for the company magazine probably would ask questions about the impact of the new equipment on the work force of the firm. The advertising interviewer might be interested in details about the effectiveness of the machine; he or she might even want to operate the equipment briefly to get a feel for the product. The news reporter might be interested in the effect of the equipment on street cleaning in the city, on the firm's profitability, or the bidding process that resulted in the selection of this particular equipment. In each of these instances, the interviewer is engaging the company representative in a dialog that recognizes the ultimate interest of the audience in particular questions about the firm's decisions and behaviors. The information objective in this type of interview might be getting hard facts, opinions, attitudes, or anecdotes.

The use of interviews for initial information gathering will be more about open-ended questions and giving the interviewee room to discuss angles of interest to them. You don't know where they might lead you. A good question to ask in the information gathering interview is "What is the most important thing for me to know about this…" and at the end of the interview, "What else should I be trying to find out about this."

Human Interest. Interviews can provide insights about people and give you the detail that adds appeal to your story or copy. Human interest interviews are less about facts and figures and more about impressions, ideas, and emotions. In human interest interviews, journalists look to get a good story, get the flavor of an experience and, possibly, get some ideas on how to proceed with the writing. Advertisers interview people who might become part of a testimonial ad. Public relations practitioners look for stories that they can pitch to feature segments of morning television shows or features sections of newspapers.

Corroborating. Sometimes an interview can be a followup to another interview. This can serve the function of *he said*, *she said* and provide you with corroborating or conflicting opinions and information. Journalism, in particular, is often said to be about truth-telling—in fact, it needs to be about truths-telling (plural). The truth according to different constituencies in an issue might be very different. Corroborating interviews might involve having the interviewee reflect on what another interviewee said.

For example, to learn about public officials' responses to a proposed federal tax reform, interviews would be essential. Through interviews, you would learn which governors think that their states would suffer and which think that their states would gain from a particular tax proposal.

Investigative Interviews. Multiple interviews are the rule for investigative journalism. In addition to extensive use of records and documents, investigative journalists try to run down all relevant leads and double- or triple-check all facts. Good investigative reporters are characterized by their excellent information-finding skills and their tireless checking of often dull material. Interviews often lead to additional sources that must be checked out. The investigative report provides perhaps the widest range of interviewees of any type of reporting. Brian Brooks and his colleagues cite the following potential interviewees for a story on under-the-table political contributions: enemies, friends, losers, victims, experts, police, and people in trouble.[10] Neighbors, coworkers, government officials, waiters and bartenders, and relatives of those involved or affected by the story also are potential sources.

Methods of Interviewing

Face-to-Face.   For reporters, the face-to-face interview is the preferred method of information gathering. In the personal interview, you are able to pick up many clues about the person, beyond what they say. Tone of voice, body language, even the surroundings in which the interview takes place can add to the message the interviewee is delivering. For broadcast journalists, needing visual as well as verbal material for their story, filming the interviewee is essential.

Face-to-face interviews are also a popular method of conducting surveys in the strategic communications arena. This method of survey interviewing involves trained interviewers meeting individually with the survey respondents and asking the survey questions in person. This method can accommodate longer and more complex questions and questions that require the respondent to react to visual images (charts, drawings, photographs). Well-trained interviewers note how the interview is proceeding by observing respondents' nonverbal behavior.

Some disadvantages of the face-to-face interview method are that the labor and transportation costs for the interviewers' training and travel to and from the respondents' locations are very high. Finding appropriate respondents can be difficult because many people are unwilling to allow strangers into their homes. Interviewer selection is critical because the appearance, age, race, sex, dress, or nonverbal behavior of the interviewer may have subtle effects on respondents' answers to survey questions. For instance, when conducting the door-to-door census, the Census Bureau is careful to choose interviewers whose background and race are appropriate for the neighborhoods in which they will be conducting interviews. Because of the cost and the importance of interviewer training, the face-to-face interview method for surveying is less popular than it once was.

Telephone.   For journalists wanting to get information from busy or distant experts, the telephone interview is the second-favorite method for interviewing. Disadvantages are that some of the visual clues are missing and it is easier for an interviewee to cut short an interview by hanging up if it becomes uncomfortable or confrontational.

E-mail.   E-mail interviewing is becoming a popular method for initial contact with a prospective interviewee. It is easy to establish basic information exchange without playing phone tag. Some interviewees are more comfortable writing out a response to a question than saying something off the cuff. The dangers of the e-mail interview are obvious, though (remember the cartoon about the dog at the computer). It is hard to be sure the person from whom you want the response is actually responding. Also, all sorts of visual and auditory clues are missing, making the information gathered through the written word interview easier to misinterpret.

Group Interviews.   Up to this point, only two-person interviews have been discussed. However, group interviewing also is prevalent in mass-communication research and in the mass-communication industries. One form of group interview is known as the focus group. In focus groups, you meet with a small group of interviewees who have agreed to discuss a topic or a product. You have a list of questions you present to the interviewees, probing for details and encouraging those in the group to respond to other interviewees' comments. Subjects for discussion arise from the group, as well as from your agenda of questions. A special strength of the focus group is its capacity to raise issues and enlarge the scope of the discussion. In academic research, for example, focus group interviews may precede survey research, assisting those doing the study by identifying important questions and issues that might have been neglected otherwise. Also, focus group participants may correct researchers' misinformation and may suggest appropriate sets of responses to be offered in closed survey questions.

Focus-group interviews are prominent in advertising and marketing research and less frequently used in news and public relations work. Potential members of focus groups can range from grade schoolers, gathered to taste and judge a new snack, to retired people who discuss the services of travel agencies.

The moderator of a focus group lets the discussion range while it is moving productively and producing useful comment. Tasks include making certain that main points are covered, being receptive to new points that arise, and making sure that each respondent has a chance to talk. The moderator also has the task, at the outset of the discussion, of telling the group how the interview works, of setting up recording equipment and explaining its use to members, and of collecting any permissions that are required of the participants. Focus-group sessions typically are tape recorded and transcribed for ease of later analysis. Group members are told the method of recording and the subsequent use of their comments. Paying participants a small sum is a typical practice.

The advertising industry makes frequent use of focus-group interviewing. For example, a travel firm's ad agency may wish to learn what services are especially appreciated by retirement-age people, who constitute a sizable proportion of those who travel and who use travel agencies. For this purpose, interviewees may be sought from among those who are retired, have traveled recently, and are in a particular income bracket. The ideas gleaned from the focus-group discussion may be used as the basis for an advertising campaign directed at retired people. An intermediate step might be to use the discussion points as the basis for a survey that would provide numerical data on the major questions.

Group interviewing is also used in news reporting. For news work, where direct quotes generally are required, group interviewing presents some difficulties. Even if the session is tape recorded, identifying the voices accurately is difficult. Under some circumstances, however, group interviewing has advantages. You may find that individuals are unwilling to be interviewed for attribution but are willing to have their stories told as a part of the group's story. For a story on alcoholism, members of Alcoholics Anonymous may relate their experiences to one another while you listen. Employees of an adoption agency who counsel groups of unmarried mothers or adopting parents might permit a group interview, on the condition that individuals' names not be used.

Having permission to tape record the discussion is important in such group interviews, although the recording generally is flawed by extraneous sounds and inaudible voices. As a precaution against flaws in the tape, you should take as many notes as possible. Further, you should, at the end of the session, pass around paper and a pencil, requesting names, telephone numbers, and e-mail addresses to contact for later clarifications and as a check on accuracy. While this may seem to violate the anonymity provision, group members may have come to trust you during the meeting and some may be willing to be called so their comments can be clarified or verified before the story is written. In addition, telephone calls may elicit other important information that did not emerge during the group interview.

News Conferences.   News conferences range in style and size from televised presidential news conferences with hundreds of reporters assembled, to informal sessions with one source and a handful of questioners. The news conference undoubtedly is the journalist's least-favorite method of news gathering. From the viewpoint of the source, the news conference is a timesaving convention. But from the reporter's perspective, there is little to recommend it. If the news conference is televised, reporters for newspapers find that their questions and the answers to them have been broadcast on television or placed as a video file on a news Web site before they can write their own stories. Followup and clarification questions are difficult at large news conferences. Reporters who have prepared particularly well often do not reap the benefits of their preparation. They may not have a chance to ask their questions and, if they do, they reveal the lines of their inquiry to competitors.

Despite the limitations of news conferences, they continue to be a standard method that busy or celebrated people use for giving information to the media. Behind the scenes at press conferences, the work of public relations staff members is critical. For many conferences, PR staff have prepared handouts that give the essential information about the announcements to be made that day. In these packets, reporters find the basics related to the announcement—names, titles, dates, places, and decisions—that free them to ask more substantial and interpretative questions than they otherwise would be able to ask. From the viewpoint of the public relations staff, these information packets are designed to promote accuracy in the news reports that follow the conference.

Grant Winter, a television journalist, emphasized the particular needs of the broadcasting industry in his advice to public relations people on how to improve broadcast-news conferences. Planning for broadcast equipment, including phone jacks, lights, microphones, tripods, and parking spaces for trucks is part of the public relations specialist's responsibilities. Winter recommended that handouts include news releases, biographies of speakers, texts of speeches, and visuals such as charts. Winter also asks that a speaker be available for separate one-on-one interviews following the news conference and that the public-relations office be prepared throughout the remainder of the day for followup questions by telephone. He points out that unless reporters have the opportunity to check for accuracy before a broadcast, a story may be scrapped rather than used on air.[11]

Questions in news conferences should be short. Reporters who seem to be making speeches instead of asking questions draw the anger of their colleagues. So do unprepared reporters whose questions do not advance the topic but require the source to repeat information that well-informed reporters have already acquired. Well-prepared and attentive listeners are in the best position to present important followup questions during news conferences.

Verbatim Interviews.   In the verbatim interview, the dialog of the interview is reproduced for the reader. The interviewer's question is printed as it was asked, followed by the response. The technique is used principally in magazines, usually with a source who is very newsworthy or who is a recognized expert.

For example, verbatim interviews in *Newsweek, Wired, U.S. News & World Report,* and *Playboy* usually present the views of political figures, celebrities, or experts on a controversial topic. The interview itself is preceded by a short introduction that establishes the context of the interview and gives background material on the interviewer and the topic.

Survey Interviews.   Survey interviews are widely used in many facets of mass-communication work. Advertising and public relations professionals made extensive use of survey research earlier than news workers did. In the 1960s, Philip Meyer led the way for journalists' use of surveys in his studies of Detroit residents' views of the crisis in race relations. Subsequently, he was influential in persuading news organizations that they could effectively use social-science methods to improve the information in news reports. In his book *Precision Journalism,* Meyer proposed a plan for journalists' use of scientific methods in reporting. The same methods had been in use for decades in other organizations that provide media content—for example, national polling organizations, such as Gallup, that serve individual metropolitan, state or regional clients.

Survey interviews both differ from and resemble other types of interviews in a variety of ways. In scientific interviewing, the interviewees are selected according to principles of tested sampling procedures. The interviewers are trained to work from identical interview forms. Most often, the questions are structured so that the answers can be analyzed statistically. Standards for interviewers are similar in survey research and in other, less formal methods. All the cautions about advance preparation, careful use of language and nonverbal communications, and self-control apply.

Much mass-communication survey research is done by the firm that needs the information. However, some is commissioned by the media and executed by research firms that specialize in particular types of research. In addition, media organizations subscribe to the reports issued regularly by other research organizations. For example, a newspaper may use survey research to develop material for news reports and may regularly publish the Gallup opinion columns, but may commission an independent firm to do its readership or marketing studies.

Selecting Interviewees

The first step in preparing for solid interviews is choosing those to be interviewed. Social scientist John Madge classified interviewees into three categories: the potentate, the expert, and the people. Potentates are, of course, those who have authority or power. Experts have special knowledge of a subject. People have experiences in life that allow them to give direct testimony on the effects of the potentate's actions and on the matters the expert studies.[12] Madge's distinction about types of interviewees takes into account their position in society, their experience with media attention, and the types of information they can contribute to the message. Let's look at the types of interviewees that might fall into these categories.

Potentate Category

Celebrities. Celebrities are good interviewees if it serves their purpose, not necessarily yours. Celebrities with something to promote will be available; otherwise, they can be reluctant. Usually you have to go through their agent—direct access to big stars is virtually impossible. For celebrities an interview is promotional and they will rarely be entirely forthcoming about themselves. They want to put a positive spin on themselves and their activities. Celebrity endorsements might also involve an interview.

CEOs and Leaders of Industry. You might get a good interview from a major business executive if there is an official statement, particularly with good news about their company, or if they will be the subject of a profile. Otherwise, you will probably be steered through the public relations office. Interviewing the business leaders of an account you might be involved in as a strategic communicator will be more about strategizing and eliciting information.

Government Officials. The leaders of government departments, legislators, and other elected officials can be considered potentates. They might well be experts, too, though it is more likely that those who work for them are the most informed.

Experts Category

Subject Experts. Experts are people who, through their training, position, or education, are highly knowledgeable on a certain subject. Experts want to be interviewed; it enhances their own sense of their expertise and provides more credibility of their knowledge base. Industry experts also have an imperative to share their expertise. For the most part, experts are the easiest interviewees because of their personal and professional interest in having their expertise known and used. Experts can provide you with solid background on the topic, insight into the issues involved, historical and contextual information, and leads to others you might want to talk to or resources you might want to read. Experts might also fall into the informal sources category when the expertise is more esoteric. These are experts who, through their own obsession or interest, have steeped themselves in a particular subject. These are the people who probably have a Web site devoted to the subject. To determine if they are true experts, you need to research their credentials carefully.

Academics. You'll read more about academic experts and how to approach them for interviews in Chapter 9. Like other experts, they are motivated to speak because being interviewed enhances their own image and provides greater credibility to their expertise.

People Category

Eye-Witnesses. Eye-witnesses were *there.* They saw the train wreck, they were on the line fighting the fire, they heard the explosion. These are ordinary people put in extraordinary situations. They are the lifeblood of the reporter and can be important resources for the strategic communicator. Eye-witnesses might well be traumatized by what they saw. Some may find it cathartic to recount their experience, others will find it too upsetting. Handling eye-witness interviews is a delicate art. There are special ethical considerations when interviewing people who have personally witnessed newsworthy events.

Eye-witness interviews will provide you with the color and details that you missed if you weren't there yourself, but eye-witness accounts must be taken with a grain of salt. Witnesses can be unclear in their recollections or may embellish the story to make it more interesting.

People with Experience.   They had been taking the medicine that was just taken off the market. They worked for the company that just declared bankruptcy. They are single moms working two jobs. They have been through what you're interested in and they can provide context for your messages. People with experience come to their knowledge through life's chances. They are informal sources, in that their knowledge and experience is through their life, not necessarily through any training or job position. People with experience are particularly important interviewees to the strategic communicator. They are the people who have used the product or service and can give you valuable insights into their experience with it.

Evaluating Interviewees

Evaluating the credentials of those who might be interviewed is a small research task in itself. During the earlier steps of the information strategy you developed a potential roster of interviewees. A sensible next step is to review all the background material and make a list of those who have written or spoken on the subject. For example, consider the background research for an advertising campaign on behalf of the Coalition for Literacy. The coalition seeks volunteers to work with functionally illiterate adults. Potential interviewees include officials of the coalition and of other groups concerned with adult illiteracy. Annual reports, newsletters, and boards of directors' minutes of meetings also reveal names of important individuals in this field. Government documents display the names of members of Congress who have shown concern about the problem and the identities of specialists who have testified before congressional committees. Some of these specialists have published articles on the subject in scholarly journals and have been quoted in news magazines.

Another type of expertise you might seek is that of people who have themselves experienced the disability of illiteracy. Their expertise may not be evident in the indexes and journals, but members of the literacy organizations probably can help you locate them. Perhaps some of the formerly illiterate adults have gone on to become volunteer teachers or members of the groups combating illiteracy. The ad campaign may permit a photo, a headline, and a copy block of 350 words for each of several ads to be produced for the campaign. The limited space available makes each bit of material to be included highly significant. The facts, ideas, and experiences presented must be accurate and compelling if the campaign is to succeed.

After drawing up a roster of promising interviewees, you need to check the reputation of those on the list. You can do this by checking such standard reference sources as *Who's Who*. In this case, *Who's Who in Education* may include biographical information on some of those who have written on the subject or spoken before congressional committees. Or the Authors volume of *Books in Print* may reveal titles of relevant books written by these people. Some checking can be done through informal and institutional sources. For example, such informal checking can help you identify persons who are notorious publicity hounds or who are known as liars.

Once the interview roster is ready, you can determine the willingness and availability of the sources. Some potential interviewees may be unavailable—out of town or tied up with other responsibilities. Others may be unwilling to be interviewed. Some may have research results that they do not wish to make public yet. Others may prefer to send you a copy of their testimony before Congress and save the time an interview would take. Some specialists who are unavailable will suggest others as substitutes. However, a good percentage of people on a well-constructed source list should be available. Enriching and supplementing the fruits of the earlier steps in the information strategy is a consistent goal.

Planning Interviews

Careful planning of interviews involves a number of steps and almost innumerable considerations. In some cases, the interviewee stipulates some conditions for the interview. For example, the interviewee may limit the time available to you, may require either a face-to-face or a telephone conversation, may refuse to speak either with or without a tape recorder, or may ask to have another person present. Plan the interview around any conditions that were established when the interview was arranged. In the case of an e-mail interview, pose questions and arrange them in an effective order to be sent to interviewees who have agreed to answer the e-mail request. You need to respect the fact that many busy people ignore unexpected e-mail messages.

Planning face-to-face and telephone interviews is similar. Some interviewers believe they get better results from telephone interviews because the potential distractions of personal appearance, race, and age do not intrude. Some nonverbal cues that are helpful in the face-to-face interview are missing, however, and you must substitute for these cues. For example, in face-to-face interviews, the interviewee's facial expression tells you when he or she is puzzled. The interviewee who notices that you are struggling to keep up with your note taking may pause or speak more slowly. When you are conducting a telephone interview you should provide plenty of "um-hums" to reassure your source that you're still there.

For extended survey research interviews, computer-assisted telephone interviewing (CATI) software is available. Using this software, telephone interviewers can read the survey questions from the screen and enter codes for the responses directly into the computer. Complex branching in questionnaires is simplified and, following completion of the interview, results can be speedily obtained with the application of a statistical package.

Interview planning requires a thorough review of all material gathered earlier in the information process. From this review, you can list needed material and devise a strategy for using interviews to meet the need:

- What material is agreed on? What patterns of consistency exist?
- What is disputed? Can inconsistencies be explained or resolved? What is the significance of the disputed facts?
- What unexplored aspects of the subject should be developed? What is new information that should be reflected in my questions?
- What questions are appropriate to each interviewee?
- What sensitivities and special perspectives should I be aware of in asking questions of each interviewee?
- What information in my files may need updating or confirming?
- What human-interest information can be elicited from the interviewee?

In preparing questions that will bring forth information, you naturally stress the content you hope to get from your interviews. However, interview preparation also involves getting ready for the social and psychological aspects of the interview. Before you draft your questions, consider the situation of the interviewee. Raymond Gorden cites eight inhibitors that you should be aware of in your interview strategies.[13] Four of these inhibitors may make sources unwilling to give information:

- Competing demands for time
- Ego threats that make the respondent fear loss of esteem or status
- Standards of etiquette that put some topics off limits in certain circumstances
- Trauma, the reluctance to return to a painful situation

The other four inhibitors affect the speaker's ability to respond adequately:

- Forgetfulness
- Chronological confusion
- Inferential confusion
- Unconscious behavior

Memory fades, sometimes to be stimulated by conversation about an event. Thus material that is most remote in time may—or may not—be recalled better if it is requested after conversation is under way and the interviewee's recall has been sharpened by reminders about the event. Chronological confusion can take on a number of forms. It is common for people to recall two or more events, but forget the order of their occurrence. They also may recall a situation, but incorrectly recall when it happened. For example, a person citing family history might believe that all parcels of the family farm were acquired at one time, since in his memory that has been the case. Inferential confusion results from faulty reasoning rather than faulty memory. The interviewee may not be able to relate his own experience to abstract questions presented in the interview unless you are patient and provide a step-by-step approach linking the experience of the interviewee with the generalizations. Unconscious behavior also influences interviewees' ability to respond accurately. People under stress or in a crisis frequently are unaware of their own behavior in these circumstances.

Fortunately, you can count on other factors that facilitate interviews. Confident interviewers who approach potential interviewees expecting their cooperation find that many people are willing to help. People appreciate the recognition that interviews bring them, another factor that paves the way. Altruistic appeals and sympathetic understanding for the prospective interviewee also affect willingness to be interviewed. Interviews can be stimulating new experiences for the respondent. Finally, interviewees who have suffered in a crisis often realize the cathartic benefits of discussing their situations. The news media frequently are criticized for interviews with people experiencing tragedy or crisis, but the testimony of those interviewed shows that many victims appreciate the chance to have a larger segment of society understand their position. The effects of inhibitors and facilitators vary, depending on interviewee and subject. You can prepare for an interview with the recognition that these factors are likely to affect its quality. You can be sensitive in determining what questions to ask, what language to use in asking them, and the best sequence for asking each question.

Developing Questions

Having assessed both the information needs and the interviewee's potential to respond, you are ready to develop an agenda of questions. This is a comprehensive list of questions, setting forth everything you would like to know. Some of these questions might be asked of a number of respondents. Others might be asked of only one interviewee. Except in survey research interviews, open-ended questions are most common. In the closed-ended question, the respondent must select one of the responses provided by the interviewer. For example, most questions asked in Gallup and other polls are closed-ended: "How do you feel about the economy of the United States at this time? Very optimistic, Somewhat optimistic, Neutral, Somewhat pessimistic, or Very pessimistic?" An open-ended interview question asks, "What is your feeling about the United States economy at this time?" One advantage of closed-ended questions is that a large number of interviews can be analyzed relatively quickly and inexpensively. Open-ended questions have the advantages of completeness, specificity, and depth. In journalistic interviews, open-endedness is stressed, for it leads to spontaneity, interpretation by sources, cues for additional questions, and quotable phrases.

Whether closed- or open-ended, clear questions are required for successful interviews. Social psychologists Eleanor Maccoby and Nathan Maccoby developed six points to assist question writers.[14]

1. *Avoid words with double meaning.* Even such simple terms as *dinner* can confuse and result in error. Residents of a nursing home, for example, may refer to dinner as either the noon meal or the evening meal, depending on custom and social class. The interviewer in such a situation might conclude that people did not know what they were eating, since they gave different answers to the question "What was served for dinner?"

2. *Avoid long questions.* Use a carefully crafted question to open the subject and a series of separate followups that will cover the material. Instead of saying, "Tell me about your experience in Central America, why you decided to go, what you found when you got there, and how you escaped your captors," the questioner should break up the string of questions and begin with, "Why did you go to Central America?"

3. *Specify the time, place, and context in which the interviewee should answer the question.* Once an interview has touched on a variety of topics, the interviewee might get off track. Keep the interview on track with specific questions such as, "Now, once you escaped your captors, you were back in Panama at your company headquarters. What happened at that point?"

4. *Either make explicit all the alternatives that the respondent should have in mind in answering or make explicit none of them.* For example, you might want to guide the interviewee through some alternatives but could easily fail to suggest the one that matches what the interviewee had in mind. "Once you were safely back in the United States, did you want to call the FBI or the CIA, or did you decide to let your company take over?" Recognizing the incomplete alternatives presented, the source might say, "Well, actually, neither of those." But some respondents might not correct you and simply evade the question or respond vaguely.

5. *When the interview concerns a subject that is unfamiliar to the interviewee, offer an explanation before presenting the question.* "While you were held captive, some new legislation was introduced in Congress. The provisions include.... How might that have affected your situation?"

6. *It is often helpful to ask questions in terms of the respondent's own immediate (and recent) experience, rather than in terms of generalities.* The respondent may resist such a general question as "Is the State Department doing a good job in these kidnapping cases?" A specific question—"In your case, how effectively did the State Department work toward your release?"—is more to the point.

Question Strategy

Arranging the questions into an effective agenda is the next step. Many interviewers use a strategy of beginning with reassuringly easy questions. Some may be questions verifying that what has been learned through earlier parts of the strategy is, indeed, still accurate and up-to-date. Although the opening questions may be simple, experienced interviewers are aware of overly broad questions that send the interviewee off the topic or set off an avalanche of irrelevances. Generally, experience suggests that embarrassing, touchy, or ego-threatening questions best be kept until late in the interview. By then, the context is well established, and you have had a chance to develop a persona as a fair, accurate, and sensitive individual. Touchy questions always bring about the possibility that the subject will declare the interview to be at an end. In that event, at least you have the earlier portions of the conversation for the record.

Each question in the interview agenda gives rise to additional questions. Some of these are followups, that is, requests for more information based on the idea just stated by the source. If you are too tightly tied to your own interview agenda you may neglect to use appropriate followups. On the other hand, it is possible that you will forget your original question agenda once the followups begin. Rigidly adhering to the question agenda promotes one kind of completeness, at the expense of expanding the topic and developing its new dimensions. Experienced interviewers learn, in time, to walk the line between the two hazards.

Conducting Interviews

Because almost all interviewing takes place away from observers' gazes, it is difficult to establish standards for interviewing. The time pressures of broadcast-news interviewing, for example, make that variety of interview too specialized to serve as a model for general interviewing. Thus you are left to develop your art through study, trial, and experience.

That said, there are some rituals and routines for interviews that will help ensure a successful session. Many of them are common sense, the kinds of things that you know, as a person, about a successful conversation. Rituals assist the conversation and do much to help establish the roles that people will play in the interview. They can help you understand the process and save both time and stress for the participants.

- Telephone in advance to arrange the interview. This gives the interviewee a chance to ask about the topic you want to discuss. It's only fair that both sides have an opportunity to prepare for the interview.
- At the start of an interview, establish that you have an agenda of questions. This will indicate to the interviewee that you have carefully prepared and will suggest your professionalism.
- Avoid having your opinion, as the interviewer, solicited. Interviewees might ask your opinion, or seek reinforcement of their own viewpoint. Have stock phrases available, such as, "It's not proper for me to disclose my opinion about this to you. Studies show that my neutrality here will give the best atmosphere for an interview. However, you can see that the subject is one that interests me greatly."
- When an interviewee strays from a subject, steer them gently back. Acknowledging that the topic has moved off the key points you are interested in exploring must be done carefully: "I wonder if we could finish talking about the cost of this program, and then get back to the comment about the application process."
- Develop an effective leaving ritual. Many interviewees who had indicated they had only a few minutes available for the interview end up wanting to continue. They see the end of the interview as the end of their opportunity to be heard. Have a phrase available like, "You have been more than generous with your time. Let me leave you my office number and e-mail address in case you think of something else I should know."
- Reassure the interviewee you are concerned with accurately presenting the interview. End the interview with the statement, "If I have any questions later, I will telephone or e-mail you to check the facts again."

Contract with the Interviewee

Perhaps the most crucial step in planning and conducting interviews is establishing the contract with the interviewee. The contract with an interview source is a legal contract that must be upheld once it is agreed upon. This was established in *Cohen v. Cowles Media Co.*, a case that is discussed more in Chapter 13.

> During the 1982 Minnesota gubernatorial race, petitioner Cohen, who was associated with one party's campaign, gave court records concerning another party's candidate for Lieutenant Governor to respondent publishers' newspapers after receiving a promise of confidentiality from their reporters. Nonetheless, the papers identified him in their stories, and he was fired from his job. He filed suit against respondents in state court, alleging, among other things, a breach of contract. The court rejected respondents' argument that the First Amendment barred the suit, and a jury awarded him compensatory damages."[15]

There are different levels of source attribution. You need to be aware of them, your interviewee must understand this, and you both need to agree upon the level of attribution to be used. The types of attribution in messages are listed here:

- For Attribution. Everything the interviewee says will have his or her name attached.
- Attribution by Title Only. The interviewee's identity is protected, identified only with something like "a highly placed official" or "sources close to the president."
- No Attribution. The interviewee agrees to talk but the information will not be attributed in any way: "CBS News has learned…"
- No Publication, Off the Record, or Deep Background. The information cannot be used in any way except to inform the communicator.

Your goal is to be sure your source understands how the information from the interview is going to be used before you ask any questions or start to gather any information. For most types of interviews, a "for attribution" agreement is the appropriate arrangement. Most news interviewees want to be recognized for their expertise or input into a story. Participants in a strategic communications focus group sign releases indicating that they understand the terms of the interview and how the information will be used. Interviewees who seek to avoid a "for attribution" agreement may be doing so because they want to protect themselves from the consequences of their words. Or they may be floating a trial balloon to gauge public opinion in advance of an official announcement. Or they may be leaking damaging information about a competitor. Any agreement other than a "for attribution" interview should put you on alert to be especially vigilant about checking the interviewee's information against independent second and third sources for verification.

Some interviewees, particularly whistle-blowers with controversial or damaging information about an organization with which they are affiliated, might seek an "off the record" status for their interview with you. Journalists normally attribute all information in a story, because without attribution the reader or viewer cannot judge the validity of the information presented. So before you agree to this condition in an interview ask yourself these questions:

- Do I have enough information to make this decision?
- Is this story important enough to justify using an anonymous source?
- Is this anonymous material confirmed by a reliable second and third source?
- Can I explain in the story the reason for the anonymity?
- What is the journalistic purpose of reporting this information without attribution? Is this a story that simply cannot be gotten or told without use of anonymous sources?
- Would more reporting get this material on the record?
- Does my editor or producer know enough about this source to justify my offering a verbal contract?
- If the story quotes an anonymous source, will it still be accurate, complete, fair, and balanced? (Some reporters have a rule that they will not use comments or personal attacks about another person from an anonymous source.)
- Does the source understand the meaning of anonymity? Does the source know that at least the editor will need to know his or her identity?
- How far will I and my organization go to protect this person's identity? To jail?
- Can I tell enough about the anonymous source so readers can judge the validity of the comment?
- Would this story be improved if I cut the anonymous material?

Be sure you understand the policies of your media organization before you give *any* promise to a source. Sometimes you can get a reluctant source to agree to attribution of a quote. Try reading back individual quotes and point out that each one is not so damaging or problematic. A good reporter can sometimes get an entire interview back on the record. This is not generally recommended practice, however. Anything that confuses the clarity of the contract you made with the source at the start of the interview should be avoided. That way, there can be no disputes with sources or supervisors later about the terms under which the interview was conducted or the agreements that were made about use of the information.

Rights of the Interviewee

The importance—and hazards—of the journalistic interview have led some organizations to provide interviewee training to representatives of their organizations. These range in scope from elaborate and expensive seminars in which executives are coached in answering (and evading) reporters' questions, to pamphlets containing guidelines for dealing with reporters. Many organizations require potential interviewers to go through a corporate Public Affairs officer to arrange an interview. Others have established their own guidelines for interviews that are given to interviewees. As a communicator, you need to understand what the interviewee might have been told about talking to you. Understanding the interviewee's agenda and expectations is a crucial part of conducting a successful interview. This list of Rights of the Interviewee from the U.S. Air Force gives insight into the expectations that interviewees might have of their interviewer.

> "In interviews of a spontaneous nature (at a crash site or natural disaster when approached by Public Affairs for an on-the-spot interview with reporters).... You have the right...
>
> 1. To know who is interviewing you and who he or she represents.
> 2. To have complete agreement by both parties on the ground rules (the boundaries or types of questions you will answer and those you will not), no matter how hastily the interview is arranged.
> 3. To be treated courteously. The questions can be tough, but the reporter's demeanor should not be abusive.
> 4. To have everything you say "on the record." There is no such thing as "off the record" comments. Keep in mind that although the reporter's tape recorder may appear to be off, it may in fact still be recording. Treat all microphones and cameras as if they were "hot."
> 5. Not to be physically threatened or impaired by lights held too closely or microphones shoved in your face (ask the reporter to adjust the lights and move the microphone back).
> 6. To conclude the interview after a "reasonable" amount of time, but only after important questions have been answered (when the reporter starts repeating questions or starts asking dumb questions, conclude the interview).
> 7. To not answer questions that are not related to the purpose of the interview.
> 8. To not answer questions for which you are not the subject-matter expert (but offer to help arrange through public affairs an interview with the expert on that subject.)
>
> In pre-arranged office or TV-studio interviews.... You have the right...
>
> 1. To all the above.
> 2. To know the general content, subject, or thrust of the interview so you have time to research the appropriate information.
> 3. To know approximately how long the interview will last.
> 4. To know if there are other people being interviewed at the same time and if so what the nature of their interview will be.
> 5. To require a public affairs representative be present.
> 6. To make your own audio or videotape of the interview.
> 7. To physical comfort during the interview (appropriate seating, comfortable chair, etc.).
> 8. To be allowed to answer without constant interruptions (as long as your answers are brief and to the point). To ignore editorial comments by reporters or others being interviewed with you.
> 9. To have the time to get some of YOUR points across during the interview (be sure to have some positive points ready and work them in during the interview).[16]

Recording the Interview

Think about how you will record the interview. Will written notes, a tape recording, video tape, or e-mail transcript of questions and responses be the best way to keep track of what goes on during the interview?

You must let your interviewee know how the interview will be recorded. It is a breach of ethics, and in some states illegal, to record someone without their knowledge. If you use a tape recorder, always use it in conjunction with a notebook.

Focus-group sessions are almost always recorded for later review by the ad and marketing researchers. Participants must sign a release indicating they understand the session is being recorded and how the information will be used.

CONCLUSION

Let's review the types of information gathering techniques and think about them in the context of the forms in which you will find information: people, paper, and digital. If you are going to a people source you will want to search for the right person, you can observe the actions of people through monitoring, and you can interview the individual person to elicit fresh information and perspective. With paper, you will likely be searching for documents. With digital information, monitoring through tracking of records or news items and searching for specific documents or materials will be the techniques you use. Within each of these forms of information the type of contributor they represent will determine the best approach to take for getting information from them in an efficient, ethical, and effective way.

In the next chapter we look at libraries as information sources.

SELECTED ADDITIONAL READINGS

Adams, Sally with Wynford Hicks. *Interviewing for Journalists*. London: Routledge, 2001.

Krueger, Richard and Mary Anne Casey. *Focus Groups: A Practical Guide for Applied Research*, 3rd edition. Thousand Oaks, CA: Sage Publications, 2000.

Metzler, Ken. *Creative Interviewing: The Writer's Guide to Gathering Information by Asking Questions*, 3rd edition. Boston: Allyn & Bacon, 1996.

Murray, Donald. *Writing to Deadline*. Portsmouth, NH: Heinemann Publishing, 2000.

Sherman, Chris and Gary Price. *The Invisible Web: Uncovering Information Sources Search Engines Can't See*. Chicago: Independent Publishers Group, 2001.

NOTES

1. Michelle Faul. "Thousands Gather to Mark End of U.N. Decade of Women." *The Associated Press*. Nairobi, Kenya: 10 July 1985, Wednesday, AM cycle.

2. Malcolm Gladwell. "Medicaid Politics and Alzheimer's Realities: How Spending Winds Up Saving Money." *The Washington Post*. 11 June 1995, Sunday.

3. Mike Hoyt. "Just How Far Is Too Far?" Columbia Journalism Review. Sept.–Oct. 1998. From www.cjr.org/year/98/5/hoyt.asp.

4. Susan Banda. "Working Undercover." *IRE Journal*. Jan–Feb 1995, 14.

5. Douglas McLeod. "Exclusive: The Loneliness of a Lock-up, Or a Night in Detention." *Regent Review*. 24 February 1977, 8–9.

6. Everette Dennis. "Touchstones: The Reporter's Reality," *Nieman Reports*. Autumn 1980, 40–45.

7. Andrew Stern. "Ad Agency Seeks Small-town Guide to Consumer Taste." *Star Tribune*. 29 April 1991, p. 3D.

8. "Web Logs: A History and Perspective." 7 September 2000. *Rebecca's Pocket*. From: www. rebeccablood.net/essays/Weblog_history.html.

9. Danny Sullivan. *Search Engine Watch*. From: www.searchenginewatch.com.

10. Brian Brooks, George Kennedy, Daryl Moen, and Don Ranly. *News Reporting and Writing*. New York: St. Martin's Press, 1980, 394–395.

11. Grant Winter. "Improving Broadcast News Conferences." *Public Relations Journal*. July 1990, 25–26.

12. John Madge. *The Tools of Social Science*. Garden City, NY: Doubleday, 1965.

13. Raymond Gorden. *Interviewing: Strategy, Techniques, and Tactics*, 4th edition. Homewood, IL, Dorsey Pr, 1998.

14. Eleanor Maccoby and Nathan Maccoby. "The Interview: A Tool of Social Science." in Gardner Lindzey, ed., *Handbook of Social Psychology*. Vol. 1. Reading, Mass: Addison-Wesley, 1954, 449–487.

15. Cohen v. Cowles Media Co. From: www.freedomforum.org/fac/opinions/90-91/90-634.S.htm.

16. Public Affairs Handbook for Engineering and Services. From: www.afcee.brooks.af.mil/ mmgpg/documents/acrobat/pa_hbook.pdf.

CHAPTER SIX

THE LIBRARY AS AN INFORMATION SOURCE

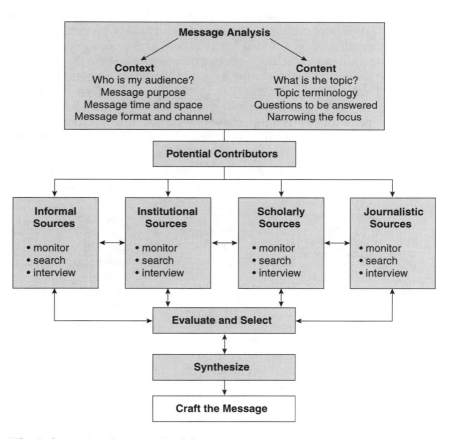

The Information Strategy Model

People, paper, and digital information are the three forms in which information contributors—informal, institutional, scholarly, and journalistic—make their information sources available. But there is another essential resource for information in all three forms from all four contributors: the library. Libraries can be affiliated with a particular contributor type, or they can be totally independent entities that contain information from different kinds of contributors. In this chapter, we discuss the different types of libraries, what you can expect to find in them, and the important role they play in your strategy for gathering information for your communications messages.

LIBRARIES

Before the Internet, libraries were the information spaces most used by, and essential to, communicators. Libraries are storehouses of recorded knowledge in print, electronic, and other formats. But with all of the electronically stored and accessible information available from any computer with access to the Internet, it may not be easy to see why you would need to use the resources of a library at all.

The main reason libraries continue to be major contributors to the communicator's information process is that library material has been organized, indexed, and coherently arranged for ease of use. Despite the best attempts of the creators of some of the exciting new electronic information services, most still lack even the more rudimentary organization schemes and retrieval systems that have been in use in libraries for centuries. Quality control is an even worse problem for some electronic services. Libraries continue to be among the few information repositories that clearly organize their collections and allow for evaluation of the relative quality and usefulness of almost everything retrieved.

Libraries are set up to preserve, collect, and make accessible recorded intellectual products. Most libraries have a computer or card catalog that lists the contents of their collections. Most libraries have both book collections and periodical collections, and they have the tools (indexes, abstracts, bibliographies) to help searchers find what they need in the collections. The libraries that can afford to do so have access to the Internet and to electronic databases of online and CD-ROM information. Some libraries allow users to tap into other electronic information services as well. And, of course, all libraries have the most important resource of all—the librarian or archivist—the person who knows the most about the collection and about how best to use it. Just as the author of a book might be more valuable than the book itself, so too is the librarian.

The information strategy emphasizes your competence as a searcher. Nonetheless, you will frequently run into dead ends in your information strategy. In these cases, the best person to consult is the librarian. Not everyone sitting behind a desk in a library or answering e-mail queries online is a librarian, however. Many libraries staff their physical and virtual information desks at off times with employees who do not have specific training in the efficient use of library materials. The librarian has a degree and professional training in the methods of organization and use of library collections. The librarian is very familiar with the special characteristics of, and collections in, the library in which he or she works. And the librarian is the one person who is trained in the area of effective information retrieval.

If you consult a librarian, he or she will ask you for specific information about your research question. It is up to you to describe precisely what you are looking for. The more specific the request, the swifter and more accurately the librarian can respond. The librarian may point to pathfinders and bibliographic guides or other online or print resources that the library staff have prepared to help with just the type of question you are asking. Web-based, online, or CD-ROM databases will be more familiar to the librarian, who can save you time in deciding where to begin a search. The librarian may also suggest files of ephemeral, fugitive, or nontraditional resources if you have been precise and specific about what you need.

For instance, if you are writing about the concept of medi-gap insurance (a form of insurance that supplements Medicare coverage for older adults), it would be wise to phrase your request to the librarian as precisely as possible. Rather than asking for information about insurance reform, you would want to ask specifically about the medi-gap idea. The librarian will then know to lead you to, among other things, the files of ephemeral materials collected from government agencies, insurance companies, consumer groups, and retired citizens' organizations designed to meet the continual requests the library has been receiving from users interested in the idea. You will also then have a glimpse into the popularity of the idea, since the librarian will have disclosed that such a file was necessary in order to meet library users' demands for the information.

It is especially important when you are working under a deadline and need accurate, appropriate, and verifiable information to understand how libraries differ from one another and how those differences affect the information strategy. Especially for freelance communicators and for those working in organizations without an in-house library, it is useful to know about the kinds of libraries that may be available in the community. There are five types of libraries that are important for communicators: public libraries, academic libraries, special libraries, archives, and media-organization libraries.

Public Libraries

Public libraries exist to serve a very special function. The need for an informed electorate is considered so important that residents are willing to tax themselves to make libraries available to the entire community. The public must be served by the collections in these libraries. Many public library collections reflect the history and makeup of the neighborhoods in which they are situated. They may include materials in the languages of the most dominant ethnic groups of that section of the city. Public libraries offer many services that are not available from other types of libraries. Reader-counseling services (helping patrons decide what the best mysteries are this week), reference and referral services, story hours for children, and Internet research classes are some of the types of services found in public libraries.

The materials you will find in the public library reflect this community mission. The books and periodicals are of a popular, ephemeral, topical, and conventional nature. The collection reflects the library's attempt to meet the recreational and day-to-day informational needs of the general public. Most public libraries are not equipped to handle in-depth or technical research projects or questions, but might well be the best source for in-depth and retrospective information about the community: telephone books and city directories, electoral-district maps, photographs of city landmarks over the years, and other community-related material.

Many public libraries have become the community resource for electronic information sources. They have developed research Web pages that help patrons link to the governmental information and regional and local sources. The electronic database services they subscribe to (databases of articles or directories of companies, for example) can be accessed through their Web page. Internet users at home can often check online the availability of a particular book they might be interested in through the library's online catalog.

Public libraries have advantages over the following libraries in that they are accessible to anyone for any purpose. Not so with the others we will discuss. They are also usually networked with a series of other libraries so if the particular item you are looking for isn't available at the library you're in, they can often find it in one of their member libraries. If you are lucky enough to be in a town or city with a strong and vibrant public library network, the first step in grounding yourself in your work should be a visit to the public library.

Academic Libraries

Academic libraries serve a very different function from the other types of libraries. These collections exist to support the teaching and research needs of the scholars, students, and researchers of the institution with which they are affiliated. Large academic libraries collect scholarly materials published in many languages and from all over the world. Even small academic libraries reflect the teaching mission of the institution. Specialized, technical, detailed materials are the norm in most academic collections of any size.

Unlike use of public libraries, use of academic library collections may be restricted to some extent. You may have to apply for a special privilege card or pay a fee in order to check out materials, or you may only be able to use materials at the library, without checking them out. In extreme instances, unauthorized users may not even be able to enter the building. However, if the topic being researched is of a national or an international nature, if it involves specialized or technical subject areas, or if it is likely to cover controversial ideas, then an academic library collection is probably one of the best places to look.

For instance, for a series of stories on the development of nuclear power in the United States, an academic library connected with an institution that has an engineering school would have much material, including current and back issues of special journals devoted to the topic, compilations of scientific papers, public-policy information, and all the indexes, reference tools, and databases necessary to locate information quickly.

The academic library user may find a welcome screen on the library's main computer catalog workstations that describes how to use both the electronic catalog and indicates how you might access other electronic collections. Most academic libraries make access to the online databases and search services they subscribe to available to authorized users through the Internet. This online, offsite access has led to a downturn in actual library visits; libraries report fewer patrons coming into the library space. This is an issue, because no library Internet site can provide the full range of access to materials and sources that a visit to the library itself gives.

Special Libraries

The term *special* refers to a broad category of various kinds of libraries. The collection, the clientele, or both may be special. For instance, most companies have some kind of library or information center that houses the books, journals, documents, and material relevant to that industry. Historical societies usually have libraries. Museums have libraries geared to the subject matter of the museum collection. The Folger Shakespeare Library is a special library in the sense that it collects books and materials by and about Shakespeare. Public and academic libraries often have special collections or rooms to house rare, fragile materials or to distinguish a particularly strong subject collection. The Kerlan Collection of children's books, manuscripts, illustrations, and research materials about children's literature is an example of a special collection at the University of Minnesota. See Box 6.1 for an idea of the scope of special libraries.

Insurance companies, law firms, churches, hospitals, oil companies, and banking institutions are other places where a special library might be located. The Special Libraries Association has twenty-four different categories of special librarians in its membership.

You may want to use these special libraries for the kinds of unique materials they make available. For instance, if an advertising campaign for a brand of beer is being prepared, you may wish to use the library collection at the brewery to get an understanding of the history of the company and the nature of past campaigns. If the information is not proprietary (that is, held by the company to be private because it involves trade secrets or financial information), you may want to look for clues about the unique brewing process or chemistry that sets that brand of beer apart from its competitors.

Special library collections are usually not organized the same as other collections. Because the materials in the collection are about the same topic, industry, or company, there is likely to be an internally designed organization system that fits the needs of the clientele. In addition, special collections may or may not be open to the public because corporate secrets are often housed alongside the usual industry or company information. The best rule of thumb is to call ahead, because the hours and visiting policies are likely to differ from collection to collection.

Archives

Archives differ from libraries in mission and operation. Whereas libraries have a selective collection development policy, archives attempt to be a comprehensive collection of a business, organization, or social movement. An archive is responsible for keeping a permanent record of the history, transactions, and operations of whatever it is that is being archived; therefore, the materials in an archive usually do not circulate.

There are governmental archives responsible for keeping the permanent record of that organization or branch. The National Archives in Washington, D.C., for example, maintains treaties, maps, photographs, motion pictures, sound recordings,

■ ■ ■ ■ ■

BOX 6.1
VALUABLE RESOURCES IN YOUR INFORMATION SEARCH

Virtual SLA

Special Libraries Association

Special Libraries Association Divisions

Advertising and Marketing (DAM)	http://www.sla.org/division/dam/index.html
Biomedical & Life Sciences (DBIO)	http://www.sla.org/division/dbio/
Business and Finance (DBF)	http://www.slabf.org/
Chemistry (DCHE)	http://www.sla.org/division/dche/chemdiv.html
Education (DEDU)	http://www.sla.org/division/ded/index.html
Engineering (DENG)	http://www.sla.org/division/deng/engdiv.html
Environment & Resource Management (DERM)	http://www.sla.org/division/derm/index.htm
Food, Agriculture & Nutrition (DFAN)	http://www.sla.org/division/dfan/
Geography and Map (DGM)	http://www.sla.org/division/dgm/index.htm
Information Technology (DITE)	http://www.sla.org/division/dite/index.html
Insurance Employee Benefits (DIEB)	http://www.sla.org/division/dieb/index.htm
Legal (DLEG)	http://www.slalegal.org/
Library Management (DLMD)	http://www.sla.org/division/dlmd
Materials Research and Manufacturing (DMRM)	http://www.sla.org/division/dmrm
Military Librarians (DMIL)	http://www.sla.org/division/dmil/index.html
Museums, Arts & Humanities (DMAH)	http://www.sla.org/division/dmah/
News (DNWS)	http://www.ibiblio.org/slanews/
Petroleum & Energy Resources (DPER)	http://www.sla.org/division/dper/
Pharmaceutical & Health Technology (DPHT)	http://www.sla.org/division/dpht/
Physics-Astronomy-Mathematics (DPAM)	http://www.sla.org/division/dpam/pamtop.html
Science-Technology (DST)	http://www.sla.org/division/dst/
Social Science (DSOC)	http://www.sla.org/division/dsoc/
Solo Librarians (DSOL)	http://www.sla.org/division/dsol/
Transportation (DTRN)	http://www.library.nwu.edu/transportation/slatran/

Source: Special Libraries Association (www.sla.org). Reprinted by permission.

correspondence files, and other documentation of the operations of the administrative branch of the federal government.

Corporations and businesses house archives that serve both a public relations function and provide historically accurate information about the company and clients. For instance, the Coca-Cola archive includes original Coke bottles, print and broadcast ads, drugstore signs, decal-covered serving trays, and other Coke-related paraphernalia. The manager of the archive is called upon regularly by the legal department to produce documentation to protect the Coca-Cola trademark.

Archives are not organized like libraries. There are special methods for recording and making accessible the files, documents, videotapes, and materials housed in boxes and vaults. This does not mean that the communicator won't be able to find what is needed. On the contrary, the archivists in charge probably have personally organized and housed the materials in the archive and are therefore the most well-versed in how to unlock the information. Archives don't contain the kinds of information found in libraries. They are full of the esoteric materials that document the history of a person, organization, business, social movement, or governmental agency. Communicators looking for primary materials can do no better than scouting out archives in their information hunt.

Media Libraries

The libraries supported by media organizations are types of special libraries. Both the materials and the clientele are unusual. As the likely first stop for the communicator during the library stage of the information search, media libraries are crucially important. Most media organizations—whether in the business of producing a newspaper, a national magazine, a local television news broadcast, advertising campaigns, or public relations materials—have some sort of library collection or research function.

The in-house library of a newspaper office may have a small, current collection of major reference tools (dictionaries, directories, almanacs), may subscribe to a handful of magazines and journals, may have access to online database services, and most likely is staffed by a professional librarian. But by far the most important resource, in the opinion of a newspaper staff, is the back files of the newspaper itself.

During the 1970s, most newspapers switched their mode of production to computers. Instead of banging out each story on a typewriter and editing it by hand, the newspaper staff prepares each story, ad, obituary, and column on a computer screen. The material is edited on the screen, and the information is sent to computers that set the type and print the paper that is delivered to the subscriber's doorstep.

Newspaper staffs soon figured out that the product that was created electronically could also be stored that way. Instead of filing hand-clipped articles from each paper, it became simple to store in the library's computer the computer files that contain each edition of the paper. The year 1985 was a watershed in the installation of electronic library systems at newspapers.[1]

Today, every large-circulation newspaper has its content stored and searchable through an electronic library system. With the growth of online news publications, the challenge of reconciling the archive of the print edition of the newspaper and the electronic version of the newspaper online has grown. Often, news organizations have two separate and not entirely equal electronic representations of news products they create.

Broadcast news libraries may not have as many of the print and electronic reference tools as are found in a newspaper or magazine library, but they do have a major resource for their employees—the archive of tapes or digital files of previous broadcasts. When you see *file footage* flashed on the screen during a television news report, you are seeing one use of this archive of materials. Broadcast news organizations keep archives of their own broadcasts, but journalists also have access to Web-based archives of streaming audio/video files through services such as those provided by ABC News Video Search, C-SPAN, PBS, and others (mentioned in Chapter 10).

Strategic communications agency libraries are designed to meet the information needs of communicators creating ads or news releases, preparing media kits, conducting market research, studying audiences or clients, and developing new business pitches. The library for an advertising agency or department, for instance, may include *tear sheets*, pages ripped out of magazines and newspapers that serve as examples of ads for particular products or services. The library may have files of pictures and photos so artists have examples if they need to draw a cheetah or a space shuttle. The library has industry and trade information so communicators can do background research on potential and current clients and their products and services. And these libraries have all of the specialized market and audience research tools we mention in Chapter 8. A public relations agency library will subscribe to the important media tracking services (see Chapter 10) and provide access to online databases and Web services that help the PR professionals follow news about their clients.

Media organization libraries, then, serve a special function. Those creating messages must have at their fingertips examples of the organizations' own output; materials produced by other communicators around the country or the world; information about the industries, products, and audiences for whom messages are produced; and general fact-finding sources for quick reference.

MAJOR SOURCES OF INFORMATION IN THE LIBRARY

There are two main categories of library sources: one-step tools and two-step tools. The one-step tools contain the information in one place. In other words, you can turn to one of these tools and quickly locate a fact, an address, a statistic, an overview or the full text of a record or article. The information you need is right there. Two-step tools, on the other hand, point you in the direction of material that might have the information you need. You will need to go to another place to get it. These categories are not hard and fast, however. Even the one-step tools might be considered two-step. Sure, the phone book will give you immediate information—the number of the person you are looking for, but not until you take that second step of calling will you be able to find out if that person knows, and will share, the information you need. Nonetheless, it helps to categorize the hundreds of library sources using the one-step and two-step heuristic to make these collections more understandable.

One-step library tools are encyclopedias, dictionaries, directories, almanacs, and yearbooks. Two-step library tools are library catalogs, indexes, abstract services, and bibliographies. Some newer versions of two-step tools, spawned digitally, are aggregation services and Web logs.

One-step and two-step tools can be found in both paper and digital form. The way you search these tools might vary slightly, depending on the form in which you find it. For example, the *Encyclopedia of Associations*, in book form, will let you look up an association by name or keyword, by geographic area, or by executive's name. The digital version of the same material will let you search for an association by any word in its description or across the indices. Looking in the book for associations in California with an interest in health topics would take much flipping back and forth, while the online listing of items with both *health* and *California* would be quickly compiled.

There are distinct advantages and disadvantages with both print and digital versions of library tools. In terms of cost, going to the library and using the print version of a reference tool is certainly cost effective, but might be time consuming. Having access to some of these core library tools online is a great boon to researchers. However, many of the most well-respected and well-researched tools are available online only on a subscription basis. The price is usually reasonable, often much cheaper than purchasing the print version, and often can be accessed for a short term (a monthly subscription, for example). As mentioned before, the advantage of digital over print versions is usually in the searching capability.

Another advantage of the online version over the print edition is updatability. The print version is static once it is published. Online, the material can be updated, appended, and edited. Some encyclopedias offer CD-Rom versions of their publications. These are handy reference tools that can be used offline—and the full capabilities of their multimedia features are not hampered by slow modems or inadequate online access.

One disadvantage of some online sources is that they contain only the text that appears in the printed book. Items like illustrations, added material, charts, and tables might not be available online. In contrast, sometimes the online version is augmented to take advantage of the online environment—for example an online dictionary may have a pronunciation audio file for each word.

For the most part, these tools will provide either a direct entry look-up or look-up through an index. When searching in any of these library tools, print or online, be sure to find out how they are organized. If you don't understand how the tool is organized, you might miss important material or not find anything when there actually is something there. Online, look for the Help file. In the print version, the front matter usually includes an overview of how best to use the resource.

Each of these one-step and two-step tools is useful at various stages of the information process. At the beginning, some of the uses might be checking terms so you know what you are talking about, finding contacts that will be useful to talk to, locating facts and figures that might give you an interesting angle. During the search, these tools will be fact-checkers and reality checks for the things you hear and discover in your research. When you are at the point of writing or developing the final message, these are the tools that will help you tie up loose ends and find interesting facts to brighten the piece or give it context. Let's look at each of the library tool categories and what you'll find in them.

One-Step Tools

Encyclopedias.   As the first step in the search for an overview of a topic, an encyclopedia article is an excellent choice. A reporter once had to cover the horse shows at a state fair. After reading the article on horses in a general encyclopedia, she was able to do a creditable job of understanding the various types of horses, interviewing the horse owners, and covering the competitions.

General Encyclopedias.   Cover a wide range of topics and can appeal to different audience levels. *World Book Encyclopedia* is aimed at a young audience and has a simple reading level and less detail; *Encyclopedia Britannica* is written for a more mature audience and is written with much greater authoritativeness and detail.

Subject Encyclopedias.   Allow greater depth and specificity and more detailed entries on narrow topics. Examples: *Encyclopedia of Pop, Rock, and Soul,* the *Catholic Encyclopedia, Stanford Encyclopedia of Philosophy.*

To find encyclopedias, any library catalog will list the print and digital encyclopedias in that collection. Several Web sites help identify encyclopedias of all sorts (there are thousands in print and online). Check the Open Directory Project: Encyclopedias (dmoz.org/Reference/Encyclopedias) or Google (directory.google.com/Top/Reference/Encyclopedias).

Dictionaries.   Since the communicator's stock in trade often is the word, the usefulness of a dictionary may seem obvious. Just as with encyclopedias, not all dictionaries are the same. For instance, the *Oxford English Dictionary* is recognized as the most authoritative source for looking up the etymology, or origin and evolution, of words. Many dictionaries include (in addition to the definitions of words) summaries of rules of grammar, perpetual calendars, tables of weights and measures, radio frequencies, constellations, ranks in the armed forces, and a variety of other facts and figures. Some dictionaries are illustrated, so you get not only the definition of the word *escutcheon,* for example, but you also get an image of one. Listed here are types of dictionaries you will find useful:

General Dictionaries.   These are your standard dictionaries of words in use in a language. Whether online or in print, pocket-sized or weighing 10 pounds, dictionaries will be important resources for you in your message creation work.

Specialty Dictionaries.   There are rhyming dictionaries, dictionaries of acronyms and abbreviations, anagram and homophone dictionaries.

Subject Dictionaries.   Law, medical, science and technology, slang, engineering, biographical, music—these are some of the types of special dictionaries that deal specifically with the language of a discipline, science, or topic.

Translation Dictionaries.   There is a translation dictionary available for virtually every language which lets you look up a term in one language and get the equivalent term in another language.

To find dictionaries, use the library catalog or check the Web site YourDictionary (www.yourdictionary.com).

Directories.   Among the most useful kinds of one-step tools in the library are directories. Whether it is a familiar telephone directory, the ZIP Code directory, or something a bit more esoteric—such as the *Directory of Alternative Spiritualities in New*

Zealand (www.aasr.org.au/aasr/directory.htm)—the directory is an important source of information for mass communicators. Because so much time is spent trying to identify the organizations or individuals connected with a particular subject area, directories can be invaluable. A range of directory types is described here:

Association and Organization Directories. Most groups with a fairly sizable membership publish a directory. The *Encyclopedia of Associations* is perhaps the best place to begin a search for any type of organization or association. Whether for snowmobilers, matchbook collectors, or chiropractors, if there is an organization, the *Encyclopedia of Associations* is the directory to use to find it.

Telephone Directories. Telephone and city directories provide contact information—to a limited degree. No directories give unlisted phone numbers, and telephone books do not include cell phone numbers. *Criss-cross* directories let you look up a telephone number and discover who it belongs to, and city directories make it possible to look up an address and find out who lives there. The trouble is that these types of printed directories are quickly outdated as people move. Furthermore in many cities, the cost to produce city directories has caused publishers to discontinue their compilation.

There are online services which provide nationwide criss-cross directories and telephone lookups. They allow you to specify an address and get information on who lives there, the telephone number, and other residents at the address. These services usually have a feature allowing you to see the names of neighbors with their phone numbers and addresses.

Biographical Directories. The *Who's Who* volumes (*Who's Who in America, Who's Who in the Midwest, Who's Who in the Press,* etc.) are sources of biographical information about an entrant. These are good resources only if you have a specific name you are looking for. There also are biographical directories for specific disciplines, such as *American Men and Women of Science.*

Publication Directories. These will help you locate daily, weekly, monthly, and less frequently published newspapers and magazines and broadcast outlets. The *Gale Directory of Publications and Broadcast Media,* for example, is organized by geographic area in the United States and Canada and by media outlet name or call letters under each location. Market and economic data for each city and town, summaries of population, statistics on agriculture and industry, and maps are included, making it of tremendous value for advertisers trying to identify how best to reach a community or learn about the characteristics and media outlets of a town.

To find directories, check the library catalog or the reference shelves or use the Web. All Web Directories (www.allwebdirectories.com) or Telephone Directories on the Web (www.teldir.com) are good sources.

Almanacs and Yearbooks. An almanac is one of the most likely reference tools to find in a media-organization library, even if there are no other references at all. The old-fashioned almanacs predicted the coming year's weather, offered advice to farmers and housewives, included stories and poems, and served as general entertainment books for the families in the early United States. Modern almanacs have a different purpose and character. Most are single-volume, annual compendia of facts, figures, and tidbits of information about a country and society. Most of the information in almanacs is reprinted from other sources such as census reports, sports statistics, lists of prize winners, data about officials and personalities, and astronomical tables. The types of almanacs are described here:

General Almanacs.   These cover popular information. Examples include *The World Almanac*, the *Information Please Almanac*, and the *Reader's Digest Almanac.*

Subject-Specific Almanacs.   In these almanacs, such as the *Almanac of American Politics*, you can find an item of information or biographical data about a topic or person not included in more general almanacs.

Yearbooks.   Often published in affiliation with an encyclopedia, these are the year-end wrap up publications that cover the latest developments. The *United States Government Manual* is the annual yearbook of the United States government organization, activities, and chief officers of all agencies within the legislative, judicial, and executive branches. Many professions and industries also have yearbooks. For example, the newspaper industry has the *Editor & Publisher International Yearbook;* book publishing has *The Bowker Annual of Library and Book Trade Almanac.*

There are also subject-specific yearbooks, such as the *Statesman's Yearbook*, the *Europa World Year Book* or the *CIA World Factbook*, which provide current information on countries and international organizations arranged according to standard subheads: head of government, area and population, constitution and government, religion, education, transportation and communication facilities, and diplomatic representatives.

To find yearbooks and almanacs, check the library's catalog and on the reference shelves. Examples on the Web include *Information Please* (www.infoplease.com), *Old Farmer's Almanac* (www.almanac.com), and the *CIA World Factbook* (www.cia.gov/cia/publications/factbook).

Two-Step Tools

Library Catalogs.   The library catalog is the key to the entire collection of information. The catalog details the holdings of the library and includes information about how each item may be located. Chapter 5 discussed some of the conceptual skills you need to successfully search library catalogs, including understanding classification systems and subject heading schemes. In addition to providing records of every item owned by the library, the catalog for most libraries now also serves as the gateway into the other electronic resources and services the library may provide for patrons. The library catalog, then, is one of the most important two-step tools you use in your search for library materials.

Indexes and Abstracts.   The index is the classic two-step tool. The index is nothing more than a listing, usually alphabetically arranged by subject categories, of articles and materials that have appeared in other publications. There are indexes to magazine, newspaper, and journal articles, and to poems, plays, songs, speeches, pictures, essays, short stories, and a variety of other items that are hidden away in library sources. The index helps the communicator ferret out, from piles of sources, that elusive item that would otherwise be lost.

Once you've located a citation to an article you are interested in, you must locate the article itself. In recent years, many of the electronic indexing and abstracting services have moved to full-text and provide a direct link to the article from the citation. This has been a huge time- and frustration-saver for researchers who (in the past) would frequently locate the perfect article title, only to find that the needed issue was missing—or worse, the page was torn out!

The abstract is an index with a brief, non-evaluative summary of each article being described. Oftentimes, the well-written abstract has the substance of the article so you can get what you need simply from the brief description, you don't need to find the article itself. Abstract services tend to be more specialized by subject or topic area than general indexes. Also, the arrangement of information in the abstract service is a little more complicated, but it is fairly easy to learn. Publications that are abstracted are usually scholarly or specialized, thus favoring the needs of the expert searcher.

There is a serious drawback with abstracting services—there is a very significant time delay between the appearance of material and its inclusion in an abstracting service. Because someone has to read and summarize every item that appears in an abstracting service, it can be months or even years before an item is included. Many abstracting services have bypassed the labor intensive abstracting process and have gone to direct access to the full text of the article they are indexing. Types of indexes and abstracts are described here:

Periodical Indexes and Abstracts. These give access to a wide range of articles in magazines and journals. The most useful indexes and abstracts for communicators are described in Chapters 7 through 10.

Newspaper Indexes and Abstracts. These locate past articles in newspapers. Again, the best newspaper indexes and abstracts for your purposes are described in Chapter 10.

Broadcast-News Indexes and Abstracts. These provide information about when news programs were broadcast and who was on them. Chapter 10 summarizes the most useful of the broadcast-news indexes and abstracts.

Biographical Indexes. These can help you locate biographical information published in various books, magazines, and newspapers. Biographical indexes are valuable resources for communicators because they provide supplemental or supporting information about individuals beyond what you can get during an interview. If some facts have to be verified, if the person in question will not agree to an interview or is unavailable, these biographical references are often the only method for gathering the required biographical information. The most useful of these are described in Chapter 9.

Picture Indexes. A number of two-step tools in libraries can help you locate pictures. Pictures of current or historical people, places, and events can be very important for news stories, creative elements of ads, and media kits. As we've said, many media organizations have their own extensive files of visual materials, but libraries also provide tools for locating pictures. Some of these include *Index to American Photographic Collections* (3rd edition, 1995), *Illustration Index* (8th edition, 1998), and *Picture Researcher's Handbook* (6th edition, 1996). Many sites on the Web are also useful for locating visual images, including Google Images (images.google.com), Weststock (www.weststock.com), Corbis (www.corbis.com), and Blackstar (www.blackstar.com). Before using *any* image you find, however, be sure you understand the terms and conditions for use, and that you make arrangements to pay the royalty fees, if any, for permission to use the image in your message.

The library catalog is the most useful tool for locating the appropriate index or abstract for your information need. Many library Web sites provide an electronic link to the free and subscription-based online index and abstract services they offer patrons, along with helpful descriptions of each index or abstract tool and how best to use them.

Bibliographies. A bibliography is a list of publications—books, articles (magazine, journal, and newspaper), documents, and Web sites. The Library of Congress publishes a huge bibliography called the *National Union Catalog: A Cumulative Author List*, which lists by author every work published since 1956 that is in the Library of Congress. A bibliography may also be a single publication that includes a list of many information sources on the same topic. *A Bibliography of Bioethics* is an example of an entire volume listing sources on one topic.

When starting a library search, it is not a bad idea to check to see whether a subject bibliography is available on the topic being researched. So many bibliographies exist that it is foolish for you to do an information search from scratch that may have been done recently by someone else. The two-step tool titled *Books in Print* is a bibliography of all fiction and nonfiction titles in print that may be available on your topic, even if the library you are using doesn't own them. If you find a book on a topic you are interested in, checking the bibliography at the end of the book is another way to locate valuable listings of resources. These can provide great leads to materials you should not miss. A reference tool (in both print and online versions) titled *The Bibliographic Index* helps you locate bibliographies that have been published as separate books or as articles in more than 2,200 periodicals.

THE LIBRARIAN IN THE
MESSAGE-MAKING PROCESS

You have access to so much information and to such powerful library and electronic tools that it might be tempting to ask what role there might be for the librarian in the message-making process. Media professionals recognize that the expertise of librarians can be of great value when information must be quickly located or verified. In many media organizations, librarians have become part of the message-making team. Many large newspapers, for instance, have the news librarian sit in on the daily budget meeting at which stories are assigned, so the library staff knows what the editorial staff is working on that day and can be ready to offer help and resources. News librarians are assigned to special project teams working on long enterprise or investigative stories. Librarians may receive byline or story credit for their contributions to news projects.

Public relations firms ask the library staff to become the intelligence operation for the firm, seeking information about clients, potential clients, competitor companies that might affect client firms, and information about the industries and services for which the public relations staff do their work. Advertising agency library staff perform many of the same functions, seeking both business and creative information for the many accounts that the ad staff handle.

Media organizations that have sophisticated libraries encourage their staffs to make better use of the resources that are available. You may not have to refer to any outside collections for routine information. The media library staff may already have prepared an intranet of resources available for you to use through your media organization's internal computer system. Intranets may provide access to work in progress by everyone in the firm; back files of previous news stories, ad campaigns, or public relations efforts; contact lists with names and descriptions of helpful people you need to talk to as you prepare your messages; and a screened and organized listing of Internet Web site links that the library staff have deemed most useful for your purposes.

For communicators who do freelance work or for whom a well-stocked and well-staffed media organization library is not available, it is important to make friends with the librarian at the public library who is most attuned to the deadline demands, accuracy requirements, and information evaluation needs of mass communication message-making work. The wide availability of electronic library catalogs, e-mail reference help, and Web site access to many reference tools has greatly enhanced the accessibility of library resources for communicators who cannot rely on in-house collections or specially trained media librarians.

It is important for you to learn how to accurately and precisely describe your information needs so the librarian with whom you are working can be of most help to you. In all cases, be sure you indicate your deadline and clearly describe how the information is going to be used. This will help the librarian make decisions about the quality and usefulness of the material he or she finds in response to your information request.

THE LIBRARY IN THE INFORMATION STRATEGY PROCESS

As we've indicated, the library houses information in all three forms—people, paper, and digital—and from all four contributors: informal, institutional, scholarly, and journalistic. No matter what you are looking for, a library is likely to have at least a portion of what you need. As such, the library is an integral part of your information-gathering routine.

By applying the information-gathering techniques we've outlined in Chapter 5—monitoring, searching and interviewing—you can unlock these storehouses of the entire intellectual output of society. Libraries make accessible the materials you need for your initial message analysis work, for your topic-specific information gathering, for your in-depth information evaluation requirements, and for your synthesis work as you create the message. In other words, libraries contribute to every step of the information strategy.

In the next four chapters we look at each of the four contributors of information: informal, institutional, scholarly, and journalistic, and discuss the types of information you can get from them, the forms in which you will find the information, and the best methods for eliciting what you need in your information quest.

SELECTED ADDITIONAL READINGS

California Media and Library Educators Association. *From Library Skills to Information Literacy: A Handbook from the 21st Century*, 2nd edition. Hi Willow Research & Pub., 1997.

Mann, Thomas. *The Oxford Guide to Library Research*. New York: Oxford University Press, 1998.

Rubin, Rebecca B., Alan M. Rubin, and Linda J. Piele. *Communication Research: Strategies and Sources*, 5th edition. Belmont, CA: Wadsworth, 1999.

NOTES

1. Marcia Ruth, "Electronic Libraries Reach Watershed Year," *Presstime* (July 1985): 10–11.

CHAPTER SEVEN

INFORMAL SOURCES

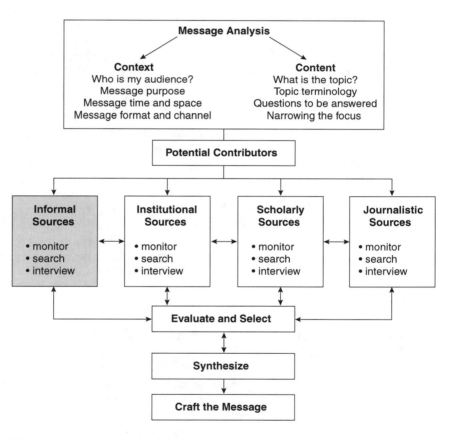

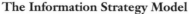

The Information Strategy Model

Getting started on a new subject and grounding the information in reality are just two challenges you'll face early in the information strategy. The best route to meet both of these challenges can be consulting people informally and observing the world around you.

In the following chapters you'll be reading about institutional, scholarly, and journalistic sources of information. The people in these roles differ from informal sources because the information that formal sources gather and distribute is tied to the work they do, the knowledge they've gained through study, and the interests of the organizations they represent. When talking about informal sources, we are talking about what people know, feel, and believe from their life experiences. A person you might consult as an informal source might also be an institutional, scholarly, or journalistic source in another research context—one in which the information you are trying to get from them is related to their work.

Informal sources can also be your own personal observation about what is going on around you. Having a nose for news generally means that you are tuned in to your surroundings and can gauge when something is "off" or different and worth checking into. Noticing the long lines in front of the automatic teller machines, for example, may be the start of a news story on fundamental changes in bank services. Observing that the lakeshore has been eroded by runners can lead to a series of articles on conflicts between the goals of recreation and preservation in park systems. Seeing "teachers wanted" classified ads may signal the education reporter that a decade of teacher layoffs is ending. Standing in the grocery checkout line behind teenage shoppers can alert the advertising researcher to do further study on which family members purchase the groceries.

You'll go to different types of sources during different stages in your information gathering. In the case of observing lines at the teller machine, talking to the people in line about their use of the teller machines would be tapping into another informal source. Talking to the bank president about changes in bank services would be using an institutional source, checking stories in the newspaper about the bank itself would be using journalistic sources, and talking to a business and finance professor would be a scholarly source.

TYPES OF INFORMAL SOURCES AND HOW THEY KNOW WHAT THEY KNOW

Informal sources are your neighbors and friends, your colleagues and family, people you see at the market, the football game, or the Y. Informal sources, for news, are the eyewitnesses to the event, the friends of the victim, the participants at the rally. In strategic communications, informal sources you'll want to tap into are the consumers of the product or service. These are the people you'll want to observe when looking into different kinds of behaviors. Informal sources get their information and opinions from their daily life and experiences.

Using Yourself as an Informal Source

What you know, think, feel, and believe are going to be foundations to the work you do as a communicator. Tapping into your own internal and physical resources as you begin a reporting job or a strategic communications campaign will start you on the course of your work. Tapping into the network of people you know through your work and your life will lead you to who they know. These connections will dictate the path of your information strategy.

Do not underestimate the powerful resources you have at hand. Languages you speak, places you've been, books you've read, hobbies you enjoy will inform you at the onset of your work as well as when you process the information you get from others.

Inventory your personal store of knowledge (see Box 7.1). This inventory will serve as a guide to your own areas of personal expertise. It gives you a map of your personal information universe. The newspapers, magazines, and computer services you see on a regular basis form part of your casual reading base. The places you've visited and the groups you regularly associate with are part of your network of contacts and sources. The way you organize your personal files tells you something about the topics that are important to you, and the information in your files can serve as starting points for an information strategy.

You should now accept that you are a research resource because of what you see and do, what you know, and what you keep. This is how most successful communicators think of themselves. Let's say that you need to begin work on a news story, advertising message, or public relations news release about the role of charities in your community. The communicator starts by asking two questions: "What do I need to know?" and "What do I already know?" The first question is covered in the message analysis stage of the information strategy. The second question involves you as an informal source.

■ ■ ■ ■ ■

BOX 7.1
USING YOURSELF AS AN INFORMAL SOURCE

Here's an exercise to help you get used to thinking about yourself as a resource. Fill out a form that includes the following information:

■ Your job or occupation
■ Your major in college, or any courses you've taken since high school
■ Five books you've read in the past year
■ Newspapers you read regularly
■ Magazines to which you subscribe
■ Magazines you buy occasionally
■ Listservs or discussion groups to which you belong or monitor
■ A list of the subjects about which you have some knowledge, either because of your job, schooling, or outside interests

■ A list of associations or clubs to which you belong
■ A list of five places you've visited outside your home state
■ The categories you use in your personal filing system for things you've read, clipped, and collected

What does this form tell you? For one thing, it serves as a guide to your own areas of personal expertise.

Source: This exercise is adapted from Mara Miller, *Where To Go for What.* Englewood Cliffs, NJ, Prentice-Hall, 1981.

You may already know quite a bit about various charities' role in your community. You may volunteer yourself for one or more charitable events at your church, your children's school, your tenants' association, or your social club. There may be a food shelf located in your neighborhood that you pass by each day. You may see solicitation messages from charities seeking your financial contribution, and you may keep a personal file of your own contributions to charities for tax purposes. You may also know whether all of these signs of charitable activity have increased or decreased in the past few years.

But even if you aren't that familiar with charities in your community, you have other sources of information to help you. You may know someone who spends every other weekend volunteering with a youth club or working at a shelter. Someone you know may work for a social service agency in the community. Here's an exercise to help you see how extensive your own network of informal sources is.

Make a list of twenty people you know. You can include your family and friends, your job or school colleagues, and people you've met but don't know very well. For each person, write down a brief description of what they do for a living, and under a separate heading write down what you know about their outside interests. In cases where you know a bit more about someone's personal history (previous jobs, where they're from, where they've traveled), include another heading for that type of information. With this list you'll quickly see that the network of people you know will tap you into an ever-expanding realm of personal expertise and contacts.

There is an even more interesting way to think about your networks of sources. Let's say that you have to start your informal search on the work of charities in your community by using only people you *don't* know. Try to think about who you might contact to talk about the topic. You might decide to talk to the person who runs the local food shelf. Or you might try to call the local newspaper reporter whose byline you regularly see on stories about charities and their activities. The point is not that these are necessarily the best sources, but they are starting points, places you already know where you might find informal sources to talk with about your topic.

Informal networks of sources do not replace the experts with whom you must conduct formal interviews at a later step in the information process. However, your contact with individuals who have experiences, authority, opinions, and a different perspective on an issue or about a product gives you the ability to approach the more formal sources of information with a better idea of what to look for and how to structure the rest of the strategy.

Observation as an Informal Source

As we discussed in Chapter 5, skilled observers are trained rather than born. With observation, as with all other skills, practice precedes proficiency. The novice can practice observing, making notes, and drawing conclusions without risking mistakes or embarrassment. Television affords the learner numerous opportunities to practice. During a televised sports event, parade, or similar nonverbal production, you can turn off the sound, observe, make notes, and summarize the main points. Your version of the event can then be compared with the next day's newspaper account.

Beginning observers typically experience a number of difficulties. One is their inability to organize their perceptions, to see anything interesting or important. They have neglected to prepare their perceptual apparatus before getting to the scene of the action. Veteran observers, though, arrive ready to see, hear, smell, and sense the activity. Skilled observers have an established system of items they have learned to put into play. They use—although many do not know the term for it—a *heuristic*. Heuristics are intellectual tools for discovering subject matter. The familiar news formula of who-what-when-where-why is one heuristic.

For observers, the news heuristic is a reasonable beginning. But each opportunity for observation offers much more than the news formula might ordinarily elicit. For example, consider the communicator who has to observe a speaker. The speech might be attended by a news reporter who intends to write an account of the talk, a public relations specialist who helped to arrange the speech, and an advertising staff member whose clients are interested in what is being presented. Each of these observers would have a slightly different focus in the observation. Thus each might arrive with a slightly different heuristic. The following heuristic covers much that each would want to record:

1. *The event.* What is the occasion? What is its significance? Is anything unique? Who sponsored the event? Why?
2. *The speaker.* Who is the speaker? What are the speaker's credentials? Is the speaker an expert, a celebrity, or an ordinary person? What is the speaker's purpose? How are the speaker and the sponsor related to each other?
3. *The message.* What is the main idea? What are the supporting points? Does the speaker cite evidence? From whom? Does the speaker illustrate with examples? How are they significant?
4. *The delivery.* What style or tone does the speaker use? What rhetorical devices are employed? Does the speaker use humor, repetition, emphasis? What nonverbal language is noticeable? Does it support or contradict the verbal message? Does the speaker use audiovisual aids?
5. *The audience.* For whom is the speech intended? Are there social, political, and psychological factors among audience members that the speaker plays to? Are there some unfavorable psychological elements between speaker and audience? How does the speaker adapt the main idea to this audience? Does the speaker approach this same subject similarly or differently with a different audience? How does the immediate audience respond? How can other audiences—for example, those hearing a broadcast of the speech—be analyzed for their response? What evidence is there that the speaker affected the audience or motivated it to action?

Before arriving at the observation site, you should have completed much of the information strategy that involves institutional, scholarly, and journalistic sources.

Informal sources may be used at any point in the strategy; they often are used during preliminary survey of a topic. However, you might return to them at a variety of points in the information strategy. Observation, especially random and casual observation, also is used early in the process. Along with generating ideas for a story or an ad, informal sources and observations can lead to additional sources, especially institutional sources.

TAPPING INTO INFORMAL SOURCES

Monitoring Informal Sources

Among the riches of the Internet for communicators are the variety of places where you can monitor informal sources. Newsgroups and listservs are treasure troves for tapping into the thoughts and opinions of people. No matter what topic you are doing your research on, you will find a newsgroup where people are discussing the issue and their feelings about it. Google Groups (groups.google.com) has over 700 million messages in its twenty-year archive of Usenet messages. You can go into the advanced search portion of Google groups, put in the name of your company or the subject you are interested in, and get messages that people have posted about it.

Say you are assigned to the White Castle account. Searching in Google Groups for "White Castle" (putting quotes around the words ensures you are doing a phrase search) will get you a variety of messages that might inspire some ideas about how to advertise White Castle burgers. There are recipes using White Castle burgers, nostalgic stories about trips to White Castle during school, a history of the burgers, and this message:

> "Eating at White Castle is just like drinking—you pile into a car, drive a distance, indulge too much, and get sick. Then the next morning in the can you swear to yourself you'll never do that again, and then you're off to…White Castle a few days later. Men are stupid and weak, and White Castle knows this. I tell you this because I KNOW."[1]

Certainly that little quote could generate some ideas for an innovative ad campaign, but if you intended to use the actual quote in your ad copy you would need to contact the source of the quote for permission.

Monitoring does not have to be done virtually. Find the actual places where the kind of people you need to stay in touch with hang out. If you are the education reporter, wander the halls of the high school (with permission, of course), go to the PTA meetings, listen in at the teachers' union gatherings. Even if you aren't covering a specific story, you'll get ideas and insights. If you are assigned to a specific advertising account, find the places where you can observe people using the product or service. Keep up with teen fashion trends by frequenting the mall and seeing which stores the 15-year old girls are hanging out in.

Monitoring also involves paying attention to the casual information sources you see around you. Flyers on telephone poles, bumper stickers on cars, t-shirt messages— all can provide clues about current trends and opinions. Unofficial communications such as graffiti can alert you to societal trends. A recent visit to Stockholm revealed numerous tags of Nazi symbols—this should give a reporter a clue to a subcurrent of feeling in the population that might be well worth reporting on.

Searching Informal Sources

Searching for informal sources might include a search in a newsgroup message area or trying to find someone's personal homepage. The main searching you will need to do when using informal sources is to locate them. There are a wide variety of resources available on the Internet that can help you locate specific people and unknown people who might have an interesting insight into the topic you are researching.

People.   Here are some tried and true methods for finding people resources.

Locating Specific People.   Among the most valuable people-finder resources on the Internet are the telephone directory services. Infobel (www.infobel.com) allows you to look up by name, by phone number, and by address.

Locating Types of People.   Newsgroups, listservs, and subject-focused Web sites are great places to track down people with particular interests or backgrounds. There are two ways you can use these resources to locate relevant informal sources for your research. You can troll the sites and find the names of people you might then contact, or you can post a message saying you are looking for particular types of people who might want to contact you. When a *Miami Herald* reporter was doing a story on the census-based statistic that there were more single-person households than at any other time in history, she posted a message to a singles discussion group asking people who had some comment to contact her. She was overwhelmed with responses.

Trolling newsgroups to find relevant people is a good technique when looking for people otherwise difficult to identify. If you are covering a story about a disease you might contact an association that has expertise about that disease to see if they will give the names of some people to contact. Be aware that the people suggested by the association are likely to have been pre-screened and coached on how to talk to the media. If you want truly "person on the street" sources to talk about their experience with a disease, you're better off going to a discussion group on that topic and either identifying some people through their posted messages or by sending an "I'm interested in talking with...." message to the group.

Discussion Lists, Newsgroups, and Forums.   Although discussion lists (sometimes referred to as *listservs* or *distribution lists*) and newsgroups or forums are good ways to read what people think about a vast variety of topics, there are differences between them that you need to keep clear.

You subscribe (usually for free) to a discussion list. You have to submit your e-mail address to get your name placed on the distribution list for messages. Messages posted to the discussion list will come to your e-mail box. The discussion list community is self-regulating. If members disobey the rules of the group (No posting of spam or advertising, No posting messages that are off-topic for the discussion), they may be ejected from the group. Some lists are for discussion, such as the Online News Listserv, others are just for distribution of a newsletter such as the E-Media Tidbits List. If you want to subscribe, unsubscribe, or perform other business with the discussion list, you send a message to the administrative address listed at the site. If you want to post a message, you send it to the discussion list address. A good source identifying appropriate discussion lists is Liszt, available at www.liszt.com.

Newsgroups are more like bulletin boards: you go there to look at the messages. You don't have to be a member of the newsgroup to post a message. The membership is more transient and less regulated than discussion lists. Newsgroups were originally called Usenet messages, but now they are just referred to as newsgroups. Google Groups, groups.google.com, has twenty years' of worth of Usenet archives—more than 700 million messages.

Newsgroups are categorized. The prefix gives the general category; it is followed with a period (dot). After the dot is the subgroup. For example, the *rec.* newsgroup category has seventy-four subgroups: animals, antiques, art, birds, juggling, puzzles, and so on. Some of these subgroups have further subgroups. *Rec.crafts*, for example, has twenty subgroups: beads, carving, pottery, quilting, woodturning, plus fifteen more. Figure 7.1 illustrates some popular newsgroups' prefixes.

Messages on a specific topic are referred to as the message *thread* and the messages themselves are called *articles*. (These should not be confused with a news article. Remember, these messages have not gone through any kind of editorial filter.)

Forums can be found on many news and corporate Web sites. These are areas where people can post messages discussing issues, stories, or products. Forums can be either unmoderated or moderated. Unmoderated forums allow anyone to post any kind of message. Moderated forums will have someone who reviews the message for content

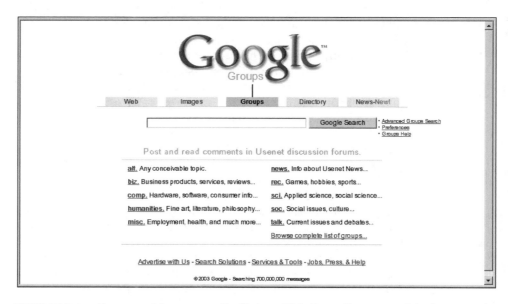

FIGURE 7.1   Common Newsgroup Prefixes.   This figure lists some of the largest and most common of the nearly 850 newsgroup prefixes that exist.

Source: Google, Inc. Reprinted by permission.

before it is allowed to be posted. Sometimes you have to register to the site to be able to post messages to the forum, but usually you can read the messages without registration. There is no standard way to locate forums, they are just a feature on particular sites. Whether you are using a discussion list, a newsgroup, or a forum you should be able to find one related to your area of interest and track them on a regular basis. People interested in bicycling might track the newsgroup illustrated in Figure 7.2.

Interviewing Informal Sources

When interviewing informal sources you need to consider their state of mind, their motivation, and your reason for wanting to talk to them. Interviewing an eye-witness to an accident who might be traumatized by the event is very different from talking to an excited observer of a parade or a participant in a focus group who has just sampled the new brand of frozen peas. You will need to adjust the manner in which you approach each of these informal sources according to their state of mind.

Trying to determine what motivates the source to talk with you is another important consideration. Are they outraged at something and want to get their viewpoint heard? Are they concerned and want to help tell the story? Have they been paid a stipend

Date	Topic	Author
Oct. 27, 2002	Heart rate monitors (12 articles)	nobody
Oct. 27, 2002	The parkway is not the place for bicyclists (30 articles)	David Reuteler
Oct. 26, 2002	The parkway is not the place for bicyclists (28 articles)	Matt O'Toole
Oct. 25, 2002	San Diego cyclists - Camp Pendleton access (7 articles)	TJ
Oct. 25, 2002	Riding around Tiburon (3 articles)	Dennis P. Harris
Oct. 25, 2002	SAG definition (5 articles)	Bob
Oct. 25, 2002	Greenbrier River Trail (WV) (7 articles)	Oliver
Oct. 25, 2002	The climbs of the 2003 Tour de France (5 articles)	Paul Southworth
Oct. 25, 2002	Anyone ever rode 17 mile drive? (17 articles)	Tom Kunich
Oct. 24, 2002	Puerto Rico (3 articles)	Luis Anaya
Oct. 24, 2002	Cycling in France during TdF (4 articles)	rstandring
Oct. 24, 2002	2003 Tour Itinerary (1 article)	CTRDY01
Oct. 23, 2002	Wanted 2003 Midwest ride info (1 article)	Mike
Oct. 23, 2002	Ireland (27 articles)	Garry Lee
Oct. 23, 2002	DC area riding in the age of the sniper (1 article)	Jim Flom
Oct. 22, 2002	Pasadena, CA riding? (4 articles)	BikerX
Oct. 21, 2002	FAQ Location and Weekly posting for Rec.Bicycles.* (321 articles)	Mike Iglesias
Oct. 21, 2002	Ramona, CA (3 articles)	Jim
Oct. 21, 2002	Chicago Critical Mass Ride - October 25th (2 articles)	Risto S Varanka
Oct. 21, 2002	Mallorca for a week (5 articles)	logarto
Oct. 20, 2002	Bike access to the Orlando FL airport? (2 articles)	George
Oct. 20, 2002	I got fixed (gear)! (4 articles)	R42Pilot
Oct. 19, 2002	New Missouri Bicycle Federation Web Site (1 article)	Brent Hugh
Oct. 19, 2002	our inappropriate tour of France (10 articles)	Steve Juniper
Oct. 18, 2002	Cycling in Toronto?? (10 articles)	Brian Huntley

FIGURE 7.2   A Bicycling Interest Newsgroup Found on Google Groups, rec.bicycles.rides.

Source: Google, Inc. Reprinted by permission.

to participate in your focus group? And why do you want to talk with them? Are you try-ing to fill in the details about an event, in which case you need to talk with several sources? Are you interested in opinions to give a broader perspective to the topic you are covering? Are you looking for a better way to reach your audience for an ad campaign? The art of interviewing is complex and your approach to different kinds of sources will be different. With informal sources, the better you can determine motivation and mood, the better you'll be able to figure out what to do with the information and reactions you get.

Many of the informal sources you might want to interview will be inexperienced. When interviewing these sources, understand that they may not appreciate the impli-cations of talking with you. Recall back in Chapter 5 when we discussed the impor-tance of your contract with the interviewee. It is even more important, then, to disclose to the inexperienced source exactly how the information revealed during the interview will be used. In the news setting, interviewees must understand that what they say can be used in the news report with their name attached. In the case of a focus group, the participants are asked to sign a release stipulating that they understand how the information is going to be used.

CAUTIONS FOR USE

Since you will constantly rely on informal sources and observations made by a variety of people, including yourself, you have to recognize the potential for distortion by these sources and observations. Distortion is relative. Ideas about what is "real" differ from culture to culture, from time to time, and from place to place. Communicators who live in a given culture in a specific place and time should understand that the con-ditions of their culture influence their own definitions of a situation, as well as the def-initions of their sources and their audiences. Within their cultural framework, communicators hope to avoid the most obvious and serious distortions.

Prominent causes for distortion include the following:

1. *Source reactions to the communicator.* Those who give you tips or who serve as in-formal sources are usually quite familiar with the content of mass communication. Often they know, or think they know, what you are looking for. Based on these ideas, sources select what they disclose and what they withhold. If you are talking with someone who is part of a particular organization, they might well obscure information that they suspect is better kept secret by the organization of which they are a part.

2. *Selective perception.* Both you and your sources are, like all other humans, prone to perceive selectively. Selective perception is rooted in our experiences, our preju-dices, and our expectations. Overcoming some of the distortions caused by selective perception lies in training, as well as in understanding the occasions when such selec-tivity is most damaging to accuracy. When you are using ideas from informal sources learn, with experience, to avoid consulting those most prone to selective perception.

3. *Selective recall.* Recalling events, conditions, and factual information is tricky in many respects. Memory fades quickly. What remains may have been selected for its interest value, its amusement quotient, its quotability, or its sensationalism. Taking the most complete notes possible helps overcome some of the problems of selective recall. But sources you consult may be relying on selective memory when they talk to you. Some are aware of the need for accuracy and offer to consult records that may aid their recall or, at least, warn that memory may be incomplete or faulty.

4. *Institutional bias.* Informal sources and communicators themselves owe allegiances to a variety of institutions. Some of their perceptions inevitably are shaped by institutional factors. Recognizing that this is so is the first step to reaching beyond the bias of the institution. Even sources speaking to you outside their "official" capacity may have concerns about how what they say might reflect on or be perceived by the organization they work for.

5. *Ego-involved bias.* Human beings naturally protect their egos and identities. Their testimony and observations frequently reflect strategies, conscious or unconscious, of self-protection. You need to watch for signs that your informal sources are excessively ego-involved in their subjects. And on your part, you need to guard against taking on topics in which you feel your own ego might interfere.

6. *Inaccurate observation.* Mechanical or technical errors abound. Each moment in the day presents us with more stimuli than we can possibly perceive. With so much around us to observe, errors are inevitable. That is why double and triple sourcing information is critical. You'll want to check with as many observers as possible to eliminate ordinary errors. You'll give more credibility to trained observers with no obvious personal or institutional biases and attempt to verify what observers tell you, especially when precision is critical.

Although informal sources may be the easiest to find—they are truly everywhere—they are often the most complex for interpreting what they tell you. If you are looking for color, reaction, and interesting anecdotes, informal sources will be your best bet. If you are looking for solid and informed input, you might be better off going to institutional, scholarly, or journalistic sources. Remember, too, that informal sources might well be a different type of source in a different situation. Be sure you know what role they are playing when you go to an informal source for information.

The information you get from informal sources via news groups or by overhearing conversations must be used carefully. Even though this may appear to be casually gathered, you still need to get permission to use the information you find.

CASE STUDY OF INFORMAL INFORMATION SOURCES

When Minneapolis-based Campbell Mithun advertising agency was asked by Burger King to compete for a new advertising campaign, their first step was to check in with informal sources. This gave the account team a better understanding of what stands out to customers about their Burger King experiences.

Brittany Leigh, a Campbell Mithun team member, began her information search using Google's search engine to identify Web sites where Burger King was being discussed. This led her to epinions.com, where participants review and write about brand name companies, products, and services—including Burger King. Leigh began monitoring the virtual discussion about fast food restaurants and paid close attention to attitudes and themes that were expressed repeatedly. She learned what attracted these brand-focused discussants to Burger King, what things were important to them, and whether there were any differences in what particular groups of people said—men versus women, for example.

Leigh and her Campbell Mithun team members immersed themselves in their work—living, breathing, and most importantly, *eating* whatever they could in relation to the subject at hand. The Campbell Mithun pitch team relied on personal observation, making frequent trips to Burger King as they were preparing the pitch. They talked to friends and family about their fast food insights. They conducted informal interviews with average Joe customers, offering to pay for a person's meal in exchange for that person taking time to sit down in a BK booth with a Campbell Mithun team member to talk about why they ordered what they ordered, how they felt about the service, and so on. The ad agency staff even handed out video cameras to self-professed burger-lovers who captured their day-in-the-life experiences on their own—without a Campbell Mithun representative in tow.

The information Campbell Mithun gathered using these techniques highlights some of the benefits informal sources offer. First, informal sources help you determine where to start your information search—and often lead to information search questions you might have otherwise missed. For example, one message that came out on the epinions Web site was the importance of Burger King's Birthday Club to particular customers. Without monitoring this source, the ad team might not have focused part of their search on finding information that would help them create messages that would appeal to an important Burger King audience—kids. What's more, Campbell Mithun chose interviewing and monitoring techniques that allowed them to capture real or authentic attitudes and opinions. Although we have listed some of the cautions to keep in mind when using informal sources, one advantage is that you often gain candid feedback from informal sources who are not concerned with sticking to the party line—in contrast to formal representatives who are speaking on behalf of particular organizations.

The ad team used these experiences to shape a campaign they felt would appeal to the target audience they had learned so much about through Web postings, conversations, and video diaries. The result? Campbell Mithun was selected by Burger King to provide some of its advertising.

SELECTED ADDITIONAL READING

Agar, Michael H. *The Professional Stranger: An Informal Introduction to Ethnography*, 2nd edition, San Diego, CA: Academic Press, 1996.

NOTES

1. Evan Dorkin, "White Castle." Google Groups: *rec.arts.comics.xbooks*. 2 May 1995. From: groups.google.com

CHAPTER EIGHT

INSTITUTIONAL SOURCES

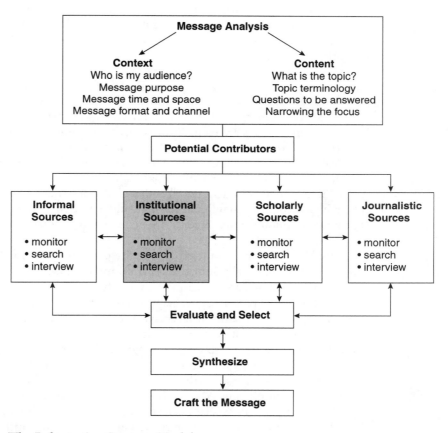

The Information Strategy Model

Institutions are among the most prolific information factories in modern society. The metaphor of a factory suggests the dynamic, deliberate creation of information that churns through the system and affects everyone both within and outside the institution. Information does not exist like some raw material in nature—it is a deliberately manufactured entity, and institutions are key manufacturers.

The term *institution* covers highly diverse concepts and organizations. All societies have conventional social arrangements such as the institutions of marriage and the family, and legal and economic arrangements such as property inheritance standards and free-market behavior. All individuals exist during much—if not all—of their lives in relation to these fundamental social, legal, and economic institutions. But beyond that, people also relate to the more specific and visible institutions of their particular societies—governments, religious organizations, unions, political parties, schools, corporations and businesses, neighborhood associations, and hobby groups are among many that can be cited.

Each of us in society leaves a paper and electronic information trail that represents our interactions with institutions. For example, a couple who marry begin a series of interactions with many institutions which keep records that reflect that couple's married status—a marriage license is purchased, sworn witnesses confirm the alliance, insurance beneficiaries are named, surnames may change. When land and a house are acquired, records establish the sales price, method of payment, and terms of ownership. When children are born, their births are recorded and files relating to the births are kept by hospitals, insurance companies, and the attending physician or midwife. The U.S. federal government requires that all children have a Social Security number. If a savings account is established for the child, another set of tax and income records is generated. Immunization records are generated to confirm that the child's health is being protected.

For the children and their parents, these records are just the beginning of the paper and electronic trails of institutional information that follow them through their lives in society. Public and quasi-public records confirm that they attend school, play tennis in the public park's league, acquire a driver's license, buy a car, get arrested for speeding, apply for a credit card, receive a scholarship, earn money and pay taxes, inherit money from a relative, purchase property, file for bankruptcy, go to court to recover damages in a legal dispute, and a myriad of other activities, including dying!

Just as individuals leave traces behind, so specific institutions leave distinctive marks. Institutions have a "birth" record in the articles of incorporation that bring a new institution into being. More records are created as that institution hires people, pays them and pays the Social Security, insurance, and retirement benefits taxes for them. If that institution goes to court as a defendant or a plaintiff, there are records of the dispute. The institution's compliance or noncompliance with licensing and regulatory requirements is recorded. As that institution purchases property or merges with other institutions, there are records of the financial transactions. If the institution sells stock to the public there are more records. When an institution "dies," there are bankruptcy or dissolution records.

In other words, information generated by and about institutions makes up an enormous category of material, much of it extremely important for communicators.

Much of what is produced is for internal use only, but some is created for use both inside and outside the institution. Some of the major reasons that institutions generate so much information are:

- To operate the institution itself
- To cooperate with other institutions, including government at all levels
- To make decisions and set policy
- To justify policy and operational decisions
- To administer policy
- To communicate with interest groups and the general public about activities and positions on issues
- To raise money or finance activities

For example, a small retail store creates and keeps many records for its own use. The inventory of goods ordered, received, and sold is essential for the orderly conduct of business. So are records of employees' work hours and pay rates. These types of records are generally for private use in the firm. However, they may become part of the public record if there is a dispute about whether an employee was properly paid for hours worked, or a dispute about payroll taxes that ends up in court.

Other records kept by this same small firm include more public information such as the sale of taxable goods and the amount of sales tax collected, which are forwarded to tax collectors in the state. Then those sales tax data are compiled and become part of the measure of economic activity in the community. Regulations about sales of certain items such as firearms or state lottery tickets require additional public record filing. Thus, even the relatively simple and straightforward information collected by a small retail store has some public dimensions and larger significance.

You enter the picture when you understand the process through which institutional information is produced and take advantage of the fruits of that process for your message-making tasks. Voluminous records result from the process outlined just above. Many of these records are available for the asking if you know where to look and who to ask. Some are kept within the institution, and some are publicly promoted by the institution through news releases, letters to the editor, advertisements, and Web sites. It is your job to know how to move efficiently and effectively through these information factories to get what you need.

TYPES OF INSTITUTIONAL SOURCES
AND HOW THEY KNOW WHAT THEY KNOW

Institutions are divided, broadly, into two sectors: the private and the public. Private institutions are funded with money and other resources from private individuals, acting singly or in association with one another. Public institutions are funded with tax money and other resources from local, state, and federal governments. Thus, the corner drug store is in the private sector, whereas the police precinct station next door is in the public sector. The elementary school maintained with tax revenues is part of the public sector, the church-affiliated school is in the private sector. These lines are hardly neat, however. Almost all private colleges, for instance, enroll students whose financial support comes partly from state and federal sources. Most corporations are in the private sector, but some operate with charters from the federal government, such as Amtrak (rail service), Fannie Mae (home mortgages), or the Corporation for Public Broadcasting.

For our purposes, the private sector institutions we will discuss include businesses and corporations; market and audience information sources; trade associations; union and professional associations; foundations and nonprofits; religious institutions; political, citizen-action, and policy associations; and interest and hobby associations. Public sector institutions include municipal and county governments, state government, federal government, and international agencies.

Both public sector and private sector institutions generate public and private records about their activities. For example, the public sector police precinct station includes much information that is part of the public record: arrest and detention records, firearm registrations, incident reports, calls for service, police vehicle maintenance records, budget requests. But some records in this public sector institution are private: internal investigation reports, disciplinary actions against individual police officers, some types of personnel files (medical histories, etc.).

Likewise, the private sector business or corporation generates private information such as internal correspondence, proprietary product recipes or unique manufacturing processes, marketing research about their customers, business plans for product line expansions and so forth. But some public records are also generated about these private-sector institutions. If they sell stock to shareholders, they must create and maintain public financial disclosure documents. If they operate in an environment that requires licenses or regulatory oversight, they must demonstrate that they are in compliance with these requirements. They must report tax information for, and about, their employees. If they are engaged in international trade they must demonstrate they are complying with federal and international commerce laws and regulations.

You have legal and legitimate access to much more information from both public sector and private sector institutions, through public and private records, than you ever think to request. In fact, the danger in seeking institutional information is that you will be overwhelmed by the quantity and complexity of it all, rather than that your requests will be denied. The competent communicator understands what is legitimately considered public and what appropriately remains private, and has a clear picture of institutions as important information factories that help societies accomplish their work.

You can reasonably expect institutions to be reliable, accurate, and complete in their information-producing and disseminating functions. But you should not expect the information to be neutral in respect to social values and social structures. Nor should you expect that institutions will not alter their methods as laws change and as social values and structure evolve. Rather, you should recognize that when you use information from institutional sources, you have to decode the biases, assumptions, and vested interests inherent in the information.

There is, in fact, competition among institutions that try to produce a "definition of the situation" that will be adopted in society. As part of such competition, institutions provide information to communicators as they attempt to influence prevailing ideas and policy. Despite the competition, the most powerful of the institutions often have overwhelming advantages in having their perspectives adopted. For measuring national economic conditions, for example, there is no close competitor to the United States government. The government has the power to require public and private sector institutions to file financial data; they collect more information, generate more statistics, track more industries and generally monitor the economic situation far more extensively than any other institution would ever be able to do. Hence, they get to set the agenda and dominate the discussion about national economic conditions.

Since communicators play significant roles in distributing information in society, they naturally end up adopting much of the information produced by institutions. Your skill in making full use of what is available from many sources, as contrasted with simply using what a single association promotes, can make an important difference in how audience members are informed and how members of society understand their common life together. It is tempting to use the *information subsidies* (discussed in Chapter 3) that institutions provide without seeking additional, perhaps contradictory, material. But it is your responsibility to put your full information strategy skills to use, to be sure you can provide your audience with a full and complete picture rather than just one corner of the scene as provided by one powerful institution.

As we've already discussed, institutions generate information for a wide variety of purposes. The types of information subsidies you can expect to get from institutions include:

- *Statistics.* Governments, businesses, advocacy groups, think tanks, political parties and many other institutions generate statistics to bolster their positions, lobby for change, defend their actions, and communicate with the public. Many times, institutions will take statistics from a source such as the federal government (census data, for instance) and massage the data for their own purposes by reinterpreting the figures, adding analysis, or selectively choosing the evidence that supports a position or point of view. Chapter 11 includes a full discussion about how to interpret statistics for mass communication messages and audiences, regardless of the source.
- *Media kits.* Prepared on paper or in digital form, media kits include information that is both informational and promotional. The sponsoring organization understands that it helps to present its facts in a manner that aids its reputation or position. By providing ready-made fact sheets, photos, video, biographical information, quotes, contact lists, and other material designed to be easily incorporated into a news story, advertisement, or public relations message, the institution advances its goal of getting its point of view accepted as the right picture of reality. Advertising professionals are targets of elaborate media kits sent by media outlets (magazines, television stations, Web sites) trying to convince the ad professionals to place ads there. News professionals receive hundreds of media kits designed to convince them to write or broadcast a story using the information subsidies therein.
- *News releases.* Again, news releases arrive via paper, satellite feed, videotape, or Web site. News releases help communicators by providing routine information

about meetings, speakers in the community, elections of institutional officers, stock offerings, road construction announcements and countless other institutional events and activities that have to be monitored by communicators. But the news release also may serve the purpose of setting an agenda or a perspective that favors the institution that issues the news release.

- *News conferences.* These work much the same way as news releases and media kits; in fact, many news conferences use news releases and media kits as integral parts of the news conference presentation. In addition, a prominent person or celebrity usually presents information designed to liven up the material being promoted and to give the material either authority or human interest.

- *Evaluation reports.* The federal General Accounting Office and individual state auditors' offices do countless investigations on the efficiency and effectiveness of government programs. They issue reports that would be otherwise prohibitively expensive for news organizations and political parties or candidates to undertake. These reports are usually designed to be neutral in their approach, seeking to simply provide accurate oversight and evaluation of sometimes very expensive government activities. Obviously, these evaluation reports can be creatively used by other institutions as a source of evidence for a point of view or position on an issue if the findings support that institution's take on the topic.

- *Policy documents.* Institutions issue policy statements and white papers on topics of interest to them and their members. These policy documents provide an insight into the priorities and perspectives of the sponsoring institution, as well as a statement about the institution's stand on an issue, a piece of legislation, a proposed rule change, a social policy, and myriad other activities. Because our interactions with institutions are so tightly woven into our social fabric, it is very important for communications professionals to track these policy documents to understand how and why institutions are influencing public debate or private activities. Many times, these policy documents arrive in a form that very much resembles a more independent scholarly study of the topic, so your antennae need to be finely tuned to recognize the difference. Scholarly sources are discussed in Chapter 9

- *Offers to provide spokespersons and experts for interviews.* Institutions have become very savvy about how dependent media professionals are on getting good quotes and providing good sound bites in their messages. Hence, many institutions do their best to provide communicators with ready-made experts and spokespersons to bolster a message. These individuals are sometimes extremely well-qualified to speak on behalf of the institution and about the topic, so we are not suggesting that these offers should be dismissed. However, you need to use your information skills to determine the qualifications of these people and make your own judgments about their appropriateness for your message.

Because institutions are such prolific information factories, they devote substantial resources to organizing and maintaining the information they have generated. They keep their collections in libraries or archives and on Web sites run by knowledgeable staff members. They have a staff that provides information to communicators from outside the organization who request material. Many institutions have a public information office designed specifically to meet these requests. Small institutions, of course, have less elaborate services available. But even small institutions try to cooperate with requests for information because their staff understands how powerful the media can be in disseminating a point of view or perspective.

TAPPING INSTITUTIONAL SOURCES

As with the other contributors to the information strategy, you can tap into institutional sources through people, paper, or digital means. You might *monitor* institutional sources by regularly scanning the news releases and Web sites they issue and support, you may *search* for relevant institutional documents and reports using the tools in libraries or databases, or institutional spokespersons may share their knowledge through in-person, telephone, or e-mail *interviews* with you.

Monitoring Institutional Sources

As discussed in Chapter 5, monitoring involves observation and tracking of information in order to gain a preliminary sense of what is going on in your information topic area. This is an especially important strategy for institutional information sources. Ad professionals working for a retail store or a restaurant client certainly want to visit those locations regularly to observe how business is doing, what customers seem to be engaged with or in, and to talk regularly with the proprietors. Public relations professionals working for a chain of nursing homes want to visit the facilities to observe patient care and infrastructure conditions in order to be fully informed about their client's performance as a health provider. News professionals monitor the schedule of public meetings of the government agencies in their communities and attend those gatherings where public policy is being made.

Specific alert or tracking services also help you monitor public and private institutions. Several that are especially useful for advertising and public relations professionals include Business Wire (www.businesswire.com) and PR Newswire (www.prnewswire.com). Both services allow you to customize your search preferences so that you automatically receive information (news releases, stock price information, analysts' reports, alerts of news stories about those companies or organizations you are interested in) every time something important happens. Many federal and state government agencies also offer alert or tracking services for which you can sign up electronically to automatically receive information.

Businesses issue many publications designed to inform various groups about their products, services, and activities. Among the types of publications that you would find useful to monitor are annual reports, house organs, newsletters and magazines distributed to clients and customers, and reports circulated to others in the industry. Many of these are posted on the company's Web site or can be obtained through the company's corporate information office.

Many companies have also created their own information services. For instance, the Gatorade Sports Science Institute (www.gssiweb.com), a division of the beverage company, produces sports and nutrition information and publishes materials in bulletins and newsletters that are sent to thousands of sports medicine professionals. Trade associations, political parties, lobbying organizations, and citizen-action groups issue newsletters, support Web sites, and generate news releases, to advance their agendas. Public sector institutions also generate their own media kits, news releases, and public relations packages to garner attention. Monitoring the offices with which you have regular contact for these types of routine communications is essential for you to keep up with your media assignments.

Searching Institutional Sources

Private Sector Institution Searches.   There are thousands of library tools and electronic sources to help identify and locate information from and about private sector institutions. Searching for information from these institutions can sometimes be an overwhelming task because of the sheer immensity of information generated. However, there are some logical ways to organize your thinking as you begin any private sector information strategy. Just keep in mind why an institution is generating information, and why or how they might want you to know about it.

Business and Corporate Information Searches.   As we've already discussed above, businesses produce a wealth of information they are willing to make public, and you can keep track of much of this material through your monitoring activities. However, there are times when you need to conduct a focused search for information about a business or a corporation. This is when the myriad of information-finding tools (print and electronic) can provide the best strategy for success. Table 8.1 provides examples of business and corporate information and some access points for locating that information.

Generally, businesses are willing to provide information from their own research if doing so does not undermine their competitive advantage. For example, a sporting goods manufacturer may disclose some statistics it has compiled about changes in U.S. lifestyles that it has used to understand how customers make clothing choices. It would not, however, be likely to reveal those portions of the research on which it is basing a new product line or manufacturing plan. Beyond the research information, however, firms also offer to provide a wide variety of publications and services about their activities. Typical offerings include industry statistics, biographies of officials, photos, media kits, brochures, and offers for interviews. The public relations office typically handles preliminary requests for this type of information.

In addition to the information that businesses disclose voluntarily, either as a courtesy or in response to a request, you should be aware that the law requires many disclosures. Businesses intersect with government at all levels. In many instances, a license is required to conduct business. This "permission" to do business affects business people, from the ice-cream vendor on the street corner to multinational companies that have contracts with the Department of Defense. Many public records (discussed later in this chapter) result from the licensing power of governments, and all of them are available for inspection by communicators.

TABLE 8.1   Business and Corporate Information

EXAMPLES OF BUSINESS/ CORPORATE INFORMATION	SOME ACCESS POINTS FOR BUSINESS/CORPORATE INFORMATION
Background information about an industry	Newspaper, business journal, and trade publication articles indexed in print and electronic tools such as *ABI Inform; Business & Company Resource Center; Business Source Premier; General BusinessFile; National Newspapers; Lexis Nexis; ECONLIT*
	Reference tools such as *Dun and Bradstreet/Gale Group Industry Reference Handbook; Encyclopedia of American Industries; Standard and Poor's Industry Surveys; U.S. Industry and Trade Outlook; U.S. Industry Profiles*
	Trade and industry associations, identified through tools such as *Encyclopedia of Associations* or Web sites such as info.asaenet.org/gateway/ OnlineAssocSlist.html or www.associationcentral.com
	Investment surveys and analysts' reports found in tools such as *Value Line Investment Survey* and *FINDEX: The Worldwide Directory of Market Research Reports, Studies and Surveys* and online sources such as *First Call Analysts, Investext* or *Multexnet*
	Federal Department of Commerce at www.doc.gov; Small Business Administration at www.sba.gov
	Chambers of Commerce in specific communities
	Proprietary research done by a company and repackaged for public consumption
General information about a specific company or firm	Annual reports issued by the company
	Newspaper and magazine articles from the region in which the firm operates
	Investment analysts' reports (see tools above)
	Reference tools such as *Wards Business Directory of U.S. Private and Public Companies; Thomas Register of Manufacturers; Hoover's Handbook of Private Companies; Directory of Corporate Affiliations;* and Web sites such as www.corporateinformation.com
	Company Web sites, found using search engines such as Google (www.google.com)
Executives/corporate officers and their compensation	Securities and Exchange Commission filings for publicly owned companies (in print or from www.sec.gov; www.tenkwizard.com or www.freeedgar.com
	Internal Revenue Service filings for nonprofit companies (IRS form 990s are required for all nonprofits); available from www.guidestar.org or www. nonprofits.org or from IRS regional offices or state attorneys general offices
	Company annual reports

(continued)

TABLE 8.1   CONTINUED

EXAMPLES OF BUSINESS/ CORPORATE INFORMATION	SOME ACCESS POINTS FOR BUSINESS/CORPORATE INFORMATION
Company financial information, ownership changes, mergers	Securities and Exchange Commission filings for publicly owned companies Internal Revenue Service form 990s for nonprofit companies Company annual reports Reference tools such as *FIS Online; Mergent's Manuals; Moody's Industry Review; Market Share Reporter; Business Rankings Annual; Almanac of Business and Industrial Financial Ratios*
Labor relations, unions, worker safety	National Labor Relations Board files, available from regional offices or www.nlrb.gov Federal Occupational Safety and Health Administration public records, available from www.osha.gov Federal Bureau of Labor Statistics, available from www.bls.gov State labor and industry departments Union offices in all communities
Consumer safety, regulatory, and licensing issues and compliance	Consumer Product Safety Commission public reports from www.cpsc.gov Federal Trade Commission reports on companies under investigation, merger applications, when advertising claims are challenged, from www.ftc.gov State and local licensing agencies such as Health Department, Commerce Department, City Clerk, Public Utilities Commission, Pollution Control Agency Private oversight agencies such as the Better Business Bureau or Chamber of Commerce
Corporate newsletters, magazines, news releases, media kits, promotional materials	Corporate communications offices Corporate Web sites Wire services such as *Business Wire* www.businesswire.com, *News Alert* www.newsalert.com, or *PR Newswire* www.prnewswire.com Reference tools such as *O'Dwyer's Directory of Corporate Communications*
International trade issues	Federal Department of Commerce's International Trade Administration at www.ita.doc.gov for profiles and analysis of companies conducting international trade, trade agreements, and treaties between the United States and other countries, compliance records, etc. ITA's Trade Information Center at www.ita.doc.gov/td/tic for information about trade opportunities in specific countries Reference tools such as *Encyclopedia of Global Industries; Exporters' Encyclopaedia;* Dun and Bradstreet *Principal International Businesses*
Legal issues or court cases involving a company or industry	Public records filed with the court in which a case is tried *Lexis* or *Westlaw* online services for legal information News reports about lawsuits or settlements

In addition to licensing power, the federal government also requires that publicly held companies (that is, companies that sell stock to the public) file quarterly and annual reports on their financial condition. The reports include the names of corporate officers along with their salaries, bonuses, and certain fringe benefits. Additional content of these reports includes information on new products and services; acquisition, sales, divestiture or merger plans; major lawsuits in which the company was engaged; and government actions or regulations that affect business. These reports are available through the company's annual reports, or through the Securities and Exchange Commission directly at (www.sec.gov, www.tenkwizard.com, or www.freeedgar.com).

Privately held companies are not required to file such reports. However, both privately held and publicly held companies get involved in lawsuits, trade disputes, and criminal complaints that bring them into courts of law. And court decisions, along with the records introduced as evidence, are publicly accessible. Court records, then, reveal much information about businesses and corporations that was hidden.

Market and Audience Information Searches. A particular class of institutional search tools is vitally important for the day-to-day activities of advertising and public relations professionals: sources that include information about the characteristics of audiences and markets. Subscriptions to many of these tools are very expensive, so they may be found only in the libraries of ad or PR agencies or departments within a company. Other important audience and market information can be gathered from specialized periodicals, industry reports, government documents, and other more easily accessible sources. These tools provide you with some of the most important information that is used in creating ads or news releases and messages that influence public opinion and preferences, and that eventually affect the kinds of entertainment that society has available to it through the media.

A number of these tools help you identify the *size of a market for a brand and its competitors.* They help you prepare the product and market *situation analysis* required to understand the product or service characteristics of the things about which you are creating messages. Tools that are useful for this type of information include *Market Share Reporter,* the *Encyclopedia of Consumer Brands, Brands and Their Companies, Public Company Analysis, Privately-Owned Companies,* and *Directory of Corporate Affiliations.* Most of these tools are updated at least annually.

Another set of tools helps you locate information about *audience characteristics:* demographic information (age, income, education level, etc.), psychographic information ("Do you prefer to read a book or go wind-surfing on your day off?") and media use information ("What magazines do you read? What television programs do you watch? Which Web sites do you visit regularly?"). Two major sources for this information are the syndicated services *Mediamark Research Inc. (MRI)* and *Simmons Study of Media and Markets.* Each company conducts more than 20,000 personal interviews annually in which they ask participants to record their product-purchase habits, their media-use habits, and their demographic characteristics. This information is compiled into massive data sets, published in electronic form. The reports are used by magazines, television and radio, Internet and other media, leading national advertisers, and hundreds of advertising agencies to help determine what kinds of people purchase which kinds of products and use which types of media to learn about trends, styles, new products, and events. If you want to reach people who use mopeds or motor-scooters, or who shop in health food specialty stores, these tools will help you identify them and understand how best to reach them with messages.

Likewise, *broadcast audience information* is available from the research services that collect and compile ratings services. Arbitron collects information about radio audiences and Nielsen collects information about television (broadcast and cable). The ratings volumes and reports generated by these two companies include a wealth of information about the geographic markets surveyed, the demographic characteristics of the households and individuals surveyed, the time of day when people watch television or listen to the radio, the types of programs that attract the largest audiences, and the time spent by different types of people using broadcast media. While it is not necessary for every communicator to learn to decode the ratings volumes, it is important to understand how this information is used. Ratings information determines the advertising rates charged by broadcast and cable stations, helps communicators understand something about the characteristics of media consumers, and gives a snapshot of the types of media programming that are popular or influential among audiences. The Internet has become an important advertising medium and both Nielsen and Arbitron, along with a number of new companies, provide ratings services for Web advertising. These companies track usage of Web sites based on factors such as the number of unique visitors to a Web site on an hourly, daily, weekly, or monthly basis. They also can provide basic information about how users move around at a particular Web site. Many Web sites ask users to provide additional information about themselves such as demographic information (income, family profiles, spending habits). That information can be combined with the tracking of site visits to provide advertisers with a powerful form of tailored audience measurement for this medium.

Psychographic information about audiences is collected by many institutions as well. One of the best-known is a company called SRI Consulting Business Intelligence. Their product, called VALS (for Values and Lifestyles), divides consumers into eight mutually-exclusive groups based on their psychology and several key demographic characteristics. You can use VALS data to identify who to target with your messages, uncover what your target group buys and does, locate where concentrations of your target group live, identify how best to communicate with your target group, and gain insight into why the target group acts the way it does. For instance, people who are categorized by the VALS system as "Makers" are the most likely among the eight types of consumers to purchase hand tools, camp, or hike. This insight into consumer psychology can be very useful for an ad team creating ads for hiking shoes, for instance. Using the information provided by VALS, the message creators might decide to incorporate an appeal to the hands-on, do-it-yourself attitude of the target audience members in their ad for hiking shoes.

A great many services reveal to advertising professionals *where ad dollars are spent*. Media analysis is a research-intensive aspect of work in strategic communications. It involves deciding on an ad budget, how to determine competitors' ad spending, how best to reach the target audience with specific ad purchases of time or space, how to locate sponsors, and the most effective means for communicating your client's message. One important set of tools to help with this task is the *Multi-Media Service: Quarterly Reporting of Brand Expenditures*. Published by CMR, the *Multi-Media Service* reports advertising expenditures in ten major media: consumer magazines, Sunday magazines, newspapers, outdoor, network television, spot television, syndicated television, cable television, network radio, and national spot radio. For instance, you could learn how much Proctor & Gamble spent on advertising for all its products in any year, or how much they spent on advertising for just their Head & Shoulders® shampoo brand, and how those ad dollars were apportioned among the different types of media (mostly magazine and network TV ads, it turns out). You could also learn the total number of ad pages and total dollars spent in specific magazine titles (how much does *Cosmopolitan* magazine bring in from P&G product ads each year?) or the amount of money spent on advertising for particular categories of products, such as personal care products.

Previously mentioned *MRI* and *Simmons* also provide information to help with media analysis tasks, as does a service titled *Standard Rate and Data Service*, which provides extensive information about advertising and marketing opportunities, costs for placing ads, and technical specification information for advertising in print publications, on television, and on the Web. The *IGE Sponsorship Sourcebook* helps you identify possible sponsors for your client's messages, and the Web site www.tsnn.com provides a comprehensive database of tradeshow and exhibit opportunities where your client's products or services might be showcased.

Trade Association Information Searches.   Individual business firms generally belong to associations of companies in the same industry. Through the association, they exchange information, lobby for favorable legislation and administrative rules, and promote their industries as a whole. They produce an enormous amount of information that can be useful to you, and they usually have Web sites that make it easy for you to get the information they offer.

The best way to locate the trade association that is most useful for your message task is to use one of the print or online directories, such as the *Encyclopedia of Associations*, the *ASAE Gateway to Associations* (info.asaenet.org/gateway/OnlineAssocSlist.html), or *AssociationCentral* (www.associationcentral.com). You should be aware, however, that trade associations release information to the public with an eye toward protecting members' interests, so you need to evaluate the material carefully for point of view and perspective.

Unions and Professional Association Information Searches.   Workers in every field from the arts to zoo-keeping are organized into trade and professional associations. Like industry associations, they offer facts and views to the public on issues that concern them. They provide biographies of their leaders, statistics on wages and benefits, media kits, position papers, annual reports, and assistance in gathering information at their conventions or during labor negotiations. The tools listed in Table 8.1 under "Labor relations, unions, and worker safety" are most useful for locating information about these organizations, along with the association directories and Web sites listed above.

Foundations and Nonprofit Institutions Information Searches.   More than 44,000 foundations fill a variety of roles in American life, spending billions of dollars on activities they deem important. In addition, there are more than 1 million institutions with nonprofit status in the United States (everything from local cemeteries or credit unions to the March of Dimes and the National Football League!). These nonprofit institutions not only wield substantial power, but vary in purpose. Some support causes and classes of people, conduct or sponsor research, promote viewpoints, or subsidize activities that are not supported in the marketplace. They issue annual reports on their expenditures, invite grant submissions, and report to federal and state governments about their financial affairs.

Foundations are among the most prolific institutions providing information subsidies to communicators. Foundation spokespersons and researchers make themselves available for interviews, and many of them are eager to share their point of view. Tools such as the *Foundation Directory* and the *Foundation Grants to Individuals*, produced in print and online by the Foundation Center (fdncenter.org), provide extensive information about these thousands of organizations. Foundation information is also available from the Council on Foundations (www.cof.org) and the Independent Sector (www.indepsec.org).

Additional information about foundations can be located by using the IRS Form 990-PF, which is much more detailed than the simple IRS Form 990 required of all nonprofit organizations. Foundations are required to provide these forms to the public at a reasonable fee. The forms are also available through a number of regional offices of the IRS or The Foundation Center, online directly from the IRS (www.irs.treas.gov/tax_stats/exempt), or from the National Center for Charitable Statistics (nccs.urban.org).

Information about the more than 1 million nonprofit institutions in the United States can be found by asking the institutions themselves for their IRS form 990s, by contacting the attorney general in the state where the nonprofit organization operates, or by searching Web sites such as those provided by the Center on Nonprofits and Philanthropy, a program of the Urban Institute (www.urban.org/centers/cnp.html) or Guidestar (www.guidestar.org). In addition, the nonprofit industry is covered by special trade publications such as *The Chronicle of Philanthropy* (philanthropy.com) or the general business trade press.

Religious Institution Information Searches.   Among the oldest institutions are religious organizations, which touch the lives of many individuals and intersect with other institutions at all levels. In the local congregation are found records of births, deaths, and such rites of passage as baptism, confirmation, bar and bas mitzvah, and marriage. Other records preserve details about selection of clergy, financial matters, membership and locally sponsored groups such as youth clubs, missions, and prayer and study groups. Locally, regionally, and nationally, religious organizations hold conventions, keep minutes of their meetings, and issue news releases, publications, and position papers.

Because of the strict separation of church and state in the United States, religious organizations are not required to file very much information with local, federal, or state government authorities. However, they must register ownership of property, vehicles, and other real assets with the appropriate state offices. And if a religious organization supports a political action committee (PAC) or owns a license to operate a broadcast facility (which many do), they must file the appropriate records with the Federal Elections Commission or the Federal Communications Commission, respectively.

Additionally, religious organizations affiliate in associations that represent their common interests. For example, the National Council of Churches of Christ, the National Conference on Christians and Jews, B'nai B'rith International, and the National Association of Evangelicals are examples of national associations that provide information and seek to influence communicators. As always, you can check their Web sites or request information from their public information offices.

Political, Citizen-Action, Policy Association, and Think Tank Information Searches. Political parties have been significant almost since the birth of the United States. They are not provided for in the Constitution, but they vitally affect local, state, and federal government. The national parties all host Web sites (www.democrats.org, www. nrc.org, www.reformparty.org, www.libertarian.org, etc.), and individual state and local party organizations also provide extensive information to the public, especially during election campaigns. Searches for political party information may include the need for materials about campaign financing for specific candidates or causes. Institutions such as the Center for Responsive Politics (www.opensecrets.org) and the Campaign Finance Information Center (www.campaignfinance.org) provide useful information about how to track the actions of political parties and candidates using public records and data that must be filed with state and federal government agencies.

Politicians also receive help from political action committees, which raise and spend money to elect and defeat candidates. Most PACs represent business, labor, or ideological interests. A PAC must register with the Federal Elections Commission within ten days of its formation, providing name and address for the PAC, its treasurer, and any connected organizations. Many politicians also form Leadership PACs, which are not technically affiliated with the candidate, as a way of raising money to help fund other candidates' campaigns. Leadership PACs are often indicative of a politician's aspirations for leadership positions in Congress or for higher office. The Center for Responsive Politics tracks PAC activities (www.opensecrets.org/pacs/index.asp).

Citizen action groups monitor the life of the nation and suggest and argue for changes they think will benefit society or some segment thereof. These groups may ask for change in private sector institutions such as corporations or foundations, or in public sector institutions such as local or state government agencies or law enforcement agencies. They study issues, conduct research, engage in advertising and public relations campaigns, and try to influence policy wherever they think change is needed. Organizations such as the League of Women Voters (www.lwv.org) and Project Vote Smart (www.vote-smart.org) work to provide independent information about candidates, the political process, and good government best practices. Specialized groups such as the Project on Government Oversight (www.pogo.org) or the New Millennium Young Voters Project (www.stateofthevote.org) carve out particular areas where they want to make an impact—exposing government fraud and abuse, and encouraging youth to vote, respectively.

Some organizations have much narrower and more specific goals than do good-government groups. Among these are associations that monitor the private and public sectors for infringements of laws or constitutional rights. The American Civil Liberties Union (ACLU), the Urban League, the National Association for the Advancement of Colored People (NAACP), and the Southern Poverty Law Center work to publicize civil rights violations, file lawsuits, and support local and state affiliates with the same mission. Much of the material generated by these policy associations can be located using the *PAIS International* print or electronic library tool that indexes reports of public and private agencies in the areas of public affairs and public policy.

Countless groups fulfill similar roles on behalf of innumerable ideologies and causes. These may be associations as diverse as the National Rifle Association, the Sierra Club, or the Computer Professionals for Social Responsibility, or they may be think tanks such as the Heritage Foundation, the Brookings Institution, or the Cato Institute. These associations and think tanks conduct research and publicize results selectively as they seek to influence public opinion, legislation, and administrative actions. Many of them maintain offices in state capitals and in Washington, D.C., and they lobby with their own staff members or with the assistance of lobbyists. They generate news releases and cultivate relationships with media professionals to better communicate their point of view.

If these groups lobby in the U.S. Congress, they have to file semi-annual reports with the Secretary of the Senate and the Clerk of the House of Representatives identifying their clients, the lobbyists working for each client, and the amount of income they receive (sopr.senate.gov). Companies have to report their overall lobbying expenditures and the names of any lobbyists employed as part of an in-house lobbying effort. These reports are also collected by the Center for Responsive Politics and made available on their Web site at (www.opensecrets.org/lobbyists/index.asp). We discuss how to evaluate information from these interest groups and think tanks at the end of this chapter.

Interest and Hobby Institution Information Searches.   In addition to the policy-oriented and interest groups, the private sector includes thousands of associations whose members pursue more personal interests. Some people join to indulge their interest in a sport or travel; others to associate with like-minded button-collectors, restorers of antique cars, and breeders of toy poodles; still others to share skills and equipment. Such hobby groups maintain organizations chiefly to serve their members rather than to promote an organizational ideology or influence public opinion on issues. Thus, they are less active in seeking attention from communicators. You may have to make relatively greater efforts to get information from these associations than from those whose mission includes influencing public policy or opinion.

Once again, tools such as the *Encyclopedia of Associations* or Web sites such as info.asaenet.org/gateway/OnlineAssocSlist.html or www.associationcentral.com can help you identify associations appropriate for your information searches. Many of these groups also publish newsletters or magazines for their members. While most of these publications are not included in periodical indexes, specialized periodical directories such as *Ulrich's Periodical Directory* (www.ulrichsweb.com) or the *Standard Periodical Directory* list basic information about publishers and subscription prices.

Many of these interest and hobby associations also have started Web-based *zines*, or electronic magazines. You can find zines in your particular search area by using tools such as the Ezine Directory (ezine-dir.hypermart.net) or EzineSearch (homeincome. com/search-it/ezine). A site that includes background information and hundreds of links to additional information about zines is the Book of Zines (www. zinebook.com).

Public-Sector Institution Searches. Institutions in the public sector—governments, particularly—are among the most prolific producers of information used in mass communication. There are a number of reasons why governments are such enormous information factories. Some information is collected for internal record keeping and decision making and for creating a permanent record of government activities. Some is collected on behalf of other institutions: the statistical material collected by the federal government alone is critical to the operation of traditional commerce, manufacturing, and services. Much information is generated as a way of keeping track of government-sponsored or -commissioned research. Also, some government agencies serve as clearinghouses for the collection and dissemination of information that is produced by other institutions in society. The Educational Resources Information Center (www.eric.ed.gov) and the National Technical Information Service (www. ntis.gov) are examples of clearinghouses at the federal level. One way to picture the complex organization of public-sector information is to visualize the information as it is presented in Table 8.2.

Information is generated at each level and in each branch of government. The information sources are so voluminous that it would require a book for each of the branches to discuss comprehensively the material available at each level and in each branch, and the tools to locate that material. The important thing for you as a communications professional is to understand that each level of government generates information that is likely to be important for most messages you will work on, and that there are efficient and effective ways to locate that information if you know how and where it is generated.

Each piece of information collected or produced by a public institution has either a public or a private character. By definition, some information must be public. The clearest example is laws. Obviously, laws enacted by legislatures, signed by executives, and interpreted by courts cannot be obeyed unless they are made public. Conversely, some information has little or no significant public character. For example, public clinics treat patients who have no way to pay their own medical bills, but these patients' medical records are considered private even though they receive care at

TABLE 8.2   Organization of Public-Sector Information

BRANCH	LOCAL	STATE	NATIONAL
Legislative	Council	Legislature	Congress
Judicial	Municipal courts	State courts	Federal courts
Executive	Mayor	Governor	President

public expense. Medical information about individuals is aggregated into statistics that register the state of public health at all levels of government. In each local community, contagious diseases and causes of death are recorded, tabulated, and analyzed. Thus you have access to government-produced documentation about public health matters in the community, the state, and the nation even though individual medical records are private.

The distinction between public and private information in the United States is reflected in legislation that provides both for access to information and for privacy for individuals and institutions. Legislation at the local, state, and national levels specifies what is protected as private and what must be disclosed as public.

At the federal level, the Freedom of Information Act (FOIA), passed in 1966 and amended in 1974, 1986, and 1996, ensures that individuals may have access to information generated by all executive branch departments, agencies, and offices of the U.S. Federal Government. The law does not cover Congress or the federal judiciary, however. The 1996 amendment to the FOIA explicitly extended the provisions of the law to cover records stored in electronic form and ordered executive branch agencies to construct Internet sites to make it easier for the public to search for, and gain access to, information.

Requests for information under FOIA provisions must be specific enough that the agency can identify what is being requested. A sample request letter is shown in Figure 8.1. The FOIA identifies nine exemptions designed to safeguard national security, trade secrets, law-enforcement investigations, foreign-policy actions, and privacy rights of government officials, along with geological information about the location of oil wells! All states have their own versions of the FOIA.

Some independent organizations collect information using the FOIA and make that material available to the general public. One such organization is the National Security Archive housed at George Washington University (www.gwu.edu/~nsarchiv). The Archive collects and publishes declassified documents acquired through the FOIA and accepts no government funds to operate. Since its founding by a group of journalists and scholars in 1985, it has become the world's largest nongovernmental depository of declassified government documents.

Another federal law, the Government in the Sunshine Act, provides for open meetings of any federal executive branch commission, committee, or other "collegial" body. Among the agencies covered are the Securities and Exchange Commission, the Federal Communications Commission, and the Federal Trade Commission. Agencies are expected to announce scheduled meetings one week in advance and to publish meeting agendas so that interested persons may attend. All states have their own versions of open meetings laws, as well.

The Federal Advisory Committee Act (FACA) mandates that meetings of special federal task forces be open to the public. Since Congress and the President have recently delegated more and more highly controversial decision-making to these task forces, it is especially important that their activities and proceedings be scrutinized. There are also federal laws that address particular kinds of records. For instance, the Presidential Records Act specifically addresses how and when presidential papers are made available under the FOIA.

FIGURE 8.1   Sample FOIA Request Letter

Freedom of Information Officer
Public Affairs Office
Name and Address of Agency

RE: Freedom of Information Act Request

Dear _____ :

Under the provisions of the Freedom of Information Act, 5 U.S.C. §552, I am requesting access to…(identify the records as clearly and specifically as possible. If requesting electronic records, be sure to include a request for the code guide as part of the material sought).

If there are any fees for searching for or copying the records I have requested, please inform me before you fill the request. (Or,…please notify me if the expenses for processing my request exceed $_____)

As you know, the Act permits you to reduce or waive fees when the release of the information is considered "primarily benefiting the public." My interest in the requested information arises solely from a desire to increase public awareness of the activity of our federal government. Therefore, I ask that you waive any fees.

If all or any part of this request is denied, please include in your response the precise exemption(s) which you think justifies your refusal and inform me of your agency's administrative appeal procedures available to me under the law.

I anticipate a response within the 20 working-day statutory time limit. Thank you for your assistance.

Sincerely,

[Your name, affiliation, address, telephone number, fax number, e-mail address]

The privacy issue is governed by the federal Privacy Act, passed in 1974 and amended in 1986. The Privacy Act is intended to give individuals some control over the personal information that is collected by the executive branch agencies of the federal government. The act guarantees two rights: the right of individuals to see files about themselves, and the right of individuals to sue the government for permitting others to see information about them without their permission. Most states also have a version of the Privacy Act that covers state records about individuals. Your ability to collect information from public sector institutions is affected by these laws, along with a large number of other statutes and regulations governing electronic information-gathering, hacking, credit-reporting services, electronic fund transfers, and (especially after the 2001 terrorist attacks), a growing number of homeland security orders, laws, decrees, and regulations.

Since it is impossible to commit to memory all the sources of governmental information, you have to learn how governments operate, how they produce information, and what portion of the information is available in public records, documents, and publications. In addition to general background on governmental operations, it is useful to maintain a file of material that is specific to your local area. Such a file should include organization charts of municipal and county governments; state government organization charts; the state versions of the FOIA, open meetings, and privacy laws; and contact information or Web browser bookmarks for the public sector institutions you deal with most often.

Municipal and County Government Information Searches.   You may receive information from local government institutions when an agency wants to publicize its actions or decisions. For example, when a paving crew plans to interrupt traffic for a week, the city or county Public Works Department will issue a news release. When a public immunization campaign is scheduled, the Public Health Service will try to get the word out by producing public service advertisements and placing them on radio and local television. In most instances, you will take the initiative in searching for information from these local and county entities.

Local governments provide substantial help to communicators and community residents who search for information. Many maintain municipal reference libraries, which exist chiefly to help public employees research topics connected with their department jobs. Many local governments also maintain Web sites that allow citizens to search for information; fill out applications, license and permit requests; send e-mail messages to city officials and staff; and learn of city activities, proposals, development plans, and other important aspects of civic life.

Table 8.3 provides some examples of city or county information and some access points for information searches. Much of the information is still available only in paper form, but more and more local and county government offices are using electronic records systems to maintain their recordkeeping and provide access to information. City and county Web sites usually follow a standard URL format: www.ci.[city name or abbreviation].[state abbreviation].us. For example, www.ci.austin.tx.us is the URL of the Web site for the city of Austin, Texas. County Web sites usually follow this format: www.co.[county name].[state abbreviation].us. For example, www.co.king.wa.us is the URL for King County, Washington.

Several reference tools help you locate information generated by city or county governments. The *Index to Current Urban Documents* (www.urbdocs.com) publishes a guide to the reports and research that are generated by local government agencies, civic organizations, academic and research organizations, public libraries, and metropolitan and regional planning agencies in approximately 500 selected cities in the United States and Canada. They index more than 2,400 documents yearly, providing a spectrum of access to local information. The *County and City Data Book* and the *State and Metropolitan Area Data Book* (both published by the U.S. Census Bureau) provide extensive statistical information about U.S. cities and counties. The *Sage Urban Studies Abstracts* provides access to some municipal and county documents and scholarly studies about urban issues.

State Government Information Searches.   State governments resemble the federal government more than they do local governments. All three branches of state govern-

TABLE 8.3   Municipal and County Government Information

EXAMPLES OF CITY/COUNTY GOVERNMENT INFORMATION	SOME ACCESS POINTS FOR CITY/COUNTY INFORMATION
Building permits and applications	City Clerk or Public Works Office
Inspection of new construction reports	City or county public works offices
Master plans, zoning information	County planning departments; county clerks, assessors or recorders of deeds; local planning and zoning commissions
Property ownership	Recorder of deeds
Property tax and valuation records	County or city assessor
Fire safety citations, inspection reports	Chief Fire Marshal or Warden
Autopsy reports	Chief Medical Examiner
Animal licenses and citations, garage sale permits, nonprofit solicitation permits, burn permits	City Clerk
Criminal, civil, small claims, and traffic case files, search warrants, felony arraignment, and preliminary hearing case files	District Court Clerk
Superior court files (civil, criminal, divorce, probate)	County Clerk
Police blotters, portions of arrest reports, and booking information	Station house records
Jail logs	County Sheriff
Birth, death, marriage certificates	County recorder
City/county publications	*Index to Current Urban Documents; Sage Urban Studies Abstracts;* municipal or county reference libraries
City/county statistics	*County and City Data Book; State and Municipal Area Data Book;* www.firstgov.gov/Government/ State_Local/Statistics.shtml

ment are rich sources of information for communicators. Typically, state governments employ many public relations staffers who help provide information to residents and to media professionals. Advertising agencies have contracts with state governments to produce print, radio, television, and Web ads for such purposes as promoting tourism. Each state maintains a legislative reference library that is usually open to the public as well as to the public officials it is designed to serve. States issue hundreds of publications, many of which grow out of research done in state agencies.

Like cities and counties, states have established Web sites where they provide access to information and allow citizens to conduct public business. All state Web site URL's follow a standard format: www.state.[two-letter state abbreviation].us. For example, the state of Minnesota's Web site is found at www.state.mn.us. Visitors to the state's Web site can renew their vehicle registration online; search the Department of Corrections' offender locator database of public information about adult offenders under its jurisdiction; generate tailored reports about higher education enrollment in the state's secondary education system; search the state Department of Agriculture's licensing database for information about the quality, condition, labeling, advertising, and the sanitation of premises, equipment, and vehicles used for selling, storing, or distributing foods and beverages; and much more. State and local government information on the Web is indexed (www.statelocalgov.net/index.cfm).

You will usually seek information from a limited number of state offices rather than from a wide range of them. The ad agency that has the tourism account might do most of its business with the departments of tourism, economic development, and natural resources. A public relations staff member with the Association for the Blind may have frequent contact with the state departments of health and education administration. Legislative reporters, obviously, will be broadly familiar with the state legislature as an institution. They frequently seek information from both the legislative and the executive branches of the state government.

State constitutions specify the system of courts for each state. The systems differ substantially from one another. Thus, you must become familiar with the provisions of the state constitution where you work and learn the court system of the states from which you are serious about gathering judicial branch information. Searching for legal information is discussed later in this chapter.

As is the case with city and county information, there are a number of reference tools that provide access to information produced by state governments. Until 1994, a publication titled *Monthly Checklist of State Publications* was produced by the Library of Congress. However, that publication was discontinued and now the only way to locate comprehensive listings of state publications is to search the state's Web site or contact the state document publications office, or to check a Web site titled "The StateList Project" (gateway.library.uiuc.edu/doc/StateList/check/check.htm). This site offers timely, centralized access to state checklists and shipping lists of state documents that are currently available on the Internet (a total of 32 states at the time of this writing). Some state documents and publications are also included in the *PAIS International* index or *Sage Urban Studies Abstracts*. Table 8.4 provides some examples of state government information and some access points for that information.

Federal Government Information Searches.   The federal government of the United States has no close competitor as a generator of information. Its information production takes place not only in the nation's capital, but also in federal offices in all fifty states and at diplomatic posts and military installations around the globe. In fact, the federal government produces so much information that it is impractical to try to enumerate all the types of materials that are generated. It is easier to discuss the types of information functions the government fulfills (see Table 8.5). The federal government is willing, and in some cases eager, to provide some information to all who seek it. This is especially the case with consumer information (through the Federal Consumer Information Center at www.pueblo.gsa.gov) and with statistical information that is collected specifically to monitor such important economic indicators as agriculture,

TABLE 8.4 State Government Information

EXAMPLES OF STATE GOVERNMENT INFORMATION	SOME ACCESS POINTS FOR STATE GOVERNMENT INFORMATION (ALL DEPARTMENTS ARE AT THE STATE LEVEL UNLESS NOTED OTHERWISE)
Bank examination reports and statistics, business licensing records	Commerce Department
Prison inmate information	Corrections Department
Civil and criminal appeals court cases	Courts of Appeal
Drivers' licenses and vehicle registration (states now limit access to this information to comply with federal legislation)	Driver and Vehicle Services
Statewide birth, marriage, death, divorce records	Health Department or Vital Statistics Department
Inspection reports for restaurants, nursing homes, hotels, hospitals, recreational camps	Health Department
Wage and workers' compensation information, labor law compliance, OSHA compliance	Labor and Industry Department
Licensed health care providers	Medical Practice Board
Corporate statutes, statements of officers, articles of incorporation, name changes, Uniform Commercial Code filings, limited partnerships, notary public files	Secretary of State
Statewide voter registration files	Secretary of State
Public utility financial reports and rate change requests	Public Utility Commission; service providers
Environmental regulation compliance records	Pollution Control Agency; business records
Bids, performance bonds, contracts, vouchers, payment records	Responsible agency or State Auditor
Education statistics, budgets	Education Department
Legislative actions, statutes, legislator voting records	Legislation tracking sites; state *Blue Book* or legislative manual; *StateLaw* (www.washlaw.edu/uslaw/statelaw.html)
Campaign contribution and finance records	Ethical Practices Board; Secretary of State; candidate records; Federal Election Commission (www.fec.gov)
Agency publications	State government printing office checklists and catalogs; state legislative reference libraries; StateList (gateway.library.uiuc.edu/doc/StateList/check/check.htm)
Statistics at the state and local level	www.firstgov.gov/Government/State_Local/Statistics.shtml

TABLE 8.5 Federal Government Information

FEDERAL GOVERNMENT INFORMATION FUNCTIONS	EXAMPLES OF FEDERAL GOVERNMENT INFORMATION	SOME ACCESS POINTS FOR FEDERAL GOVERNMENT INFORMATION
1. Collecting and producing statistics	The decennial census of population, and all other census information	Print, online, or CD-ROM census files (www.census.gov)
	Business, labor, trade, agricultural, health, environmental, criminal, educational, military, and other types of statistics	FedStats (www.fedstats.gov) *Statistical Abstract of the United States;* Bureau of Justice Statistics on the Web at (www.ojp.usdoj.gov/bjs); LexisNexis Statistical Universe database (www.lexisnexis.com)
2. Keeping a record of government activities	Hearings before congressional committees	Senate and House Web sites (www.house.gov and www.senate.gov); the Library of Congress' "Thomas" Web site at thomas.loc.gov; LexisNexis Congressional Universe database
	Legislative actions, including budgetary appropriations	U.S. Government Printing Office online (www.access.gpo.gov/su_docs/index.html); Thomas, House and Senate sites (above); LexisNexis Congressional Universe
	Regulations issued by executive branch regulatory agencies	*Federal Register* online (www.access.gpo.gov/su_docs/aces/aces140.html); LexisNexis Congressional Universe
	Presidential speeches and executive orders	*Federal News Service* (www.fnsg.com); Whitehouse Web site (www.whitehouse.gov)
	Judicial actions, case law decisions	*Westlaw* (www.westlaw.com); LexisNexis; court digests and reporters; court Web sites; *Current Law Index; Legal Resources Index*
3. Tracking research activities funded by the federal government	Reports prepared by agencies or organizations engaged in government-sponsored research	National Technical Information Service (www.ntis.gov); *Federal Research in Progress* (grc.ntis.gov/fedrip.htm); LexisNexis Congressional Universe
	General Accounting Office, Congressional Research Service oversight reports	www.gao.gov; www.house.gov/rules/crs_reports.htm
4. Publishing general information for citizens	Publications covering topics such as federal benefits, health and nutrition issues, child care, consumer protection advice, money matters, careers, travel and hobbies, small business	Federal Consumer Information Center (www.pueblo.gsa.gov); FirstGov (www.firstgov.gov) or (www.scitechresources.gov/scitech-popular.htm)
5. Serving as an information clearinghouse	Educational Resources Information Center; National Technical Information Service; National Library of Medicine	FirstGov; www.eric.ed.gov; www.ntis.gov; www.nlm.nih.gov

manufacturing, and commerce. Other information is difficult to extract and some is impossible to obtain, such as documents that are classified on national security grounds.

A solid understanding of the relationships within and among the three branches of the federal government allows you to make the most speedy and effective use of the vast information resources of the U.S. federal government. A novice discovers that the government itself publishes comprehensive manuals and supports Web sites that specify how each agency operates, what its responsibilities are, and how to contact that agency. Federal offices employ public information officers who are responsible for assisting information searchers in locating material.

In addition, each member of Congress has an office and staff that constitute a separate information factory. Each legislative committee has a research staff that generates information and produces reports on behalf of the committee. The Congressional Research Service (CRS) (www.house.gov/rules/crs_reports.htm) was created by Congress in order to have its own source of nonpartisan, objective analysis and research on all legislative issues. Their reports are sometimes available to those who request them or conduct a search on the CRS Web site.

Another major research arm of the Congress, the General Accounting Office (www.gao.gov), has a reputation in both the public and private sectors for its meticulously produced, independent and nonpartisan studies of any subject for which a request from Congress or any other federal agency has been made. Again, many of the GAO's reports can be obtained by searching the agency's Web site or contacting the public information office.

Information about Congressional activities can also be found using one of several Web sites established by the House, Senate, or the Library of Congress (www.house.gov; www.senate.gov; thomas.loc.gov) or by tapping into some of the independent watch-dog agencies mentioned earlier. Washington correspondents enjoy a number of courtesies that help them as information searchers. Official accreditation as a journalist opens the doors of the Congressional galleries, the White House, and various executive departments. Working space is provided for accredited reporters. More informally, if you are an accredited Washington journalist, you will receive assistance in gathering background information and arranging interviews from many personal contacts—public relations and news colleagues; congressional staff members; political party workers; lobbyists. In addition, you might be a guest at the many social events that are viewed as essential information-swapping sessions in the nation's capital (see the Monitoring section of this chapter).

Anything published by the federal government qualifies as a government document. A "document" can have any form—print, map, graphic, film, photographic, database, CD-ROM, Web site. Libraries that receive federal documents are called *depository libraries*. The federal government describes the depository library as a "library within a library," reflecting the fact that the documents in the federal depository system are distinct from those in the rest of the library collection where they reside. Both federal documents and selected international documents are forwarded to depository libraries. There are more than 1,350 libraries that receive materials judged to be of public interest and educational value. At least one library in each state, the library of the state capital, receives federal documents. Other recipients may include two libraries in each Congressional district, two libraries selected by each senator from each state, and libraries in public colleges and universities and government agencies.

Depository libraries employ staff who can assist users, because the cataloging system for these materials differs significantly from those most users are familiar with. Government documents are assigned a Superintendent of Documents (SuDoc) classification number that corresponds to the issuing agency for that document. Since the logic of the SuDoc system is radically different from that of other classification systems, you should always take advantage of the government documents library staff who can help you locate the materials you need. Tools such as the *Catalog of U.S. Government Publications* (www.access.gpo.gov/su_docs/locators/cgp/index.html), the LexisNexis *Congressional Universe* (www.lexisnexis.com), and many other sources can help you locate government documents, reports, and testimony transcripts (refer back to Table 8.5).

International Agencies and Foreign Governments Information Searches.   You occasionally need information from international agencies such as the United Nations, the World Court, or the World Bank; or from regional agencies such as the North Atlantic Treaty Organization (NATO), the North American Free Trade Agreement (NAFTA) Secretariat, or the European Union (EU). International agencies and commissions meet regularly to deliberate on subjects such as agricultural production, the world's money supply, labor issues, nutrition, disarmament, and trade. Each agency produces information about its decisions and the reasons for its actions. These agencies also publish periodicals, generate and interpret statistics, and issue news releases about their areas of interest. This material is usually available on the agencies' Web sites or through their public information offices. Many of these international agency documents are also available in the federal depository libraries that house U.S. government documents.

Most countries with which the United States government has ongoing relations establish consulates and embassies in the United States. These consulates and embassies can assist you with questions about many aspects of their countries' activities and interests. The United States Department of State (usembassy.state.gov) maintains lists of names and addresses of embassy and consulate personnel. Many foreign governments have also retained the services of United States public relations agencies or private consulting firms to represent them and their interests with the U.S. federal government. Political lobbying activities at the federal level must be registered with the Secretary of the Senate or the Clerk of the House of Representatives in the U.S. Congress (sopr.senate.gov). Public relations firms working for foreign governments can be identified using that Congressional Web site or by using *O'Dwyer's Directory of PR Firms*.

Court Records and Legal Information Searches.   If you remember your grade school civics class lessons, you will recall that there are three bodies that can issue laws and regulations. Legislatures create *statutory* law by passing bills that become law when signed by the executive. Administrative agencies create *administrative* law, consisting of rules and regulations issued by each agency (for example, the Environmental Protection

Agency at the federal level issues regulations concerning disposal of hazardous wastes). The judicial branch of government issues *case law*, which is found in the court decisions written by judges or justices of the court system.

Sometimes you may have to find an actual legal decision or regulation. Sometimes you may be able to settle for an interpretation of that statute or regulation prepared by experts whose job is to comment on the law. In any case, there are certain characteristics of legal and court record information that you must be familiar with before attempting to search for a specific topic or case.

Federal statutory, administrative, and case law applies to every state court and agency in the country. Statutes, regulations, and case laws written by individual state governments apply only to courts and agencies within that state. In order to determine where to look for information about laws at the federal or state level, you need to understand how the court and regulatory systems are organized at the federal and state level.

United States statutory law, created by the U.S. Congress, is found in sessions laws, which collect the statutes in chronological order, and is found in a tool called *Statutes at Large*. These statutes also are compiled in the *United States Code*, which is organized according to the topic of the law. So if you are looking for any law written and passed by Congress, you have several ways to find it (by date of issue or by topic).

Federal administrative law is found in both chronological and topical order, as well. The *Federal Register* arranges in chronological order all regulations issued by federal regulatory bodies. The topical arrangement of federal regulations is found in the *Code of Federal Regulations*. These tools help you locate rules and regulations issued by agencies such as the Environmental Protection Agency, the Federal Communications Commission, the Department of Defense, and the Securities and Exchange Commission.

The judiciary, or courts, make case law, interpret the Constitution, and make other legal determinations. The appellate courts establish precedent, or rules, that all lower courts must abide by. Depending on whether a decision was written by a federal court or a state court, the precedent value of the decision applies to either the entire country's courts or just the state's courts. When looking for case law, you need to distinguish between laws that apply to only one state or federal court district and those that apply to all the states in the country.

Federal case law is found in a series of *case reporters*, which organize the laws chronologically, and *case digests*, which organize the laws topically. Within the federal court system, there are three levels of courts performing different functions and writing different kinds of laws. These three levels are the trial level, the intermediate appellate level, and the final appellate level.

Federal trial courts are called United States District Courts. Each state has at least one federal judicial district, and some states have several districts. There are dozens of library and database tools that help you locate past and current decisions of the U.S. District Courts. The most recent decisions can be found chronologically in *West's Federal Supplement*, and topically in *West's Federal Practice Digest 4th*.

The second federal court level is the intermediate appellate level, the United States Courts of Appeals. There are thirteen federal courts of appeals, each of which covers a particular geographical area known as a circuit. For instance, the Eight Circuit includes the states of Minnesota, Iowa, Missouri, Arkansas, Nebraska, North Dakota, and South Dakota. Decisions written by judges at this level are also collected in both chronological and topical order. The most recent decisions can be found chronologically in *West's Federal Reporter, Third Series* and topically in *West's Federal Practice Digest 4th.*

The third federal court level, and the court that sets precedent for the entire country's legal system, is the United States Supreme Court. Again, the decisions of the Supreme Court are arranged in both chronological and topical order. Two tools provide chronological access: the court's own official tool titled *United States Reports* and *West's Supreme Court Reporter.* Topical access is provided through the *Supreme Court Digest.* In addition, starting with the 1990 session, the Supreme Court began issuing rulings electronically just minutes after decisions were announced (www.supreme-courtus.gov). Each of these tools will help you locate the decisions of the Supreme Court with the verbatim wording of the Court's opinion, along with the facts of the case, the names of the lawyers who argued the case before the Court, other legal decisions that were referred to by the justices in reaching their decisions, and any dissenting or minority opinions.

When the 2000 U.S. presidential election was thrown into chaos by vote count irregularities in Florida, it was the U.S. Supreme Court that ultimately decided who won the presidency. The December night that the decision was issued, television reporters from around the world stood on the steps of the Supreme Court building in Washington, rifling through the pages of the court's complicated and contentious decision as they tried to provide instant interpretation for their audiences who were waiting to learn who the new president was going to be. Many of those reporters no doubt wished then that they had brushed up on their legal decision interpretation skills before being thrust into the spotlight.

Courts at the state level also write decisions that affect state legal activities. Indeed, it was a decision of the Florida Supreme Court that was under review by the U.S. Supreme Court in the 2000 presidential election controversy. Decisions of state courts are collected in a series of state reporters, many of which are published by the West Publishing Company. Each state has at least one official high-court reporter; some states have separate reporters for the appellate courts; and a few states have reporters for the trial courts. West publishes a series of regional reporters, each of which reprints the full text of opinions from courts in a specific geographical region.

Two online database services provide extensive access to all of the types of information we've mentioned in this section, and to the hundreds of legal periodicals and law journals that provide commentary on legal decision making. Westlaw (www. westlaw.com) and LexisNexis (www.lexisnexis.com) are the premiere resources for online access to the actual texts of decisions, regulations, statutes, and legal documents. In addition, they provide indexing and in many cases full texts of the articles that are published in journals and magazines by legal scholars, lawyers, law students, and commentators about all aspects of law and legal decision making. A good Web site for locating legal information is *FindLaw* (www.findlaw.com), which helps locate the Web sites of courts at all levels, along with many other legal resources.

Once you understand the relationship between government organization and the legal research sources that correspond to each area, finding the actual court opinions at any level should be fairly straightforward. However, doing legal research is not for the novice information searcher. All law libraries have legal reference librarians who can help you locate the actual legal opinions that often serve as the subjects of news, commentary, and social furor. Most media organizations have a legal counsel who helps professionals make day-to-day decisions about the legality of certain kinds of messages and activities. The legal information search tools mentioned here are really for the communicator who has to understand the atmosphere in which certain public policy decisions are being made and who has to be able to independently locate and interpret information that the public might need to make informed decisions.

Another type of court record besides case law includes the material that is generated any time two parties go to trial, whether for a criminal or civil suit. Unless specifically sealed by the court, all of the evidence (documents, photos, reports, witness testimony, etc.) generated as a part of the trial is public record information. That means that you can have access to that material. Sometimes, court records of this type provide the only insight you may have to certain types of organizations or institutions. For instance, privately held companies are not required to file very much information with government agencies (meaning there are few public records about them). But if they are in court, as a plaintiff or a defendant, their activities are laid bare as a part of the evidentiary process.

Public Records Information About Individuals.   We've already mentioned that you leave a paper and electronic trail of public records about your life and activities. When you are born, there is a birth certificate registered with the county and state. If you have a license to drive or hunt, own a gun or a pet, operate a boat or plane, sell liquor or dispense prescription drugs, operate a restaurant or beauty parlor, work as a health-care provider or a real estate broker, or any one of a hundred other types of licensed activities, there are public records of your license holding. If you served in the military, there is a record of your service and the type of discharge you received when you left. When you are married there is a public record. When you have children, their births and school registrations are recorded. If you register to vote, there is a record of your name and address in the state voter registration files (therefore making you eligible for jury duty). If you divorce, there is a public record of the dissolution of the marriage and terms of settlement. If you own real estate and pay taxes on property, there are public records. If you go to court for any reason—as a defendant, a plaintiff, or a witness—there is a public record of your participation in the proceedings. If you work for a public agency and are injured on the job, your worker's compensation claim is a public record. When you die, there is a record of the death.

All of this means that public records are extremely valuable information sources about individuals. News professionals need to conduct background checks on people in the news. Public relations professionals need to conduct research about their clients. Advertising professionals need to locate information about their audiences for messages.

Paul Grabowicz, director of the New Media Program at the University of California at Berkeley Graduate School of Journalism, published a two-part article titled "Researching People on the Internet" that we reprint here in Box 8.1 (with permission, of course!). It summarizes some of the main sources of public record information about individuals. Certainly, many public records are not available via the Internet, and must still be searched using the old-fashioned method of thumbing through paper files and drawers of 3-by-5 cards in public agencies. However, Grabowicz's article provides an insight into the types of public records that are accessible and outlines a general strategy for getting started.

Interviewing Institutional Sources

Institutional interviewees pose special challenges for communicators. Many interviewees are well-trained to talk to communication professionals, wary of saying too much, and sophisticated in their ability to take control of an interview. Particularly for institutional sources such as politicians, business executives, and government spokespersons, you have to be diligent in your preparation and persistent in your questioning to generate anything new or useful from an interview.

As with any other interview, the best strategy for institutional sources is to go into the interview extremely well-prepared. Because they are savvy interviewees, institutional sources will try to take your measure and determine how likely they are to be able to dominate the interview. They can usually tell within the first few questions whether you've done your homework. The best advice is to know your stuff and approach the interview with an attitude of professionalism seasoned with empathy and friendly openness. Assume that institutional interviewees are talking to you in good faith and with the intention of being forthcoming unless and until they prove otherwise.

Sources such as politicians and senior business executives are likely to be surrounded in their day-to-day activities by people who defer to them. They are not used to being asked rude or challenging questions, or to being subjected to criticism about their actions. Therefore, you need to phrase your interview questions in a way that demonstrates respect. It is possible to ask difficult questions while still remaining on friendly terms. For instance, you can ask a politician about a controversial decision by phrasing a question such as, "Some of your critics suggest that your tax proposal will provide huge advantages to the wealthiest citizens at the expense of those in the bottom third of the earning brackets. How do you respond?" This type of question phrasing helps you retain your neutral stance, without putting you in the role of adversary and forcing the interviewee into seeing you as the enemy.

Business executives are especially well-trained not to reveal too much information. They are concerned about revealing something that might affect a company's stock price, about not providing information that might advantage competitors, and about putting their company in a bad light. Assume that a business interviewee has been briefed about you and your media outlet before the interview. Before you can even schedule an interview, you may be asked to provide information about the topic of the interview and some of the questions that might be asked. This forces you to think carefully about your interview purpose and to structure your questions for generating the information you need in the most efficient manner. You will rarely have the chance to go past the allotted amount of time with a business interviewee, so you need to get into the substance of your interview quickly.

■ ■ ■ ■ ■ ▬▬▬▬▬▬▬▬▬▬▬▬▬▬▬▬▬▬▬▬▬▬▬▬

BOX 8.1
SEARCHING PUBLIC RECORDS FOR INFORMATION ABOUT INDIVIDUALS

RESEARCHING PEOPLE ON THE INTERNET—PART I

by Paul Grabowicz

Whether you're working on an investigative project or a breaking news story, one of the most common tasks a reporter faces is doing a background check on a person. Researching public records—property ownership, business ties, professional licenses—is a central part of that.

Those public records databases are increasingly being put on the Internet by government agencies. Finding them is another matter. There is no master database for all the records—you have to go to the Web site of a particular agency to see what's available.

But there are numerous Web sites that track the different public records databases and help you more quickly find what's accessible online in a particular state or locality. This is a guide to how to do a background check on a person that takes you through the different kinds of public records databases, describing what's available and the best Web directories to assist you in locating the records. The services I list here are free—not commercial research sites that charge a fee to do a search for you (which are fine if you have the money—they can be a real time-saver).

Starting Out
It's wise to start by running a person's name through some general Web search engines, especially someone with a common name, to see if you can find any identifying information on the person. Where a person lives or works, their age, or their affiliations with corporations or associations will help you decide which databases in which states, counties or cities to try.

If you can identify someone's profession, for example, then you know to go to the online database of a state agency that license professionals. If you identify where someone lives,

then you'll know which county to check for online property records databases.

Identifying information also will help you sort out which records pertain to the person you're researching and which ones relate to someone who just has the same name. Keep in mind that even a seemingly uncommon name may belong to several people, and you have to be very careful to make sure a public record pertains to the person you're researching.

Search Engines
As a first step, I recommend just typing the person's name into the Google search engine, which has a special ranking system for Web pages that gets high marks from researchers for returning relevant results. There's even a new verb for this kind of search—"googling" someone to find whatever information you can on him or her.

You might also try the same search at *AllTheWeb*, which now claims to have a database of Web sites larger than Google's. And because *AllTheWeb* uses a more traditional method of ranking pages, you may find different Web sites at the top of its list than Google's, especially more obscure sites that may just have a key scrap of information on a person. Again, look for identifying information that turns up in a search, such as age, address and affiliations.

Phone Directories
I also recommend running the person through one of the big online phone directories, again so you can try to find a specific address for the person that might come in handy later in your research.

A good online phone directory is Switchboard. Just type a first and last name into the "White Pages" section at the top to do a nationwide search. Another online white page directory is Bigfoot, which also lets you do a reverse directory search, typing in a phone number or address to see who it belongs to.

(continued)

BOX 8.1   CONTINUED

Now armed with a little more information on the person you're researching, you can start to mine the more specific records databases.

Property Transactions

Some county agencies put their property transaction databases online, usually a summary of property sales or mortgage loans that can be searched by the name of a person.

A good index to these databases is the Web site for NETR Real Estate Research and Information. NETR has a map of the United States you can click on to bring up a list of all the county agencies in a particular state that record property sales (usually recorder's offices). Agencies that have Web pages are noted, and if their property records are available online that is flagged with a "Go to Data Online!" link.

Some counties just list the parties involved in a transaction, such as the buyer and seller of a piece of property or the lender and borrower in a mortgage loan, the date and maybe an identifying number such as an assessor's parcel number for the piece of property.

If you want to look up more specific information you'll have to contact the county office directly. To get phone numbers and addresses for county recorder's offices all over the country, go to Peelle Management Corporation's National Recorders Directory.

Property Ownership

County property ownership records also are frequently available online. But many don't allow a search by a person's name. Instead searches can only be done by street address to find the assessed value of a property (and not ownership information).

Privacy concerns are part of the reason for this, and, in the case of California, legislation that barred release of property ownership records for public officials. Many counties in California simply don't post any ownership records because of the time it would take to sort out which property owners are public officials.

A good index to these county property ownership databases again is NETR. Click on a state in the map of the United States to bring up a list of all the county agencies in that state that track property ownership (usually assessor's offices). Agencies that have Web pages are noted and online databases can be accessed through the "Go to Data Online!" link.

Another index of county assessor's office Web sites is at Portico's Real Estate Online Assessors.

Professional Licenses

All kinds of professions require state licenses—doctors, nurses, accountants, psychologists, contractors, veterinarians, security guards, geologists and so on. Many of these licensee databases are online, sometimes including addresses and information on disciplinary or enforcement actions.

A good index for the state licensing agencies that have online databases is Pacific Information Resources' SearchSystems.net. Pick a state and then scroll down to the entries for "Licenses" for the list of state licensing agencies and links to their online databases.

Another site that has an index of licensing agencies is CLEAR's Directory of Boards of Professional and Occupational Licensure. You also can browse this index by type of professional license.

Lawyers

Probably the best searchable directory of attorneys is the *Martindale-Hubbell Lawyer Locator database,* which is also used by the Web site for the American Bar Association. You can type in an attorney's name and search for a listing anywhere in the United States.

The FindLaw site also has a database of attorneys. At the main FindLaw page scroll down to the "Business" section and click on "Lawyer Directory" on the bottom right. At the new page, in the tab above the main search box, click on "Search by Name."

Doctors

Information on doctors is available at the American Medical Association's Physician Select Web site. Click on the "Search for a Physician" button, accept the terms at the next page, click on the "Physician Name" button at the following page and you'll get a search box. There you can type in a physician's name and the state he/she practices in to get an office address and information on his/her educational background.

For information from state medical boards try the Association of State Medical Board Executive Directors' DocFinder service. This has links to state licensing agencies that have online databases of physicians practicing in those states, sometimes including information on disciplinary actions.

Pilot Licenses and Aircraft Ownership

The Federal Aviation Administration keeps databases on licensed pilots and owners of aircraft. A searchable version of the FAA databases is available on the Web at Landings.com.

To check if someone has a pilot's license, click on "Databases" in the menu at the top. At the new page in the left menu under "Certifications," click on "Pilots."

To check if a person or corporation owns a plane or helicopter, at the Landings home page again click on "Databases" in the menu at the top. At the new page in the left menu under "Registrations" click on "US." At the next screen scroll down on the right and click on "Owner Search."

For ownership information on aircraft in other countries, at the Landings home page again click on "Databases" in the top menu. At the new page in the left menu under "Registrations" click on "World." Then scroll down on the right through the list of countries that have searchable databases available.

Federal Judges

The Federal Judicial Center's Judges of the United States Courts database has biographies of federal judges from district court on up to the U.S. Supreme Court, dating back to 1789. It's searchable by name.

Other Professions

Many other professions have membership organizations that put searchable databases of their members on their Web sites. You often can use these sites to get contact and biographical information on a person (such as schools attended). For a list of the Web pages of professional associations try Yahoo!'s Professional Business Organizations directory.

AllTheWeb.com
www.alltheweb.com/

American Medical Association's Physician Select
www.ama-assn.org/aps/amahg.htm

Association of State Medical Boards Executive Directors' Docfinder
www.docboard.org/docfinder.html

Bigfoot.com
bigfoot.whitepages.com/

CLEAR'S Directory of Boards
www.clearhq.org/boards.htm

FindLaw
www.findlaw.com

Google.com
www.google.com

landings.com
www.landings.com

Martindale-Hubbell Lawyer Locator
lawyers.martindale.com

NETR
www.netronline.com/public_records.htm

NETR Real Estate Research and Information
www.netronline.com/public_records.htm

New Media Program at UC Berkeley
journalism.berkeley.edu/program/newmedia.html

Pacific Information Resources' Searchsystems
www.searchsystems.net

Peelle Management Corporation
www.zanatec.com/multiwin.html

Portico's Real Estate Online Assesors
indorgs.virginia.edu/portico/personalproperty.html

(continued)

BOX 8.1   CONTINUED

Switchboard.com
www.switchboard.com

The Federal Judicial Center's Judges of the United States Courts
air.fjc.gov/history/judges_frm.html

Yahoo!'s Professional Business Organizations
d2.dir.scd.yahoo.com/business_and_economy/
organizations/professional

RESEARCHING PEOPLE ON THE INTERNET—PART II

Now we'll look at researching the businesses and organizations with which a person might be affiliated, as well as checking on political contributions they may have made. And we'll go through other public records that aren't as readily available online, but you can order them over the Internet or at least find where they're physically located.

Business Records

Most states have electronic databases of incorporated businesses and partnerships that file with a Secretary of State's Office or a Department of Corporations. The filings usually include addresses and the names of key executives.

While the databases often are searchable only by the name of a business, some let you type in the name of a person to see if he/she is an officer, director, agent or partner in some business.

A good place to find the state business databases that are online is *Pacific Information Resources' SearchSystems.net* Web site. Click on a state and then scroll down to the listing for "Corporations," which will link you to the online database for that state.

Another index to the Secretaries of State offices with corporation/partnership databases is the *National Association of Secretaries of State.*

Some businesses such as sole proprietorships or small partnerships file "fictitious business name" statements, usually at a county level. These often can be searched by either the name of a business or the name of an owner/partner.

A smattering of online databases of fictitious businesses, especially in California, are available online, and SearchSystems.net is again your best bet for tracking these down. In the "Public Record Locator" search box type the words "fictitious business" (without the quotation marks) and to the right select "Match exact phrase." You'll get a list of the states and counties that have their databases on the Web.

For publicly traded companies (those that sell their stock on a public stock exchange), you can search by corporation name at the U.S. Securities and Exchange Commission's EDGAR Database.

There are many other databases of corporations put online by private organizations and publications that compile information on businesses. Among the most popular are the *Better Business Bureau's Check out a Company, Hoover's Search by Company Name* and the *Thomas Register of American Manufacturers* (you'll have to register to use the Thomas site, but it's free). At each you'll get an address and phone number for the company and the type of business it conducts.

For an extensive list of the various Web sites and services for finding background information on businesses, try CorporateInformation.com's links for privately held companies and for publicly traded companies.

Uniform Commercial Code Filings

Uniform Commercial Code filings are records of loans extended to businesses or people, usually with equipment of some type pledged as collateral. States keep databases listing these UCC creditors and borrowers, and some of those databases are online. To see what's available go to SearchSystems.net. In the "Public Record Locator" search box type "uniform commercial code" (without the quotation marks) and to the right select "Match exact phrase." You'll get a list of states and some counties that have online UCC databases.

Non-Profit Organizations

If the person you're researching is affiliated with a non-profit organization, you usually can find detailed information online on that non-profit, including its annual filing with the IRS. The best site for locating these filings is GuideStar.

GuideStar lets you search by the name of a non-profit organization to get a general description of it, a link to the group's Web site if available, and financial data on the organization such as the detailed Form 990 report that non-profits file with the IRS. For the Form 990 information, after doing a search and calling up the page with the general information on a particular non-profit, look on the left under "Contents" and click on the link for "Form 990." At the new page you can download a copy of the 990 form in Adobe's pdf format.

Many state agencies also keep records on non-profit charitable organizations, and some have put their databases online. In California, for example, that agency is the Registry of Charitable Trusts. For a list of some of the other states that have online databases of charitable groups go to Portico's State Non-Profit Databases.

Political Contributions
Another important step in researching a person is to check for campaign contributions the person has made. Besides getting a list of elected officials the person supports, the campaign contribution filings also list an address for every person making a donation and often a business affiliation.

For contributions to federal campaigns, probably the best site is FECInfo. At that page on the left click on "Donor Name Lookup." At the new page type the name of the person you're researching into the search box and below that select the years ("election cycle") you want to search. If you get a listing showing the person made a donation, click on the "View Image" link at the end of the listing to see a copy of the actual contribution report that includes the donor's address.

To check for databases of donors to state elections, try Investigative Reporters and Editors' Campaign Finance Information Center. There you'll see a list of the state agencies that compile campaign contribution reports and links to their Web sites.

Web Site Registration
Sometimes you'll come across a Web site for a person or for an organization with which that person is affiliated. You can get more information on who is behind that Web site by doing a search at one of the Internet's "whois" sites, such as Allwhois.

Just type the address or URL for the Web site into the search box to get the registered owner of that site, their mailing address, and contact information for the administrator of the site (note: this search is only good for people or organizations that have registered their own Web domain addresses, not for people who use Internet service providers to host their pages, such as Yahoo!'s GeoCities, EarthLink, etc.).

Now for the not so good news—public records databases that are not readily available on the Internet.

Court Records
Court records, especially criminal court documents, are only very slowly going online. Generally only federal and state Supreme Court and appeals court decisions are accessible on the Web. Some federal district courts, federal bankruptcy courts and state superior courts have put their dockets of cases on their Web sites, but those usually are only for pending cases, and the actual documents filed in court are not online. On the other hand, a high profile case sometimes will prompt a court to put some of the major filings in the case online.

A good site for tracking down the Web sites of courts at all levels is FindLaw. The FindLaw site has listings for the Web pages of federal, state and local courts across the country, as well as a multitude of other legal resources.

For federal courts, at the main FindLaw page on the right under the heading for "US Federal Resources" click on "Judicial."

For state and local courts, at the main page click on the right on "US State Resources." At the new page select a state, and at the next screen look for a link to courts.

One Web site does put actual court filings online—for federal class action lawsuits involving allegations of securities law violations by corporations. That's the Stanford Law School Securities Class Action Clearinghouse. At the site there's an alphabetical index by company name to see if a firm has been involved in a securities lawsuit.

(continued)

BOX 8.1   CONTINUED

Vital Records

Only a relative handful of states and counties have free online databases for searching marriage, divorce, birth or death records. The information provided also is often very sketchy, with a fee required to get the full document (some sites have an online order form).

One index to what is available on both the state and county level is Virtual Gumshoe. Scroll down on the left and click on "Vital Records." At the new page click on the right on "United States."

If the vital records database you need is not online, go to the U.S. National Center for Health Statistics' Where to Write for Vital Records Web site. There you'll find instructions on how to order such records along with the addresses, phone numbers and fees charged for the state agencies that have the records.

Voter Registration Records

Only a few counties scattered around the country have their voter registration databases online (in large part because of privacy concerns). One site that has a list of the available databases is Virtual Gumshoe. Scroll down on the left and click on "Voters Records."

Motor Vehicle Records

I don't know of any state motor vehicle departments that have free searchable online databases for obtaining license and registration information. Most DMV's charge a fee for such information and require a request in writing.

For a list of state DMV Web sites and contact information try The Auto Exchange or Virtual Gumshoe (at the Virtual Gumshoe site scroll down on the left and click on "Motor Vehicle Records").

Military Records

I'm also unaware of any free online databases for searching for military service records. But there are a lot of Web sites that assist military personnel and veterans that you can use to try to track down information on someone's military service.

One of the most extensive lists of those sites is again at Virtual Gumshoe. Scroll down on the left and click on "Military." You can order military service records in writing from the federal government. For help on doing that go to the National Personnel Records Center's Access to Military Records by the General Public Web site.

Closing Note

None of the indexes I've listed here can possibly keep up with the constant flow of public records databases online. So if you don't find a particular public agency listed in any of the above resources, try doing a Google search by the name of the agency to locate its Web site. Then prowl around the site—you may find the agency has just put online exactly the records database you're looking for.

Paul Grabowicz is director of the New Media Program *at the University of California at Berkeley Graduate School of Journalism, where he has taught computer-assisted reporting since 1995. He has been a journalist for more than 25 years, for much of that time as the investigative reporter at the* Oakland Tribune. *He has also co-authored* California Inc., *a book describing how entrepreneurism has shaped the politics, culture and economy of California.*

Allwhois
www.allwhois.com

Better Business Bureau
search.bbb.org/search.html

Corporate Information.com
www.corporateinformation.com/uspriv.html

Corporate Information.com: publicly traded companies
www.corporateinformation.com/uscorp.html

FECInfo
www.fecinfo.com

FindLaw
www.findlaw.com

GuideStar
www.guidestar.com

Hoover's Search by Company Name
www.hoovers.com

Investigative Reporters and Editors'
Campaign Finance Information Center
www.campaignfinance.org/linksstate.html

National Association of Secretaries of State
www.nass.org/busreg/busreg.html

National Personnel Records Center's Access
to Military Records by the General Public
www.archives.gov/facilities/mo/st_louis/
military_personnel_records/general_public.html

New Media Program at UC Berkeley
journalism.berkeley.edu/program/newmedia.
html

Pacific Information Resources'
Searchsystems.net
www.searchsystems.net

Portico's State Non-Profit Databases
indorgs.virginia.edu/portico/nonprofits.
html#stdb

Registry of Charitable Trusts
justice.hdcdojnet.state.ca.us/charitysr/default.asp

SearchSystems.net
www.searchsystems.net

Stanford Law School Securities Class
Action Clearinghouse
securities.stanford.edu/companies.html

The Auto Exchange
www.autoexchange.net/dmv

Thomas Register of American Manufacturers
www4.thomasregister.com

U.S. National Center for Health Statistics
www.pueblo.gsa.gov/cic_text/misc/vital-records/
w2welcom.htm

U.S. Securities and Exchange Commission's
EDGAR database
www.sec.gov/edgar/searchedgar/webusers.htm

Virtual Gumshoe
www.virtualgumshoe.com

Paul Grabowicz (grabs@uclink.berkeley.edu) posted: 2002-07-24 modified: 2002-08-01

Source: USC Annenberg Online Journalism Review. Reprinted by permission.

A very important strategy for successful interviews with institutional sources is to gain the trust of your source. That is why it is so important for you to cultivate sources even when you aren't seeking something specific. In other words, identify the people you are likely to need to talk to on a regular basis in your line of work (your ad clients, the government officials on your beat, the PR officers in the businesses you interact with). Talk to those people on a regular basis, just to check in and touch base, and to let them get to know you as a conscientious and professional practitioner. Then, when you need to conduct a formal interview with that person, he or she knows you and knows that you can be trusted to do a good job.

No matter how hard you try, however, there are times when you will need to talk to someone you haven't previously interviewed or who is well-trained to resist your questioning. The most important strategy for you is to stay in control of the interview.

Asking vague questions or demonstrating that you aren't well prepared assures that your savvy interviewee will be in control. Avoid this. Good interviewers know how to establish rapport without fawning, know how to admit when they don't understand something without sounding ill-prepared, and know how to ask sophisticated questions without sounding too clever for their own good.

Well-trained institutional sources can avoid answering questions in any number of creative and frustrating ways. Author Sally Adams lists the strategies that institutional sources (in this case, politicians) use to deflect questions:

- Ignore the question
- Acknowledge the question without answering
- Question the question
- Attack the question
- Decline to answer
- Make a political point, for example attack an opponent
- Give an incomplete answer
- Repeat a previous question
- Claim to have answered the question already[1]

The sophisticated interviewer understands ahead of time that his or her source may use these tactics and knows how to counter. In almost every case, you can get the interviewee back on track by using some stock phrases or understanding responses that demonstrate that you are going to be persistent. For instance, in response to an interviewee who gives an incomplete answer, you can use the stock phrase, "Tell me more about…." In response to an interviewee who ignores a question or acknowledges a question without answering, you can use the stock phrase, "Let's return to the issue of…" And always, ask every institutional interviewee, "How do you know that? What is your evidence?"

Another set of institutional interviews involves the use of surveys or focus groups in advertising and marketing message-making. Many of the tools we discussed earlier in this chapter rely on information generated by survey or focus group interviews with consumers or audience members. More and more strategic communications professionals are relying on online tools to conduct these types of interviews. Online focus groups provide a way to reach participants who might otherwise not be available.

Although the techniques vary slightly, an online focus group is usually conducted as a chat session in a secure (password-protected) area of a company's or agency's Web site. An experienced moderator keeps the session focused and sees that all participants have a chance to contribute. This method of conducting a focus group allows for a geographically diverse set of respondents to participate, eliminating time-consuming travel and reducing costs. Also, certain types of institutional sources are more likely to participate in an online focus group than one conducted in person. For instance, many professionals such as lawyers, doctors, business executives, and managers are comfortable using this type of technology and find this method more convenient than meeting with a group in person.

Researchers using this technique have found that the optimal online focus group calls for six to eight participants who work for no more than 90 minutes in an online discussion. The moderator sees everyone's comments and encourages participants to interact and share their views. The online environment allows the researcher to reproduce high-quality printed information such as ads, logos, and Web pages, and get respondent reactions immediately.[2]

Strategic communications professionals rely heavily on information generated by institutions that use interviews with consumers as the basis for their data collection. Data about audience media habits such as that collected by Simmons or MRI, ratings data collected by Nielsen and Arbitron, and psychographic data collected by companies such as SRI Consulting Business Intelligence, are all generated using interview techniques. Research companies specialize in gathering information using these techniques and sell their interviewing expertise to the agencies and firms that need such data.

CAUTIONS FOR USE

Institutional sources are among the most useful and important information contributors for media practitioners. However, you must use caution with these sources as with any other. In particular, many of the institutions we've identified in this chapter have vested interests in providing you with a particular set of facts or pointing you in a specific direction for your information strategy. Institutions such as trade associations, businesses, lobbying groups, political organizations and government agencies all want to set the agenda in their subject areas and control the parameters of public discourse. For this reason, they will go to great lengths to provide some types of information and withhold other types.

Your job as a communications professional is to understand how to dissect the information you are provided, and how to seek material that you may be steered away from. In Box 8.2, Pulitzer Prize–winning investigative journalist Eric Nalder has advice about how to independently gather information from institutional sources.

In addition to the concerns outlined by Nalder, you must also acknowledge that many of the public records sources we've discussed in this chapter contain errors, omissions, and inaccuracies that can lead you into making serious mistakes. Many public records are generated from handwritten applications or registration cards submitted by hurried citizens and keyboarded into computer files by underpaid and overworked public servants. It is not uncommon to find outdated and superceded information in government databases. The rule of thumb is to check multiple sources, triangulate your information, and reject information if you cannot verify it is recent, accurate, and reliable.

Additional concerns spring up around certain types of institutional information. For instance, the television industry has long complained about the reliability and validity of ratings data. Television professionals argue that the methods for gathering reports about viewers' behavior are, at best, spotty and highly subject to human error.

■ ■ ■ ■ ■

BOX 8.2

INDEPENDENTLY GATHERING INFORMATION FROM INSTITUTIONAL SOURCES

Breaking and Entering
How to Dissect an Organization

by *Eric Nalder*
San Jose Mercury News

In our bellicose jargon, we refer to them as targets...as in "the target of my investigation." Perhaps that's because they pop up like shooting gallery icons in the course of a newspaper reporter's life.

One day a tipster introduced me to the fascinating world of nuclear weapons plants, and then a faulty o-ring sent me packing to a Utah rocket plant. The errant crew of the Exxon Valdez redirected my attention to tanker companies, a screwed up deregulation program in California switched me to electricity and the attack on the World Trade Center caused me to examine airport security. I learned about Coast Guard, the University of Washington football team, the Seattle Fire Department, a bunch of crime labs, the U.S. Department of Housing and Urban Development, the California Governor's office, the Federal Energy Regulatory Commission and the FAA.

If our best stories are told through people, our toughest reporting tasks often involve cracking the associations they form. The challenges are myriad since the 265 million people in this country have created—so far—6.5 million businesses, 1 million non-profit organizations and 85,000 state and local governments. Each has its own culture, and more are being formed every day.

Ergo, the first rule for investigating organizations is to be flexible.

The second rule is that you must stop thinking of them as targets. After all, you are not going to shoot the organization. You will lift off the lid, pull out the parts, read the operating instructions and discover how it works.

Then you may expose its flaws, and in the process write some meaningful poetry.

First, though, you must lift off the lid.

The manual for dissecting an organization starts with basic questions:

- Who are the players?
- Who is in charge?
- Who are the regulators?
- What are the rules?
- How are things done?
- Where are the mistakes recorded?
- Where is the spending recorded?
- Who knows the story and how can I get it?

To answer these questions, here are some suggestions.

WHO ARE THE PLAYERS?

Lists: Every organization and government agency has payroll lists and phone books, which are frequently available on computer disc or online (one example: The California On-Line Directory, www.cold.ca.gov). Scan government agency phonebooks for a library or research center and contact the record keepers to learn more about what is in their files and data collections. Visit them if possible. For the government agencies you cover, routinely make FOIA or state public disclosure requests for the best documents and databases, as well as the job-application resumes and personnel files. At private companies, cultivate helpful employees to provide the same. A company librarian might be helpful. In all cases, be sure to ask for outdated payroll rosters and phone books to get the names of former employees (a computer can be used to compare the lists and pop out the names of ex-employees).

Newsletters: Most organizations publish internal newsletters that contain employee names, and other bonus information. Writing about a secretive Army Ranger battalion—which had a classified roster—I gleaned a third of the names from a year's worth of the post newspapers at the Ft. Lewis library, just because the Rangers were frequently mentioned as accomplished athletes.

Associations: Contact professional associations and unions since they sometimes give out rosters, and they publish newsletters. They also hold annual conventions where you can meet lots of potential sources. Books on file in the library have lists of professional associations.

Courts: Check the local courts for lawsuits that might list employees, and keep in mind that disgruntled workers who have sued the firm or agency are sometimes good sources of information. Even an innocuous suit involving a land dispute might contain helpful names. Be on the lookout for depositions.

Whistle-blowers: State personnel boards and the U.S. Merit Systems Protection Board in Washington D.C. have on public file the names of government employees who have appealed disciplinary actions. Some cases involve whistle-blowing. For towns and counties, check the local civil service commission. To contact people who have submitted confidential ethical, consumer, environmental and-or safety complaints to state, federal or even private agencies (like the Better Business Bureau), try getting around the confidentiality requirements by asking the agency to forward a letter from you to the complainants.

Licenses and Permits: State licensing bureaus provide lists of a wide variety of professionals who have state permits, including real estate agents, surveyors, undertakers, manicurists, architects, and nurses. You can frequently search for them by company name. The FAA has the names of pilots employed at an airline. The Coast Guard registers crew members on U.S.-flagged merchant ships, but don't overlook information available from companies representing international flags like International Registry Inc. in Reston, Va. (Marshall Islands) and the Liberian International Ship and Corporate Registry in Vienna, Va.

Contracts: Contracts with government agencies frequently include the names of the employees who work for contractors. For example, a housing authority applying for a HUD grant often includes resumes of key employees and officers.

Bankruptcy: Federal bankruptcy court records are a gold mine, since they contain, among other things, the names of employees who were stiffed for their wages and lists of creditors who might know the names of other sources.

Newspaper morgue: Stories mentioning the organization will contain useful names, and don't ignore obituaries which will open the door to family connections or routine lists in the business section of people promoted, etc.

Old city directories: Newspaper and public libraries have old copies of the city directories that list the place of employment of local residents.

Newsroom sources: Interview your fellow reporters because they might know of people in the organization or other sources.

Outsiders: You can get information on employees from a company's customers, suppliers and competitors. And remember, too, union leaders and shop stewards. Companies have lawyers and accountants, and sometimes they have ex-lawyers and ex-accountants. Ex-wives of company bosses can also be helpful. And don't assume that a banker won't tell you anything.

Gripes: Try the people who register their gripes with the Better Business Bureau, or the city licensing agency, or the licensing department, or in letters to the editor.

Hangouts: To meet sources, hang out at the restaurants, bars and cafes located near the company office. Or maybe there's a gym where the troops play basketball.

Tour: Take a tour of the agency. Meet people. Take note of the names you see on desktops and on those little magnetized "in" and "out" signs that are frequently located at the receptionist's desk.

Interviews: The best sources, of course, are the employees themselves. When you interview them, ask each one to tell you what they know about the others. You can quickly build a roster this way. Ultimately you want to know how people interact, and who is the best source for each type of type of information. If you already have a payroll list or phone book, or you have built a dossier (see next item) read out the names to prompt your interview subject's memory. During one recent investigation, I had each

(continued)

BOX 8.2   CONTINUED

interview subject go through a roster and by do-ing so I developed very useful dossiers.

When an employee tells you something important, always follow-up with the question: "How do you know that?" The answer will frequently include the names of other players.

Dossier: Enter all the information you gather on each person into a computer database. I use Excel. On my database, from left to right, I provide cells for last name, first name, middle initial and a code word for the person's role (i.e., "manager", "supplier", "union"). Going further right, I provide a cell for comments that includes information on their likes, dislikes, any behavior or act that is significant to my story, connections and notable quotes, etc. Next are cells for date of birth, phone numbers (office, home, cell, fax, etc), address, employer and perhaps other identifiers.

WHO IS IN CHARGE?

Government: It's relatively easy to obtain a roster of bosses at government agencies. Resumes should be available and much of the personnel file should be open for your perusal. Pay attention to the place where the bosses formerly worked, because you can learn a lot about them there. Verify what they have said on their resume. Do background checks on former employees using on-line resources.

Disclosure: Elected officials, of course, file documents disclosing their finances and campaign contributions, but keep in mind that the top appointed officials at the federal and local level must frequently do the same. Check out your state, county or city ethics commission. Do background checks on major campaign contributors. Use a database to group contributors by industry and-or interest group. Arrange contributions by date and look for clusters that might indicate who is influencing the person in charge.

The unofficial hierarchy: Learn about the shadow bosses. Sometimes a member of the city council runs the show at city hall more than the mayor, or a particular contractor has more power within a state agency than the director. Ask employees about this. Request the desk calendars of the bosses to learn who they meet with regularly, and get travel records along with an itinerary.

Private companies: One of the best resources is Dun and Bradstreet. The free version of a Dun and Bradstreet report has bare bones information, but the $100 version is much better. Another source of the names is your state's corporations office. In addition, the county recorder keeps records regarding limited partnerships. Loan documents on file at your state's Uniform Commercial Code office frequently contain names and social security numbers. Credit reports are available online. The local Chamber of Commerce might have information as well. Of course, the company phone book is a key. Service club directories contain names of company leaders. Bankruptcy records point fingers of blame when a company gets into financial trouble. Keep in mind as well that employees, suppliers and customers can provide additional information on informal hierarchies. Who does it/he/she contribute to? How much? Why? What do the politicians who received donations say about your subject? Does the business have its own PAC? Many large companies, including privately held ones, do. And if they've got a PAC, they've got to file with the FEC and, often, with state and municipal authorities as well (often there'll be two PACS, one for federal elections, one for state). If a company has its own PAC take a close look at who contributes to it. You'll most likely find key company officers and, perhaps, friends or business associates who can offer other avenues for reporting. A particularly good web site for FEC data is: www.tray.com/fecinfo.

Publicly traded companies: The Edgar site operated by the Securities and Exchange Commission (www.sec.gov/edgar.shtml) provides valuable documents such as the 10K and the proxy (known as Def 14A). These have names of executive officers including their wages and perks, age, title, time with the company, familial relationships and a brief biographical description. Annual reports, available from the company's investor relations office, contain more puffery but have additional valuable information. Ask the relations office for resumes on company officers. Stock analysts are a great source of information on company bosses and on the informal hierarchy. Lists of stock analysts are available in *Nelson's Directory of Investment Research* and *Bloomberg News*. Be aware of possible bias if the analyst works for a brokerage house that serves as the company's investment banker.

Non-Profits: The IRS 990 form contains the names you want plus financial information. Non-profit organizations are required to release the 990 if you ask for the document at the office during normal business hours. You can also fax your request to the IRS. The proper address in our region is the office of Return and Income Verification Services, Ogden (Utah) Service Center, 801-620-6671. The reply should take 30 days. Dan Langan, formerly with the National Charities Information Bureau, says you'll get quicker service from the IRS if you cite the IRS code and **do not** cite FOIA. Keep in mind that some 30 states require charities to keep their 990s on file with the state, and you will frequently get quicker service there. The agency in Washington is the Charities Division of the Secretary of State. GuideStar (www.guidestar.org) is a good online source for 990 forms. It contains PDF images of actual 990s filed by many non-profits.

Other sources: Nothing is more valuable than the contacts you make with secretaries and clerks. Take a tour of the company. Sometimes these are offered to the general public. Talk to competitors, suppliers and customers. Check court files and interview the litigants. Talk to the boss' neighbors and his buddies at the golf and country club.

WHO ARE THE REGULATORS?

Federal government: The inspector general offices for each federal agency have web sites, and a directory for them is located on Ignet at www.ignet.gov. You can search inspector general reports by key word or topic. The General Accounting Office is a good resource, as are the internal audit agencies (i.e., the Army Audit Agency, etc.). Cultivate sources at the audit agencies. Staff members from congressional committees are sometimes helpful, and there are directories that can help you locate them. The U.S. Merit Systems Protection Board and the U.S. Office of Special Counsel receive complaints on personnel issues. Check the court files and the Federal Election Commission.

State and local governments: The state auditor's office is a good starting place, but don't forget legislative committees and the city council staffers, as well as the various offices of internal audit. The state attorney general's office and the state police conduct investigations at state agencies. Each government agency has an office that answers complaints and claims. Remember the personnel office, the unions and OSHA. For police, there is the office of internal investigations and frequently there is an ombudsperson.

Private companies: You might locate some government audits if the company has a government contract. The GAO and the IG might also get involved. The SEC acts as a regulator for publicly traded companies and, in an ad hoc way, so do the various stock analysts. What kind of business is your company engaged in? If it is involved in a regulated business—as most are—then you can get information from a variety of sources; i.e., for transportation companies you can get reports from, among others, the FAA, ICC, NTSB, local state highway police and (if waterbourne) the U.S. Coast Guard. The city business registrar will have some basic information. The city engineering and building departments, and the county assessor, will have data on the structures that the company owns. As mentioned before, the state licensing department might have complaints filed against licensed professionals. The Uniform Commercial Code Office keeps a record of loans. The state revenue department will have some releasable information. OSHA and your state labor office will supply reports on safety and wage-and-hour complaints (you can also look up OSHA inspection reports online at www.osha-slc.gov/oshstats). It might even be relevant to ask the police and fire departments for records on emergency calls to the business location. Check the court files for lawsuits, of course, and the Better Business Bureau for complaints. (Council of Better Business Bureaus has information on businesses and charities at www.bbb.org.)

Non-profit: While the IRS 990 form is one good source of information, an even better

(continued)

BOX 8.2   CONTINUED

one is the audited financial statement. Under some circumstances, charities are required to release their financial statements. Langan gives the example of public TV and radio stations which are required by agreement with the Corporation for Public Broadcasting to make their financial statements publicly available. In some cases, charities file their audited financial statements with the state. Or you can always ask the people at the non-profit agency to give you a copy. If they don't, ask them why they are not willing to release it.

Watchdogs on the perimeter: Organizations like the Government Accountability Project receive whistleblower complaints, while environmental organizations take care of the dirty discharges and poisonous products. Your library will have a list of private organizations that watchdog various businesses. Lawyers who have sued the company might also be aware of organizations, and-or groups of complainants. Canvass the neighborhoods surrounding a company for activists who might keep an eye on the place, and cruise the Internet. Think about the work that the company performs, and imagine what kind of people might come in contact with that work. I found information about tanker companies among the ship pilots, tugboat drivers and oil terminal operators. Use your imagination.

WHAT ARE THE RULES?

Government agencies: You'll be buried for too long if you try to read every law and regulation that affects your agency. Learn to use the indices in the federal law, and the code of federal regulations, to more precisely locate the sections that apply to your subject. For a shortcut, watchdog agencies and organizations can point you to the relevant language. You can get a government agency to do the work for you by filing a FOIA request asking for any and all laws, regulations or internal policies that apply to whatever you are writing about.

Private companies: Use the same process, but in this case go to the government regulators who oversee the business. Find the laws and reg-

ulations that they are empowered to enforce. Remember, too, that there are general laws governing the operation of a company—taxes, unfair consumer and labor practices, wages, etc.— that might be relevant. Various agencies, like the Labor Department, administer those laws and they can help you with the details.

Internal regulations: Agencies, non-profit organizations and companies all have their own internal policies and regulations. Request them from government agencies and get someone inside the private organization to provide you with the rulebook.

The history: When you find the rules and regs you are looking for, read the legislative history and interview the experts to learn how the law or regulation came into being. Local county law libraries are a good source for looking up older state-level statute changes. In California, the Senate and Assembly websites contain information on legislative histories. You might find that the old problems that were supposed to be fixed by the new law haven't gone away. Or you might find that new problems have arisen as an unintended consequence of the law. You can also locate the people who spurred the change in regulations, and get their perspective on current events.

HOW ARE THINGS DONE?

Tactical plan: Once you have a grasp of your subject, sketch out a plan for figuring out how the organization works. As a general rule, you should file your FOIA requests to the government agencies early in the process. While the agency is deciding whether to honor your request, you will be getting to know some employees who will leak the documents to you.

People trail: Decide who you are going to interview and in what order. Sometimes you must catch certain people quickly before they are scared off. Other times you must circle them, talking to their friends and associates. Also decide where you are going to interview people. It is frequently best to talk with them at the place where they are doing the thing you are writing about. But sometimes you might want to surprise them at home, where they are likely to be more candid. Talk over the plan with your editor and your fellow reporters.

Getting the inside story: Once you have your roster of players, you'll need an insider to guide you to the players who are most likely to talk freely about the hidden stuff. Find the home addresses for those people and visit them at a convenient and non-threatening time (7 p.m. is often good). Tell them you are working on a story and you could really use their help. Offer a brief rundown of the story you are working on because, sometimes, their curiosity about your story will get you in the door. And telling them something about your story is a good way to prompt them to give you more information. It also helps to use your roster and ask the person about others in the company. People are sometimes more comfortable talking about others rather than themselves. If that doesn't work, apologize for the intrusion and appear as though you are backing off. Get the person to talk about something else. Anything else. Maybe you noticed an unusual plant next to the walkway, or the family dog, or something on the wall that indicates a hobby. Say something about it. As a general rule, if you can get people talking about anything, you can gently move them back to the subject you are interested in. As you move back to the subject that interests you, start with non-threatening questions. Ask the person about their work, and then ask what they know about the person or the problem you are interested in. If the interview subject balks, reassure them that they are not the only person you are talking with and "it's really no big deal." You explain that what you need as a reporter is a little help. Be honest. As you get to the most important stuff, it's important for you to organize your approach. Follow a chronology. When the person says something significant, always ask—"How do you know that?" That question is a perfect door opener to other sources, and for some reason it usually gets people to say more. Also ask for examples. When a person tells you that the bosses are unfair, ask for an example. And always ask people to suggest other ways of getting the information you need, and other sources. "If you were working on this story, how would you do it?"

More on the paper trail: Get your hands on the memo traffic, the emails and the internal letters, whether you are using FOIA with a government agency or a mole at a private company. If the agency or company is in trouble, or if rules are being violated, there will be plenty of memos. Make sure you follow the memo trail to the end. Audits, of course, are helpful. Travel records and desk calendars are good sources of information. It is very important, at some point, that you visit the department that keeps the records and meet the record keepers. Drop in unannounced, if that's possible, and do so in a friendly and casual manner. Ask for a tour. Your goal will be a detailed explanation of the records system in the agency or company. An alternative is the midnight visit. If a source works the graveyard shift, ask if they can bring you to work one day and give you a tour (as long as it is legal).

WHERE ARE THE MISTAKES RECORDED?
Anecdotal: As you meet with sources, ask people to tell you where the mistakes are written down. Every company and government agency has a system. Sometimes there is more than one place where the mistakes are recorded. At Department of Energy nuclear weapons plants, for example, some screw ups were described in "Unusual Occurrence Reports" and others were memorialized in "Off Normal Reports." There were also audits, internal memos, internal letters and surveillance reports.

Paper Trail: Government agencies are required to release lists of relevant documents. With private companies, you've got to ask people to describe the system (more on that later).

WHERE IS THE SPENDING RECORDED?
Anecdotal: Besides the obvious internal sources, you might find yourself a friendly private auditor who has dealt with the company or agency you are examining. Be wary of organizations that keep two sets of books. It does happen. If necessary, try to find a mole within the bookkeeper's office by visiting people at home.

(continued)

BOX 8.2   CONTINUED

Paper trail: Reading a balance sheet is never easy. Find yourself an expert, maybe an inside source or perhaps someone from the accounting office in your own newspaper. Remember that a balance sheet shows you how the money was spent, and a budget shows you how they planned to spend the money. You'll want both. Be sure to follow the budget trail. Get the budget proposal made by the agency head to the agency chief executive, and the one submitted by the CEO to the council or legislature. Look for stuff that gets lopped off or added, and read the narrative to learn more about the agency's needs.

WHO KNOWS THE STORY AND HOW CAN I GET IT?

After you have made your document requests, and toured the plant, you need an excuse to move in. Sometimes the best excuse is the simple act of copying documents.

Whether you have made a FOIA request of a government agency, or talked a company into sharing some of its records with you, you can win friends by offering to help with the copying. Once you get there, get yourself assigned to a table, and ask directions to the restroom and the soft drink machine. Be courteous and don't get in the way. Meet people. Chat. Listen to conversations. Basically, you want to become a part of the operation. Doing so, you will witness stuff you would never see in the annual report.

Come up with an excuse to return several times. Move around with confidence. Act like you belong. Act like they are lucky to have you there.

Ask people to retrieve records for you, and accompany them to the file cabinets. Learn how the filing system works, and offer to pull out the stuff yourself. Pretty soon you'll get direct access to the records.

Drop in on the bosses several times. Have valid questions, don't be a pest, but get them accustomed to talking with you several times. Ease them into informal conversations.

If something important happens—a critical meeting, an accident or a major incident—be there. Instruct your sources to inform you whenever they expect a significant event. If necessary, ask sources to keep diaries for you on what goes on in the office.

If your story involves a factory, get down on the floor and learn how to operate the machinery. Don the protective clothing that the workers wear, and handle the same tools. If you are writing about crooked cops, hang out with the cops. It pays to be on the scene. The best interviews are conducted with the eyes, as well as the voice and ears. Be there, and you will be aware.

If people are nervous about giving you access, explain to them that you can write more accurately about their operation if you have firsthand knowledge.

Organizing your material is your best method for cracking the code inside any establishment.

As you collect information, organize it into two major files. One is a chronology and the other is the dossier, which I described earlier.

I usually start building a chronological database when I begin reporting. I use an Excel database. The chronology will contain an entry for every event, large or small, that is described or simply mentioned in records, clips or interviews. On my Excel file, from right to left, I have a cell for the date when something happened and another for code words describing where in my story that event might be relevant (i.e. "Governor" for anything pertaining to the Governor). Next is a cell that describes any information I have on the event or on the people involved in the event. Next is a cell describing where in my files or interview notes that event is mentioned. You can have other cells as well. For example, another cell might remind you of reporting tasks (I also make "to do" lists separately).

You can organize the chronology by date or subject matter. You can create small subchronologies. Scanning them, you will discover relationships between events. It may tell your story for you. And as you write, it is a powerful writing tool.

Before you write, decide what the story is. A poorly written investigative piece is usually the work of a disorganized reporter who is not sure of the point.

If you cannot write with authority, then you are not ready to write. Do more reporting.

Thanks to the following people for their help: Leigh Poitinger, Rick Tulsky, Pete Carey, Mark Gladstone, Duff Wilson, Stanley Holmes, Tom Boyer, Tom Brown, Dan Langan, Deborah Nelson, Greg Heberlein and David Boardman.

Source: Eric Nalder, *San Jose Mercury News.* Reprinted by permission.

Asking viewers to keep detailed diaries about programs they watched, or asking them to use devices such as the people meter which requires viewers to punch in and punch out as they come and go from the television viewing room, begs for trouble. The selection of the households used in the samples is also problematic. There has always been a bias toward households with more urban, more technically savvy, and younger viewers, because they are more likely to agree to have their houses wired for data collection and participation in the process. And Nielsen is only now starting to address how to measure television viewing that takes place outside the home—in bars, offices, student lounges, and so on. The ratings service providers argue that they strive mightily to adjust their samples and weight their data to provide a fair representation of the overall viewing population, but there is always room for criticism.

What this means for you as a communications professional is that you have to analyze these information sources with an eye toward understanding their weaknesses as well as their strengths, and try to supplement your information searches with as many different sources of evidence as possible. We discuss more specific techniques of evaluating information in Chapter 11.

CASE STUDY OF INSTITUTIONAL INFORMATION SOURCES

The article in Box 8.3 that appeared in the *Sun-Sentinel* (Ft. Lauderdale, Fla.) is a good example of the use of public records and institutional sources on deadline. Note that the writers used monitoring, searching, and interviewing techniques when tapping into the institutional sources.

SELECTED ADDITIONAL READINGS

Burwell, Helen, Carl R. Ernst, and Michael Sankey. *Online Competitive Intelligence: Increase Your Profits Using Cyber-Intelligence.* Facts on Demand Press, 1999.
Business Information Handbook: Munich, Germany: K. G. Saur, 2002.

■ ■ ■ ■ ■ ▬▬▬▬▬▬▬▬▬▬▬▬▬▬▬▬▬▬▬▬▬▬▬

BOX 8.3

USING PUBLIC RECORDS AND INSTITUTIONAL SOURCES ON DEADLINE

Lost Kids Easily Found: Sun-Sentinel Turns Up Nine of DCF's Missing Children

By Sally Kestin, Diana Marrero, and Megan O'Matz, Staff Writers
Posted August 11 2002

Florida's child welfare system has been unable to locate more than 500 children under its care, some of them missing for a decade or more.

But a Sun-Sentinel search for 24 South Florida children on the missing list turned up nine—two in under three hours.

The Department of Children & Families has been a target of intense criticism and scrutiny since April, when the agency admitted it had lost 5-year-old Rilya Wilson of Miami, who is still missing. No caseworker had checked on her for 15 months.

As of last month, DCF could not account for 532 children who the agency said had run away from foster homes or had been abducted by parents against court order

The Sun-Sentinel, however, discovered that it is possible—even easy—to locate some of the youngsters.

The newspaper examined 24 cases involving Broward, Palm Beach and Miami-Dade county children primarily under age 4 whose profiles were available through the Florida Department of Law Enforcement. Although the paper did not have access to more detailed DCF files, by using public records and interviewing relatives the Sun-Sentinel found more than one-third of the 24 children in four weeks.

Two sisters missing since 1997 have been living in Wisconsin with their mother, whose phone number is listed in directory assistance.

Four Miami brothers missing since January are routinely seen in their Overtown neighborhood—a mile from DCF offices. The boys are playing football in a city-sponsored league and have not been in school for at least half a year.

The newspaper found a Miami boy who was missing for almost two years visiting a relative at the same North Miami Beach address DCF had given to police after the child disappeared.

One youth, reporting as missing in February, was found with his mother in Miami.

Another boy was located in the Dominican Republic by calling two relatives and a friend. DCF has been unable to find him for almost eight years.

'UNDER OUR NOSES'

"It's such an indictment of the department and our system," said state Rep. Nan Rich, D-Weston, a member of the child and family security committee. "To think they're right here in our own community, listed in a phone directory or playing football, and somehow the department has not taken the resources to find these children. They're right here under our noses."

DCF officials in Tallahassee and Miami did not respond to repeated requests for interviews. The agency released a statement Friday evening, saying that in the cases of four children found by the Sun-Sentinel, "appropriate actions had already, in fact, been taken and the locations of the children are known to DCF personnel."

The statement did not identify the four children, and DCF officials did not respond to messages seeking comment.

All nine children were still considered missing by police, and as of Saturday, remained on the Florida Department of Law Enforcement's missing children Web site.

DCF administrators in Broward County said they do look for missing children. "I believe we treat [the cases] seriously enough, but it's apparent there are efforts that we haven't made or could be making," said Mary Allegretti, DCF deputy district administrator in Broward.

The agency's limited resources make searching for children difficult, said Jack Moss, DCF district administrator in Broward.

"If we had one person working on it for three weeks, what do we forgo?" he asked. "We have a fixed amount of assets."

Top DCF officials and the governor have insisted that Rilya's disappearance is an isolated case. Her caregiver claims a DCF worker took the child and never returned her. The department has no record of moving the girl.

"Have other children been lost for 12 or 13 months? No," Gov. Jeb Bush said on a television talk show in May.

Yet some of the 532 children DCF lists as runaways or victims of abductions have been missing for as long as 14 years. Eight are considered endangered, meaning police believe their physical safety is at risk.

When a DCF child goes missing, the agency's policies require caseworkers to immediately notify law enforcement and missing children centers. They must also obtain a "pick-up" order from a judge, authorizing law enforcement to take a child into custody.

But the Sun-Sentinel found repeated violations of those policies:

- In 20 of the 24 cases reviewed by the newspaper, DCF waited at least a month to file police reports. In six cases, the delay was four to seven years.
- In more than half the cases, it took the agency up to four months to obtain a court pick-up order.
- In 10 cases, DCF waited a year or longer to notify the Florida Department of Law Enforcement's missing children center.
- In only one case did missing children centers have a usable photo of the child, despite a DCF policy in effect since March 1999 requiring workers to have current pictures of youths under their care. Without a picture, authorities lose a valuable tool in locating missing children.

"The intent here is to get a poster [on a missing child] up on our Web site as soon as possible," said Ben Ermini, director of the missing children's division of the National Center for Missing & Exploited Children. "That's really how we find kids. Somebody thinks they know the child and calls us."

Delays in notifying authorities often leave a cold trail.

"Every minute that a child goes missing determines whether they live or die," said Sherry Friedlander, founder of A Child is Missing, a Fort Lauderdale agency that assists law enforcement in finding missing children.

MISSED OPPORTUNITIES

Teenage runaways and children thought to be abducted by parents often are low priorities for police and social workers nationwide, Ermini said.

"Very often, they take a police report, enter the child into [a national crime database] and very little follow-up is done," he said. "They should be investigated just like any other case. Every year, we have cases where children are injured or killed because they're in danger with a parent."

Keylan Golden, 4, of Hollywood, is an example. He has been missing for more than two years, but the Sun-Sentinel learned he has been living in motels and apartments with his drug-addicted parents who are in and out of jail.

Authorities missed several opportunities to find the boy, considered by police to be endangered. Atlanta police have arrested his parents at least three times this year, but officers had no way of knowing about Keylan because authorities in Florida failed to obtain warrants.

The boy's aunt, Robin Dillon of Boynton Beach, said she called the child's DCF worker and supervisor in May to tell them that his mother, Regina Fisher, was in an Atlanta jail.

"I told them the name of the detention center, and I gave them the [phone] number," Dillon said. "I had peace of mind knowing they're finally going to pick this child up."

At DCF's request, the social services agency in Georgia went to an address where

(continued)

BOX 8.3   CONTINUED

Fisher had been living but did not find the child, Allegretti said. She did not know whether anyone contacted Fisher in jail.

Hollywood Detective Timothy McKenna, who is investigating Keylan's case, said the child's caseworker never notified him about Fisher's arrest in Atlanta. "Gee, I wish I would have known that," he said. "If we would have known that, we could have contacted officials in Atlanta."

Unlike the nationwide, high-profile cases of children who were snatched from their beds or a sidewalk, children who disappear from the child welfare system do not get search parties, public TV announcements or widespread news coverage. Police say they try to find the children, but by the time DCF reports them as missing, the leads are often cold.

"They don't have pictures. They don't have dental records," said North Miami Police Officer Lucrecia Burleson. "The addresses they were missing from, no one of course lives there anymore."

Efforts to find the children are further hampered by DCF's sloppy record keeping.

Since the beginning of the year, FDLE's Missing Children Information Clearinghouse has received more than 450 reports from DCF. The clearinghouse was unable to enter 64 of those cases because DCF failed to provide adequate or legible information about the children.

"We couldn't read the forms," said Pat Rutherford, a clearinghouse analyst. "A contact person wasn't there. The name was misspelled."

In the case of missing Vanna and Zachary Ward, ages 9 and 2, FDLE lists their mother as Stephanie Ward, but a Miami Police Department report has it as Shaphen Wade.

FINGERPRINTING

DCF's internal tracking log for missing children in Miami-Dade County conflicts with police reports on critical information, such as birth dates and when the children went missing. In June, DCF revised its policy on missing children in part to help reduce errors. Each of the 15 regional districts must now designate an administrator to ensure that information sent to FDLE's clearinghouse is complete and accurate.

The National Center for Missing & Exploited Children recently has been getting reports from DCF faster than in the past, Ermini said.

"I think it's getting better," he said. "I think it's probably a result of the Rilya Wilson case."

Statewide, DCF is in the process of fingerprinting all children in its care, Allegretti said. In Broward, the Sheriff's Office has agreed to assist DCF by assigning analysts to do record searches on missing families. "We need to have trained investigators that have the ability and time to concentrate on looking for the children," Moss said.

Miami Police Detective Angel Travieso said the number of missing children cases has spiked since Rilya Wilson's disappearance. Seven detectives on the force, he said, devote at least some of their time to trying to find missing children, but more are needed.

"Really, we need about 20 detectives to look for these kids. We do the best we can do with what we have."

The state's continued inability to find the children shows Florida's child protection system is failing, Rep. Rich said.

"The system is broken, and we need to start over. How much does it take for the governor and legislative leaders to say this is enough?"

Source: Sun Sentinel (Ft. Lauderdale, Fla.) Reprinted by permission. *Sun-Sentinel* researcher Kathryn Pease contributed to this report.

Crittenden, Pam and Michael Sankey, Eds. *The Sourcebook to Public Record Information: The Comprehensive Guide to County, State & Federal Public Records Sources*, 3rd edition, Business Resources Bureau, 2001.

King, Dennis, *Get the Facts on Anyone*, 3rd edition, Arco Pub, 1999.

Sankey, Michael L., Peter J. Weber, and James R. Flowers, Eds. *Public Records Online*, 3rd rev. edition. New York: Facts on Demand Press, 2000.

NOTES

1. Sally Adams, *Interviewing for Journalists* (London: Routledge, 2001): 106.

2. Paul Jacobson, "Focus on the Consumer," *American Advertising* 12, no. 4 (Winter 1996–97): 28–29.

CHAPTER NINE

SCHOLARLY SOURCES

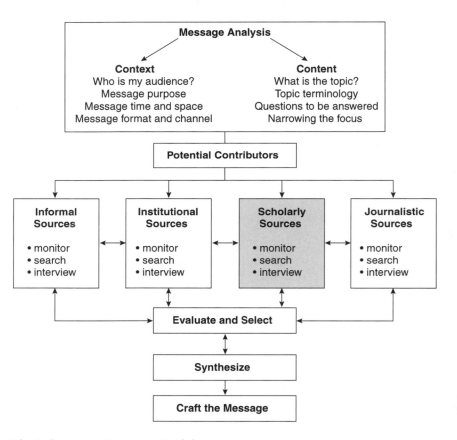

The Information Strategy Model

As we discussed in Chapter 2, scholarly sources include materials produced by subject experts working in academic institutions, research centers, and scholarly organizations. Most information created by scholars is produced, collected, and arranged according to subject areas, or *disciplines*, which are knowledge-producing and -disseminating systems. Scholars have their own ways of sharing information among themselves and with their audiences. Sometimes referred to as the *invisible college*, these are groups of scholars who talk with one another on the telephone and at conferences, exchange e-mails and listserv messages, review first drafts of one another's papers, share progress reports, and publish informal newsletters for the in-group of people working on an idea. As with the other contributors to the information strategy, scholarly sources exist in their own universe and you need to know how to unlock the information that is most useful for your message.

TYPES OF SCHOLARLY SOURCES AND HOW THEY KNOW WHAT THEY KNOW

The main objective of scholarly sources is to report on new knowledge or experimentation and to share that information with the appropriate specialist audiences. Scholarly journal articles, research reports, conference papers, books, reference guides, and the myriad of other formats for scholarly information delivery reflect this purpose. As discussed in Chapter 5, scholarly sources undergo the process of *peer review*, during which the ideas are subjected to close scrutiny by experts in the field, who decide whether the information is fit to be published and shared with the scholarly audience.

In an extensive research study that examined how scientists use scholarly scientific journals, Tenopir and King found that scientists consistently say scholarly journal articles are the most important information resource for their field. The amount of scientific knowledge recorded in these journals doubles every fifteen to seventeen years, and scientists must keep current or risk failure in their profession. Scientists use journals for research, teaching, current awareness, background reading, and many other purposes. Use of peer-reviewed electronic scholarly journals is escalating. Readers expect that the work they find in these publications, print or electronic, has undergone rigorous review.[1]

Making distinctions between types of disciplines may help you determine the types of scholarly information sources that are most useful for your purposes. The clearest distinction is between the sciences and the humanities. The scientist and the humanist use different research methods and study different phenomena. They publish their findings in forms that are characteristic of their disciplines and make these documents available through a variety of print and electronic tools.

Scientists seek experimental validity by studying the natural world and examining the regularities or irregularities that seem to govern natural phenomena. Their methods must be open to scrutiny and, in the best of circumstances, must be reproducible by others following the same procedures. Experimental validity, rather than individual interpretation of events or phenomena, is paramount. Immediacy in sharing results is very important for professionals in the scientific fields, so scientists rely on the research report and journal article.

The humanist's method is shaped for interpretive validity; that is, the humanist tries to interpret a poem, a painting, a novel, or a musical score by presenting an interpretation that will be considered valid. Humanists study the products of human imagination and combine a personal, unique perspective with the framework of accepted concepts and knowledge that their discipline provides. Humanists rely on books as the primary method of expressing their knowledge of a field because the book allows the in-depth exploration of context that characterizes humanistic investigation.

Social and policy scientists rely on a combination of experimental and interpretive methods. They have adopted the scientific method for much of their work and exhibit the same concern for openness and validity exhibited by scientists. However, because the subject of much of their study is human social activity, social scientists work interpretively as well. For the most part, they are concerned with the present and with the implications of their work in social organizations and in public decision making. Social and policy scientists publish their findings in a number of forms. Journals are important, but research reviews, yearbooks, and handbooks are also valuable.

It is easy to understand why scholars share their work among themselves, but why would scholars want to share their information with you as a communications professional? For one thing, scholars are as eager as anyone else to have their work recognized and appreciated. Taking a call from a reporter or public relations specialist seeking the most reliable expert on a particular subject is an ego-boost for the scholar who is used to toiling in relative anonymity in the quiet of the academic or research center environment. Another motivation for scholars to talk to you is that they might be conducting their work with the help of a grant or financial backing from a foundation or research organization that would appreciate wider distribution of the findings and a larger public audience for the organization's work.

In fact, it is your job as a communications professional to ask scholars who is supporting their work financially. It is not unusual for scholars to have grants from large companies (pharmaceutical companies, for instance) or government agencies (the U.S. Department of Defense, for instance), and the work they do may reflect the interests or priorities of the funding source. Scholars typically must reveal their funding sources in manuscripts they submit to journals for peer review so the experts reviewing the work know who "paid the piper" and who may be "calling the tune." This is not to disparage the independence of scholars who work with grant funding, but to alert you, as the information seeker, to ask for full disclosure about the nature of the funding of the scholarly work you intend to use in your research.

Much of the work you do as a communications professional requires you to range across many disciplines of knowledge and skim across many fields of expertise. That usually means that you will not, yourself, become an expert in any one subject area. You must rely on scholars to help you accurately interpret information for your audience. You seek the help of scholarly sources to identify emerging social or scientific trends, to decipher specialist information or jargon that you cannot understand, to comment on the work of other scholars, to critique institutional policies or procedures, and for a wide variety of other purposes. The main use of scholarly sources in mass communication messages is as a source of expertise and knowledge about audiences, subject matter, or the effects of messages.

As you move through the information strategy process, you will begin to identify the individual scholars and the scholarly publications or resources that are most appropriate for your message task. For instance, if you are working on the advertising account for a new type of low-fat snack food, your initial discussions about the product with the client may direct you to several researchers whose work documents the dietary effects of the new food. If you are writing a news story about the possible effects of a new government-imposed tariff on imported steel, you are likely to want to discuss the policy with economics scholars whose names you find in the transcripts of testimony before Congress about the policy. If you are preparing a news release about the introduction of curtain airbags (those that inflate in front of vehicle side windows to provide passengers better head and neck protection) in next year's models, your supervisor may ask you to seek the expertise of a scholar studying the effects of the new devices on auto accident injury rates.

In every case, the scholarly source is intended to provide credibility, depth, balance and expertise to your message. Rather than asking your audience to trust that you, the communicator, just happened to get it right, you seek the help of scholarly sources to ensure that audiences are receiving complete, accurate, and fair information in their news stories, advertisements, and public relations messages. If you choose your scholarly sources carefully and with attention to their credentials, expertise, and relevance for your topic, you are likely to produce a much more reliable and credible message for your audience.

TAPPING INTO SCHOLARLY SOURCES

As with the other contributors to the information strategy, you can tap into scholarly sources through people, paper, or digital means. You might monitor scholarly discussions by subscribing to listservs or attending conferences to hear the presentations by those who are sharing their work; you may search for relevant published work, using the tools in libraries or databases; scholars may share their knowledge through in-person, telephone, or e-mail interviews with you.

Monitoring Scholarly Sources

As we've said, much of the work that scholars engage in takes place in the invisible college network of informal contacts, discussions, and idea exchanges that defines scholarly endeavor. It is difficult for an outsider to gain an insight into this world. However, the observation and tracking techniques discussed in Chapter 5 can be useful.

Journalists on a specialty beat (science, business and economics, politics, etc.) know that the scholars who work in that area gather on a regular basis to share their work with each other and a wider audience, if they can generate one. For example, astronomers meet twice a year through the auspices of the American Astronomical Society and share their latest discoveries through scholarly paper presentations, exhibits, and news conferences for the media. The conference organizers choose several presentations each day that they believe will generate journalistic coverage, they prepare news releases, they make sure the scientists are available for interviews, and they help reporters interpret scientific findings. If you were covering the science beat, you would want to regularly monitor these conferences (by attending in person or checking the AAS Web site) and stay in contact with the scientists whose work you want to understand. Asking the scholars you speak with to suggest the one or two most important conferences or meetings in their field will give you a start on penetrating this part of the scholarly world.

Scholars also conduct ongoing discussions through their specialty listservs and discussion groups in the virtual world. Most of these groups are open to anyone who signs up to receive the messages. A number of online services keep track of the thousands of discussion groups that exist in all of the scholarly disciplines. One of the more useful at the time of this writing is *The Directory of Scholarly and Professional E-Conferences* (www.kovacs.com/directory) which screens, evaluates, and organizes discussion lists, newsgroups, mailing lists, and interactive Web chat sessions on topics of interest to scholars and professionals for use in their scholarly, pedagogical, and professional activities.

You can tap into these discussions by searching the *Directory* for the group that is most relevant for the subject area in which you're interested; subscribe to the group and then regularly monitor the discussions that take place. These groups can also give you leads to individual scholars you might want to interview or use as a source for your messages. By noting the individuals who seem to have an interesting perspective or a new point of view on the topic, you can be alerted to someone you will want to put in your index file of interviewees.

Searching Scholarly Sources

Scholars share their knowledge through the publication of books, journal articles, conference papers, research reports, and a variety of other means of knowledge dissemination. One of the hallmarks of scholarly work is the expectation that one's findings are reproducible—in other words, a scholar using the same method should be able to repeat someone else's experiment and generate similar findings. This is the foundation of the scientific method. It explains why publication of results is so important, and why the peer review method for deciding what to publish is so prized. It is also one of the reasons documentation of scholarly work is so highly developed. There are hundreds of indexes, abstracts, citation guides, bibliographies, review services, and other such tools to help you locate and evaluate scholarly work.

These sources can be of immense value to you as a nonexpert searching for scholarly information. There are some standard tools you should know about when beginning the search for this type of material. We will discuss a few of the more widely available and generally useful here, with the caveat that for every source we mention, there are five or ten others that we could have included if this book were about nothing except scholarly sources!

Indexes and Abstracts of Scholarly Sources.   As we've discussed, scholars share much of their most recent work through the articles they write for scholarly journals.

The articles in these journals are extensively indexed and abstracted to facilitate knowledge dissemination. Although many print and digital indexes include more than just scholarly articles, we've included those that have a large proportion of scholarly work that is useful for communicators.

1. *America: History and Life*, 1964 to date (monthly), print and online. Covers materials on U.S. and Canadian history from prehistory to the present in more than 2,000 journals published worldwide. In addition to covering all key English-language historical journals, it also includes selected historical journals from major countries, state and local history journals, books, dissertations, and a targeted selection of hundreds of journals in the social sciences and humanities.

2. *Applied Science and Technology Index*, 1958 to date (monthly); online from 1983 to date. Indexes more than 300 international and English-language periodicals in the areas of engineering, mathematics, physics, and computer technology; includes articles, interviews, meetings, conferences, exhibitions, new product reviews, announcements, and more.

3. *Art Index*, 1929 to date (quarterly); online as *Art Abstracts* from 1984 to date. Indexes journals in the fields of fine arts and performing arts: advertising, antiques, archeology, architecture, art history, city planning, computer graphics, crafts, design, folk art, graphic arts, industrial design, interior design, landscape architecture, motion pictures, painting, performance arts, photography, sculpture, television, textiles, and video.

4. *Biological and Agricultural Index*, 1964 to date (monthly); online from 1983 to date. Indexes professional and scholarly publications in subjects such as agriculture, environmental science, forestry, microbiology, plant pathology, and zoology.

5. *Business Source Premier*, 1990 to date (daily); online. Provides full text for more than 2,710 scholarly business journals covering management, economics, finance, accounting, international business, and much more. Coverage is especially strong for materials in advertising, public relations, and marketing.

6. *ComAbstracts*, varies but generally 1982 to date (irregularly) (see Figure 9.1), online. Contains abstracts of articles published in the primary scholarly and professional literature of the communications field.

7. *Criminal Justice Abstracts*, 1968 to date (quarterly), print and online. Comprehensive coverage of the major journals, books, and reports on criminology and related disciplines, including crime trends, crime prevention and deterrence, drugs, government, juvenile delinquency, juvenile justice, law, police, political science, public administration, courts, punishment, and sentencing.

8. *Dissertation Abstracts*, 1861 to date, print and online. With more than 1.6 million entries, the *Dissertation Abstracts* database is the single authoritative source for information about doctoral dissertations and master's theses. The database represents the work of authors from more than 1,000 graduate schools and universities. Some 47,000 new dissertations and 12,000 new theses are added to the database each year.

9. *EconLit*, 1969 to date (quarterly), online. Indexes the world's economic literature (over 300 major economic journals and collective volumes), compiled from the American Economic Association's *Journal of Economic Literature* and the *Index of Economic Articles.*

10. *Education Index*, 1929 to date (monthly); online as *Education Abstracts* since 1983. Indexes materials from journals, conferences, proceedings, bulletins; yearbooks and book series in education administration, preschool, elementary, secondary, and higher education; teaching methods and curriculum; literacy, government funding, physical education, and more.

11. *Humanities Index*, 1974 to date (quarterly); online as *Humanities Abstracts* since 1984. Covers journals in the arts, archaeology, architecture, area studies, classical studies, communications, dance, drama, film, folklore, history, journalism, language, literature, music, performing arts, philosophy, photography, religion, and theology.

12. *PAIS International*, 1915 to date (monthly); online since 1972. Covers articles, books, conference proceedings, government documents, book chapters, statistical directories, reports of public and private agencies, and materials from the U.S. Congress in public affairs and public policy in the areas of business, economics, law and legislation, government, political science, international relations, public administration, banking and finance, environment, agriculture, health, education, demography, statistics, sociology, and other social sciences.

13. *PsycINFO*, 1887 to date (monthly), online. Covers articles from more than 1,300 international journals in psychology and related fields, including experimental and developmental, communications, social processes and issues, personality, physical and psychological disorders, professional issues, applied psychology, educational psychology, and behavioral literature in such related fields as law, business, and medicine.

14. *Sociological Abstracts*, 1952 to date (bimonthly); online since 1963. Covers articles, conference papers, dissertations and books in sociology, including social psychology, mass phenomena, social change and economic development, political interactions, rural sociology and agricultural economics, urban structures and ecology; sociology of the arts, education, religion, science, health, medicine; social welfare, clinical sociology, family studies, women's studies, gay and lesbian studies, and criminology.

15. The *InfoTrac* database provides access to more than 4,200 full text periodical files and five newspaper indexes with more than 20 years of coverage. Content includes newswires, newspapers, general interest magazines, refereed scholarly journals, business publications, and specialty publications in law, health care, and computers.

Reviews of Scholarly Sources. We've already mentioned that a search in the library catalog is a good first step toward locating books written by scholars. You can also use subject bibliographies, directories such as *Books in Print*, or online booksellers such as Amazon.com or BarnesAndNoble.com. But how do you know whether a book you find listed in the catalog or in an online source such as Amazon.com is a well-

Hits	Author	Year	Title	Journal
15	Coombs.	1998	An analytic framework for crisis situations: Better responses from a better understanding of the situation.	Journal of Public Relations Research
9	Coombs, &	2001	An extended examination of the crisis situations: A fusion of the relational management and symbolic approaches.	Journal of Public Relations Research
8	Coombs	1999	Information and compassion in crisis responses: A test of their effects.	Journal of Public Relations Research
7	Benoit	1997	Image repair discourse and crisis communication.	Public Relations Review
7	Seeger &	1998	Communication, organization, and ...	Communication Yearbook
7	Penrose	2000	The role of perception in crisis planning.	Public Relations Review
6	Kauffman	1999	Adding fuel to the fire: NASA's crisis communications regarding Apollo 1.	Public Relations Review
6	Egelhoff &	1992	An information-processing model of crisis management.	Management Communication Quarterly
6	Coombs &	1996	Communication and attributions in a crisis: An experimental study in crisis communication.	Journal of Public Relations Research
6	Rogan &	1995	Assessing message affect in crisis negotiations: An exploratory study.	Human Communication Research
6	Atwater	1987	Terrorism on the evening news: An analysis of coverage of the TWA hostage crisis on "NBC Nightly News".	Political Communication
6	Kauffman	1997	NASA in crisis: The space agency's public relations efforts regarding the Hubble space telescope.	Public Relations Review
6	Blumler	1997	Origins of the crisis of communication for citizenship.	Political Communication
6	Sen &	1991	Six years and counting: Learning from crisis management at Bhopal.	Public Relations Review
6	Williams &	1998	Expanding the crisis planning function: Introducing elements of risk	Public Relations Review

FIGURE 9.1 ComAbstracts indexes scholarly journals covering public relations, advertising, journalism and communications.

Source: ComAbstracts. Reprinted by permission.

respected treatment of the field? These resources provide reviews that can help you determine that.

1. *Book Review Index,* 1965 to date (quarterly). Covers book reviews that have been published in more than 200 periodicals. Before you use the information you find in a book or decide to interview the author, you want to know how that book was received by experts in the field. This tool will help you locate the reviews of the book that appeared in the specialty literature in that field.

2. *Book Review Digest,* 1905 to date (monthly). Covers 100 journals and magazines in which reviews have appeared. This tool actually includes summaries of the reviews as well as full citations for locating the entire review, so you can save some time by using the *Digest* if you just want the summary of the review.

3. Search engines such as Google.com can help locate book reviews of particular titles or sites that feature hundreds of reviews of recent titles. You may also find the online versions of the *New York Review of Books* or the *New York Times Book Review* useful for some scholarly books. (Amazon book reviews might sometimes be useful for scholarly books.)

4. Conference papers and presentations are frequently reviewed by discussants, scholars who appear on the panels where the researchers present their findings and who give a critique of the paper(s) in that session. You can monitor these critiques if you attend the conferences in person, or you can find the name of the discussant listed in the conference program and contact that discussant individually before or after the conference to find out how a researcher's work was received by the experts in that field.

Directories of Scholars. As we've said, there are many instances when you will want to interview a specific scholar about his or her work. There are other times when you know you should talk to a scholarly expert about your search, but you don't know who. Again, there are a variety of searching tools that can help you locate the scholars who will be most appropriate for your information need.

1. *American Men and Women of Science,* first published in 1906 and now updated every few years in print and on CD. Identifies and profiles more than 126,000 leading experts from North America in all the physical, biological, and related sciences from acoustics to zoology.

2. *Directory of American Scholars,* first published in 1942 and now updated every few years. Identifies and profiles more than 30,000 leading experts from North America in the humanities and social sciences.

3. *The Media Resource Service.* A nonprofit telephone and e-mail service that maintains a database of 30,000 (primarily U.S.) scientists, engineers, physicians, and policy makers who have agreed to provide information on short notice to communicators who request a referral to an expert in a specific subject area. Full contact information is found at Mediaresource.org.

4. *ProfNet.com,* an online and telephone service that helps communicators locate experts at universities and research centers who provide information through their institution's public information office. The service requires communicators, public information officers, and experts to register through a subscription with the PR Newswire company, thereby providing some quality control assurances for all who use the service.

5. *The Research Centers and Services Directory,* online (updated annually). A comprehensive source of information on more than 27,500 organizations conducting research worldwide. It corresponds to the print *Research Centers Directory* family of publications: *Research Centers Directory,* which covers more than 14,000 university-based and other nonprofit research facilities in the U.S. and Canada; *International Research Centers Directory,* which covers more than 8,200 non-U.S. research organizations in approximately 145 countries; *Government Research Directory,* which covers more than 4,300 research units of the U.S. and Canadian federal governments, and *New Research Centers,* an inter-edition update covering some 800 newly identified research centers. The *Research Centers and Services Directory* database and print counterparts provide full contact information for the scholars who lead these centers, thus giving you a scholar's name and area of expertise in hundreds of different disciplines.

6. *Who's Who* volumes (*Who's Who in America, Who's Who in the Midwest, Who's Who in Medicine and Health Care, Who's Who in Finance and Industry*, etc.) provide solid background information about 900,000 leaders and significant achievers from every field of endeavor. The family of *Who's Who* publications is in print and online editions that are updated frequently.

7. Contact the public information office of your local university or community college campus to ask for a referral to a local expert in your subject area. Many times the public information office maintains an internally generated database of scholars at that institution who have agreed to speak with communicators on a variety of topics. Some universities now post a list of subject experts publicly on their Web sites (e.g., www. usc.edu/experts, experts.wsu.edu, www.vega.org.uk/info/media/experts.html).

Interviewing Scholarly Sources

As we've discussed in Chapter 5, conducting an efficient and focused interview requires considerable preparation. This is especially true for the interviews you do with scholars. The worst thing you can do in an interview with scholarly sources is ask the interviewee to "teach me the topic." Someone who has spent a career studying a specialized and focused sliver of a complicated discipline will not appreciate being asked to summarize his or her entire field in a few convenient sound bites. On the other hand, scholars usually delight in being recognized for their expertise and sharing their knowledge in a discussion with a communicator who demonstrates some familiarity with the field. So you need to do some background work before you ever pick up the phone or send that e-mail query.

Many of the monitoring and searching strategies we've already discussed help you prepare for your interview with scholars. If you've done your homework, you will know something about the main trends and ideas in the discipline you're tapping. In other words, you will know what scholars in that area have been talking about with each other recently, at their conferences, on their listservs, in their informal newsletters and publications. You will have some familiarity with the main peer-reviewed publications in that field, and will know what your specific interviewee has written about in those journals or books. And you will be able to speak intelligently about the field, using the appropriate terminology and buzz words that are important to the knowledge-creators in that area.

Once again, there are several tools that can help you prepare for your interviews with scholarly sources. Most of these provide biographical information about the individual you are going to talk to, hence giving you a good start on your background work. In addition to the tools we've already discussed in the previous section that provide biographical information, there are several general sources to help with this task:

1. *Biography and Genealogy Master Index*, 1981 to date (annual updates); online since 1993. Helps you locate specific biographical information that has been published in many of the tools we mentioned in the previous section (such as *Who's Who* volumes,

Directory of American Scholars volumes, etc.). If an individual has been profiled in a biographical source, the entry in this tool will indicate where and when that biography appeared.

2. *Biography Index*, 1946 to date (quarterly); online since 1984. Helps you locate biographical articles that have appeared in 2,000 periodicals and journals, biographical books, and chapters from collective biographies.

3. *Current Biography*, 1940 to date (monthly); print and online. A magazine-style publication that includes articles about people in the news, with brief, well-documented entries and a photo for each person covered. People who may never be included in the more formal biographical sources may show up here if they are in the news.

The purpose for using these biographical tools before conducting your interview with a scholar is to be sure you fully understand that person's background, credentials, and areas of expertise.

If your source is not included in these tools, another strategy for gathering this information is to contact the public information office of the scholar's institution and ask for that person's resume, or as it is called in the academic world, his or her *vita*. This summary of a scholar's career is usually a public document and may even be found online by searching the Web site for that institution or that scholar's specific academic department. A vita typically lists scholars' degrees, their publications, the courses they teach, the research grants they've received, the conference papers they've delivered, and so on.

Researching someone's background using biographical tools helps you decide whether the potential source has the needed knowledge, expertise, reputation, background, and characteristics to warrant an interview. These biographical information searches also help you develop an agenda of questions. If conflicting information turns up in the preliminary information search about the person's background, you can use the interview to clarify and correct those problem areas.

As with any expert interview, schedule the interview with scholarly sources as far in advance as possible. At the time the interview is arranged, explain the topic, the context, and the probable use of the information. The interviewee will spend some time preparing, and may be willing to share additional information if she or he is aware of the topic before hand. Also, ask permission to record the interview on audiotape or videotape if that is what you intend to do. It is not always possible to prearrange an interview, but try to give the source as much lead time as you can.

Again, as is the case with all interviews, use all the principles of interpersonal communication that can make the exchange successful. Be cordial, smile, make eye contact right away, start with some small talk or make a personal observation ("I see you have a picture of a cat on your desk. I'm a cat lover, too."), appear curious but not pushy or cynical. The opening of your interview is where some of your background biographical information can come in handy. If there is time, ask about something you know interests your source to break the ice and put him or her at ease.

A common novice's mistake is to talk too much. Remember that you are there to get the *source* to talk, not to show off your scintillating personality. Most people are uncomfortable with silence. They tend to want to fill the silence by talking, which can work to your advantage. Resist the inclination to jump in and ask the next question as soon as your source is finished speaking. One interviewer recommends waiting at least four seconds before asking the next question. Four seconds may not seem like a lot, but if you count it out to yourself using the standard schoolyard trick ("one Mississippi, two Mississippi, three Mississippi, four Mississippi"), you will usually discover that your source will carry on, amplifying his or her answer and filling the space.[2]

Ask questions that will generate the most information and keep the interviewee talking. Don't ask yes/no questions. Don't ask about things you should already know from your background information unless there is some discrepancy you need to clarify. Ask lots of How? and Why? questions. Especially with scholarly sources, use summary questions throughout the interview. These includes question such as, "Let's review what we've covered...," "I want to be sure my notes are accurate. First,...," or "Let me check to make sure I understand your points...."

Don't let pride get in the way of a good interview. Don't be afraid to ask if you don't understand something. There are no dumb questions when it is in the context of avoiding a misinterpretation or a mistake. Keep asking until the material is clear, so you can make it clear to your audience. Especially with scholarly sources, you may find yourself listening to a lot of jargon or specialized terminology. A good question to ask in that situation may be, "How would you explain that to a layman?"

Many scholarly sources are not experienced interviewees. You may be the first person who has ever called or e-mailed to ask for an interview, which puts you at an advantage in one sense, but poses some special problems in another. The advantage for you is that, unlike highly coached institutional sources from business or politics, your scholarly source is usually not polished in evading or skirting difficult or provocative questions, meaning that you are likely to get an honest view of their expertise and opinions. The disadvantage is that the person may be nervous, apprehensive about how you are going to conduct the interview and use the information, and fearful of saying or doing something that will hurt his or her reputation or standing in the academic community.

There are several ways to deal with this particular problem. The most effective, as we've already said, is to be totally prepared for the interview by knowing as much as possible about your source and the topic before you ever make the call. A nervous interviewee will be put very much at ease when he or she realizes that you've done your homework in advance.

Another strategy is to use an interview technique in which you demonstrate that you understand the interviewee's agenda. The source has probably been thinking about the interview, rehearsing what to say, feeling nervous about making the right points and being clear. How do you let your source know you understand his or her agenda? You might start this way: "I have six questions I think are important for you to answer. After we finish with those, I will ask you whether we've left out any important information. And I will make sure you have my phone number and e-mail address so that if something occurs to you after I leave, you can contact me."

This saves time and prevents a "filibustering" interview, in which you ask your first question and your source, thinking "I'll never get a chance to say what *I* think is really important," immediately goes off on a tangent from which it is nearly impossible to get back to *your* point. When you explain your procedure in advance, the source knows that he or she will get a chance to identify important information even if you miss it in the first pass.

CAUTIONS FOR USE

As we've already discussed, the scientific method is designed to generate publicly verifiable results. Scholars are supposed to do their work under conditions that are reproducible by others. Scholars also try to minimize factors that affect the accuracy and interpretation of their results. Hence, they try to conduct their work under controlled circumstances as much as possible. This is sometimes easier for physical scientists than for social or policy scientists, however. Physical scientists can do their work in the laboratory and with multiple observations of the phenomena they're studying. Social scientists do much of their work in the social environment and are studying complex human behavior, thereby making control harder to achieve. Nonetheless, all reputable scholars strive to be precise in their methods and careful in their interpretation of research findings.

As much as scholars want to achieve this perfection of the scientific method, they are, in the end, human beings. The evidence they generate must be scrutinized and used with caution, as is true with any other source of information. Critical thinking experts M. Neil Browne and Stuart Keeley suggest that you keep a number of factors in mind when you are considering using scholarly research findings as a source of information.[3] These include:

1. Research varies in *quality*, and because the research process is so complex and subject to so many external influences, even well-trained scholars sometimes make mistakes. Just because something was published in a peer-reviewed journal does not mean it is not flawed in other important ways. This is why it is important to try to interview several scholars about the findings of a particular study in order to understand the *reputation* of that work.

2. Research findings often contradict one another (see Box 9.1). Thus, *single* research studies presented out of the context of the body of work in that area often present misleading conclusions. You should look for studies that have been repeated by more than one researcher or group of researchers.

3. Research findings *do not prove* conclusions. All someone can do with a set of findings is say it does or does not *support* a particular conclusion. Scholars must always interpret the meaning of their findings, and all findings can be interpreted in more than one way. Thus, when you see the statement, "research findings show…," you should translate that statement into "researchers interpret their findings to show…"

4. Despite best intentions, scholarly work is not neutral and value free. Scholars, along with the rest of us, have emotional investments in particular ideas and ways of

■ ■ ■ ■ ■ ▬

BOX 9.1
RESEARCH FINDINGS OFTEN CONTRADICT ONE ANOTHER

New study questions whether previous research pointing out the evils of fat in the diet is correct after all.

**STAR TRIBUNE (MINNEAPOLIS, MN)
JULY 13, 2002**

OUR PERSPECTIVE: FAT; WHAT IF IT'S NOT ALL THAT BAD?

For two decades, Americans have been preached at from almost every corner to reduce their intake of fatty foods in order to lower the risk of heart disease and keep their weight at appropriate levels. Over those two decades, the rate of heart disease has failed to fall, the rate of Type 2 diabetes has skyrocketed and begun to appear more frequently in children, and the nation has become the land of the large and home of the obese. What gives?

Writer Gary Taubes, correspondent for the journal Science, and the experts he consulted think they know the answer, and it is a shocker: Americans would have been better off staying with their higher-fat habits. Writing in the *New York Times Magazine*, Taubes puts forward the view, gaining ground in the scientific and medical communities, that Americans have substituted loads of refined carbohydrates and starches for the fat they have given up. The effects have been disastrous: greater obesity, higher levels of dangerous triglycerides, an epidemic of what used to be called "adult-onset diabetes."

Put simply, Taubes' tentative conclusion is that if you have a choice of sausage and eggs or a muffin for breakfast, you'd be better off choosing the sausage and eggs. And don't even look at one of those Big Gulp soft drinks.

It appears to work this way: People like food that tastes good, and fat tastes good. So as Americans worked to reduce the fat in their diets, they looked for substitutes that appealed to their taste buds. Starch and carbohydrates, especially refined carbohydrates, were the substi-tute of choice: pasta, bread, sodas, potatoes. The shift was reinforced by government urgings to eat less fat and meat, and by a low-fat food industry that necessarily turned to refined carbs as a fat replacement.

Refined carbohydrates move quickly into your bloodstream, sending your blood sugar level into a spike. That triggers the release of lots of insulin to bring the sugar level down; some of the sugar gets burned, some gets stored as fat. You get energy that is quick but short-lived. Soon you are hungry again, but your insulin levels are still high, and that prevents your body from reaching into its stores of fat to burn them. So you eat more carbohydrates and go through the cycle again.

But when you eat, say, a steak that has a high fat level and lots of protein, the food is broken down more slowly. You feel full longer, and your blood sugar avoids the roller coaster, so insulin levels remain lower. As the effects of your meal wear off, your body begins to burn fat.

What about cholesterol? Taubes and the experts he talked to say that the link between cholesterol and heart disease was never actually proven a–controversial assertion–and that at any rate the health threat from a high-carbohydrate diet is much greater than the threat from a high-fat diet. In other words, Robert Atkins and his carb-averse, fat-embracing diet may have been right all along or at least closer to right than just about every other dietary authority.

"More than two-thirds of the fat in a porterhouse steak, for instance," Taubes writes, "will definitely improve your cholesterol profile (at least in comparison with the baked potato next to it); it's true that the remainder will boost your [bad cholesterol], but it will also boost your [good cholesterol]. The same is true for lard. If you work out the numbers, you come to the surreal conclusion that you can eat lard straight from the can and conceivably reduce your risk of heart attack."

(continued)

BOX 9.1   CONTINUED

But it's not necessary to go that far. The key to the problem Taubes lays out is the substitution of carbs and starches for fat. The diet Americans ate before the low-fat boom may be better than a high-carb diet, but the best diet may be something altogether different: lean meat, fish, poultry, legumes, vegetables, whole grains, select fruits and unsaturated oils like olive oil. One *Wall Street Journal* writer calls this the "caveman diet" because it more closely resembles what human beings ate before the development of agriculture.

The central premise of Taubes' assertion is breathtaking: that the dietary change pushed on Americans to get control of weight and heart disease has made things much worse. If that's so, why are Americans learning about it chiefly from diet books and the popular press? Taubes' Times article is an updated and popularized version of a report that appeared in *Science* magazine more than a year ago, but to most Americans this will come as a complete and infuriating surprise.

Why is that? Taubes suggests two reasons: First, because the American medical community, having spent three decades vilifying Atkins, now finds itself paralyzed by the idea it must embrace his heresies and admit that the low-fat orthodoxy may have caused great harm. And second, only recently have the Atkins-type diets actually been studied against traditional low-fat diets.

Initial results support Atkins, but studies supported by the National Institutes of Health and others are incomplete. If the low-fat dietary recommendations resulted from bad science, the error can't be rectified with more bad science and a leap to conclusions.

But as the headline on Taubes' *Times* piece asks, "What if it's all been a big fat lie?" Then health-conscious Americans are in for a big adjustment in their eating habits. So are many American dietary experts: They're going to be eating an awful lot of crow.

Source: Star Tribune Editorial: "Our perspective: Fat: What if it's not all that bad" July 13, 2002, A20. Reprinted with the permission of the Star Tribune.

understanding the world. Regardless of how objective a piece of scholarship may appear, subjective elements are always involved. Therefore, you must always try to put an individual scholarly finding or piece of evidence into the larger context of what we think we know about that topic, and try to understand the full set of influences on that scholar's work.

5. A scholar's work may be mischaracterized by another scholar who is citing or using that original piece of evidence in a new study. Do not rely on someone else's characterization of another person's findings. Look at the original piece of scholarship yourself and make sure you understand what that particular scholar said he or she found.

6. Research findings change over time. What we once thought we knew is no longer true, or has been superceded by more recent scholarship. As with so many other sources of information you will use for your messages, be sure you have the most *recent* findings in front of you.

7. Some studies are done using artificial circumstances because trying to do the study in the "real" world would be impractical, unethical, or otherwise not feasible.

For instance, many studies about the effects of media messages on children involve exposing kids to messages with particular characteristics (violence, pro-social behavior, etc.) and then studying how the children interact with one another or with dolls or toys in a laboratory setting. How do we know that this artificial setting isn't affecting the outcome? Other studies are conducted with research subjects chosen because of their easy availability rather than their appropriateness for the study. An example is when an advertising scholar uses a classroom full of freshmen advertising students to study the effects of several different commercials for house paint (some using humor, some using a more rational appeal, etc.). How many of the freshmen in the room are actually in the market for house paint (in other words, how many of them are in the target audience for that product)? You need to ask whether the scholarly study you are thinking of using is flawed by the artificiality of the research setting or the selection of research subjects.

8. As we've already said, many scholars do work that is funded by outside sources, such as research grants or contracts from large companies or government agencies with an interest in the outcome of the work. This does not, of course, automatically mean that their findings are biased. However, it is not uncommon for drug companies, for instance, to require a scholar funded with one of their grants to seek permission from the company before submitting any findings to academic journals for peer review. Understandably, the drug companies are unlikely to give permission for studies that are not favorable to their products or treatment regimens. The U.S. Department of Defense (DOD) spends upwards of $1.38 billion a year on basic research, much of it done by academic scientists. In the aftermath of the September 11, 2001, terrorist attacks in the United States, the DOD was considering new restrictions on scholars working with DOD grants, including criminal sanctions against individuals who publish unclassified studies involving basic research.[4] All of this is a long way of saying that as a communicator considering using any type of scholarly research findings, you need to know how the work was funded, and by whom. You also need to ask the author(s) what restrictions they might have been working under as a result of that funding source.

As Browne and Keeley advise, you should approach any scholarly study with the skills of a critical thinker. We will discuss specific types of information evaluation techniques in more detail in Chapter 11. Suffice it to say here that just because you are not an expert in the subject area, you are not relieved from the responsibility to make sure you get your facts right and your interpretations verified.

A particularly vexing problem for media professionals who are searching for appropriate scholars to help with their messages these days is what is sometime referred to as the "golden Rolodex™" syndrome. It works like this: an enterprising journalist discovers a good scholarly source who returns phone calls on time, who speaks in clear language rather than obscure jargon, who has impeccable credentials in their subject specialization, and who knows how to provide provocative quotes and soundbites. That source gets interviewed and quoted in the journalist's work. Soon ten or twenty more journalists will find that interview archived in a database or on a Web site and call the same person. Pretty soon, that scholar is a recognized pundit in his or her area and gets more opportunities to interact with media professionals than his or her expertise or credentials may warrant. Remember, it is hard for any human being to resist the urge to respond to the promise of flattery, attention, and wide recognition. Especially with scholarly sources, who are usually not celebrities and who are sometimes diffident and hard to interview, it is tempting to use the same people over and over because they make the journalist's job easier.

This is a serious error. Most scholars work in highly specialized subfields of widely disparate disciplines of knowledge and expertise. An expert on the political situation in Iran is usually not qualified to speak equally authoritatively on the political situation in Afghanistan. Do not fall for the easy, lazy way out. You need to use the sources we've mentioned throughout this chapter and in Chapters 5 and 6 to identify the scholars who are truly appropriate for your message, not those who have become pundits for one reason or another.

Another serious error is to assume that anything or anyone associated with a research center is producing independent scholarship. Quite the opposite. There are myriad numbers of think tanks, research centers, institutes, and foundations that publish journals that *appear* scholarly, provide "fellows" for interviews with communicators who ask, write briefing papers and call news conferences to announce their findings, and otherwise mimic scholarly endeavors. But their purpose for being is to advance a particular point of view, usually politically or socially aligned with one side of the opinion spectrum or the other, and they are perfectly willing to let you *believe* their work, publications, and fellows are independently scholarly.

Don't be fooled. As we discussed in Chapter 8, these institutions have an agenda and are operating with a different set of standards and procedures than do legitimate scholarly institutions or scholars. Remember that true scholarly work is characterized by peer review of findings—independent authority to conclude what the findings and evidence support regardless of sponsorship or ideological concerns—and something called "academic freedom." Once again, asking how a particular research center or individual scholar's work is funded and how their work is reviewed before publication is the best method for ferreting out these differences and nuances. If you want help determining whether a publication or journal is peer reviewed, you can also turn to an independent reviewing source such as *Magazines for Libraries*. This resource (despite its title) is not just for librarians, but can help anyone determine whether a particular title is a popular, scholarly, or trade publication.

CASE STUDY OF SCHOLARLY INFORMATION SOURCES

Journalists were faced with a significant challenge in using scholarly sources for their storytelling when, in the summer of 2002, a new federally sponsored study raised serious questions about the safety and risks of hormone replacement therapy, a treatment that more than 13 million U.S. women were using. Every major news organization scrambled to cover the alarming news that, contrary to conventional wisdom, researchers had discovered that the hormones in one of the most widely prescribed drugs, Prempro, actually raised the risk of heart attack, stroke, blood clots, and breast cancer among the women on the treatment.

Newsweek magazine ran their cover story on the findings in the July 22, 2002, issue.[5] The lead article, "The End of the Age of Estrogen?," and accompanying sidebar and companion articles in the issue, ran for eight pages. The articles provide a powerful example of the use of scholarly sources in a publication intended for a general, nonspecialist audience. Of course, the articles also demonstrate the use of institutional, informal, and journalistic sources. But our focus for this example will be on the scholarly sources used for the cover pieces.

The main article, by Goeffrey Cowley and Karen Springen, begins with this lead:

> Menopause may be a natural event, but the medical establishment has never viewed it as an auspicious one. "The years of the climacteric are the most troublesome in married life," the Czechoslovakian physician Arnold Lorand declared in his 1910 classic *Old Age Deferred*, "not only for the wife, who is directly affected by it, but also in almost equal degree for her husband, who must show the greatest forbearance." Luckily there was good news for the menopausal woman, "if only she be a clever member of her sex." Lorand had discovered that extracts from pigs' ovaries could "put off old age for a score of years," or at least "mitigate its effects when it has asserted itself with all its terrors." By the early 1940's drugmakers were mass-producing estrogen from pregnant mares' urine. And by 1960 the august New England Journal of Medicine was recommending the stuff for "everyone with evidence of an estrogen lack"—which is to say virtually every woman over 50.

This lead quotes from a classic medical textbook, refers to the conventional wisdom about hormone therapy in the medical sciences, and quotes an article in one of the leading scholarly journals in the medical field—all in the first paragraph of the story! The main article went on to describe the findings of the study that had been conducted by observing more than 16,000 women for roughly five years. The study was orchestrated by the federal Women's Health Initiative and conducted by researchers and physicians across the country. Federal health officials announced on July 18, 2002, that the study indicated that Prempro did significantly more harm than good when taken for long periods. The study was supposed to run for eight years, but the five-year results were so decisive that the researchers cut it short and urged women to stop taking their pills. The article acknowledged that this was an astonishing occurrence in a field that is known (and derided) for its hedging, confusing, and sometimes outright contradictory advice about medical decisions and practices. The journalists quoted Dr. JoAnn Manson, a women's health expert at Harvard Medical School, as saying it was "the most dramatic sea change I've seen in clinical medicine."

The journalists covering the story for *Newsweek* knew they had to clarify the story for their readership, many of whom would be directly personally affected because they were taking the drug. The third paragraph of the story described the panicked calls to doctor's offices and the overnight drop in the stock price for Wyeth Pharmaceuticals, the maker of Prempro. But the very next sentence qualified the findings by assuring readers with a quote from another scholarly source, Dr. Jacques Rossouw, the acting director of the Women's Health Initiative. Rossouw said, "This is not like an urgent medical alert or the withdrawal of a drug from the market." The journalists explained that the study did not uncover huge, unimagined dangers to patients, but rather provided evidence about the relative benefits and risks for patients who use the drug long term.

The next several paragraphs went on to explain why it has taken the medical establishment so long to assess the risks of such a widely prescribed treatment such as hormone replacement therapy (HRT). The journalists summarized the available research that had for so long suggested that HRT was a boon to women's health. They cited the 1966 "ode to estrogen," the book *Forever Feminine* by Dr. Robert Wilson that helped sell a generation of women on estrogen therapy. They described the "once-authoritative 1992 guidelines" of the American College of Physicians that had advised most postmenopausal women to take HRT unless they were at high risk for breast cancer. They quoted numerous physicians and researchers who provided context for the decades-long attachment to HRT as a medical wonder treatment.

Then, in language the average reader could understand, the journalists wove together a narrative of how the current study was conducted and the details of the findings, interspersed with descriptions, photos, and quotes from typical HRT users. Quotes from the chairwoman of the Women's Health Initiative from Stanford University helped the reader understand the decision to stop the trial. The journalists boiled down the scholarly findings to this pull quote, "The danger to an individual woman is small. But small risks can have large consequences when a lot of people take them."

Summarizing four decades of scholarly work in a highly technical and contentious area of research certainly required considerable skill on the journalists' part. The story included quotes from five scholarly experts and one physician who was quoted as an HRT patient rather than as a scholarly researcher (in other words, she was used as an informal source rather than as a scholarly source). No doubt these experts helped the journalists understand the subject area, the immediate story, and the historical context for the findings. But the journalists also demonstrated skill in locating relevant scholarly articles (some that were decades old) and the ability to put the risk information in its proper perspective for the lay audience.

The companion article to the cover story reviewed ways to treat menopause that don't involve the use of HRT. Journalist Claudia Kalb used the direct address form of writing in her lead:

> No doubt you're confused about hormone-replacement therapy. And, like thousands of women who bombarded their doctors' offices and sent HELP! messages to Internet bulletin boards last week, you're probably wondering what to do.[6]

That lead demonstrates the use of the monitoring technique of information gathering. Kalb clearly checked Web discussion groups to listen in on how HRT users (informal sources) were reacting to the news. But the article went on to describe alternative therapies for many of the symptoms that menopausal women say make their lives difficult. In colorful sidebars that accompanied the article, Kalb and the other *Newsweek* journalists outlined how various symptoms such as osteoporosis, hot flashes and night sweats, mood swings, and heart disease might be treated without resorting to HRT.

The journalists did not come up with these alternative therapies out of their own heads. They cited the National Heart, Lung and Blood Institute and the North American Menopause Society for the sidebar materials. They quoted five medical experts and provided a review of the latest thinking on alternative therapies from the scientific research literature. They described the National Institutes of Health's trial of two herbs for treatment of hot flashes. They referred to menopause research being conducted by the National Institute on Aging. In short, they provided the kind of advice about what to do next that was not provided by the study sponsors, who simply said, "Stop taking the drug."

Now, most of us would not take medical advice about life and death decisions from *Newsweek* magazine, or at least we wouldn't take it as the only source of information we use to make decisions. However, the journalists used scholarly sources (research articles, interviews with scholars and physicians, books on the subject) to provide a comprehensive overview of the main issues and possible alternatives. This gave the reader enough information so that she could make some informed decisions about what to discuss with her doctor. And that is an important service of high-quality journalism—providing us with the information we need to conduct our lives as individuals, as citizens, and as consumers.

We next turn our attention to the use of journalistic sources as contributors to the information strategy.

SELECTED ADDITIONAL READINGS

Girden, Ellen R. *Evaluating Research Articles: From Start to Finish*. Thousand Oaks, CA: Sage Publications, 2001.

Hart, Chris. *Doing a Literature Review: Releasing the Social Science Research Imagination*. Thousand Oaks, CA: Corwin Press, 1998.

Locke, Lawrence F., Waneen Wyrick Spirduso, and Stephen J. Silverman. *Reading and Understanding Research*. Thousand Oaks, CA: Sage Publications, 1998.

NOTES

1. Carol Tenopir and Donald W. King, "Use and Value of Scholarly Journals," International Federation of Science Editors, Rio De Janeiro, Brazil, August 2000.

2. Sally Adams, *Interviewing for Journalists* (London: Routledge, 2001), 34.

3. M. Neil Browne and Stuart Keeley, *Asking the Right Questions: A Guide to Critical Thinking*, 6th edition, (Upper Saddle River, NJ: Prentice Hall, 2001), 130–131.

4. "Pentagon Considers Tighter Control of Academic Research," *Chronicle of Higher Education*, May 3, 2002. chronicle.com/weekly/v48/i34/34a02401.htm

5. Geoffrey Cowley and Karen Springen, "The End of the Age of Estrogen?" *Newsweek*, July 22, 2002, 38–41.

6. Claudia Kalb, "What's a Woman to Do?" *Newsweek*, July 22, 2002, 43–45.

CHAPTER TEN

JOURNALISTIC SOURCES

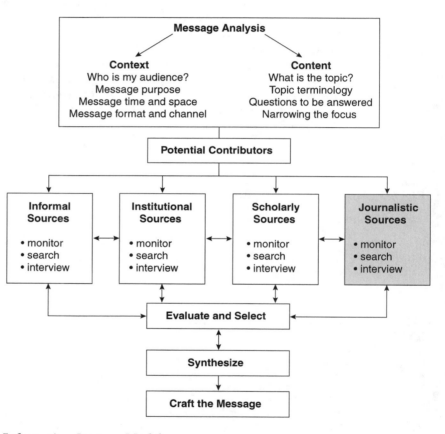

Information Strategy Model

In Chapter 2, we described journalistic sources as mass media content produced to inform, educate, or persuade and intended for a mass audience with a generalist background in the subjects explored. Traditionally, journalistic sources are newspapers, magazines, broadcast and cable news programs, and radio (particularly public radio) program transcripts. In the past decade, digital delivery of news has expanded the availability and the types of journalistic sources. The alternative press, zines, news aggregators, and Webloggers are redefining the notion of mass media news.

News is sometimes described as the first take on history. Unlike the scholarly source which is the product of deep research, a thorough canvassing of previous knowledge on the topic, and long, considered writing and thinking, journalistic sources are written in the heat of deadline, using the available "facts" and, often, cursory examination of background material. So, while the information in a news report may not be "vetted" to the extent that scholarly sources are, it is similar in that news reports strive to be objective reports of people and events (unlike the very subjective informal sources or the institutional sources which are supporting a particular organization.)

TYPES OF JOURNALISTIC SOURCES
AND HOW THEY KNOW WHAT THEY KNOW

There are several important considerations when looking at journalistic sources: the type of source, the type of story, and the type of reporter. Let's look at each of these categories and describe their differences.

Types of Sources

In the opening paragraph we listed the types of journalistic sources. There are distinct differences in the purposes and methods of each type.

Newspapers.   These are generally broad but shallow chroniclers of the news of interest to readers in a general circulation area. Local and regional newspapers can be daily or weekly. Newspapers have a combination of staff written material—generally those news items of local interest, and wire service stories—ones available for publication by any subscribing newspaper. National newspapers, like the *New York Times* or *USA Today*, or those focused on a particular sector, like the *Wall Street Journal*, have less of a geographic interest and are written to appeal to a wide audience. There are mainstream newspapers and alternative newspapers—the difference being the tone, the subject matter covered, and the intended audience. Alternative newspapers are usually weeklies and focus more on the arts and entertainment and social issues in an area.

Most newspapers of any size have an online version. Usually, the online version is essentially *shovelware*—the electronic representation of the print product. In some cases, the newspaper's Web site has material that never was printed on paper—particularly as newspapers start to experiment with some new forms of stories online using Flash animations or multimedia presentation of text and graphics.

Source for Locating Newspapers.   Editor and Publisher International Yearbook:

www.mediainfo.com/editorandpublisher/business_resources/yearbook.jsp

Source for Locating Online Newspapers.   Online Newspapers:

www.onlinenewspapers.com

Magazines.   Magazines have more in depth coverage of the stories that fit the magazine's editorial direction. News weeklies take those stories covered in a newspaper and go into deeper detail about the significance of the event. Subject focused magazines, weeklies or monthlies, cover a wide variety of angles and stories on their area of interest (technology, business, computer games, music, etc.). There are magazines that are published by institutional sources; they will generally be produced in order to promote the organization that publishes them. Take care in looking at a magazine source to determine whether it is, in fact, journalistically produced or is serving more of a public relations function.

One of the publishing sectors that has boomed because of the World Wide Web is *zines* or *e-zines*—electronic magazines that have no print equivalent. These zines provide an alternative voice and an edgy point of view that make them more informal sources, perhaps, than journalistic. Other zines, like Slate (slate.msn.com) or Salon (www.salon.com) are backed by mainstream media organizations. Many print magazines have an online version of their publication—often, however, they provide only a few of the articles and fewer photos as an incentive to subscribers to continue to get the print version.

Source for Locating Magazines.   Publist.com has more than 150,000 magazines, journals, newsletters, and other periodicals.

www.publist.com

Source for Locating E-zines.   The Book of Zines has links to a number of directories of zines:

www.zinebook.com

Broadcast and Cable News Programs.   Just as with local versus national newspapers, there is a difference in the scope of news coverage between local and national television news programs. Local programs tend to cover crime, traffic, events, and politics of the viewing area, whereas national news focuses on bigger national and international news events. Local television is often accused of shallowness in its coverage, depending on sensational and breaking news rather than providing much in the way of context or depth in their reporting of events. National news, particularly the news magazine programs, go more deeply into the story they are covering.

Online, television news stations are evolving. In the early days of the Web, the television news site was primarily promotional material about the anchors and, perhaps, a link to the weather. Now you may find transcripts of the news stories available online and, in some cases, the video. One television station in Minneapolis, KSTP-TV, has a service called *5Cast*, which lets you click on specific news stories in any order and essentially create your own newscast of previously aired stories.

Source for Locating Television Stations.   Gebbie Press—All-in-One Media Directory:

www.gebbieinc.com/tvintro.htm

Source for Locating Television Stations Online.   News Directory:

www.newsdirectory.com/tv.

Organized by state, then city.

Radio.   Most local "top of the hour" newscasts on commercial radio are of the "rip and read" variety—often the news reader is simply taking stories from the newspaper or wire service. Public radio is like the broadcast version of magazines—they will cover a news story in great depth. The transitory nature of the radio program was a problem for information gatherers in the past. Now, the transcripts and, often, audio files of programs can be found on the radio program's Web site.

Source for Locating Radio Stations.   Radio-Locator provides links to more than 10,000 radio station Web pages and more than 2,500 audio streams from radio stations in the United States and around the world.

www.radio-locator.com/cgi-bin/home

News Aggregators.   Ask teenagers for their favorite journalistic source and they might well say "Yahoo." Yahoo, NewsTrove (www.newstrove.com), Google News (news.google.com) and NewsNow (www.newsnow.co.uk) are examples of news aggregators. A news aggregator is "software that periodically reads a set of news sources, in one of several XML-based formats, finds the new bits, and displays them in reverse-chronological order on a single page."[1]

News aggregators don't have their own staff of reporters and writers, they compile the work of other journalists. The power of these aggregators is in their wide coverage of news and in the special features they offer for customized searching and delivery of news topics (see more about these in the section on monitoring journalistic sources).

Webloggers.   Webloggers are an online combination of news aggregator and commentator. Webloggers provide their own editorial view on the news and scan for items of interest from both mainstream and alternative sources to provide a referral list and commentary on the news items selected. Webloggers have loyal audiences who have come to rely on their take on the news and their eye for finding interesting sources.

Source for Locating Weblogs.   EatonWeb:

portal.eatonweb.com

Those are the forms in which journalistic sources might be presented. Now let's look at the types of stories that will be found in journalistic sources.

Understanding the differences between these types of stories is important for you as you select information to use in your own quest. The motivation and intention of the type of journalistic stories will make them more, or less, valuable to you in your information quest.

There are many ways to categorize the types of material that you will find in the journalistic source. Whether it is being presented in newsprint, on air, or online, the following are the types of stories or content that you might encounter. Most of these will not be labeled as such, so it is important that you understand the characteristics of each type of story—it will help you decide how to use the information you find in the story.

Types of Journalistic Stories

You'll remember back in Chapter 1 that we discussed the information standards for specific types of news stories you might be responsible for creating. The types of material we are talking about here differ slightly because we want to focus on the types of information you can find as a researcher rather than the types of messages to be crafted as a communicator. It is important to know the distinctions between the following:

Breaking News.   The quintessential "first take on history," the breaking news story is the kind that will interrupt the TV show you are watching or will be the lead story in the online news update. The publishing cycle of newspapers make the concept of covering breaking news impractical, so you will generally find newspapers have the followup story on news that broke the day before. Breaking news will often be sketchily reported and updates will be provided as they come in. On September 11th, 2001, the first reports of something happening at the World Trade Center speculated it was a small private plane that had accidentally flown into the skyscraper. The number of people killed or the extent of damage had to be revised as more facts and more time to report was available. Breaking news is important for communicators to keep track of, particularly those covering a particular market segment or industry.

Follow-Up or Second-Day Story.   As the details of a breaking news event become clearer and more depth is available, the second-day story is written to put the event into better context. These stories generally interview more experts and informal sources for reaction and background information. The followup story is a more reliable source to go to when checking on the facts or sequence of an event, because more was known to the reporter when the followup was written.

Analysis.   The analysis story will be the most in-depth coverage of a news event. The reporter assigned to the analysis piece is generally a subject specialist or has covered the beat being written about. Analysis pieces are written to put a news event into context and are valuable sources when you are trying to understand the "who, what, when, where, and whys" of a news story.

Investigative Report. These are the in-depth studies that uncover coverups, expose wrongdoing, and bring things to light. These rely on data, documents, and multiple interviews. Strategic communicators monitor investigative reports to keep track of industry issues they may need to respond to. Journalists monitor investigative reports in other markets for ideas about the kinds of investigations they can do in their own communities.

Profile. Profiles are pieces written about interesting or newsworthy people or organizations. Profile pieces generally have an interview with the person and with others who know the person or organization. These can be great background pieces for the communicator looking at covering or investigating that person or organization.

Review. The review, whether it is of a restaurant, a movie, a band, or a play, is a critic's subjective view of the experience. Reviewers will often bring in some objective information, background on the writing or the business or the inspiration behind the thing they are reviewing, but most of the information will be their own opinion. For the person creating an ad campaign for a new nightclub, the review will be a valuable source for background on how the entertainment reviewers in town assess your client.

Feature. Feature stories are like the profile. These are not necessarily "news driven" but are enterprise stories written to tell about something of interest to the community. PR and advertising professionals monitor feature stories to help them understand audience characteristics and emerging trends.

Editorial. The editorial board of a publication or program is separate from the newsroom. They set the editorial or philosophical position of the organization and will offer opinion, whereas the newsroom is more about objective reporting of facts. The editorial's purpose is to persuade and to influence the opinion of the reader, viewer, or listener to a particular point of view. Editorials are generally well researched and written, but keep in mind that they present the facts in a way that supports the opinion they want to promote. Looking at the editorials might help you understand the political viewpoints of the publication, which might, in turn, color your decision about how to use other information from that source.

Types of Reporters

The news story is the journalistic source that we are primarily referring to, but it is also important to consider journalists themselves as journalistic sources. As a communicator, you will often go to the news story to get the information you need, but you might also want to go to the person who reported or wrote the story. When we get into talking about how to monitor, search, and interview journalistic sources we will talk about both the story and the creator of the story as sources. So, knowing a little about the different types of journalists might be helpful.

General Assignment Reporter.   These are the reporters who are on call to pick up and cover various news events. One day it might be a kidnapping, the next day a sewage leak into a local lake, and the next a report of the problems of potholes on a particular stretch of road. These are the generalists of the newsroom and they are rarely subject specialists. General assignment reporters are good journalist sources if you want to talk with someone who knows the issues and interesting news angles in a community.

Beat Reporter.   News organizations usually have reporters assigned to cover certain types of stories: business, crime, education, city hall, environment, and so on. These reporters are subject specialists who know the local and national experts, follow trends, and anticipate the next important stories in the area they cover.

   The specialist reporters that work for industry publications such as *Advertising Age* or *PRWeek* fall into this category as well. These journalists are particularly good sources for communicators wanting to get informed background on a topic.

Investigative Reporter.   The investigative reporter is the one who covers stories before they break. Investigative reporters are charged with digging deeply into structures and functions of a community to root out problems or to report on anomalies. They are the watchdogs of the community and provide the most in-depth take on issues specific to the community. Investigative reporters frequently make use of the technique of interviewing *data* through computer-assisted reporting techniques. For example, they might obtain a data file of bridge inspections, cull through to find problems such as bridges that haven't been inspected in years, and produce an investigative piece that brings these problems to light. Investigative reporters, if you can get them to agree to an interview, are great resources for the communicator because of their

Source: Non Sequitur. Reprinted by permission.

ability to dig deep. They generally know about the more esoteric files and data that can be valuable to the communicator.

Editorial Writer.   The editorial writer is responsible for the columns and items on the editorial page. They are opinion writers and are often considered the "scholars" in the news organization, in that they usually deeply research and think about the issue they are editorializing on before they write about it. They are also excellent resources for the communicator in that they are not just opinionated, like the informal source, they are also well-versed, like the scholarly source.

Photojournalist or Videographer.   The photojournalist is often the most "on the scene" of the reporting team. They are there in the midst of the action trying to capture a visual record of the event. Photojournalists are the eyes and ears of the news organization and, in partnership with the reporter, make for a complete record of the news event.

Graphics Reporter.   Graphics reporters are concerned with visualizing information in a way that makes it more readily understood. They take complex data and create charts that let you see the significance of the numbers. They diagram news events through maps and drawings that make the unseen visible. If you are trying to understand the structure and sequence of news events, the graphics reporter can be an excellent resource to talk to.

News Researcher.   Although news researchers only infrequently get bylines for their work, their support of the reporting effort is essential. News researchers track down the secondary sources—past articles, relevant statistics, and facts—and identify experts for the reporter to interview. News researchers often find the leads that reporters then follow in their reporting of the news story. Getting to the researcher who has worked on a big story can be better than talking to the reporter. While the reporter's knowledge of the story often begins with the assignment and ends with the publication of the story, news researchers tend to continue their interest and attention to news topics.

News Uses of Journalistic Sources

For journalists, the news archive is their primary resource. At each stage of the reporting process journalistic sources will provide ideas, insights, facts, and background.

Getting Story Ideas.   When you are assigned a story, looking at previous stories on the topic or event in the files can give you an idea about angles to take, or ones to avoid because they have already been done.

Beginning the Reporting.   At the start of your reporting project you need to get up to speed on the topic you will be writing about. Getting a sense of the issues involved, the names of important players, and key facts and figures will help you as you go out to update the story. Checking national and international journalistic sources will give you a sense of context and perspective for the story you are covering.

During the Reporting.   In the midst of the reporting process you'll need to verify what you hear from people you've interviewed and you'll want to follow up on leads you may get as you uncover new information.

During the Writing.   As you write your story, you'll want to get specifics—facts, quotes, dates—that will add detail and depth to your report.

In addition, accessing journalistic sources of information can be a great way to get regional angles on a story. Hopping around to different news sites can quickly give you a sense of how stories are playing and what angles are being covered on a story you are doing. If you are going to a new town, checking the local media in advance of your visit is a way to see what is going on there. At all these stages of reporting, journalistic sources will be invaluable to the reporter.

Strategic Communications Uses of Journalistic Sources

For strategic communicators, journalistic sources will be just as important in various stages of the campaign development or in tracking an industry or organization you might be responsible for. Journalistic sources, particularly for locally covered news, might be the only source for information about local companies, people, and events. When dealing with national or international companies, people, or events, the vast archives of news stories will provide the strategic communicator with background, statistics, and leads to other issues that might be relevant.

Campaign Development.   You can monitor journalistic sources to get an idea of what the trends are; what has happened before; to get background on a product, service, or industry; and to help identify how your client should be positioned. It will also help you identify the news environment within which your campaign will be placed.

Competitor Information.   Journalistic sources will help you keep abreast of what competitors are doing and how the product you are promoting might be different than your competitors'. In industry-related sources you can learn specifics such as what agencies are working on which accounts, and what they are spending.

Ad Placement.   Although the ads (produced by institutional sources) are not themselves journalistic, their placement within the news publication or program can give valuable insight to strategic communicators. You can see the creative strategy, and infer the media strategy and product or service claims used by the advertiser.

Media Relations.   Before you pitch a story, you need to familiarize yourself with the publication, the writing styles of the reporters, and the types of stories they are likely to be interested in.

Issues Management and Crisis Communications. If your client is in the news for some reason (usually bad), you need to be vigilant about monitoring journalistic sources for every news story about the breaking problem.

For both journalists and strategic communicators, talking to the journalist who has been covering the story can be valuable. Getting the "first person" account of a trained observer who was on the scene or the inside knowledge of someone who has been steeping themselves in the issues and details of a particular type of story can be an important first source as you start your own research.

TAPPING INTO JOURNALISTIC SOURCES

Before messages in most media were created digitally, it was difficult if not impossible to get access to previously created messages. In the mid-1990s, the World Wide Web brought in a revolution in production. Newspapers, magazines, television stations, and radio programs began to use the Web to provide electronic access to current and, in some cases, past news stories. In the early days of the Web many of the television and radio stations online used the space primarily to provide promotional material rather than actual access to news stories they had run, but as the Web matured and the stations found ways to improve their packaging of materials online, they began to make video and audio as well as text versions of their stories available.

With online newspapers and magazines, there was a wide range of availability to previously published stories. Some publication Web sites had the policy of having only current stories online (and in the case of magazines, many only had a selection of stories from their current issue available). Others had current and a few days' worth of previous stories available. Others had a link to the full database of previously published stories ready for a user to search, for a fee. While the access to journalistic sources has certainly improved, the complexity of this access has increased. Figuring out who has what, where, and for how long—and how much they'll charge—can be a complicated process.

The digital revolution also made available some new methods for accessing journalistic sources, both stories and the people who write them. In the following section we'll discuss the ways you can monitor, search for, and interview journalistic sources of all types, online and offline.

Monitoring Journalistic Sources

- You're a reporter who covers health care. Your particular interest these days is the cost of prescription drugs.
- You're a public relations officer at a major drug company. Your responsibility is keeping up with the latest information (and disinformation) about drug prices.
- You're an advertising account executive with a pharmaceutical company client. Your responsibility is to understand your client's market and the unique selling proposition for that firm's products.

Whichever type of communicator you are, monitoring news sources will be essential in keeping up with your job, ensuring you are up to speed on the latest issues, players, and developments, and hearing about emerging trends.

In all three cases, you'll want to monitor not only news stories on the issue of prescription drug pricing, but also tap into the journalists who are writing the stories.

There are different intents and purposes for the monitoring of news sources. In an article that appeared in the Association for Computing Machinery's publication, *netWorker: The Craft of Network Computing*,[2] six types of users of monitoring services were identified:

Competitive intelligence "need-to-know" users: Must find out everything reported or rumored to be happening at companies in their market. These are the elite "power users" of news clipping services, often with licensing and purchasing budgets in excess of their own annual salaries. These users find LexisNexis or Dialog very useful services for their more complete coverage of events and giant background archives.

Competitive intelligence "nice-to-know" users: These folks aren't as dedicated to market analysis as they are to managing the relationships that touch the company and its marketplace, such as a sales manager in charge of a sales force in a market where buyers use multiple vendors of similar components.

Industry intelligence users: Mostly marketing and advertising people who need to position the company and differentiate it from others in a market. Also, salespeople who watch key customer relationships and look for new opportunities. These types of users will want to be able to sort items specifically by industry, using free services such are PRNewswire, Business Wire or IndustryWatch. However, it should be noted that many such services function merely as news release and PR vehicles for industry companies, meaning that the "news" being delivered is specifically crafted by the competitor to convey the message it wants the market to understand.

Technical intelligence users: Product development, R&D, engineering and design personnel will be more interested in the evolving technologies necessary to come up with better products and services than their rivals, as well as respond to new customer needs. Generally, technical journals and industry-specific publications can provide a solid foundation for technical intelligence customers.

Topical intelligence users: Those interested in a single area of interest that is less mission-critical than the previous types of users outlined. Perhaps they're simply checking stock prices to keep abreast of analyst perceptions of new competitor initiatives. Dow Jones, Reuters or Hoover's would fill the needs of this type of user, coverage that might be described as "a mile wide and an inch deep."

General news awareness users and personal users: These users are typically less concerned with a complete picture of a market or company than they are with just being informed about what's happening in the marketplace and the world. Usually, these users are unwilling to pay fees in the form of licensing the news they consume, and will instead select a delivery mechanism from one of the Internet search engines, such as Yahoo, Excite, or Go.com.

The article goes on to explain the differences in monitoring services: "Each service offers a different mix of price, quantity and quality of sources, frequency of updates, areas of coverage, chronological depth of archives, scalability for integration with your intranet, and search and delivery options."

As you explore and evaluate different ways to monitor journalistic sources, it will serve you well to keep those criteria in mind.

Types of Monitoring Services

Clipping Services. Prior to the Internet, there were services that would monitor particular publications for you. You could sign up with a clipping service: they would scan a wide range of publications and provide a folder of articles, on a weekly or monthly basis, that matched your interest. Companies still use these services, but some electronic services have also emerged, many of whom can provide updates on a daily basis.

NewsAlert is a service provided by Burrelle's, a print clip indexer, and VMS, a long-time indexer of broadcast programs. Its clipping report contains *"news segment summaries from the latest broadcast news and full text articles from today's domestic and foreign news wire services, newspapers, magazines and newsletters. NewsAlert can even search Internet news groups"* (www.vidmon.com/newsservices/na.htm). This sort of custom service will cost you and is the kind of service that the *"Competitive Intelligence 'Need-to-know' Users"* find valuable and economically justifiable.

Dialog's *NewsEdge* (www.newsedge.com) is another type of high-end online custom clipping service that provides both updates of news stories and access to the archives of thousands of news sources.

ClariNet (www.clari.net) offers keyword filtered news from all the major wire services and quick subject searching of newsgroup postings for about $10/month.

NewsAlert (www.newsalert.com), not to be confused with the "for fee" monitoring service provided by VMS and Burrelle's, lets you enter a portfolio of up to 100 company stock listings or use their news manager function to put in up to 25 industry sectors for which they will filter their news feed. This service is free.

News Web Site Filters. Many of the major news organizations' Web sites offer customization features. The Washington Post.com's "MyWashingtonPost" (www. mywashingtonpost.com) lets you customize the categories of news you see, select stocks to monitor, and displays weather for your region. At MSNBC.com you can put in your ZIP code and get news specific to your area.

Other sites will send you alerts when breaking news happens. CNN's site will send an e-mail to you if you subscribe to their "Breaking News Alerts" service. Even news aggregators, such as Yahoo, which take news stories from a number of news services and repackage them, offer customized pages with just the news you are interested in monitoring. Yahoo's News Clipper service lets you put in specific terms and locate articles that are relevant. If you make a News Clipper profile on "prescription drugs," you get articles from AP, USA Today, Reuters, New York Post, the Daily Press of Hampton Roads, and WCVB—the Boston Channel.

Weblogs. Using Webloggers to monitor the news for you can be an interesting approach. On the EatonWeb Portal (portal.eatonweb.com), there are 9,400 Weblogs categorized by topic. Under "news" there are 105 Weblogs listed, many of them from non-U.S. bloggers interested in tracking news about news in their countries. But there are also subject specific blogs like nature/environment (including Bird Stuff which links to stories in the news about birds). These bloggers keep their eyes out for interesting news items and Web sites and provide personal commentary about the items.

Monitoring Journalists.   Journalists rely on their network of other journalists. Professional colleagues can give tips on how to cover a story, advice about pitfalls to avoid, leads to people who should be interviewed. In the past, journalists only networked with other journalists in their newsroom or with members of professional organizations. Now there is unprecedented opportunity to hang out with journalists, virtually. News groups and message lists let you listen in on conversations between journalists. These can be great ways to track issues in the areas of interest that the journalists are talking about. Journalism.net describes more than forty lists, ones for investigative reporters, literary journalists, copyeditors, foreign correspondents, and health reporters.

Journalists use their network to get advice, exchange ideas, and share gossip. The etiquette of mailing lists can be delicate and you need to make sure, if you are not a journalist, that you are welcome to the group. Often, the best use of journalism lists is to get the names of journalists who post some interesting message that you might want to follow up with offline. The thing to remember about mailing lists is that usually only a small percent actually contribute to the discussion. According to an article in *e* magazine, "It seems that no more than 17 percent of the membership base is made up of babblers. And the remaining 83 percent is composed of lurkers."[3] So, it might be a good idea to use the mailing list community by throwing out a question and asking people to respond to you offline.

There are also some newsgroups focused on journalism. These may attract more news consumers than news creators, but they can also be interesting places to monitor. The easiest way to browse messages in journalism-related newsgroups is to go to Google Groups (groups.google.com) and type *journalism*. You'll get messages from alt.journalism, alt.journalism.criticism, alt.journalism.freelance, alt.journalism.students, and so on.

Monitoring the reaction to news coverage can also be of interest, particularly to public relations professionals. You can usually find discussion about major news stories in a newsgroup on that news story's topic. This is a good way to combine journalistic and informal sources of information and comment.

Newsgroups also serve as informal distributors of articles of interest. A search for messages in Google Groups on *prescription drug prices* provides links to stories from institutional and journalistic sources:

- AARP Bulletin
- Families USA Report
- The Congressional Record
- McClatchy Newspapers

Searching Journalistic Sources

The first thing to determine when searching for journalistic sources is the time frame within which the stories you want were produced. This will help you decide which route you need to take in locating the materials you need.

Before digital production of content, you needed to use a printed index and microfilm to find previously published stories in print; broadcast stories were essentially lost. Or you could call the news library and hope you could get the news librarian to look something up for you in the clip files. Then, as databases of news stories were sold through large commercial vendors, you could—in one search—access the archives of hundreds of news publications and shows. Now individual news Web sites have their own archives of news stories, and in some cases, there are two databases of news stories on the site—one which is an archive of the content of the Web site, usually searched for free, and another which provides access to the newsprint publication's stories—usually for a fee.

All of these options for searching for materials from worldwide publications and broadcasts certainly enhance the communicator's range of access, but they also complicate the information process. If you are going to do a thorough job of searching journalistic sources you might have to use a variety of methods—contacting the news researcher to check backfiles, checking through print indexes and microfilm, searching through commercial databases, and checking individual news Web sites.

Let's look at different types of reference tools and sources you can use to find journalistic materials.

Indexes. These standard references to articles in publications have gone through their own revolution in the past two decades. For years, indexes were printed on paper and you usually had to search multiple volumes of the index if you wanted to cover a span of years. Then, in the 1980s, many supplemented their paper editions with CD-ROM versions of the same material. Some even expanded their "citation only" information to include an abstract of the article's contents. Then, with the growth of the Web, many of the major indexing services moved to online database versions, many of them with full text of the articles they cite. Here are some of the major indexes to newspapers, magazines, and broadcast programs.

- *The Reader's Guide to Periodical Literature*, 1890 to date. Digital since 1983. *The Reader's Guide* is probably most familiar to any schoolchild who uses the local public or school library. This index covers material that has appeared in about 275 general and popular magazines. Few technical, specialized, or subject-specific journals are included. In the past, paper editions of the index required you to look in each volume issued during the year; these would then be compiled into an annual volume.
- *Business Periodicals Index*, 1958 to date. Digital since 1982. This Index includes both journalistic sources and institutional sources. There are citations to articles in 594 publications that cover business and industry, as well as journals published by trade associations or industry-specific organizations. The articles you'll find in the *Business Periodicals Index* are valuable for information about industries, markets, population characteristics, trends in business, or biographical information about people in business.
- *Alternative Press Index:* 1969–present. Digital since 1991. A quarterly subject index to more than 250 alternative, radical, and left-wing periodicals, newspapers, and

magazines covering topics such as gay rights, socialism, the women's movement, and minority rights. If you are looking for information from non-mainstream publications, this index is one of the best sources. A listing of the publications it indexes can be found here:

www.altpress.org/direct.html

- *The New York Times Index:* 1851 to date. (Semimonthly with quarterly and annual cumulations). Digital since 1969. Perhaps the most sophisticated of the printed newspaper indexes, the *New York Times Index* includes not only the date, page number, and column information needed to locate an article, but also a brief summary of the articles. For some items, the index actually reproduces a photo, graph, map, or chart that was important in the article, making a trip to the microfilm issues unnecessary. Interpreting a *New York Times Index* entry is a little different from interpreting a periodical index entry, but is just as simple once the basic elements are known. Citations to articles in the *New York Times* are available back to 1969 and full text of articles from 1980 forward are available on LexisNexis. The *New York Times* Web site has the past week's worth of articles searchable for free, and back to 1996 for a fee.
- *Wall Street Journal Index*, 1955 to date. Digital since 1990. Indexed in two parts, "Corporate News" and "General News," with brief summaries of each article.
- *Official Washington Post Index*, 1979 to 1988. Digital since 1990. Monthly publication with annual cumulations.
- *NewsBank:* monthly. 1970 to date. Digital since 1980. Selected articles from more than 450 newspapers are indexed in this printed tool, with the full text of the articles.
- *ABC News Index:* 1969 to date. Digital since 1990.
- *CBS News Index:* 1975 to date. Digital since 1990.
- *NBC News:* Full-text Nov. 1, 1989, through *Burrelle's.*
- *CNBC News:* Full-text March 1, 1994, through *Burrelle's.*
- *Summary of World Broadcasts:* 1973 to date. Weekly. Transcripts of news broadcasts monitored and translated into English by the BBC.
- *Foreign Broadcast Information Service Daily Reports:* 1975 to 1996. Digital since 1996 through *Global NewsBank.* Transcripts of news broadcasts monitored and translated into English by the U.S. government.
- *Television News Index and Abstracts:* 1967 to date. Digital since 1993. Printed index to the videotapes of national evening news as broadcast by ABC, NBC, and CBS, with CNN broadcasts added starting in 1989. Collected by the Vanderbilt University Television News Archives. Users may conduct searches by name, subject, or reporter. The tapes themselves are available from the Vanderbilt Television News Archives in Nashville, Tennessee; the archive will loan tapes, duplicate news broadcasts, or compile items from various broadcasts upon request from the users. Beginning in 1993, the entire contents of the Index and Abstracts were also transferred to an electronic database, now searchable on the Internet (tvnews.vanderbilt.edu).

Database Services. The bread and butter of news searching has been the large commercial database services such as Dialog (www.dialog.com) and LexisNexis (www.lexisnexis.com) or Factiva (www.factiva.com). These provide cross-title searching of multiple news organizations' materials—for a fee. These large subscription database services are best accessed through a public or university library.

News Web Sites. The growth of news Web sites has been a boon to the researcher. Even publications too small to have been attractive to the major news database vendors in the past now have their articles available in electronic backfiles.

- *NewsLink:* newslink.org—Find newspapers, magazines, and radio/tv sites by region and by category.
- *MediaInfo* from *Editor & Publisher:* www.mediainfo.com/editorandpublisher/business_resources/medialinks.jsp. Links to more than 3,500 newspaper sites from around the world.
- *News365:* www.news365.com. More than 10,000 news media outlets lists. Organized by 300 topic areas.
- *News Archives on the Web:* www.ibiblio.org/slanews/internet/archives.html. Listing by state and country of news archives, how far back they go, and the cost of searching them.
- *Ultimate Collection of News Links:* 64.227.22.235/links/news/. Organized by continent.
- *Radio-Locator:* www.radio-locator.com/cgi-bin/home (see Figure 10.1). Links to more than 10,000 radio station Web pages and more than 2,500 audio streams from radio stations in the U.S. and around the world.

News Aggregators. News aggregators are great resources for staying up on a particular breaking or current news story. They compile information from a number of publications and programs and make them available. Google News (news.google.com), News Hub (www.newshub.com), NewsTrove (www.newstrove.com), and News Now (www.newsnow.co.uk) are examples of news aggregators that track stories by topic. Checking in each day on those topics can be a great way to both monitor the news and search for current stories.

Directories of Journalists. Most strategic communications firms subscribe to directories that help them locate journalists. These include *Bacon's Media Directory* (www.bacons.com), *Burrelle's Media Directories* (www.burrelles.com), *Editor and Publisher Yearbook*, and *MediaMap* (www.mediamap.com). You can find names, addresses, and e-mail addresses for reporters, information about the publications they write for, and the specifics about the beats they cover. Especially for public relations professionals who need to place stories in news media or interview journalists, these resources are crucial.

Interviewing Journalistic Sources

Journalists, for whom interviews are the foundation of their work, are notoriously reluctant interviewees themselves. Unless they are promoting themselves for a book or

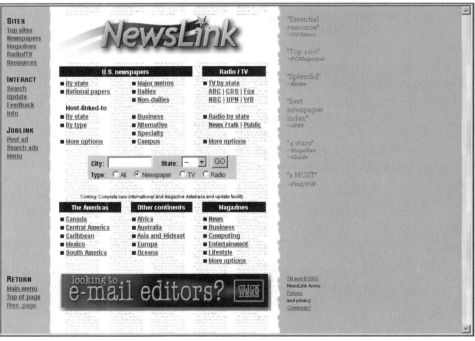

FIGURE 10.1 Web sites such as radio-locator.com and NewsLink.org are convenient ways to find a list of news outlets—by location or format—quickly.

Source: Theodric Technologies LLC and NewsLink Associates. Reprinted by permission.

have just won an award or are one of the pundits found on Sunday morning news programs, journalists would much rather be on the interviewer side of the desk, rather than the interviewee.

If you are looking for personal commentary, insight, or advice from an individual journalist, first you have to find him or her. You might locate the name of a reporter you'd like to talk with from a byline on a story. Some news organizations include e-mail addresses on their reporters' bylines. Most news organizations have on their Web sites a listing of names and contact information for people in their newsroom. If you don't have a specific name of someone and are just looking for a journalist who has experience or knowledge about a particular story, then posting a question to a list or newsgroup where journalists correspond might be a useful tactic. Tell them you are interested in someone who has covered, say, the rising cost of prescription drugs, and ask them to e-mail you directly.

Another journalistic source you'll want to interview is the news librarian or news researcher. They can be harder to get to, though, than the journalist. For years, news libraries considered allowing access to their files by the public to be a public service. As the pressures of production of daily archives and budget demands to reduce staff grew, the number of news libraries who will take calls from the public and locate articles has decreased.

The network of news researchers is strong, so use your own news researcher, if you are in a news organization, or an agency librarian to make your contact for you. The Web site for the Special Libraries Association, News Division—(www.ibiblio.org/slanews) is a good source for information about news researchers and their work.

The directories we just identified will also be good sources for locating journalists.

CAUTIONS FOR USE

- Remember, news is the first take on history, so keep in mind that the journalistic source you are referring to might not be the definitive word on the topic. Also, news organizations can be lax in ensuring that the corrections they do make to their stories actually become part of the permanent record.

- News organizations sometimes have short attention spans. They may report on a topic that flares into the public eye, but not follow up on the aftermath. If you need to follow the progression of a particular story or event, you may need to go to other sources to get the full picture.

- The perspective of the news organization will color both the tone of the reporting and the selection of news stories in the publication. An article in the *National Review* will reflect a very different ideological perspective than one on the same topic in the *Nation* or in the *Economist*. All three are popular magazines, but you had better understand the ideological point of view they represent before using an article from one of them.

- The standards to which the news organization adheres can vary from those used at the *New York Times* to those used at the *National Enquirer*, from those used on the *Daily Show*, to those used on *Nightline*. The audience is generally not as savvy about the differences in the standards used but you, as a communicator, must be able to make these distinctions. This will be discussed in more detail in Chapter 11.

- If there are competitive or personal turf issues, journalists will not be forthcoming sources. Framing your research request to be as nonthreatening as possible will be the best approach.
- Journalists skim the first few inches of a topic, they rarely dig deeply. If it is depth you are looking for, you'll need to go to scholarly or institutional sources.

CASE STUDY OF JOURNALISTIC INFORMATION SOURCES

One major U.S. public relations firm and its client, a non-profit health organization, faced a difficult media relations challenge following the terrorist attacks of September 11, 2001. Instinctively, the team knew that this unprecedented event would have serious implications on how the media, legislators, health officials, and the American public would perceive the non-profit group's planned release of the results of its annual healthcare performance survey, set for October 2001. For example, would the media see the release of this information at that time as frivolous or self-serving? The PR firm turned to journalistic sources to get a sense of the media environment in which their client's news release would be placed.

The media relations team conducted extensive, daily audits of national U.S. newspapers to examine the types of stories that were running and the extent to which reporters and publications were returning to normal coverage. The PR practitioners paid particular attention to the amount of space devoted to terrorist versus nonterrorist articles, and noted that many reporters were covering areas outside of their normal beat. They also found that many features and business sections—where healthcare coverage is normally found—were carrying national news instead. Perhaps more importantly, the team identified a theme of unity running throughout much of the coverage.

The situation was further complicated when envelopes contaminated with anthrax began appearing in U.S. mail. The PR team's daily media audit revealed that the *only* type of healthcare-related news coverage found in the newspapers it was monitoring was on the topic of bioterrorism.

The team members next used the LexisNexis database to search for news articles and broadcast coverage that had run the previous year following the release of the nonprofit organization's annual survey. They found that the tone of much of this past coverage was competitive. For example, in the stories they found from the previous year's coverage the focus was on how different U.S. states stacked up to each other in the health survey, with those states achieving the top marks pitted against those in the bottom ten positions. This analysis of journalistic sources alerted PR team members to some important insights. First, it was clear that a healthcare story that did not address the terrorist threats—and bioterrorism concerns more specifically—would be outside of the current news agenda. Second, it raised concerns that the potentially divisive nature of the survey—which positioned some states as performing better than others—was not the right focus at a time when unity was important to the nation. Clearly, the positioning used in the previous year's news coverage had to change.

The PR team (with feedback from a large group of state public health officials and public information officers) made the decision to downplay the non-profit group's role in generating the report, instead using the information to spark discussion about the importance of the U.S. public health infrastructure—especially post-September 11. The survey was used as a way to stimulate discussion about what each state was doing well, along with ways to pull together to achieve continued improvement.

The new strategy proved effective with *USA Today*, leading to an article in the national newspaper's Life section. This publication was identified as an important target through interviews conducted with broadcast journalists both prior to, and after, September 11. These interviews revealed that many television stations in smaller markets were unable to afford a reporter devoted to healthcare, especially in light of the economic downturn. PR team members learned from the reporters they interviewed that the *USA Today* Life section, in particular, was described as having a cascade effect—meaning that stations without a healthcare reporter often took *USA Today*'s lead in determining what kind of healthcare stories to air.

In addition to *USA Today*, team members used the MediaMap directory (www.mediamap.com) to compile a list of the top health and lifestyle editors and writers at national daily newspapers, daily newspapers in the top 100 cities, wire services, national and local broadcast outlets, business and trade publications, and Web news outlets. The team also proactively called a select group of these news organizations to personally pitch the story. The pitch list included top-tier media outlets (such as CNN and the *Chicago Sun-Times*), as well as media located in smaller markets. Practitioners used the MediaMap database to find background information about each of these news outlets and about the healthcare or lifestyle reporters' preferences—types of stories they're interested in, whether they prefer to be contacted by phone or e-mail. In addition, they located past articles to familiarize themselves with each particular reporter's writing style before making a pitch call or sending an e-mail.

This effort resulted in more than fifty print and 100 television broadcast stories—due in large part to tapping into journalistic sources to ensure that the messages would resonate with these gatekeepers operating in an atypical media environment.

In the next chapter, we discuss how to evaluate the information you have gathered with your successful information strategy.

SELECTED ADDITIONAL READINGS

Hane, Paula J., and Scott Simon. *Super Searchers in the News: The Online Secrets of Journalists and News Researchers.* Edited by Reva Basch. Medford, NJ: Cyberage Books, 2000.

Silverblatt, Art, Jane Ferry, and Barbara Finan. *Approaches to Media Literacy: A Handbook.* Armonk, NY: M.E. Sharpe, 1999.

NOTES

1. Dave Winer, "Radio is a News Aggregator," *Radio UserLand*, (June 11, 2002), www.radio.userland.com/whatIsANewsAggregator

2. Arik R. Johnson, "News Clipping Services," *netWorker: The Craft of Network Computing*, 3.3 (September 1999), www.acm.org/networker/issue/9903/incs.html © 1999 ACM. Reprinted by permission.

3. "Lurkers and Babblers Liven up your Web Sites Discussion Board," *e* Magazine, 10 May 2001, www.e-magazineonline.com/EBI/EBI011804.htm

CHAPTER ELEVEN

EVALUATING AND SELECTING THE INFORMATION YOU'VE GATHERED

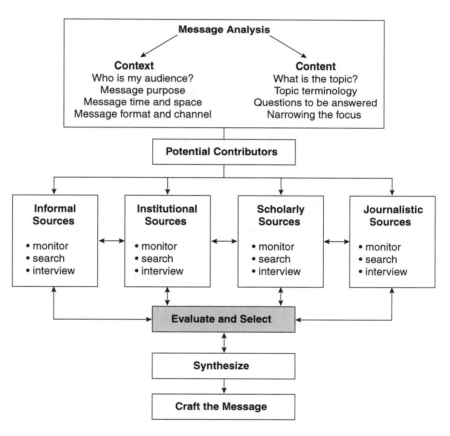

The Information Strategy Model

There is little doubt that the most challenging work in the information strategy process often is evaluating and selecting information. Of course, evaluation and selection do not occur only after all or most of the information has been collected. In fact, selections are made during earlier parts of the strategy, when you take or avoid a particular route through the information universe. For example, a news reporter may decide a potential interviewee is not reliable, based on previous experience with the person or on the individual's reputation for trustworthiness. The reporter finds and interviews others instead. Or, a public relations specialist may discover conflicting information in journalistic reports about an event and decide to seek original documents or more reliable statistical information from scholarly sources. Still, there is a special time of reckoning at the point in the search when much of the information has been collected and you must decide what it means and what the message will include. This chapter examines the judgments made in evaluating and selecting information for the message.

If you have mastered the information-gathering skills we have been discussing, you will usually find yourself buried under far more information than will ever be used in any particular message. Your powers of critical thinking and careful scrutiny are crucial at this point in the process. Evaluating information requires skills honed for analysis, skepticism, a regard for accuracy, an ear for the "false ring." Communicators ask themselves a set of questions:

- What should be verified?
- What needs to be reinvestigated?
- What is the element of *risk* involved in information revelation and use?
- What are the *consequences* of putting this information into the public arena?

By asking yourself these kinds of questions, you begin to develop patterns of verification and pathways for tracing information. You need to develop alternative interpretations of facts in order to protect yourself against being taken in, or to avoid doing the same old thing with your message. News professionals want to figure out other possible meanings of information, to avoid the *handout syndrome* (allowing an information subsidizer to frame their understanding of a topic or issue). Advertising professionals want to be creative and original in their selection and use of information for their attention-grabbing messages. Public relations professionals want to select the "best light" material so their clients' messages are targeted properly and have the intended effect.

CRITICAL THINKING

We live in a world that is inundated with information. Making sense of facts, opinions, assertions, claims, and appeals has become such a challenge that educators from preschool through higher education now recognize the importance of teaching critical thinking skills. You are especially responsible for applying critical thinking to the information you may use in messages. There are many formulas for critical thinking, but the underlying skill is the ability to ask intelligent questions that help you decide which information to accept on behalf of your audience.

M. Neil Browne and Stuart Keeley[1] provide a checklist of questions that critical thinkers pose when they are faced with the challenge of evaluating information:

1. What are the issue and the conclusion?
2. What are the reasons?
3. Which words or phrases are ambiguous?
4. What are the value conflicts and assumptions?
5. What are the descriptive assumptions?
6. Are there any fallacies in reasoning?
7. How good is the evidence?
8. Are there rival causes?
9. Are the statistics deceptive?
10. What significant information is omitted?
11. What reasonable conclusions are possible?

While it is beyond the scope of this chapter to summarize each of the questions Browne and Keeley recommend for critical thinkers, we might focus on the few that are most relevant for communicators at this step of the information strategy process. These include an analysis of the words and phrases in any source of information, an analysis of the evidence, and an analysis of the statistics.

Language Cues

Language can be a cue that helps you invoke the critical-thinking mode. Words and phrases have amazing flexibility, suggesting one meaning to some and another, very different, meaning to others. Think about the different connotations of the words *terrorist* and *freedom fighter.* Or the words *tax increase* and *revenue enhancement.* Or the words *layoffs* and *reorganization.* Each pair may be used to describe precisely the same thing by different speakers or writers. Yet they carry entirely different meanings, and the meaning changes even more when the word or words are placed in the larger context of a sentence, a paragraph, or a fully-developed document, speech, or publication.

So what is the critical thinker to do in the face of these language challenges? For one thing, you need to be able to recognize and flag the key words or phrases that are meant to convey the main point in any document, interview transcript, Web page, or other source of information. Pay attention to the role these key words play in the overall argument or conclusion the information source wants to make. Communicators writing about the 500th anniversary of Columbus' voyage to the New World noticed that some people described the trip as the "discovery of America," while others referred to it as "Columbus' invasion of the Americas." The difference between the key words *discovery* and *invasion* provided a clear signal about the overall argument different sources were advancing about that historic event. In that instance, you would be alert to the dangers of adopting the perspective and language of one source over the other without raising critical questions.

Tests of Evidence

The obvious use of evidence is in the deliberation process. Courts of law and legal professionals (law enforcement officers, lawyers, judges) are concerned about the admissibility of evidence, the appropriateness of evidence to the making of a case, and other judicial standards. Rhetoricians and scholars of debate concentrate on the types of data that can be considered as evidence, sources of evidence, and the classification of evidence for the purposes of effective persuasion or debate.

For mass communicators, the use of standards of evidence takes on a slightly different hue. Evidence can be in the form of written materials (articles, books, letters, court records, Web sites), oral communications (interview testimony, focus group sessions), or personal observation, knowledge, or experience. You can apply traditional *tests of evidence* to all the information that is gathered through the information strategy process. When skillfully applied, these tests of evidence can alert you to potential problems or inconsistencies in information, to the gaps or holes in your information search, and to areas that require further investigation.

Here are the tests of evidence[2] as they apply to mass communication information gathering:

1. *Clarity.* During an interview with a person who witnessed a holdup, you discover that the witness can be clear on just two points about the robbery and the perpetrator. You would have to evaluate the testimony of the witness on the basis of clarity and may decide that the evidence is not trustworthy and can't be used. Or, as an advertising account executive, you might decide that the advertising campaign goals of the client are unclear, requiring further information gathering before you can effectively plan the campaign.

2. *Verifiability.* A famous author may write an autobiography that includes a number of impressive claims about his or her education, achievements, and financial success. You may be unable to verify that the author actually attended the schools because enrollment and alumni records may not include the author's name. Or, an advertising client may wish to make claims about the superiority of the company's product but may not be able to provide the substantiating documents to verify the claims. If this is the case, then you can't create an ad which makes that kind of claim.

3. *Accuracy.* You are a reporter attending an event as an observer, and you count about 25 people in the audience. Two hours after you get back to the newsroom, the event sponsors sends out a news release claiming about 250 people were there. You would reject that news release on the basis of accuracy.

4. *Recency.* A public relations firm working on the problem of airport noise for an airport commission needs the most recent figures on the number of takeoffs and landings since the airport was expanded. Information about how recent flight activity compares with pre-expansion activity is also useful. Or, an ad campaign for a new brand of pizza requires the most recent information about consumer preferences and the media habits of pizza eaters. You would reject a marketing study that was two years old on the basis of the recency test.

5. *Relevance.* An advertiser evaluating market research about consumer characteristics must decide whether the research is relevant to the product or service being advertised. A study of people who buy chicken may or may not be relevant to the advertiser of turkey. Or, a reporter writing about the nation's *fiscal* policy may reject the notion of interviewing an expert on *monetary* policy, based on the relevance test. The testimony of a movie celebrity about federal research funding for a particular disease might be rejected in favor of a medical specialist's view, based on the test of relevance.

6. *Reputation.* People, institutions, and print and electronic records have reputations. A reporter might try to arrange an interview with a government official who has a reputation for being candid and forthright on the issue of tax reform. The same reporter might avoid another official because of his or her reputation for stonewalling the press. Or, a public relations practitioner may rely on a scholarly study of the effects of factory emissions on air quality rather than on a study done internally by the factory's own staff because the PR professional knows that the public will hold the independent study in higher regard.

7. *Sufficiency.* You're in charge of the ad campaign for a new chain of music stores. You get a marketing research report from a group which monitors teen spending. However, the category for teen spending in the area of music does not break down the specific music types. This report, then, would be rejected on the basis of the sufficiency test.

8. *Internal consistency.* You might decide not to use a particular document because the figures for average household income used on page 15 are inconsistent with those on page 38, indicating a serious internal consistency problem. Or, the testimony of an interviewee varies widely over the course of a three-hour interview, suggesting that the interviewee is being inconsistent in her or his story.

9. *External consistency.* Two reports on the implications of a change in property taxes come to different conclusions about the projected tax on a $200,000 house, alerting you that there is an external consistency problem with the evidence. Further information is therefore needed to clarify the inconsistency. Or, an advertising firm conducts its own research about the market for a new brand of jeans, and the conclusions differ from those of an industry-wide research project about the same project, suggesting an external consistency problem.

10. *Comparative quality.* Decisions about what constitutes good information or the best information are necessary at some point. An ad researcher preparing an ad campaign for a new line of athletic apparel might decide that in comparing two studies of teenage athletes, the study that specifically addresses athletes' leisure activities is the most useful. Or, a reporter might decide that among all the interviews she conducted with experts on the subject of rising health care costs, two stand out as being the most informative and containing the freshest perspectives on the topic.

11. *Contextuality.* All information exists within a particular context. An interviewee's comments at one point in an interview cannot be taken out of context of the rest of the interview. Isolated figures in a report about the incidence of police loafing on the job cannot be taken out of the context of the rest of the report, which might indicate that the problem is not widespread. Both the context and the time period within which information exists must be recognized and respected. If the context or time period cannot be determined, the information is suspect.

12. *Statistical Validity.* It is not necessary for you to become a statistician in order to test the validity of statistical claims. Simple questions about the method of gathering the statistics, the method of analyzing the data, and the standards for drawing the conclusions from the data are within your ability. We'll address some of these skills in a later section in this chapter.

There are many examples of how the tests of evidence are applied in mass media message-making. The extensive fact-checking of articles that appear in a magazine; the multiple methods for evaluating information about audiences and consumers for advertising and marketing decisions; verifying information for news accounts—you can apply all of these methods for the purposes of meeting *your own* need for appropriate evidence before using information in a message.

Also, however, there is concern for the acceptability of the evidence to the *audience.* Is the material understandable, believable, useful to the point being made, and from a familiar source? If not, more evidence than normally is needed will have to be gathered and presented to overcome the audiences' natural skepticism. For example, if a fast food restaurant is going to make a claim in an advertising message that its food is healthful, you need to understand that the audience will demand a higher level of evidence than would normally be the case, because it is counter to common sense that such food is healthy.

Here's an example of one of the tests of evidence—comparative quality—and how it applies in mass media message making. One of the local television stations in the Minneapolis–St. Paul area has an investigative team that regularly produces investigative reports for the local news. The I-Team actually has a hierarchy of quality for the evidence they require when doing an investigation. The I-Team tries to use their investigations to expose wrongdoing and acts of corruption.

The communicators at this station use the comparative quality standard for their evidence, and put videotape of the specific act of crime or corruption at the top of the list of information they need. A close second on their list is to have a document that lends evidence to the case they are making. Something like a cancelled check, a letter, a public record of a campaign contribution; documents like these are considered good evidence. The rest of their list includes disinterested eyewitnesses (those who have nothing to gain or lose by telling their information), interested eyewitnesses, the journalists' own observations, and, finally, anonymous tips. In fact, the I-Team producers won't use an anonymous tip as the sole source of evidence for a claim of crime or corruption because, in addition to being at the bottom of the comparative quality list, it also fails the sufficiency, credibility, and reputation tests. They have decided that they cannot trust such a tip by itself—they must have at least one other source of evidence from the preferred types on their list to confirm the tip before they will use that information.[3]

The verifiability test is another one with plenty of examples in mass communication work. The classified ad department of a local Minneapolis newspaper ran an ad on two consecutive days indicating that PC Express, a local computer retailer, had lost a class-action lawsuit in federal court and that customers were entitled to recover monetary damages. The ad said the suit involved false advertising, lack of FCC registration for computer electrical standards, and violation of Minnesota warranty laws. The ads also listed a federal court case number for the suit and suggested readers call a specific local law firm to file their claims. But it turned out that the ad was a fraud.

Here's how it happened. At 7 p.m. on a Friday night, a caller claiming to be an attorney from a local law firm telephoned the classified ad department to ask if a facsimile of a legal notice had been received. When no facsimile could be found, the classified ad staff person took the wording of the advertisement over the phone with the understanding that the law firm would be billed for the ad. The person who took the call did not try to call the law firm back to confirm the accuracy of the information because it was assumed that the firm would be closed for the weekend. No questions were raised because the information was detailed, complete, and the caller had correct information for billing.

But there was no such suit and Minnesota federal court records showed no such case number as the one indicated in the ad. The local law firm said it knew nothing about the ad until it was published. The computer company president charged that the newspaper was negligent for not checking on the accuracy of such a damaging notice. The newspaper was forced to run a retraction and apologize for the mistake.[4]

The classified ad staff have access to the news library, and there is someone on staff in the library over two shifts. Applying the tests of evidence, the ad staff person could easily have asked the news library staff to run a search in one of the legal databases to find the court case number and see if it was accurately described. When no such case number was found, the ad person would have known that there was a problem, and that the ad should be held until more evidence was gathered. This would have avoided the embarrassment of such a public mistake.

Verifying the accuracy of visual information is another challenge for communicators trying to apply the tests of evidence to information. The increasing use of freelance images and video opens the media to the possibility of fraud. With today's computer and photographic equipment, there are more and more sophisticated ways to manipulate images. Rank amateurs can use digital techniques for doctoring photos, creating video of things that never happened, and causing all sorts of mischief with visual information.

There have also been several incidents of staged photos. An infamous example occurred after the death of England's Princess Diana, her companion, and their driver in a gruesome automobile accident in Paris in 1997. Shortly after the world learned of the accident, a photo appeared on the Internet and was subsequently distributed by several news services and published on the front page of a French newspaper. The photo showed a mangled Mercedes with a blonde victim in the back seat, and rescue workers and emergency vehicles surrounding the crash site. Even the most rudimentary check of the authenticity of this photo would have revealed that the rescue workers' uniforms did not match any used by Paris fire brigades, and the phone number visible on the side of a rescue vehicle would not work anywhere in France. Similar hoax photographs appeared on the Web in multitudes after the terrorist attacks on the World Trade Center and the Pentagon in the United States in September 2001.

There is a related problem in using satellite images. Several firms now sell satellite images as a commercial venture. Interpreting information from a satellite photo requires expertise usually not available in news organizations. The old saying "A picture is worth a thousand words" was never true (photographers have always *chosen* the way to represent their images and a photo was never an objective representation of reality), but now it is even less useful as a way to think about visual information. Again, common sense and a critical mind will help avoid problems.

Analyzing Statistics

You have no doubt heard the saying, "Lies, damned lies, and statistics." Statistics do not, in and of themselves, lie. The problem with statistics is in the application or interpretation of the statistics. Most problems with statistics involve ineptitude, not deliberate lying. The numbers themselves are not even the issue. You need to evaluate how numbers are used to provide context and interpretation for an idea or trend. Some basic types of statistical interpretation problems[5] to look out for are described here:

1. The *everything is going up* statistic—More people are employed, more people are getting certain diseases, and so on. This type of statistic is usually right, but also meaningless, because the total number of people is also going up all the time. A more useful statistic is the rate or proportion of the population that is affected by something or doing something. The total number of plane crashes may be higher than the year before, but the more important figure is the one that says how many crashes have occurred *per number of passenger flights* or *per miles traveled* or some other benchmark that provides the rate or proportion, rather than the absolute raw number of crashes.

2. The *best foot* statistic—The number that best supports a case is the one that is chosen by the person making the argument. Someone may choose the worst year of a recession and compare current economic conditions to that worst year in order to make the current climate look good. Or someone may choose to use the mean family income figure when the median figure might more accurately reflect whether incomes have risen or fallen (see Box 11.1).

3. The *gee-whiz* or *half-truth* statistic—The number that tells just part of the story. If the overall unemployment figure is not dramatic enough to make the point, then the person providing the number focuses on the unemployment rate for teens, or for specific industrial states, or some other smaller or unrepresentative group. Groups that are trying to influence public debate are notorious for these types of half-truth statistics.

4. The *anecdote* statistic—The one-in-a-million exception that supposedly proves the rule. It is always crucial for you to ask how many instances or people are represented by the statistic.

5. The *everyone is average* statistic—The tendency to characterize individuals by group characteristics. For example, many argue that women can't be soldiers or firefighters because the average man can lift more weight than the average woman. But people are individuals, not averages, and many women can and do lift more than many men.

BOX 11.1
MEAN AND MEDIAN

It is important for you to brush up on your basic mathematical terminology, in order to be able to interpret the numbers you find in many reports, studies, documents, and other types of information resources. A few commonly confused terms are explained here:

Percent. A standard way of expressing a fraction, where the denominator (the bottom number) equals 100; so 1/4 equals 25 percent (4 × 25 = 100), 1/3 equals 33 percent (3 × 33 = 99 rounded to 100), 1/5 equals 20 percent (5 × 20 = 100), and so on.

Percent Change. A way to express a relationship between an old number and a change or a new number and a change. For example, last year's budget is $500,000 and the current budget is $600,000. The change is $100,000. To express this as a *percent change* from last year to this, you have to divide the change by the old number, or $100,000/$500,000 = 0.2 = 20 percent. The new budget is therefore 20 percent higher than the previous year's budget. To figure what percent of spending in the current budget is new, you have to divide the change by the higher new figure, or $100,000/$600,000 = 0.1666... = 16.7 percent.

Percentage Point. A way to compare two numbers that are already expressed as percents. For example, the March unemployment figure is 5 percent, the April unemployment figure is 6 percent, and the change is 1 percentage point. The percent change is 1 (the change) divided by 5 (the old number), or 20 percent.

Mean. The arithmetic average of a set of values.

Median. The middle value in a group, where values have been ranked from top to bottom.

Let's take the last items on the list: the difference between a mean and a median. The *mean* is the arithmetic average of a set of values. To compute a mean, you simply add up the values and divide by the number of values. For example, let's say that among 100 workers at a company, 95 make $30,000 and 5 make $300,000 a year. The mean salary is therefore (95 times 30,000) plus (5 times 300,000) divided by 100 OR 4,350,000 divided by 100 OR $43,500. This simple arithmetic average provides information about the average salary for workers at the company. But does it accurately describe salaries at this company? If you answered no, you begin to understand how important it is to evaluate how a figure is arrived at. A better way to portray salaries for this company is to use the median figure rather than the mean.

The *median* is the middle value in a group, where values have been ranked from top to bottom. A median figure is more likely to smooth out very wide differences between the highest and lowest values in the group. For example, the middle value in our group of 100 salaries in our imaginary company ranked from top to bottom is the average of the salary of the 50th and 51st highest paid people. In this case, the median is therefore $30,000. The median figure clearly tells you more accurately about the salaries for the majority of people in the company.

6. The *coincidence* statistic—When is something actually related to something else, and when is it just a coincidence? The corollary is that just because two things are correlated doesn't mean that one thing caused the other. For instance, consider a study with the following title: "Bottled Water Linked to Healthier Babies." The title invites you to infer a causal connection between bottled water and babies' health. However, think carefully about what else this might mean. Affluent parents are more likely both to drink bottled water and to have healthy children; they have the stability and wherewithal to offer good food, clothing, shelter, health care, and amenities. Families that own cappuccino makers are more likely to have healthy babies for the same reason, but we wouldn't waste time considering a study that was titled "Cappuccino Linked to Healthier Babies."[6]

Box 11.2 presents statistical terminology you should understand. An important strategy in evaluating information that includes statistics is to find out as much as possible about where the numbers were obtained. Avoid estimates that appear too precise to be true, use common sense when presented with numbers that appear counterintuitive, and maintain skepticism with claims that could just as easily be based on coincidence. A good starting question to ask about any statistical claim is, "How do you know that?" Is the person or organization that provides the statistics just telling you something they "know" or have "found to be true?" Or can they provide studies, experiments and documentation of the claim? Even if someone says, "I've done a study,"

■ ■ ■ ■ ■

BOX 11.2
STATISTICAL TERMINOLOGY

To upgrade your skill at interpreting applied statistics, you need do no more than review a few basic terms and concepts:

Hypothesis. A tentative statement of the expected relationship among variables, which must then be tested through research.

Dependent Variable. A variable that is influenced by another variable; for example, if salary level is influenced by education level, salary level is the dependent variable.

Independent Variable. A variable that influences another variable; in our example above, if education level influences the salary someone earns, education level is the independent variable.

Significance. A measure of whether the result in a study could just as likely have been found by chance; statistical significance is usually expressed as a p (or probability) value; a low p value (.05 or less, or 5 or fewer chances in 100) means there is a small likelihood that a result could have happened by chance.

Reliability. The extent to which a result can be reproduced when a test or study is repeated.

Validity. The extent to which a study measures what was intended to be measured.

Distribution of Responses. The summary of a collection of measurements or values; showing how the results of a study fall along some type of scale, for instance.

Correlation. The extent to which two or more variables are related.

you should ask, "What kind? What were the possible flaws in the study?" An honest researcher will always report the limitations of his or her data. Also, recognize that a single study rarely proves anything.

Another good question is, "How sure are you about your numbers?" There are many obstacles to gathering certain types of information. How certain can we be about the number of people in the United States who shoplift, carry the AIDS virus, are homeless, commit white-collar crimes, or drink more than three beers a day? People are unwilling to provide truthful information for certain purposes, many things go undocumented, and there are physical barriers to accurate observation of many types of activities.

Also, form the habit of blinding yourself to the information's statistics. Instead, ask yourself what kind of evidence would be convincing to prove the information's point. In other words, compare the *needed* statistics with the *given* statistics. Pay attention to whether the statistics are said to prove one thing when they could more reasonably be used to conclude something else. For example, a car dealer might claim that a particular model was widely successful because just 5 out of the 100 people who bought the car had complained to the dealership about its performance. If you blind yourself to the car dealer's statistics, you would have to ask how to prove that a particular model was widely successful. You should conclude that you would want to sample a large number of buyers of that model from many different dealerships and ask them if they were pleased with the car. Instead, the dealer heard only from those who complained, and assumed that all the noncomplainers were satisfied, an unwarranted assumption. The dealer proves one thing (few buyers complained) and concludes another (the model is widely successful).[7]

Sarah Cohen, database editor at the *Washington Post*, wrote a book titled *Numbers in the Newsroom* in which she offers some simple advice that is appropriate for all types of communicators. For instance, every one of you would benefit from memorizing some common numbers in your area of work. You probably need to know the population of the United States (about 285 million at the time of this writing) and the income of the typical household in the country (about $41,000 at this time), for example. Every sort of communications task (your reporting beat, your ad client's industry, your PR client's audience) has its own specialized numbers as well. Medical reporters need to know the annual number of deaths each year in the United States. Ad account executives need to know what rank their client company holds in its market. PR practitioners need to know how many media organizations they must contact with a client's message in order to be successful. Memorize these specialized numbers and you'll be much more comfortable in your communications work.

Another piece of advice from Cohen is to use devices from everyday life when working with numbers. Sports fans know how to calculate an earned run average even if they flunked high school math! Most of us know how to figure out the price of something that is marked on sale for 10 percent off. This means that you know how to do the math that is used most heavily in creating messages. Simply convert your questions into these types of everyday math problems. You and your audience will benefit.

Cohen also advises her readers to use the tools available to them. Anyone who works at a computer workstation has a calculator built into their desktop software.

Many will also have a simple database management system and a simple spreadsheet program on their computer desktops. These three tools can provide enormous help in working with statistics and numbers. Invest the time to learn the basics of these tools and you will be rewarded with a set of skills and confidence in working with numbers that might now elude you.

Finally, always double check your answers and ask yourself if the number you are thinking of using (as a source of evidence, as part of the copy of your message, as an argument for your story pitch) makes sense. Ask yourself if you'd believe that number if you saw it in a message. As Cohen says, some numbers just don't stand up to common sense. If the number you're working with doesn't, make sure you haven't misunderstood the calculation, mistyped the numbers, or misread the results.[8]

EVALUATING POLL AND SURVEY INFORMATION

Communicators are faced with a formidable task in evaluating and interpreting information generated from polls and surveys. To avoid some of the common pitfalls and mistakes that are possible when using poll and survey data, you must ask important questions about how the survey was conducted, how the respondents were selected to participate, and how questions were worded and sequenced.

Types of Survey Interviews

One of the crucial questions facing you when trying to evaluate the usefulness and reliability of information from a survey is, "How was this survey administered?" Three common methods are used to gather survey data: the face-to-face interview, the telephone interview, and the self-administered (by mail or online) interview. Each has its advantages and disadvantages, and each poses evaluation problems for you.

The face-to-face method involves trained interviewers meeting individually with the survey respondents and asking them the survey questions in person. This method can accommodate longer and more complex questions and questions that require the respondent to react to visual images. However, the labor and transportation costs for the interviewers' training and travel to and from the respondents' locations are very high. Respondents are also less and less likely to allow strangers into their homes, so the completion rate is low.

You must ask several questions in evaluating a survey that was done using the face-to-face method. How were the interviewers selected? Were the interviewers chosen to avoid the bias of race, age, sex or other social factors that might limit respondents' comfort level in participating? How was the work of each interviewer checked? What instructions did the interviewers receive regarding the selection of respondents? All of these questions are important guides to the quality of the firm doing the survey and to the reliability of the information gathered by the survey.

The telephone interview is a commonly used method because costs are reasonable, return calls are simple, the nonresponse rate is low because interviewers can keep calling back until the respondent is home, and interviewers can collect a large amount of data in a short time. The disadvantages are that some portions of the population do not have access to a telephone, many respondents are suspicious of telephone interviews, long or complicated questions are inappropriate, and more and more people have screening devices on their telephones that allow them to disregard the callers entirely.

If you are evaluating a poll based on telephone interviews, you must ask if the questionnaire and individual questions were appropriately brief for this method, if the telephone banks were staffed in a central location (telephone interviewers who work from home are subject to less supervision, obviously), what instructions the interviewers had about who in the household to interview, and how many call-backs were standard procedure for the survey. Without sufficient attempts to reach those selected as part of a "random" sample, the sample becomes more of a "convenience" sample, skewing the survey results to reflect the responses of those who are easier to catch at home, including stay-at-home parents, the unemployed, those who work a certain shift, and so on.

The self-administered survey is the least expensive of the three because it takes the fewest personnel to administer. A survey questionnaire is mailed to each member in the sample or is posted online, and respondents choose to fill it out and return it. Advantages, aside from cost, include the ability to cover a wide geographic area, to provide anonymity to the respondents (which encourages candid responses), and to require a less skilled staff to administer. The disadvantages are numerous, however. The response rate is usually very low because respondents forget to respond, throw it out or delete it, ignore the request, or fail to complete a usable questionnaire. There is no way to know who filled out the questionnaire unless one of the questions specifically asks for that information. For instance, a questionnaire intended for a corporate executive might be filled out by his or her secretary. Also, results may be skewed because only people who were really interested in the topic of the survey took the time to fill out the questionnaire, thereby introducing bias into the results.

When evaluating the results from a poll based on a self-administered questionnaire, you must ask what the response rate was (the lower the response, the less reliable the results), whether follow-up questionnaires were sent to those who failed to respond the first time, and how self-explanatory the instructions to the respondents were. The self-administered questionnaire obviously does not allow the respondent to ask questions of the interviewers or poll-takers, so clear instructions to the respondent are crucial.

Types of Survey Samples

A survey is usually conducted using some sample of the population that the pollsters want to learn about. You must be very careful to evaluate the sampling techniques employed in any poll or survey you are contemplating using. There are many types of samples, and some are more reliable than others.

The sample may be chosen by nonprobability or by probability sampling methods. Nonprobability sampling methods include all those in which respondents are selected without randomness. However, the word *random* here does not mean haphazard. A random sample means that every person in the population being studied had an equal and nonzero chance of being included in the sample. Nonprobability sampling is generally cheaper and easier to do than probability sampling, but causes some evaluation problems for communicators.

Nonprobability Samples.   One type of nonprobability sample is the available or *convenience* sample. Interviewers choose respondents who are readily accessible. Using people passing by a street corner as respondents is an example. One problem with an available sample is that there is no way to determine who the respondents represent. That is, it is impossible to tell if the respondents represent the larger group you want to learn something about, and the results of the survey are not generalizable to any larger group. For example, if the mall where a nonprobability sample was conducted is in an upscale neighborhood, the results might not reflect the opinions of a typical consumer for a particular product.

Another nonprobability sampling method is the *volunteer* sample, in which interviewees choose to volunteer for the sample. Using students who volunteer to complete a survey is one example. Posting a questionnaire on a popular Web site and inviting responses is another, as is any call-in survey that might be used on a television or radio show. One difficulty with this method of choosing a sample is that people who volunteer for things usually have different characteristics from those of the general population—they have more education, higher intelligence, greater need for approval, or other psychological characteristics that make them unrepresentative of a larger group. And once again, it is impossible to generalize from these results to any larger group.

For a *quota* sample, the interviewers choose respondents based on prearranged categories of sample characteristics. For instance, the survey interviewer is instructed to interview fifty men and fifty women for the survey, and finishes collecting information when those interviews are complete. This method, again, does not allow the pollster to measure the representativeness of the large group.

The *purposive* sample calls for the interviewer to select respondents from subgroups in the population being studied because they have specific characteristics or qualities. For instance, an interviewer in a grocery store might be instructed to interview only those people who say they eat yogurt and will not administer the survey to any others. Again, there is no way to know how representative of the larger group you want to learn about this purposive sample really is.

Probability Samples.   Probability sampling methods allow the survey researcher a much better chance of accurately choosing representative respondents. It is the only method that makes it possible for you to estimate the amount of error that the sample will produce. As we said, a random sample is set up systematically so that every member of the population being studied has an equal and nonzero chance of being included in the sample. There are variations of random samples, including the simple random sample, the stratified random sample, the disproportionate random sample, and more. The key for your purposes is to recognize that a random sample based on a probability sampling method results in findings that are likely to be generalizable, although several other factors, such as the wording of questions, must also be considered.

Sampling Error.   Even the most carefully selected random sample almost never provides a perfect representation of the population being studied. There will always be some degree of error. That is called *sampling error*, the yardstick that measures the potential for variation between the survey responses and what the entire population might have answered if everyone had been questioned. For instance, a poll might indicate that 46 percent of the adults polled support the governor's new tax plan, while 44 percent oppose it, and the rest don't have an opinion. The stated sampling error is plus or minus 4 percent. That means that those who support the plan may be as many as 50 percent or as few as 42 percent (46 plus 4 or 46 minus 4 percent). Those who oppose may be as many as 48 percent or as few as 40 percent. In other words, opinion is divided evenly between the two camps.

Several things determine the sampling error in a random-sample survey. One major factor is the size of the sample. A general rule is that the larger the sample, the smaller the sampling error. After a certain level, however, any increase in the sample size results in such a small decrease in the sampling error that it is not worth the effort to increase the size of the sample any further. This is why most major polling organizations use a random sample of between 1,200 and 1,500 respondents. That size sample results in a sufficiently small sampling error (roughly 2.5 to 3.5 percent) so that a larger sample size is not justified.

It is important for you to look for a stated sampling error in the results of any poll or survey you may be contemplating using. Also, when a stratified random sample or a disproportionate random sample is used, the results may include an analysis of subsamples, or responses from smaller groups within the larger sample. The margin of error for subsample results will always be larger than for the total sample, thereby requiring even more careful scrutiny to determine if differences in responses are real. For example, if a survey of 250 people shows results by region (Midwest, South, East and West), be cautious. When the sample is divided in this way, recognize that only about 62 people represent each region—almost never a large enough sample to be truly representative of a particular region.

Another factor determining sampling error is the level of confidence used with the analysis of the results. The level of confidence refers to the odds that the results of a specific survey are within the estimated sampling error range. In other words, if the survey were repeated, the researchers are 90 percent (or 95 or 99 percent) confident that they would get the same results within the same range of error.

When you are evaluating the results from a poll that used a random-sample method, you should look for the statement of the sampling error and the level of confidence. If you see these figures, you can be sure the results are based on a probability sampling method. A common goal is to look for a poll with a sampling error of no more than 5 percent at the 95 percent confidence level. If you are evaluating a poll with figures like that, the data are likely to be more credible than those from a poll with higher sampling error and lower confidence levels.

Types of Survey Questions

The types of questions, the wording of questions, and the placement of questions in the overall questionnaire can dramatically affect the results of a survey. There are four basic types of questions, some of which are more appropriate for survey questionnaires than others. The first type is the *stimulus open/response open* question. An example might be,

"What do you believe are the major problems in the city?" The question, or stimulus, does not give any direction to the respondent, and the answer, or response, is completely open-ended.

The second type of question is the *stimulus open/response closed* format. The example here is, "What do you believe are the major problems in the city?" with a list of twelve problems from which to choose. The question, or stimulus, is still very broad and undirected, but the respondent now has a set of fixed responses from which to choose.

The third type of question is the *stimulus closed/response open* format. An example would be, "Unemployment is one problem facing our city. How do you feel about it?" This is a very specific question which directs the respondent to a particular problem. However, the response is still open-ended.

The last type of question, and the format that is used most often in surveys, is the *stimulus closed/response closed* question. The question might be "Unemployment is one problem facing our city. How concerned are you about it?" with a list of seven answers ranging from Very concerned, to Not at all concerned. Both the question and the choice of answers are thoroughly outlined. There is no room for respondents to answer in their own words.

Stimulus closed/response closed questions are used most often in surveys because they provide data that are easily tabulated and analyzed. Because all respondents must choose from one set of answers, the researchers can prearrange for the coding, or analysis, of each questionnaire. When interpreting information from a poll or survey, you can request to see the questionnaire and can determine whether the questions were mostly closed-ended or open-ended. Open-ended questions are harder to code, and a good explanation of how open-ended items were coded must accompany the interpretation of the survey information.

Question Wording.   The wording of questions is another major area of concern in evaluating polls and surveys. Question bias, clarity, length, and construction can cause crucial differences in results from polls and surveys. There are a number of rules about question wording:

1. Questions should be clear, using everyday language and avoiding jargon.
2. Questions should be short, thereby reducing the likelihood of being misunderstood, especially in telephone interviews.
3. Questions should not ask more than one thing. An example of a double-barreled question might be: "This product is mild and gets out stubborn stains. Do you agree or disagree?" The respondent might agree with the first part of the statement, but disagree with the second.
4. Questions should avoid biased words or terms. An example might be: "Where did you hear the news about the president's new tax program?" The word *hear* biases against an answer such as "I read about it online." Instead ask, "Where did you learn the news...." There are even more insidious examples of bias in questions, a result of the survey sponsor's having an interest in seeing the survey produce a certain set of answers. Questions can be written to signal the respondent about *exactly* what the interviewer wishes to get as the "right" answer.

5. Questions should avoid leading the respondents' answers. For example, asking the question "Like most Americans, do you read a newspaper every day?" leads respondents to think that answering "No" puts them in the un-American group! Another example might be: "Do you believe, along with many others, that abortion is murder?" The leading question tells the respondent what the expected answer is.

6. Questions should avoid asking for unusually detailed or difficult information. A detailed question might be: "Over the past thirty days, how many hours have you spent watching TV?" Most respondents would not be able to answer that question without considerable calculation. A simpler way of gathering the same information would be to ask, "About how many hours a day do you spend watching TV?"

7. Questions should avoid embarrassing the respondent whenever possible. It is difficult to judge which kinds of questions will be embarrassing to every person, but some questions will embarrass almost everyone. For instance, questions about level of income are usually perceived as intrusive. In fact, many survey researchers put those questions at the very end of the questionnaire so that if the respondent is offended by the question, the rest of the interview is not spoiled.

8. Questions should not assume knowledge on the part of the respondent. Many surveys include *filter questions*, which help the interviewer decide whether that part of the questionnaire is pertinent to the respondent. For instance, the questionnaire might ask: "Have you purchased something online in the past month?" If the response is "No," then the questions that deal with the online purchase experience are not asked (or the respondent is instructed to skip over them).

9. Questions should avoid abbreviations, acronyms, foreign phrases, or slang. Respondents are less likely to be confused when simple, familiar language is used. Also, certain slang phrases may connote some kind of bias on the part of the interviewer, which will influence the respondent.

10. Questions should be specific about the time span that is implied. For instance, a question may ask about the respondent's approval or disapproval of a $20 billion program for road and bridge improvement. Unless the question specifies the number of years over which the money will be spent, the respondent has no way to evaluate the program's impact and the answer given will be meaningless.

11. Where appropriate, questions should attempt to gauge the intensity of feeling the respondent has about a topic. For instance, a question may ask for the respondent's preference for one product over another. Some respondents may not feel particularly intense about their preference for either, but just to be polite, they will give an answer. If an intensity question were included ("How strong is your preference for Product A?"), those who were less intense could indicate their ambivalence.

12. Questions should avoid using a forced response strategy. Respondents should have the option to say "I don't know" or "I don't have enough information to answer" to avoid the problem of respondents giving an answer, any answer, just to be polite.[9]

When you are considering the use of information from a poll or survey, you should have the questionnaire in hand in order to apply these standards of evaluation to the questions. Any evidence that the questions were poorly worded or improperly written should alert you to the possibility that the information gathered through the survey may not be reliable.

Question Order. The order in which questions appear in the questionnaire can also affect the reliability of the results. Questions should be grouped together by topic and within topic to avoid confusion. The first few questions in a questionnaire are crucial in preventing termination of the interview and in relaxing the respondent. Questions asking personal characteristics (age, education level, income level) should come in the last section. Topic questions that are likely to be objectionable (asking about touchy subjects such as sexuality, religious beliefs, or illegal behavior) should be placed just before the personal items at the end of the questionnaire.

Furthermore, try to evaluate how the order of the questions might have affected respondents' tendency to answer. For instance, a poll might ask U.S. citizens how much trust they have in the federal government. If the question is asked as a stand-alone question without any preceding set-up questions, you are likely to get a response that reflects people's general dislike of big bureaucracies. However, if the question about trust in government is preceded by questions asking about trust in a number of programs that U.S. citizens generally support (Social Security, Medicare, environmental protection, programs to help the poor), the question about trust in the government as a whole would reflect a very different response. Respondents would have been reminded about the things that the federal government does that are generally supported, and hence their answer about trust in the government would be different than it would be if that one question were asked in isolation.

Interpreting Poll and Survey Information

Evaluating the results of a survey involves both statistical analysis and interpretive skill. The person who conducts and analyzes the poll data has great sway in determining how the data get interpreted. It is up to you to carefully critique any information based on a poll or survey and apply stringent standards of evaluation. When you are considering using poll or survey information, you should have the answers to the following questions:

1. Who sponsored or paid for this poll, and who conducted it? Serious bias can enter into a survey design if the sponsoring agency or the firm conducting the poll has a particular ax to grind.
2. Who was interviewed? What population was sampled?
3. How were people selected for the interviews? In other words, was it a probability or a nonprobability sample? If a nonprobability sample was used, the results cannot be generalized to a larger population
4. How many people were interviewed? What was the size of the sample? Were there any subsamples or specific groups for which results were analyzed separately, and if so, what was the size of those smaller groups?
5. If a probability sample was used, what was the range of sampling error and the level of confidence for the total sample? What were those figures for any subsamples?

6. How were the interviews conducted? Were they telephone, face-to-face, or self-administered (mail or online) interviews? Were the interviewers trained personnel or volunteers? Were they supervised or working on their own?

7. What were the actual questions that were asked? What kind of response choices did respondents have (response-open or response-closed)? Experts know that when you ask questions about something that is potentially awkward or embarrassing, people over-report socially desirable behavior and under-report behavior that is considered antisocial. If the survey asks about topics such as sexuality or illegal behavior such as drug use, the results must be interpreted and reported upon with a great deal of caution.

8. What was the wording of questions? Were there biased, loaded, double-barreled, leading, or ambiguous questions? Even individual words can influence results. Did the question ask about *taxes* or *revenues*? *Welfare* or *assistance to the poor*? *Universal health insurance* or *managed health care*?

9. When were the interviews conducted? The results of a survey are good only for the time at which the questions were asked. *Polls do not have any predictive value and cannot and should not be used to predict anything.* For instance, a poll may ask respondents about their preferences for one candidate over another during a three-day polling window just before an election and the results may show that candidate A has a wide margin of support over candidate B. But some last-minute revelation about candidate A may change the atmosphere around the election, influencing the outcome and making the poll data irrelevant. Outside events always hold the potential to affect results of any survey. That is why polls should never be used to predict anything. The results are good for just one point in time.

These general questions must be sufficiently addressed before you can interpret the results of any poll or survey.

Many polling organizations have been conducting studies on public opinion for decades. Companies such as Gallup, Roper, Harris, and the National Opinion Research Center have archives of their studies going back, in some cases, to the 1930s. Their Web sites provide access to summaries of current studies and, for subscribers, the complete information about each poll they conduct. In addition, the Web site *PollingReport* (www.pollingreport.com) provides free information about hundreds of national polls and opinion surveys as they are released by the major polling organizations. The print tools *American Public Opinion Index* and *Index to International Public Opinion* help you locate surveys conducted by many organizations, as well.

You can evaluate the usefulness of a poll better if you are familiar with the reputation and reliability of the company that conducted the study. These nationally recognized and respected organizations have staked their firm's reputation on the quality of their studies and the *transparency* of their results. In other words, they want their subscribers to know how they conducted the survey and how they analyzed the results. For that reason, they make all of the background information about their methods and their questionnaires available as a routine part of their disclosure. If you cannot find the background information about how a survey was conducted, or if the firm that did the study will not share it, you have reason to believe that you should not use those results in any message.

EVALUATING ONLINE INFORMATION

One of the serious challenges you face as professional communicators in the current environment has to do with the evaluation of information you find using online information tools. Online information tools include proprietary databases prepared by syndicated research services such as Mediamark or Nielsen (audience and media use information), databases created by large information companies such as LexisNexis (legal information, and news and business information), databases of public records information (property records, criminal history records, auto or airplane license records, etc.), and the seemingly limitless material found by browsing the millions of sites on the World Wide Web. Much of the information in these online sources once existed (and may still do so) in print form. Now it is more easily accessible because someone has converted the material and made it available in digital form. Other information is unique to the online world. All of it requires close attention to quality and credibility.

The Internet is a major tool for retrieving information online. Before we start the discussion of evaluating online information, a few words about information found using the Internet:

- The Internet did not invent misinformation or disinformation.
- The Internet did not create rumor mongering.
- The Internet did not spawn the use of propaganda.
- The Internet is not responsible for dirty data and stupid statistics.

All of these problems have been around forever. They just have a new distribution outlet. The Internet *does* make it possible for misinformation, disinformation, rumor mongering, dirty data, and stupid statistics to be distributed more quickly and widely than in the past. But the Internet also provides many sources of help and advice about how to detect and avoid these information traps. For instance, there are a number of good Internet sites where rumors and hoaxes are exposed, such as urbanlegends.miningco.com.

Obviously, the same tests of evidence discussed earlier in this chapter must be applied to information you find online. You need to determine the reputation or authority of the information producer, the accuracy of what you find online, the recency of the information, the completeness of the data, and so forth. To help you with this evaluation, Joe Barker, one of the librarians at the University of California at Berkeley, has developed a checklist of questions to ask about anything you find on the Web. This list, found in Box 11.3, will give you a good start on your information evaluation task.

It also helps to understand that online information producers have a reason for making the information available electronically. The database or Web site's main goal might be advocacy of a particular position or point of view. The database or Web site might be primarily designed to provide business or marketing information to consumers or to other businesses. The database or Web site might be a vehicle for delivery of news or information. Or the database or Web site might exist solely as a personal expression of an individual's unique perspective. Your task as an information evaluator is

BOX 11.3
EVALUATING WEB PAGES

Evaluating Web Pages: Techniques to Apply & Questions to Ask

UC BERKELEY LIBRARY | HOME | SEARCH

Finding Information on the Internet: A Tutorial
http://www.lib.berkeley.edu/TeachingLib/Guides/Internet/Evaluate.html

Evaluating Web Pages:
Techniques to Apply & Questions to Ask
UC Berkeley - Teaching Library Internet Workshops

About This Tutorial | Table of Contents | Handouts | Glossary

Looking for the old Evaluate.html page with the rationale and sample links to try?
Looking for the Web Page Evaluation Checklist PDF form?

Evaluating web pages skillfully requires you to do two things at once:

1. Train your eye and your fingers to employ a series of **techniques** that help you quickly find what you need to know about web pages;
2. Train your mind to think critically, even suspiciously, by **asking a series of questions** that will help you decide how much a web pages is to be trusted.

This page is organized to combine the two techniques into a process that begins with looking at your search results from a search engine or other source, follows through by investigating the content of page, and extends beyond the page to what others may say about the page or its author(s).

---

1. What can the URL tell you?

Techniques for Web Evaluation :
1. Before you leave the list of search results -- before you click and get interested in anything written on the page -- glean all you can from the URLs of each page.
2. Choose pages most likely to be reliable and authentic.

Questions to ask:	What are the implications?
Is it somebody's personal page?	Personal pages are not necessarily "bad," but you need to investigate the author very carefully.
• Read the URL* carefully:	For personal pages, there is no publisher or domain owner vouching for the information in the page.
○ Look for a personal name (e.g., *jbarker* or *barker*) following a tilde (~), a percent sign (%), or or the words "users," "members," or "people."	
○ Is the server a commercial ISP* or other provider mostly of web page hosting (like aol.com or geocities.com)	
*Click on linked words for term definitions in our online Glossary.	
What type of domain does it come from ? (educational, nonprofit, commercial, government, etc.)	Look for a appropriateness, fit. What kind of information source do you think is most reliable for your topic?
• Is the domain appropriate for the content?	
○ Government sites: look for .gov, .mil, .us, or other country code	

(continued)

BOX 11.3   CONTINUED

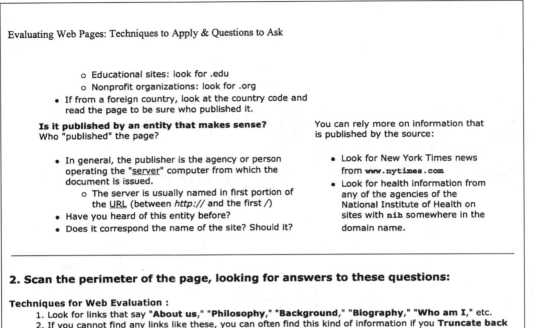

Evaluating Web Pages: Techniques to Apply & Questions to Ask

        o Educational sites: look for .edu
        o Nonprofit organizations: look for .org
- If from a foreign country, look at the country code and read the page to be sure who published it.

Is it published by an entity that makes sense?
Who "published" the page?

- In general, the publisher is the agency or person operating the "server" computer from which the document is issued.
        o The server is usually named in first portion of the URL (between *http://* and the first /)
- Have you heard of this entity before?
- Does it correspond the name of the site? Should it?

You can rely more on information that is published by the source:

- Look for New York Times news from `www.nytimes.com`
- Look for health information from any of the agencies of the National Institute of Health on sites with `nih` somewhere in the domain name.

2. Scan the perimeter of the page, looking for answers to these questions:

Techniques for Web Evaluation :
1. Look for links that say **"About us," "Philosophy," "Background," "Biography," "Who am I,"** etc.
2. If you cannot find any links like these, you can often find this kind of information if you **Truncate back the URL.**
      INSTRUCTIONS for Truncating back a URL: In the top Location Box, delete the end characters of the URL stopping just before each / (leave the slash). Press enter to see if you can see more about the author or the origins/nature of the site providing the page.
      Continue this process, one slash (/) at a time, until you reach the first single / which is preceded by the domain name portion. This is the page's server or "publisher."
3. Look for the date "last updated" - usually at the bottom of a web page.
      Check the date on all the pages on the site.
      Do not rely on a date given in IE's File|Properties or Netscape's View|Page Info displays. These dates can be automatically kept current and are useless in critical evaluation.

Questions to ask:	What are the implications?

Who wrote the page?
 	
 • Look for the name of the author, or the name of the organization, institution, agency, or whatever who is responsible for the page
    o An e-mail contact is not enough
 • If there is no personal author, look for an agency or organization that claims responsibility for the page.
    o If you cannot find this, locate the publisher by truncating back the URL (see technique above). Does this publisher claim responsibility for the content? Does it explain why the page exists in any way?
	Web pages are all created with a purpose in mind by some person or agency or entity. They do not simply "grow" on the web like mildew grows in moist corners.
	     You are looking for someone who claims accountability and responsiblity for the content.
	 An email address with no additional information about the author is not sufficient for assessing the author's credentials.
	     If this is all you have, try e-mailing the author and asking politely for more information about him/her.

Evaluating Web Pages: Techniques to Apply & Questions to Ask

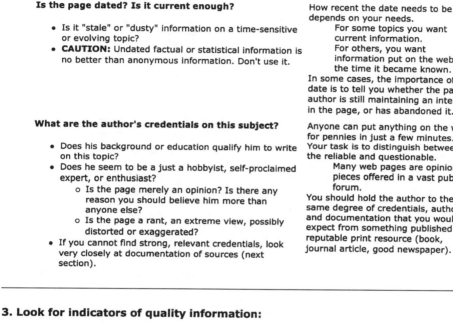

Is the page dated? Is it current enough?

- Is it "stale" or "dusty" information on a time-sensitive or evolving topic?
- **CAUTION:** Undated factual or statistical information is no better than anonymous information. Don't use it.

How recent the date needs to be depends on your needs.
> For some topics you want current information.
> For others, you want information put on the web near the time it became known.

In some cases, the importance of the date is to tell you whether the page author is still maintaining an interest in the page, or has abandoned it.

What are the author's credentials on this subject?

- Does his background or education qualify him to write on this topic?
- Does he seem to be a just a hobbyist, self-proclaimed expert, or enthusiast?
  - o Is the page merely an opinion? Is there any reason you should believe him more than anyone else?
  - o Is the page a rant, an extreme view, possibly distorted or exaggerated?
- If you cannot find strong, relevant credentials, look very closely at documentation of sources (next section).

Anyone can put anything on the web for pennies in just a few minutes. Your task is to distinguish between the reliable and questionable.
> Many web pages are opinion pieces offered in a vast public forum.

You should hold the author to the same degree of credentials, authority, and documentation that you would expect from something published in a reputable print resource (book, journal article, good newspaper).

3. Look for indicators of quality information:

Techniques for Web Evaluation :
1. Look for a link called "links," "additional sites," "related links," etc.
2. In the text, if you see little footnote numbers or links that might refer to documentation, take the time to explore them.
> What kinds of publications or sites are they? Reputable? Scholarly?
> Are they real? On the web (where no publisher is editing most pages), it is possible to create totally fake references.
3. Look at the publisher of the page (first part of the URL).
> Expect a journal article, newspaper article, and some other publications that are recent to come from the original publisher IF the publication is available on the web.
> Look at the bottom of such articles for copyright information or permissions to reproduce.

Questions to ask:	What are the implications?
Are sources documented with footnotes or links? • Where did the author get the information? o As in published scholarly/academic journals and books, you should expect documentation. • If there are links to other pages as sources, are they to reliable sources? • Do the links work?	In scholarly/research work, the credibility of most writings is proven through footnote documentation or other means of revealing the sources of information. Saying what you believe without documentation is not much better than just expressing an opinion or a point of view. What

(continued)

BOX 11.3   CONTINUED

Evaluating Web Pages: Techniques to Apply & Questions to Ask

credibility does your research need? An exception can be journalism from highly reputable newspapers. But these are not scholarly. Check with your instructor before using this type of material.

Links that don't work or are to other weak or fringe pages do not help strengthen the credibility of your research.

If reproduced information (from another source), is it complete, not altered, not fake or forged?

- Is it retyped? If so, it could easily be altered.
- Is it reproduced from another publication?
    o Are permissions to reproduce and copyright information provided?
    o Is there a reason there are not links to the original source if it is online (instead of reproducing it)?

You may have to find the original to be sure a copy of something is not altered and is complete.

Look at the URL: is it from the original source?

If you find a legitimate article from a reputable journal or other publication, it should be accompanied by the copyright statement and/or permission to reprint. If it is not, be suspicious.

Try to find the source. If the URL of the document is not to the original source, it is likely that it is illegally reproduced, and the text could be altered, even with the copyright information present.

Are there links to other resources on the topic?

- Are the links well chosen, well organized, and/or evaluated/annotated?
- Do the links work?
- Do the links represent other viewpoints?
- Do the links (or absence of other viewpoints) indicate a bias?

Many well developed pages offer links to other pages on the same topic that they consider worthwhile. They are inviting you to compare their information with other pages.

Links that offer opposing viewpoints as well as their own are more likely be balanced and unbiased than pages that offer only one view. Anything not said that could be said? And perhaps would be said if all points of view were represented?

Always look for bias. Especially when you agree with something, check for bias.

---

4. What do others say?

Techniques for Web Evaluation :
1. Find out what other web pages link to this page.
    Do a link: search in Google, AltaVista, or another search engine where this can be done.
    INSTRUCTIONS for doing a link: search in Google or AltaVista:

Evaluating Web Pages: Techniques to Apply & Questions to Ask

Questions to ask:	So what? What are the implications?
Why was the page put on the web?	These are some of the reasons to think of. The web is a public place, open to all. You need to be aware of the entire range of human possibilities of intentions behind web pages.
• Inform, give facts, give data? • Explain, persuade? • Sell, entice? • Share? • Disclose?	
Might it be ironic? Satire or parody?	It is easy to be fooled, and this can make you look foolish in turn.
• Think about the "tone" of the page. • Humorous? Parody? Exaggerated? Overblown arguments? • Outrageous photographs or juxtaposition of unlikely images? • Arguing a viewpoint with examples that suggest that what is argued is ultimately not possible.	
Is this as good as resources I could find if I used the library, or some of the web-based indexes available through the library, or other print resources?	What is your requirement (or your instructor's requirement) for the quality of reliability of your information?
• Are you being completely fair? Too harsh? Totally objective? Requiring the same degree of "proof" you would from a print publication? • Is the site good for some things and not for others? • Are your hopes biasing your interpretation?	In general, published information is considered more reliable than what is on the web. But many, many reputable agencies and publishers make great stuff available by "publishing" it on the web. This applies to most governments, most institutions and societies, many publishing houses and news sources. But take the time to check it out.

More About Evaluating Web Sources

- **Evaluating Information Found on the Internet** <*http://www.library.jhu.edu/elp/useit/evaluate/*>
  An excellent series of pages on this subject (from the Milton Library at Johns Hopkins University).
- **Critical Evaluation of Resources** <*http://www.lib.berkeley.edu/TeachingLib/Guides/Evaluation.html*>
  A broader, more theoretical look at the criteria and importance of evaluating all types of resources (also from the UC Berkeley Teaching Library).
- For annotated descriptions of many other good guides to evaluating web pages, search the subject "Evaluation of Internet Resources" in the **Librarians' Index to the Internet** <*http://www.lii.org*>.

Source: University of California Berkeley Library (www.lib.Berkeley.edu/TeachingLib/Guides/Internet/Evaluate.html). Reprinted by permission.

to be sure you understand what type of information you have in front of you before you decide to use it in any type of message.

The bottom line here is that you must remember the old computer adage: "garbage in, garbage out." If you want to ensure that you are not producing garbage, make sure you don't use it.

The next chapter discusses how to synthesize and organize all of this high-quality information you have found.

SELECTED ADDITIONAL READINGS

Alexander, Janet E. and Marsha Ann Tate. *Web Wisdom: How to Evaluate and Create Information Quality on the Web.* Mahwah, NJ: Lawrence Erlbaum Associates, 1999.

Cohen, Sarah. *Numbers in the Newsroom: Using Math and Statistics in News.* Columbia, MO: Investigative Reporters and Editors, Inc., 2001.

Katzer, Jeffrey, Kenneth H. Cook, and Wayne W. Crouch. *Evaluating Information: A Guide for Users of Social Science Research*, 4th edition. New York: McGraw-Hill, 1997.

NOTES

1. M. Neil Browne and Stuart M. Keeley, *Asking the Right Questions: A Guide to Critical Thinking*, 6th ed. (Upper Saddle River, NJ: Prentice-Hall, 2001), 13–14.

2. J. Vernon Jensen, *Argumentation: Reasoning in Communication* (NY: Van Nostrand, 1981).

3. Theodore Glasser and James Ettema, *Custodians of Conscience* (New York: Columbia University Press, 1998).

4. Steve Gross, "Computer Retailer Is Victim of Ad Hoax in Star Tribune," *Star Tribune*, 14 August 1990, 2D.

5. Victor Cohn, *News & Numbers* (Ames, IA: Iowa State University Press, 1989), 130–131.

6. John Allen Paulos, *A Mathematician Reads the Newspaper* (NY: Basic Books, 1995), 135.

7. Browne and Keeley, 168.

8. Sarah Cohen, *Numbers in the Newsroom: Using Math and Statistics in News* (Columbia, MO: Investigative Reporters and Editors, 2001), 2–9.

9. Roger D. Wimmer and Joseph R. Dominick, *Mass Media Research: An Introduction* (Belmont, CA: Wadsworth, 1983), 113–120.

CHAPTER TWELVE

SYNTHESIZING INFORMATION

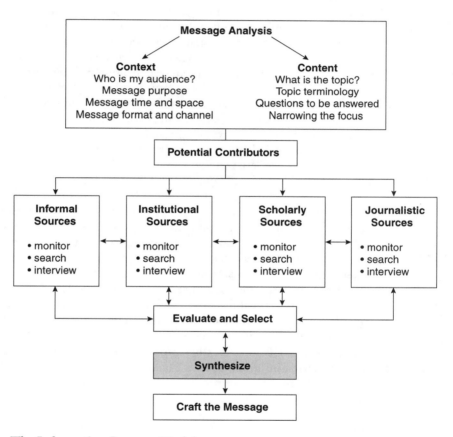

The Information Strategy Model

"How do I know what I think until I see what I say?"   —*E. M. Forster*

After evaluation and selection you have the final set of information from which you will craft the message. You have eliminated any material that you've found to be erroneous, updated facts that are not current, identified differences in viewpoints, and put into context information that reflects special interests. Even after you've sorted and selected, you will still have much more information than will ever actually be used in the message. In fact, some experts estimate that only 10 to 15 percent of a reporter's notes actually find their way into the final news story. If you don't have much more material than you need for your message, you have a different kind of problem—a faulty information strategy may be the cause. Or, if you find discrepancies in data between sources you've used, you'll need to re-examine the information you've located.

For example, if the message you're preparing is about adult illiteracy, during the evaluation step you will have reviewed the material for accuracy. Some information you found may reflect the bias of an organization trying to attract potential donors to its campaign against illiteracy by presenting alarming statistics about its prevalence in the population. If the statistics on adult illiteracy are not consistent, you'll need to go to additional sources, perhaps retracing earlier steps taken in the information strategy. At this point, you may loop back through the process as you seek to plug holes in the information you need as you prepare the message.

Once you are satisfied that the information you've gathered and evaluated is as solid and reliable as possible in the time available, you need to spend some time synthesizing and organizing all the material before actually writing the story, the ad, or the news release. This essential step of organizing the information you intend to use when writing will save you time and ensure you don't miss important pieces of the story. Just as you did as you began the evaluation and selection process, you'll keep in mind what you have established about the purpose and the intended audience for the message as you start this sorting and synthesis step.

Even with the message purpose and audience clearly in mind, the process of synthesizing all of the information and data you have gathered from different types of contributors through different methods can be a difficult process. It is also a process that is particularly hard to describe, since it takes place in many varied ways inside the minds of creative communicators. However, some writers and students of the writing process provide insights about it. For the news process, Carl Hausman provides this set of questions[1] that contribute to the decision making required for synthesizing information:

1. Is it news?
2. Is it true?
3. Is it fair?
4. Is it logical?
5. Is it distorted?
6. Is it libelous or an invasion of privacy?
7. Has the story been ethically researched and presented?
8. Is it worth the consequences?

Patrick Jackson, former editor of *pr reporter*, suggested five basic questions[2] in assessing a message:

1. Is it appropriate? For the sender? For the recipient?
2. Is it meaningful? Does it stick to the subject, and is it geared to the interests of the audience?
3. Is it memorable? Does it employ devices—including verbal, graphic, and aural imagery—that people will remember?
4. Is it understandable?
5. Is it believable? Does the source exhibit trustworthiness and expertise?

Finding the central idea, the focus, of the message involves lots of reading, re-reading, shuffling through notes, thinking about the subject, and sometimes, trying out the main idea on an imaginary audience member. A technique one editor recommends is to have writers imagine a wall-to-wall mural with a montage of every kind of face one can see on a city street: How can you select and arrange the material so it will connect with these potential audience members? Another editor prescribes: Sit down and pretend you are telling this to your mother. Another journalist and author relates that each day he writes two questions at the top of his computer screen: "What's the news? What's the point?" From examining these questions, he derives theme, focus, and (sometimes) the voice of the story. Another writer advocates making a list of the elements the story must include. Because each story, ad, or public relations release can contain only a small fraction of what the communicator has collected, these routines are designed to help establish focus and identify what is essential to the theme and what is peripheral.

PLANNING AHEAD

Writing coach Steve Buttry offers these tips for synthesizing as you gather information. For times when you need to prepare your report on a deadline, keeping these ideas in mind as you are reporting and interviewing helps in the synthesis process. Although this is framed for journalistic purposes, these same guidelines would help with the preparation of a news release, a media kit, a business pitch, a competitive analysis report, or a company newsletter.

If possible, write as you report. For instance, if you're working a story by phone, you're going to have some dead time, maybe a few seconds at a time, when you're on hold or waiting for someone to answer, maybe a few minutes while you're waiting for people to return calls.

Start putting the information from your last interview into story form. Even if you don't know where it will go in the story yet, start writing paragraphs that will fit somewhere. Write a lede based on what you know so far. In addition to starting your writing, this helps sharpen the focus of the reporting that remains.

Writing as you report allows you to continue your reporting closer to deadline. Writing in chunks, with frequent interruptions as you return to reporting, can lead to choppy writing. You need to fix this by using some of the time you save to read back through the story to make it flow smoothly. If you are at the scene and need to run back to the newsroom to report, you can't physically write as you report. But start writing or outlining the story in your head or in your notebook during moments when you find yourself waiting.

Identify the minimum story. Decide early what your minimum story is, the story that answers the basic Who, What, When, and Where questions. This is the story that meets basic levels of journalistic competence and allows you to keep drawing a paycheck next week. This is your first goal.

Identify the maximum story. The maximum story is the story that readers will be talking about at work and in coffee shops the next day. This is the story that your editors and readers will remember, that marks you as a star performer. This story may answer difficult How, Why, So what, or How much questions, or it may address the Who-What-When-Where questions in greater depth. The maximum story will have such enticing elements as setting, plot, characters, and dialogue. You are looking for elements that might make this story especially memorable.

Secure the minimum, then pursue the maximum. If you are not on deadline, you might gather the information for the minimal story fairly early, then build incrementally to the maximum story. Or you might start with some of the information for the maximum story and spend a lot of time with that, knowing you'll be able to fill in the basics later.

On deadline, you want to immediately identify the potential sources who could provide the information for the minimum story and get the information from them as quickly as possible. Then you zero right in on the sources who might provide the maximum story. Maybe you can't get the maximum story on deadline. It might be a second-day story or a Sunday follow-up. But go for it. If you don't land the maximum story, you're likely to gather material that will improve on the minimum story.

Reassess frequently. Before and after each interview, assess quickly what you still need to nail down the minimum or maximum story. Go quickly to those elements in your questioning.Go to the sources who will provide that sort of information.

If you don't have time to interview all the desired sources, avoid those who will waste your time with redundant information. For instance, in a crime or disaster story, one official source may provide all the basic information for your minimal story. Once you get that information, you might want to focus your energy on unofficial sources who can give your story greater human dimension, rather than going to other official sources. However, if you haven't identified the unofficial sources yet, other official sources may help lead you to them.[3]

PREWRITING

Synthesis for major, long-form projects in newspapers and magazines is a whole different task. In many cases, editors demand outlines of major stories or projects. They not only want to see the outlines, they want to know the writer has been able to focus and synthesize with enough skill to produce a straightforward outline of the material. Often a story pitch will require the delivery of an outline.

Much of the synthesis process involves what can be called *prewriting*. Prewriting has been described by a number of authors and refers to the steps that any writer goes through before actually beginning to write: conceptualizing the topic, planning the approach, sorting the information, and mentally writing the story, ad, news release, or other message. The prewriting process, then, is the point at which you begin making decisions about what the gathered information means and how that meaning can be conveyed. Synthesizing all the facts, opinions, views, and themes in the gathered information is an implicit part of developing the interpretation of the information for the message and the audience.

IDEAS FOR ORGANIZING INFORMATION

No matter what technique you use to categorize and organize your information, there are some steps[4] that will help with the overall organization and synthesis work.

1. Ask yourself at the outset: What is the major point I would like to get across? What are the most convincing pieces of evidence I have to back up my point? How can I divide these into subcategories? What are my most intriguing bits of information? How do they relate to each other and to my thesis? In what order would it make the most sense to put these ideas? What is my rationale for putting my ideas in this particular order? Is there another possible order to put these ideas in? Why did I choose this way of organizing my ideas as opposed to another way?
2. Use different colored highlighters to group together common ideas. You can use this method on prewriting or a rough draft.
3. Come up with subcategories, and then use a labeling system to identify the different subcategories—either in your prewriting or on your rough draft.
4. Use webbing or clustering to organize information—either at the prewriting stage or to web or cluster information already written in rough draft form.
5. Make a scratch outline—either of prewriting ideas or of ideas already written in rough draft form to see how ideas might need to be reorganized.
6. At the rough draft stage, underline topic sentences and then see if all the ideas in each paragraph reflect the topic sentence. Also check to see if any of the topic sentences are actually repetitions of the same ideas. In addition, check to see if all of your points are represented. If not, you probably need to create another topic sentence—and another paragraph. Finally, look at the order of your topic sentences. Is this the order in which you want your main points to appear in your paper? Are there nice transitions between each paragraph?

Synthesis may involve a one-shot message, such as a short news story or a retail ad intended to run for a brief period in local newspapers. But it also can involve hundreds of pieces of information, gathered over a long period of time from diverse sources. For example, someone working on a long-term campaign will have gathered focus group and survey results, industry information, comments from expert interviewees, and past media coverage of the topic. Reporters working on investigative stories or interpretive series for which extensive research is undertaken will have the same volume of material to deal with. In one such investigative project, a number of reporters for the Houston Post produced research connecting savings and loan failures in Texas, California, Florida, and Oklahoma to figures connected to organized crime and to the CIA. The complex synthesis included tips from anonymous sources, anonymously provided documents, criminal law cases, database searches, law enforcement reports, bankruptcy filings, corporate annual reports, lawsuits, tax appraisals, partnership agreements, and interviews with investors, real-estate brokers, banking experts, private investigators, FBI agents, and United States attorneys.[5]

In the case of the savings and loan project, great quantities of material were collected before the first story ever ran. Since information continued to be added by various staff members, careful examination of the collected material was required prior to each subsequent story published. The unfolding of the story illustrates the idea that you may need to retrace the path through the information strategy model numerous times.

This is the case not only in investigative journalism but also in message preparation for advertisements and public relations. The advertising campaign strategist may decide that although the information in hand is complete in providing an overview of the industry and the product category, additional information is needed to understand how a consumer is going to react to the new product. The advertising specialists on the team might not be able to craft an adequate message without that additional information about realistic consumer attitudes. This type of information is considered so useful that one very large U.S. advertising agency regularly hires actors to bring the research data to life. Dry facts and figures about the characteristics of potential target audience members do not convey very vivid information for the copywriters and art directors who must synthesize and incorporate this material as they design advertisements. So agency staff prepare actors to portray characters who display the audience attitudes, behaviors, and habits the research has identified. These portrayals give the creative staff members "real people" to focus on as they design their ads.

Aware of the need to form appropriate messages based on complete information about the topic, the audience, and the purpose of the message, you will use the synthesis process to begin mentally crafting the message. This helps you plan how the message will begin, decide what information is the most important for the audience, design the look or sound of the message, organize the logical progression of facts or persuasive arguments in the message, and so forth. When you finally reach the stage of writing the message, all the information will be organized and logically presented for the best effect.

There are some techniques for organizing your information during and after the information process that will ease the synthesis process and the prewriting work that precedes your actual crafting of the message. These can be paper-based methods such as developing a set of file folders labeled with categories into which you can put relevant notes from your search. Some experienced communicators advocate creating a set of index cards on which you note specific ideas or threads of the story. Once you have a set of cards full of information and ideas, you can sort them to organize your thoughts and to try out different sequences for the presentation of facts in the message you will create.

SYNTHESIS USING DATA-CRUNCHING TOOLS

Some communicators use computer techniques for organizing information. Particularly for stories or campaigns that have multiple threads, creating a database or spreadsheet lets you sort through information you've found and, most importantly, locate references or facts you need to get your hands on quickly. What's more, it is sometime not enough to use information that has been created and analyzed by someone else. Occasionally, it is appropriate for you to create your own databases of information, either by collecting your own data in raw form, or by doing your own analysis of data you have obtained from somewhere else. You accomplish this using the data-crunching tools that have become commonplace for many types of computer systems.

Data-crunching tools can be used for what some call computer-assisted reporting: for compiling and analyzing information about audience characteristics, keeping track of huge amounts of information gathered from many sources, and a myriad of other kinds of tasks that you face in your daily routines.

A number of computer programs and tools help with these types of information synthesis activities. One type of program is known as a database management program. These programs come under a variety of brand names and run on any desktop or laptop computer. Flat-file database management programs work like a paper index card file; each record in the file includes a selection of information, such as the name, physical and e-mail addresses, phone and fax numbers, affiliation, and expertise for all of a reporter's important interview sources. Flat-file programs can organize information in a variety of ways and can be sorted and searched by specific fields, such as by name or by source affiliation. They are fairly limited, however, in their usefulness for sophisticated analysis and synthesis.

Relational database management programs are more powerful. These programs, which also run on any desktop or laptop computer, enable you to organize many different types of information into one file and look for relationships and patterns in the information. For instance, you might obtain a computer disk from the state that includes all the death records over a certain number of years. Using a relational database management program into which the death records have been loaded, you might be able to determine which counties have the highest death rate among teenagers where an automobile crash contributed to the cause of death. After accounting for the normal variations between counties for overall numbers of teenagers residing in each county, the computer analysis might suggest that you look into the types of roads and traffic control systems in those counties, the numbers of law enforcement officers assigned to patrol highways, or other relationships that might be analyzed using the computer.

Another type of data-crunching tool is the spreadsheet program. Spreadsheet programs allow you to manipulate rows and columns of numbers (and in the more sophisticated versions, text) as a sort of very powerful calculator. You can use these programs to load large files of data, sort the records, compute averages, sums, percentages, and other figures, create graphs for visualizing the number-based information, and perform many other tasks. For instance, a small advertising firm might use a spreadsheet program to create a database that includes the circulation figures for each of the publications in which it regularly purchases ads, the costs for each type of ad, the cost-per-thousand figures for the reach of those ads, the number of audience members in certain age, sex, and income categories who see those ads, and other types of information. Using the spreadsheet program over and over, the ad professionals can tailor each of their media-buy and budget decisions for individual clients based on the results of each different shuffle of the information. Many media organizations purchase site licenses for spreadsheet software programs to be loaded on all computers so their staff members can use these tools in their routine daily work.

You face special responsibilities in using data-crunching tools in your information synthesis. First of all, new skills are required for negotiating with agencies and institutions for access to information files in digital form. Some agencies are still reluctant to provide communicators with online access or with disks, even though in its paper format the information may be considered a public record. You must develop your skills in speaking the jargon used by information technology (IT) system administrators and record managers in the agencies who have the desired information. You must also be familiar with the state laws that govern access to information in both print and digital form.

Also, data-crunching tools require you to be very scrupulous about the quality of the digital files being analyzed. A good rule of thumb when you work with digital files obtained from somewhere outside the media organization is to always request to see the paper form upon which the records in the digital file are based. If the computer file contains death records, you should request a copy of the form that is used to input the computer record. This helps you understand how to interpret records in the digital file, and can form part of the code guide necessary to use the file in a database management program.

Creating in-house databases also places special responsibilities on you and your colleagues. For instance, many large companies, including media firms and marketing or advertising firms, collect enormous amounts of information about their customers and clients. This information is exceptionally useful for internal purposes such as targeting special offers and products to specific customers. However, that database of information contains much information that would be considered private if someone outside the company were to gain access to the files. Readers of many of the largest magazines in the country, for instance, willingly provide a great deal of information about themselves to the magazine publisher in exchange for special catalogs, inserts, and merchandise offers. But those readers would be rightly angered if that information were sold to other firms without their permission or knowledge. The ability of media to compile extensive databases of information for their own, and others', data-crunching purposes is a major source of contention in our digital society.

Once you master your data-crunching skills, you have a powerful synthesis tool in your possession. Some of the best journalism of the past decade was done using these types of tools to analyze existing data and to create new databases of information that no one had ever analyzed before. Some of the most sophisticated audience and market analysis for persuasive messages is a result of original synthesis of disparate information using these tools. You will greatly improve your chances of discovering new and original perspectives on your information if you know how to use and apply these synthesis techniques.

EXAMPLES OF SYNTHESIS

Let's look at how the synthesis process works in media messages. A recent campaign illustrates some of these techniques. One important use of background information is to identify trends in population and consumer preferences in order to develop products and ad campaigns. The Dodge automobile company used changing trends in truck ownership to design an ad campaign that was a clever synthesis of several themes.

It used to be that you would see a cowboy in every new ad for a pick-up truck. But Dodge's research told them that pickups are purchased more and more often by city dwellers. The Detroit ad agency BBDO developed ads for the new Dodge pickup Dakota by putting this trend information to use. All truck makers have redesigned their pickups to emphasize curves rather than the traditional boxy lines of the vehicle. People who have always driven cars now are more likely to consider driving a truck; pickups have become fashionable for people who never have to haul hay. The ad agency personnel decided that their background research indicated that for their target audience, driving a truck is more of a statement than a necessity.

They used this information for both the content of the ads and for the placement of ads. The Dodge campaign runs counter to traditional ads for the product. The ads feature shots of cupholders and cellular phones in the trucks, not cowboys. The ads extol attributes more commonly found in cars and not often found in trucks. Safety features, roominess, nimbleness, convenient storage places, and the performance of three available engines are highlighted in the voice-over of the broadcast ads and the copy of the print ads. The ads use suburban themes—a baseball and glove, a child's bike, and a grocery cart threatening to crash into the truck, while the ad voiceover says Dakota resists dents.

The placement of ads also reflects the synthesis of information about who might be interested in buying a Dakota truck. The ads run during the usual programs such as Monday Night Football, but other media vehicles such as popular sitcoms are also used to target nontraditional purchasers of trucks. Print ads appear in *USA Today* and other print media not typical for traditional truck buyers. This example points out how the ad staff used synthesis of information about who is buying trucks to come up with a way to communicate to a new audience through new choices for creative elements and media purchases.[6]

News professionals also use their synthesis skills to tell stories. Synthesis skills help you get the story right, provide context, help the audience understand larger trends, and put things together rather than seeing things as isolated, disconnected, random occurrences.

The Minneapolis *Star Tribune* ran a story about the loss of 750 Minnesota jobs to Florida when the telemarketing firm Fingerhut decided they needed a bilingual work force in order to have successful telephone transactions with Spanish-speaking potential customers. The resultant news story used the Fingerhut incident to provide larger context for the event. Why did this major company feel it had reason to move its operation? Business forces revealed an important trend to the company's top management, and the reporter and editors thought it was also important for the newspaper audience to understand that trend. Reporters gathered background information about the makeup of the U.S. population, including census figures showing that Hispanics make up a substantial percentage of the population and will overtake African Americans in the next decade as the largest minority group. Data also showed both native-born and immigrant population growth among Spanish-speaking residents. Reporters used U.S. government figures to show that 32 million Americans speak a language other than English at home and one-third of school kids in major cities speak English as a second language.

Reporters also provided information about differences in cultures. Hispanics tend to be slower than other immigrant groups to adopt English. For evidence, reporters pointed to Spanish-language *Yellow Pages* issued in most Sun Belt cities, and the fact that the number of Spanish-language radio stations has doubled to more than 400 in the last decade. Univision and Telemundo, the top Spanish-language TV networks in the U.S., are strong promoters of culture and consumer products.

Fingerhut moved to Florida because, at the time of the story, the work force there was 18 percent bilingual, and Spanish-speaking customers were the company's fastest-growing market segment. The news story provided information about other companies that were scouting opportunities to sell to Hispanics, including local giants such as Target and Wells Fargo Bank. The news story talked about government agencies that accommodate Spanish speakers, such as the IRS offering tax forms in Spanish, communities providing ballots in Spanish, and states offering drivers' tests in Spanish. Reporters also talked about the controversy this has engendered. Reporters consulted social scientists who discussed early U.S. territorial expansion, the history of cultural integration, and close ties between the Spanish language and Mexican culture. The story also talked about laws established in 23 states to require English as the official language, and legal challenges to those statutes.

In short, reporters and editors used their information selection and synthesis skills to give an isolated news event greater context. They used their synthesis of information to provide multiple perspectives, trends, and supporting evidence. The news event was not just a one-day story about Fingerhut moving jobs, but rather an opportunity to discuss legal issues, social and cultural issues, and economic issues in a way that was engaging and understandable.[7]

The synthesis process also applies to academic reports and projects. The synthesis process in academic writing is often overlooked. When you are working on a scholarly term paper or project, you want to be able to understand and restate the meaning of all the information you have read and be able to draw conclusions from it. You need to apply the same skeptical eye when evaluating academic information as when you are judging material for a message. Try to organize material around themes, ideas, perspectives, and points of view. Also, keep in mind the requirement to use footnotes to give appropriate credit for ideas and information that you use in your writing. The issue of plagiarism is of paramount importance. It is crucial that you learn the proper method for crediting the sources of your information, no matter where it came from.

At this step in the information strategy, then, the importance of critical thinking is stressed. You must account for the accumulated *meaning* of the materials you've gathered or created from scratch. You identify common themes, discrepancies, and points that need to be verified or labeled as controversial. This step provides you with the last chance to identify missing material, catch errors, and make final decisions about the shape of the message. Along with the message analysis step that starts the information strategy, the synthesis step is the most difficult task you face in your message process.

The final chapter examines the social responsibility context in which all messages are produced. Chapter 13 reviews the societal perspectives, professional and organizational perspectives, and the individual perspective on social responsibility, as well as the legal obligations that influence the production of media messages.

SELECTED ADDITIONAL READINGS

Murray, Donald M. *Writing to Deadline*. Portsmouth, NH: Heinemann Publishing, 2000.
Stewart, James B. *Follow the Story: How to Write Successful Nonfiction*. Carmichael, CA: Touchstone Books, 1998.

NOTES

1. Carl Hausman, *The Decision Making Process in Journalism*, (Chicago: Nelson-Hall, 1990).

2. Kirk Hallahan, "Assuring Quality of Public Relations Messages," (Colorado State University, August 1997), lamar.colostate.edu/~hallahan/hquality.htm.

3. Steve Buttry, "Writing Clearly on Deadline," *Omaha World-Herald*, www.copydesk.org/words/writingclearly.htm.

4. Theresa Torisky, "How to Effectively Organize a Paper," *Bowling Green State University Writing Lab Online*, 17 March 1997, www.bgsu.edu/departments/writing-lab/how_to_effectively_o.html.

5. Steve Weinberg, "The Mob, the CIA, and the S&L Scandal," *Columbia Journalism Review*, November–December 1990, 28–35.

6. Robyn Meredith, "Advertising," *New York Times*, 30 October 1996, C6.

7. Steve Berg and Sally Apgar, "Spanish speakers are fastest-growing consumer segment," *Star Tribune*, 5 May 1996, A1.

CHAPTER THIRTEEN

LAW AND ETHICS OF GATHERING AND USING INFORMATION

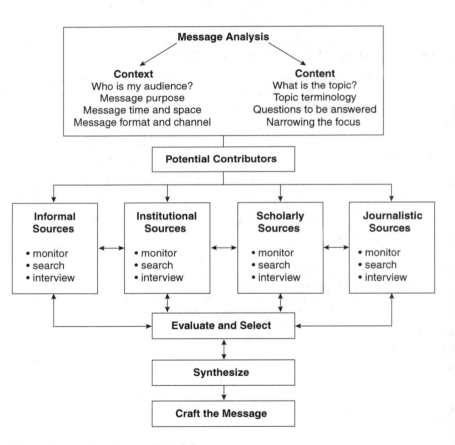

The Information Strategy Model

Dilemmas about the proper use of information are as old as the Ten Commandments, which forbid lying and false witness. But the complexity of new information technologies and their capacity to conjure up words and images at the tap of a few keystrokes are keeping critics and ethics specialists well occupied.

The senior editor of the *Online Journalism Review* posed some interesting questions for his readers in a column entitled, "A Scorecard for Net News Ethics." He asked, "Is it okay for reporters to lurk in chat rooms without identifying themselves? Can reporters quote from bulletin board postings or chat transcripts without asking the user's permission? Do news subjects have the right not to be subjected to ambushes by online journalists carrying camcorders, digital cameras or live Webcams?" His answer to the first two questions was no, and yes to the last.[1]

If a strategic communications agency assigns a college student intern to call a competitor for information, is it ethical for the intern to say she is calling for a class project and not reveal her affiliation with the firm? The Public Relations Society of America code of ethics says no.

This chapter focuses on conduct connected with the gathering and selection of materials for mass-media messages. It concerns the legality and ethics that attend activities that take place during the information strategy. Many other issues are significant but do not specifically concern the process of the information strategy: fair hiring and employment practices, media message language and images as instruments of discrimination, conflicts of interest, misleading advertising and marketing messages. Even limited in this way, this discussion can treat only in cursory fashion the issues that you and your media organization may face.

To start, we need to make a distinction between law and ethics. *Ethics* is a branch of philosophy dealing with values relating to human conduct. Ethicists concern themselves with the rightness and wrongness of certain actions, the goodness and badness of motives, and the ends of such actions. Ethical behavior is self-legislated and self-enforced. There are no ethics police.

Law stems from the ethical values in a society, but law is socially determined (legislators pass laws, the executive head of state signs them into effect) and socially enforced (through institutions such as the police and the courts). Determining what is legal is easier than determining what is ethical. Law is a matter of statute. You can look up a piece of legislation or find a federal regulation and determine the legality of an action. While there are certainly many codes of ethics that apply to the work mass communicators do, ethics is personal and self-determined.

So getting agreement about what constitutes *socially responsible communication and information practices* is difficult. It is generally conceded that socially responsible communicators are not content merely with staying on the right side of the law. While the law embodies a significant portion of our values, individuals and organizations that want to be considered socially responsible must go beyond the rough requirements of the law itself and adopt higher and more thoughtful standards.

One of the strengths of the information strategy is that it provides many alternative methods for gathering materials. This helps you avoid some of the ethical and legal problems that might arise for less skilled information searchers. If you have a variety of means for gathering information, it is less likely that you will have to resort to, or be pressured into using, a method that is unethical or that leads to charges of improper behavior.

NEGATIVE AND POSITIVE OBLIGATIONS

Communicators have obligations in their information gathering and use which may be spelled out by a code of ethics at the organizational level, at the professional level, or that may be strictly personal. In any case, there are some things which must *not* happen, and some things you should strive to always do. Let's review these.

Negative Obligations.   These are things which must not happen:

- *Privacy violations.* You must weigh the impact of gathering and using certain types of information against the possibility that someone's privacy will be violated. For instance, charges of privacy violations were at issue when the two daily newspapers in Minneapolis and St. Paul covered a kidnapping and murder/suicide. A teenager was found dead, along with an older neighbor who had been accused of molesting the teen. The St. Paul paper printed a photo on the front page of the two dead bodies in the car where they were found. The Minneapolis paper printed information that indicated the teenager had sought help from a sexuality counseling group before his death. Outraged readers demanded to know how either paper's behavior could be justified, given the privacy violations involved. Both news organizations justified themselves using one of the positive obligations we will discuss later in this chapter, the public's need for information. Privacy violations are even more problematic with electronic information. With so much personal information now stored electronically, computer snooping and privacy invasions are much more feasible, but still ethically suspect.
- *Entrapment.* Encouraging bad behavior and then reporting on it. Hidden camera investigations sometimes tiptoe on the borderline of entrapment. For instance, a local television news crew left a brand new bicycle unlocked in a public park, and then hid in the foliage with a camera waiting to see if someone would come by and steal the bike. Of course, when a hapless youngster did climb on the bike and start to peddle away, the camera crew caught it all on tape, complete with the frightened kid's reaction as the camera crew followed in hot pursuit. After howls of complaint from the community, the station declared that it was reviewing its policy regarding the use of hidden cameras.
- *Leaking of information* for the media's or an individual's purposes. Communicators are sometimes tempted to leak information to get someone to tell them something, which is a dicey tactic because it calls into question the communicator's own ethics and trustworthiness as an information collector. Another variation involves using leaked information that has not been checked for veracity and motives in other sources. Information subsidizers continually leak information for their own purposes, and you must guard against using leaked information as a dupe for someone else's agenda.

- *Concealing conflict of interest* in seeking or using information. Communicators have been accused of violating conflict of interest rules in their acceptance of speaking fees or junkets to talk to groups that they subsequently have to cover for news stories. Marketing and advertising professionals have to guard against charges of corporate espionage in seeking information about competitors.
- *Eavesdropping.* Listening in on others' conversations, electronically or otherwise, is clearly an ethical violation and in many instances is also illegal. There are devices that can be purchased in any electronics store that allow snoopers to listen in on cellular telephone conversations, monitor e-mail, and otherwise violate individuals' and organizations' privacy. And the old-fashioned method of standing outside a door where an important meeting is going on with an ear pressed to the door is also an eavesdropping violation.
- *Stealing information.* Theft is clearly an ethical and legal violation. Rifling through someone's desk drawer while they are out of the office, accepting information that was obtained through illegal means, engaging in corporate espionage, and other similar violations are going to cause problems for you no matter what the possible justification might be.
- *Plagiarism.* A variation of theft is plagiarism. It is so easy for you to gather information from so many sources. It is technically so simple to cut and paste material from other sources into your own work. You have to continually be on guard against both intentional and inadvertent plagiarism. Learn to be scrupulous about noting where information comes from as your strategy proceeds, and be sure to credit the source of anything that did not come out of your own head.
- *Using information given confidentially.* Remember the contract with your source that was discussed in Chapter 5? If you have made an offer to a source to keep that person's identity a secret, you cannot breach that promise of confidentiality without serious legal and ethical repercussions.

Positive Obligations. These are goals you try always to achieve:

- *Accuracy checks.* You are responsible for resolving issues of fact. The reporter must verify information before using it in a news story. The advertising professional must make sure client claims can be substantiated. The PR specialist must ensure that the corporate annual report accurately states the financial status of the company. These are both legal *and* ethical requirements.
- *Attempt at fairness.* You will quickly learn that there are not just two sides to a story. Fairness requires that you try to include as many perspectives and points of view as possible when compiling information for a message. The reality of most situations is that you will not be able to use in any single message everything you gather, but your information strategy should strive to uncover as many different aspects of the topic as possible so you are making an informed choice when you finally construct the message.
- *Safeguarding the public's need for information.* Despite the rhetoric of First Amendment lawyers, the public does not have a right to know *per se*. The First Amendment to the constitution of the United States says that citizens have a

right to assemble, speak, practice their chosen religion, and that the Congress shall make no law limiting the freedom of the press. It does not address the public's "right to know" anything. But most communication scholars acknowledge the role that information provided by the media plays in nurturing an informed electorate, and for helping people make informed purchase decisions. As we have already mentioned, your positive obligation to safeguard the public's need for information sometimes stands in direct conflict with your negative obligation not to violate privacy. Which obligation takes precedence? Which value is more important to you, to your media organization, to the audience, to society? These conflicting obligations are one of the reasons that you need to be systematic and clear in your ethical decision making.

- *Completeness and thoroughness.* It is not sufficient any more to claim time or budget constraints for incomplete information. Communicators who have highly developed information skills should be able, and are expected, to conduct complete and thorough information searches, and to provide complete and thorough information to the audience in their messages. This is an ethical obligation, and a matter of professional competence and pride.
- *Standing up for what is right* in the media organization. You need to be willing to be in dispute with supervisors and colleagues when there is an ethical conflict. It is not always easy to be the one who says, "Wait a minute. I think we need to examine our motives and behavior here," but you have an ethical obligation to hold yourself and your colleagues to high standards. Sometimes it means having to challenge things that others seem to accept without question.

All of these negative and positive obligations help you weigh your ethical decisions when a situation arises. Ethical thinking requires that you establish for yourself, ahead of time, how you value these various obligations, and which take precedence in your own scheme of decision making. You also must be fully aware of how your media organization has ordered these priorities for their own operations, and comply with the standards that your organization has established.

THE SOCIAL RESPONSIBILITY CONTEXT

Long-time observers of mass communication have accepted the principle that those who gather and select information for the public have enormous power to shape public discourse. Especially in the United States, you are generally free to perform your work as a communications professional without interference from the government. But you are also answerable for your actions to public opinion and to the law. This means that you have an obligation to perform your work within the context of social responsibility. There are three levels of responsibility that affect your work as a communicator. These are:

- The societal perspective on ethics and social responsibility that examines the relationships between media systems and other major institutions in society

- The professional and organizational perspective that examines your profession's and your media organization's own self-regulations and standards for professional conduct
- The individual perspective that examines the responsibility you have to society, to your profession, to your audience, and to yourself

We'll examine each of these in turn.

The Societal Perspective

Scientific study of public opinion shows that major institutions have ups and downs when public confidence in these institutions is measured. Particularly after the traumatic events of the terrorist attacks on the United States on September 11, 2001, public confidence in institutions such as the military, police, the presidency, and the Supreme Court rose significantly.[2] Of course, much of what the public knows about these major institutions in society comes from the mass communication professionals who monitor institutional activity or inactivity.

Public attitudes towards mass communication vary from one period to another. In the same opinion survey that found strong confidence in the military and the presidency, the news media (print and broadcast) ranked in the bottom third. In the 2000 version of an ongoing Gallup poll about the professions which are considered most honest and ethical in the United States, nurses, pharmacists, veterinarians, doctors, and teachers headed the list. Survey respondents said the least honest and ethical professions were car salesmen, advertising practitioners, insurance salesmen, newspaper reporters, and lawyers.[3] This reflects a consistent standard across many years of this particular survey. People tend to rate professionals who are believed to have a selfless motive higher than those who are perceived to put their own interests ahead of others'.

The fact that the communications professions rank at the bottom of the ethics scale in such surveys is troublesome, but perhaps understandable. The public is more sophisticated about media behavior than in the past, with regular insights into journalists' attitudes and views through television roundtable programs and Web chats. Advertising professionals' marketing techniques have come under scrutiny in celebrated lawsuits such as those brought against the tobacco companies. Privacy rights have emerged as a major issue that divides the populace from many media practitioners. The increasing concentration of ownership of major media outlets and its effects on the perceived diversity of media voices is another area of concern for many audience members.

Such criticism is a prod to media improvement. Many representatives of other institutions provide these societal criticisms. For example, when a judge in a criminal trial grants a motion to change the location of the trial because news coverage has made a fair trial impossible in the local community, it is an implicit criticism of media behavior. When a consumer draws public attention to an advertisement that presents what is perceived to be a harmful advertising claim, the criticism is clear and direct.

These societal criticisms and suggestions generally reflect a social-responsibility perspective. In the United States, the social-responsibility perspective affects most major institutions. Corporations, educational institutions, churches, civic associations—to name a few—are exhorted to act in a socially responsible manner. Professional education and licensing have been traditional means by which society has sought to ensure reliable practice from those who bear important social responsibilities. For law, medicine, accounting, teaching, architecture, and other fields of expertise, specific training is followed by examinations, state licensing, and the administration of oaths that include promises to live up to the standards established for the profession. However, communicators are not required to be licensed in the United States. Without the power to control entry into the field and withdraw the license to operate, society and its major power centers must exert more subtle and invisible ways to influence communication industries and those who work in them.

Certainly, one major way that the societal level of responsibility is exerted is through the laws that affect communicator choices and behavior. As a gatherer and assessor of information, you are expected to understand and adhere to your legal obligations. You cannot violate copyright laws, the laws that protect intellectual property rights, obscenity laws, or libel laws in obtaining or using information in messages. News practitioners are expected to understand how to gather the information they need without violating privacy laws that protect personal information or the trespass laws that protect private property.

Advertising practitioners are expected to adhere to federal and state regulations regarding the content of many messages. It is illegal, for instance, to discriminate in an ad for housing or employment on the basis of gender, race, or national origin. The Federal Trade Commission regulates the content of ads that might be considered false or misleading, or that makes product or service claims or comparisons. The *advertising substantiation* rule is of paramount importance for anyone collecting and evaluating information to use in a comparison ad. The advertiser must be able to substantiate any claim about a product or service with information that backs up such claims. This means that you, as the advertising professional, will follow a comprehensive information strategy in preparing the background information for any such ad.

Public relations firms increasingly are investigated along with the corporations they represent in situations of litigation, disputes about investor relations, and so on. Let's look at a few examples that illustrate how the major institutions interact in the societal-level perspective on social responsibility.

Prescription drug manufacturers are now advertising directly to the public, rather than to physicians and pharmacists who might prescribe or recommend their medications. You have probably seen the ads that tell you, "Ask your doctor about (Product X)." These ads raise questions about the ethics of providing selective, perhaps biased, information to consumers who may not have the expertise and complete information to make rational choices. Some observers express concern about patients being deceived and misled. The Food and Drug Administration has begun to crack down on some companies for false or misleading claims.

In this example, you must balance the positive value of meeting a public information need against the negative value of deception and incomplete information. As a communications professional, you also must examine your intrusion into the negotiation between the social role of physicians versus the role of pharmaceutical companies. In this case, advertising messages may play a role in upsetting traditional social arrangements between physicians, patients, drug companies, and health care organizations.

Physicians used to hold a great deal of control over patient care through their knowledge of drugs and their effects. That knowledge is now more widely accessible to the general public. But patients with an advertising-supplied level of knowledge (meaning, not much substantial information) may pressure physicians into prescribing a particular brand when a generic version of a drug might be just as effective. Or patients may insist on drug treatment when another method of treatment might be preferred. This plays into the hands of the large pharmaceutical companies, which have seen their profits soar in recent years.[4] So the complex interactions between social institutions (advertising professionals, pharmaceutical companies, physicians, and insurers) are dramatically affected by the practice of prescription drug advertising.

This requires ad practitioners to carefully examine how they craft these drug messages. In fact, the Food and Drug Administration regulates the content of these ads, and ad professionals have conducted an on-going discussion about how best to truthfully and accurately inform the public with these messages in a way that does not subvert the important relationship between physician and patient.

The use of photos and visual material in messages provides another example of the societal level of responsibility for communicators. The advertising department working on the McDonald's account in the Netherlands used a photograph of a famous French chef and four associates examining a pile of chickens from the Bresse region of France, well-known for its poultry. In the photo, there is a bubble and caption above the chefs' heads making it look like they are thinking about a Big Mac.

When the famous chef saw the posters, he filed suit against the advertising firm and McDonald's because the chef was never asked to provide permission to use his photo. When McDonald's sought to respond, they made matters worse by saying that they had asked their publicity agency to look for any photograph of chefs with tall hats. They did not recognize the famous French chef, nor any of his associates in the photograph, who were also well-known in their own right. This made the French chef even angrier. McDonald's withdrew the posters and negotiated a settlement with the chef.[5] The major issue here is that you cannot use photographic images or likenesses without permission. You cannot assume that a photograph or drawing can be used without checking the legal and ethical obligations to seek permission and provide credit, and/or payment, for the use of the image.

The Professional and Organizational Perspectives

In addition to the societal level of interactions, communication organizations and professionals engage in self-criticism and set standards for their own conduct and performance as information gatherers. One of the most conspicuous examples of this lies in the proliferation of codes of conduct for mass communication activities at all levels.

News Codes.   In the news industries, codes have expanded in number and scope over several decades. Codes have been adopted by the American Society of Newspaper

Editors, the Society of Professional Journalists, the Associated Press Managing Editors Association, the National Association of Broadcasters, the Radio and Television News Directors Association, the Magazine Publishers Association, and the National Press Photographers Association. Individual news organizations and publications frequently establish their own codes to which their staffs are expected to adhere.

One of the simpler statements of journalistic ethics is provided by the Society of Professional Journalists, whose code can be summarized in four main statements (each of which is elaborated upon in the more detailed version of the code): 1) Seek truth and report it; 2) Minimize harm; 3) Act independently; and 4) Be accountable.

The relatively new Online News Association publishes a set of guidelines in its mission statement that outlines the principles that online news providers should try to adhere to (Box 13.1). These principles do not, of course, apply only to online news, but the digital environment presents some interesting new challenges to media practitioners.

Advertisers' Codes.   Advertising codes reflect some of the specific criticism directed at the field, such as charges of deceptive advertising, unfair stereotyping, false testimonials, and misleading claims. Professional associations of advertisers, such as the American Association of Advertising Agencies, have codes that state that members will not use false or misleading visual or verbal statements; will not use testimonials which do not reflect the real choice of a competent witness; will not make price claims that are misleading; will not make comparisons that unfairly disparage a competitive product or service; will not make claims that are insufficiently supported; and will not use statements, suggestions, or pictures offensive to public decency.

The advertising industry also has a two-tiered self-regulatory mechanism. Advertising that is charged with being deceptive can be referred to the National Advertising Division (NAD) of the Council of Better Business Bureaus. Cases that are not satisfactorily resolved through NAD can then be appealed to the National Advertising Review Board. Individual advertising agencies and corporate advertising departments also have codes and standards to help employees recognize and deal with ethical questions.

Most media outlets accept or reject ads submitted to them using a set of guidelines about what types of ads are acceptable and what type of content will be allowed. Specific industries, trade associations, and professions have also adopted codes pertaining to their own groups. Drug manufacturers, automobile dealers, attorneys, and the insurance industry are examples of groups that have codes for their own advertising.

Despite all of these codes and guidelines, there is more and more agitation for government regulation of advertising because people perceive that advertisers do not police themselves enough. Several products are particular targets for self-regulation and complaint. Liquor ads are under attack, and in response, liquor bottles now include health warning labels. There is consideration of legislation outlawing liquor advertising the way tobacco ads were banned from the broadcast airwaves years ago. The example points out the negotiation that takes place among professional and organizational players in trying to meet self-regulatory demands to avoid societal level rules in the form of legislation.

Public Relations Codes.   Public relations practitioners, like advertising specialists, work closely with clients. Legal and ethical decisions often arise as clients and publicists discuss information-gathering strategies. For example, the Securities and Ex-

■ ■ ■ ■ ■

BOX 13.1
PROFESSIONAL MISSION STATEMENTS HELP PROVIDE GUIDELINES FOR ETHICAL CONDUCT

The Online News Association is an association composed largely of professional online journalists. The Association has more than 800 professional members, that is, members whose principal livelihood involves gathering or producing news for digital presentation. The membership includes news writers, producers, designers, editors, photographers and others who produce news for the Internet or other digital delivery systems, as well as academic members and others interested in the development of online journalism. ONA also, in partnership with Columbia University, administers the prestigious Online Journalism Awards.

OUR FOUNDING PRINCIPLES: We believe that the Internet is the most powerful communications medium to arise since the dawn of television. As the Net becomes a primary source of news for a growing segment of the world's population, it presents complex challenges and opportunities for journalists as well as the news audience.

EDITORIAL INTEGRITY: The unique permeability of Web publications allows for the linking and joining of information resources of all kinds as intimately as if they were published by a single organization. Responsible journalism on the Internet means that the distinction between news and other information must always be clear, so that individuals can readily distinguish independent editorial information from paid promotional information and other non-news.

EDITORIAL INDEPENDENCE: Online journalists should maintain the highest principles of fairness, accuracy, objectivity and responsible independent reporting.

JOURNALISTIC EXCELLENCE: Online journalists should uphold traditional high principles in reporting original news for the Internet and in reviewing and corroborating information from other sources.

FREEDOM OF EXPRESSION: The ubiquity and global reach of information published on the Internet offers new information and educational resources to a worldwide audience, access to which must be unrestricted.

FREEDOM OF ACCESS: News organizations reporting on the Internet must be afforded access to information and events equal to that enjoyed by other news organizations in order to further freedom of information.

Source: Online News Association. Reprinted by permission.

change Commission monitors the way corporations report their financial affairs. Information about stock offerings and financial balance sheets are scrutinized for accuracy and omission of important facts. The object is to ensure that investors and stock analysts can get accurate information about the companies that are offering securities. Public relations practitioners, along with stockbrokers, lawyers, and accountants, are increasingly being held responsible for the accuracy of information they communicate to the public. When public relations professionals find themselves on the losing side of an important ethical question with a client, it is not unusual for them to resign their positions as a matter of principle.

The Public Relations Society of America's *Code of Ethics* emphasizes honesty and accountability, in addition to expertise, advocacy, fairness, independence, and loyalty.

One provision of the Code puts forth a commitment to protect and advance the free flow of accurate and truthful information. The Code expects PR practitioners to be honest and accurate in all communications. It goes a step further by stating that professionals are expected to act promptly to correct any erroneous communications for which the practitioner is responsible.

Besides a commitment to the free flow of information, other provisions that the PRSA code addresses relate to fair competition, disclosure of information, safeguarding confidences, addressing conflicts of interest, and enhancing the profession.

The public relations code, like those for advertising and journalism, reflects the concerns of society as well as the practitioners who adopt the codes. Provisions of all the codes are designed, at least in part, to offer the public reasons to have confidence in your integrity and in the messages you create. They also are intended to help you stay out of court.

Sample Case.   A breakdown in organizational rules sometimes leads to legal action. A precedent-setting case occurred when a political operative for a gubernatorial candidate gave information about a rival candidate to four news organizations on election eve with the agreement that the source of the damaging information would remain confidential. The information involved a juvenile conviction for shoplifting against the candidate for lieutenant governor—a charge that had been vacated once the candidate had reached the age of 21. The television station staff did not use the damaging information from the operative, the reporter from the Associated Press used it in his story, but with veiled attribution, and the reporters from the two local newspapers granted anonymity but editors at both papers revoked the agreement and named the operative, Dan Cohen, in the published story. Editors claimed they felt there was a competing value involved (the negative value of not breaking a promise of confidentiality had to be weighed against the positive value of the public's need for information about a candidate's dirty trick tactics on election eve).

Cohen claimed breach of contract, sued, and his case went all the way to the U.S. Supreme Court. The Supreme Court ruled that newspapers cannot break promises of anonymity without the risk of having to pay damages to those who are hurt. The justices applied traditional *promissory estoppel* (a type of contract) law to the case and would not hear any First Amendment defenses. They turned an ethical tradition (the agreements reporters and sources make about the use of information) into a legal contract. The U.S. Supreme Court sent the case back to the State Supreme Court for reconsideration, and the state court decided the case on the basis of the state constitution and the state's freedom of the press protections. The state court ruled that "a promise is a promise," and because Cohen had lost his job as a result of the incident, the court reinstated the $200,000 compensatory award for Cohen that had been initially voted by a jury against the two papers. Thus, the professional routines and organizational responsibilities of the two local media organizations became fodder for a legal argument with wide-ranging implications for all news organizations.

There are several issues involved in this case. Think back on the negative and positive obligations we mentioned earlier. Should reporters have granted confidentiality to Cohen? What ethical obligations are in conflict? Think back to our discussion about the use of anonymous sources. Was there a different way to tell this story, or to use this information? Did editors have an ethical responsibility to support their reporters' decision on confidentiality? Did editors have an ethical responsibility to readers to identify the source of the damaging information? As a response to the fallout from the case, one of the newspapers eventually wrote formal guidelines regarding reporter and editor obligations and limitations in the use of anonymous information. The example illustrates the interaction between societal level and organizational levels of responsibility.

The Individual Perspective

The individual level of responsibility for ethical behavior is also of concern. As a communications professional, you may find yourself confronting conflicting obligations in your daily routine. You will be doing your work in a decidedly ambivalent atmosphere. News professionals are criticized for reinforcing the assumptions of those in power and ignoring reality as experienced by most of the population. Advertising is criticized for contributing to materialism, wasteful consumption, and the corruption of the electoral system. Public relations is criticized for creating and manipulating images on behalf of those with narrow interests, failing to give public interest information a priority.

Media ethics researchers Clifford Christians, Kim Rotzoll, and Mark Fackler have identified five duties that confront communicators as they follow their professional routines:

1. *Duty to yourself.* Personal integrity and conscience are paramount.
2. *Duty to clients/subscribers/supporters.* Those who pay the bills either to produce the message or to receive it command various obligations.
3. *Duty to your organization or firm.* Loyalty to the organization takes various forms, including some that may be unpopular for the moment but may be in the long-term interest of the organization.
4. *Duty to professional colleagues.* Workers in the same field stand together, often against others in the organization, when upholding work standards they believe in.
5. *Duty to society.* Social and public good are often balanced against all the other four considerations when you reflect on your duty. Advertising dangerous products, producing pornographic or violent messages, ignoring public officials' flouting of the law, and similar acts are examples of communicators' conflict with the social good.[6]

In confronting your social responsibility using the individual perspective, you are likely to place duty to yourself at the top of the list. You always need to abide by your own moral standards. But this may conflict with more worldly ambitions—desire for recognition, advancement, and financial security. The duty to the organization may be at odds with the loyalty to colleagues or to the profession. Let's look at a few examples that illustrate these tensions.

A metro newspaper was promoting an editorial series they had prepared called "Strengthening the Core," an attempt to discuss what was happening to inner city neighborhoods. They used a photograph in an ad for the series that turned out to be staged. The photo showed a graffiti-covered, boarded-up building with trash thrown about. In the lower right corner of the ad a message on a newspaper rack read, "Can we keep our cities from deteriorating?" Witnesses said they saw the ad agency photographer scatter trash he brought with him, pour liquid on the sidewalk, and break glass before taking his pictures. The newspaper company had also provided a worn-out newspaper rack to be placed in the scene for the photo. The staged photograph caused a major embarrassment for the daily newspaper when it was exposed in a monthly neighborhood paper that serves the neighborhood that was supposed to be deteriorating. The flap over the photo drew attention away from the series itself, caused the metro paper to issue an apology to readers and to business owners in the community, who were hurt by the whole process. It also called into question the metro paper's true understanding of and sensitivity to city neighborhood issues.[7]

That example points out the ethical responsibility for the paper's promotion department to supervise the work they farm out, responsibility for the editorial department to reign in the promotion department's over-zealous efforts, and responsibility for the entire news organization to understand the issues and needs of the inner city and better meet those informational needs. The individual ethics of the ad agency photographer are also at issue here. There are strict standards for news photos, which are not supposed to be altered in any way. The rules are less clear for advertising and marketing images, which typically are crafted for particular effect. In this case, however, the promotional photos and ads were being created for a *news* series. Despite the fact that the ad agency photographer might have been accustomed to operating with different standards, he should have known that staging a scene of urban decay to promote a news series was crossing the line. The rules for creating the photos for this particular ad campaign should have been spelled out by the newspaper promotion department and editorial staff, and strictly followed by the photographer.

Individual-level responsibility may arise when ad professionals object to ads they have to work on or have to accept. It is usually not necessary to violate your own standards. Let's say you are the advertising manager for a local newspaper. You receive an ad that you think is offensive, even though the product or service being advertised is perfectly legal and the company is a big advertiser in your publication. You don't have to accept that offensive ad, but you also don't have to forego the ad revenue for your publication (again, we're weighing two competing obligations—your obligation to your own standards against your obligation to your media organization to generate revenue). The way to resolve this dilemma is to call the ad agency and ask for another version of the advertisement. Advertisers almost always have another version, in anticipation that some media outlets will refuse to run a potentially offensive version of an ad. With this solution, you can adhere to your own standards and still generate revenue for your publication by accepting the more appropriate ad.

When a scathing series about the business practices of Chiquita Brands International ran in the company's home town newspaper, the *Cincinnati Enquirer*, much of the damaging information came from 2,000 internal voice mails that the lead reporter said had been obtained from a high-ranking Chiquita executive. After the company threatened a lawsuit, the newspaper's publisher and editors conducted an internal investigation and learned that the reporter was involved in theft of the voice mails. The reporter was dismissed, the newspaper paid Chiquita more than $10 million to avoid the lawsuit, and published an apology across the top of its front page renouncing the articles and the means used by the reporter to obtain the information.[8] The lapse of individual responsibility on the part of the reporter had wide-ranging implications for his organization, his audience, and the profession as a whole.

INFORMATION STRATEGY AND SOCIAL RESPONSIBILITY

All of these levels of responsibility influence how communicators weigh their actions and make their decisions. Societal expectations, organizational and professional routines and norms, and individual standards are going to play a role in each decision that faces you. As long as you have a systematic method for evaluating each situation and for applying your ethical standards, you should be able to make your information decisions in an ethical and defensible manner. The information strategy provides you with the skills to ensure that you don't have to resort to inappropriate, unethical, or illegal means to gather information. Being a highly skilled information gatherer in an information-overloaded society brings credibility to you and to your organization.

Further, using an explicit information strategy helps you explain your standards to others. When the public, colleagues, or supervisors challenge the information on which a message is based, you can present an ordered, rational account of your information search and selection process. Using the standards and methods available in the information strategy allows others to evaluate your skill and expertise as a communications professional.

The information strategy offers no remedy for offenses that originate in greed, naked ambition, low taste, or insensitivity. But most communicators' flaws are tied to other deficiencies, such as ignorance about the information universe, lack of skill in collecting information, and absence of evaluation standards. These flaws, intellectual rather than moral in origin, can be addressed by education and practice. The information strategy is designed as a powerful tool to improve the practice of mass communication.

Ultimately, personal, organizational, and public ethics return to the center of the picture. The new information age offers possibilities that frighten many: invasions of privacy, irresponsible use of information, growth of the information-poor as a segment of society. Improved information gathering methods in mass communication are small, but significant, parts of this picture. Despite improvements in information techniques, the important questions of privacy, responsibility, and equity remain to be addressed by lawmakers, judges, and the electorate. Your role as a communications professional includes the obligation to seek the most recent advice from the legal experts in your field to ensure that you are adhering to the law, and to continually examine the ethical standards in your field to ensure that you are adhering to the accepted practice for your profession.

SELECTED ADDITIONAL READINGS

Fuller, Jack. *News Values: Ideas for an Information Age.* Chicago: University of Chicago Press, 1996.

Kovach, Bill, and Tom Rosenstiel. *The Elements of Journalism: What Newspeople Should Know and the Public Should Expect.* New York: Three Rivers Press, 2001.

Seib, Philip M. *Public Relations Ethics.* Belmont, CA: Wadsworth, 1994.

NOTES

1. J. D. Lasica, "A Scorecard for Net News Ethics," *Online Journalism Review*, 2 April 2002, www.ojr.org/ethics/1017782140.php.

2. Frank Newport, "Americans' Confidence in Military, Presidency Up; Big Business, Organized Religion Drop," *Gallup Poll News Service*, 28 June 2002, www.gallup.com/poll/releases/pr020628.asp.

3. Daniel B. Wood, "Who People Trust—By Profession," *Christian Science Monitor*, 29 November 2000.

4. Robert Pear, "Marketing Ties to Increase in Prescription Drug Sales," *New York Times*, 20 September 2000, A16.

5. Roger Cohen, "Faux Pas by McDonald's in Europe," *New York Times*, 18 February 1992, C1.

6. Clifford Christians, Kim B. Rotzoll and Mark Fackler, *Media Ethics: Cases and Moral Reasoning*, 6th ed. (New York: Longman, 2001), 22–23.

7. John Yewell, "Star Tribune Admits Photo in Ad for 'Core' Series was Staged," *The Surveyor*, September 1993, 1, 14; Bob Geiger, "FM's Star Tribune Ad Was Staged, But So Are Most Ads," *Star Tribune*, 6 September 1993, 2D.

8. Laurence Zuckerman, "Paper Forced to Apologize For Articles About Chiquita," *New York Times*, 29 June 1998, A10.

FOLLOWING THE MODEL
THEN AND NOW

A CASE STUDY OF THE INFORMATION
STRATEGY PROCESS IN ACTION

When Schwan's ice cream was implicated in a salmonella outbreak in 1994 that caused illnesses in thirty-five states, the Minneapolis *Star Tribune* newspaper set out to uncover as much as possible about the highly secretive private company. The conventional wisdom about the Marshall, Minnesota, company was that it was a reporter's nightmare—difficult to cover, impossible to find information about, and, as the largest employer in the small prairie town, carefully protected by Marshall citizens.

What follows is a case study showing how the information strategy model can be used to go from a deep information deficit to an in-depth news story. Notably, this task was completed back in 1994—before the Internet as we know it today was widely available to reporters. As part of this case study, we'll also point out how this information strategy might have been different had it been developed today, what potential implications this updated approach might have had for the story, and what we can learn about gathering information from the days before Internet access was common on the desktops of the average communicator. We'll also discuss how strategic communications professionals could apply the information strategy process to their production of messages for Schwan's.

Star Tribune business reporter Tony Kennedy set out to debunk the conventional wisdom about Schwan's in 1994. He and his editor approached their **message analysis** task in the context of a breaking national story. Daily news events were helping flesh out how many people were sick, and from what kinds of Schwan's products. The U.S. Food and Drug Administration, among many public health agencies, was on the case, trying to track the source of salmonella bacteria that showed up in a number of Schwan's door-to-door-delivered ice cream products. The Minneapolis newspaper was covering the daily developments in the breaking story, but Kennedy wanted to do more. He wanted to find out as much as possible about the company and set the breaking news events in context for the readers of the largest newspaper in the state.

The news story he wrote is reprinted on the following pages. The story is a superb example of the importance of melding a rich information base with high-quality narrative. As we have said, a message is no better than the information in it. Expression and information are closely linked, and Kennedy's story demonstrates how a good writer can take a wealth of information and translate it into a colorful, well-written piece that leads readers through a complex story. The story was researched and written over five days, during which time Kennedy continued to work on other stories and assignments.

Once Kennedy and his editor settled on the type of story they wanted to do, the background-information gathering began. Kennedy did a number of important **informal interviews,** none of which show up in the story, with sources close to the food industry. Some were competitors of Schwan's, others were food brokers—the people who try to get a company like Schwan's to carry a food manufacturer's products. At the time of these information interviews, Kennedy was simply asking background questions for leads and ideas about possible formal avenues to pursue in putting together a portrait of Schwan's.

The news library staff was also involved in the preliminary background search. In addition to **journalistic source searches** in the *Star Tribune's electronic back files* for any previous stories the newspaper had written about Schwan's, the old *print clips* were also tapped. The electronic backfile began in 1986, so many pre-1986 stories about Schwan's were stored in the filing cabinet folders of old news clippings. Two library staff members also began a general **search** using other **commercial database services that index journalistic sources,** such as the *LexisNexis* database and standard business publication databases. Once again, these searches were designed to turn up any stories that had run in obvious sources such as business magazines and food industry trade publications. However, this preliminary background search did not turn up very much information, confirming the image of Schwan's as a low-profile firm.

Based on this dearth of information, Kennedy *refined the scope of the question.* He still needed very basic information about Schwan's, such as the number and location of plants the company owned, the number of brands it sold, the number of employees it had, the overall financial standing of the company, the role the company played in the industry and in the city of Marshall, and the likely response it would mount in the face of the salmonella crisis. In other words, Kennedy would have to start pretty much from scratch in order to fully understand the company and write a thorough profile.

At this time, Kennedy began to keep a file of information, including a list of the names, phone numbers, and dates for every interview he conducted. The meager background information about Schwan's also went into the file, along with notes, memos, photocopies, and work-in-progress printouts from the newsroom computer system.

It quickly became apparent that Kennedy would have to spend some time on site in Marshall (about a 150-mile drive from Kennedy's Minneapolis-based office). He ended up spending two days and one night in town, during which he gathered a wealth of information. His *professional networking* skills came in handy when he took the Marshall newspaper city editor and business reporter (**journalistic source interviews**) to lunch to talk about Schwan's. After lunch, his news colleagues invited him back to the local newsroom, where he was allowed to **search** backfiles of the newspaper. Kennedy's **observation** skills led to his notes about details of the Schwan's campus, the design of the delivery trucks, and even the grave marker for the company's founder. Kennedy was amazed to have had such a difficult time finding the gravesite, considering how prominent the company and family are in the community.

The local pub was the site for more **informal interviews** with citizens who gave Kennedy insights into the company's stature in the community, along with leads for additional interviewees and sources. One key interviewee was a former high official in the company who had retired and moved away. The locals in the pub knew that the official's daughter still lived in town, however, and gave Kennedy her married name so he could call her and get the information about how to reach her father in Florida. Other friendly conversations led to the recollection about how the company founder's funeral had been televised to the local community.

One **journalistic monitoring** source was totally serendipitous. While eating his lunch in his car parked in a supermarket parking lot, Kennedy was scanning the radio dial and happened across a local radio station that was conducting a live interview with a Schwan's spokesman. Kennedy dropped his lunch and started taking notes.

Institutional sources were a major resource. Kennedy contacted numerous city officials and perused important city and county documents for information about the public role the company played in the community. One clerk in the Marshall Chamber of Commerce had a momentary lapse and actually showed Kennedy a promotional map of the city as evidence that Schwan's was secretive. The clerk volunteered that Schwan's had specifically asked to be kept off the map in order to maintain its anonymity. Trade publications in the food industry, including one titled *Prepared Foods Magazine*, yielded valuable information about the relative standing of the Schwan's empire within the food industry. It helped that the editor of that trade publication was also Kennedy's former college roommate (another example of professional networking with **institutional sources**). The company's internal newsletter, *Schwan's News*, proved an invaluable resource for piecing together the history and holdings of the firm. Kennedy didn't get this in-house publication from the company, however. He found back issues in a file kept by the local *public library*.

The Marshall-Lyon County Library proved to be a mother lode for Kennedy's information-mining operation. He says that he has always found local libraries in small towns to be wonderful resources for information that wouldn't turn up in other ways. In this case that also proved true. The library staff maintained a file of materials about Schwan's, from many different sources and across many years, as part of the library's mission to chronicle the most important business in town. In this library file, Kennedy found private financial information about the company, backfiles of *Schwan's News*, news clippings, photographs (including one of the company founder shaking hands with President Ronald Reagan), information about the location of Schwan's plants around the country, and more. In addition, one librarian proved to be a particularly valuable source by giving him leads to people he should interview and ideas for questions to ask them.

Interviews with many sources in Marshall rounded out Kennedy's stay in the community. City and county officials, business professionals, local citizens, industry insiders, financial analysts, and Schwan's competitors filled in many blanks after Kennedy returned to his own newsroom.

Back in Minneapolis, the **institutional** sources were yielding their material. Library staff uncovered bits and pieces of information that began to paint a financial picture of the company. Using reliable business-information reference tools and databases, the librarians discovered material that ended up being reflected in the box and map that accompanied the story, as well as facts and figures that were interspersed throughout the narrative itself.

Kennedy recalls that the box was one of the most difficult parts of the story to get together. The team effort included staff members who were assigned to call every city where a plant supposedly was located to confirm the plant was still there, librarians who were gathering scattered financial data from many sources, graphic designers who helped pin down and confirm specific information for the map, and the newspaper's state capitol bureau chief. Kennedy knew that the late company founder had a reputation for supporting conservative political causes and candidates. Kennedy asked his colleague, the bureau chief, to check the election campaign finance records in St. Paul to determine whether Marvin Schwan had given money to Minnesota politicians and candidates. His name turned up in the records among contributors to an unsuccessful conservative candidate for governor. Additional information about Schwan's political activism came from the pre-1986 *Star Tribune* clips and from the backfiles of the Marshall newspaper.

The **selection and synthesis** processes included coordinating all of the information gathered by the various team members who helped work on the story. In addition, much background information never made it into story, despite the usefulness of that material in guiding the more formal aspects of the information search. Kennedy tried to weave his rich information base into an engaging narrative, rather than cramming loads of information into a dry recitation of the company's history and standing. The time he spent in Marshall, observing the community and talking to local residents, is reflected throughout the story, with telling details and anecdotes that bring the tale alive. The story flows well; every paragraph moves the story forward and provides the reader with additional information that is presented with a confident tone. There are no information holes around which the reporter is forced to write.

The resolution of the salmonella crisis came a few months after the Schwan's profile story appeared in the newspaper. Investigators confirmed that the salmonella bacteria had come from an independent contractor's tanker truck that delivered ice cream mix to the Schwan's plant. That truck had earlier carried raw eggs, a common source of salmonella bacteria, and the hauler had not properly sanitized the truck before taking on the ice-cream-mix cargo. Schwan's had already announced that it would purchase its own fleet of delivery trucks and manage all cargo tasks itself to avoid a similar quality control lapse in the future.

A final settlement with more than 13,000 people was announced a year later. Those who said they developed food poisoning because of the tainted ice cream received payments ranging between $80 and $75,000. Payment amounts depended on the severity of the victims' illnesses. Meanwhile, Schwan's settled back into its quiet ways, having handled the crisis in textbook fashion and having reassured customers that its products were wholesome and safe.

Had the Schwan's story broken today rather than in 1994, Kennedy's information strategy would have looked a bit different. The overall context and message analysis steps might not have changed much. But the convenience with which much of the information was gathered, as well as the type of information that was available, might have actually altered the final message if conducted today. In addition, the strategic communications messages produced for Schwan's (advertising messages, catalogs, news releases, consumer alerts and updates, and other persuasive messages) can also benefit from many of the sources now available.

Listservs and newsgroups are some of the *informal sources* now widely available to communicators. *Monitoring* epinions.com or Google Groups, for example, would be a good starting point for finding out what customers are saying about Schwan's. Postings on newsgroups as varied as rec.food.cooking, alt.newlywed, and kc.chat would give a reporter an overall idea about what people think of the quality of Schwan's food, the prices, the route drivers, the delivery process, similar delivery services people use (competitors) and, perhaps, the need for a second freezer. The USDA's FoodSafe listserv is an interactive discussion group that might yield some *informal interview sources* to speak with about food safety issues.

Additionally, e-mail makes it easy to tap into personal and professional networks. Communicators can use their online address books, or tools such as Yahoo! People Search, to locate friends and family who may have experience with Schwan's.

Public- and private-sector institutional sources are making more and more information available on the Web. Public-sector organizations such as the FDA (fda.gov) and the Minnesota Department of Health (health.state.mn.us) have vast Web sites containing a wealth of information resources. The foodsafety.gov site includes timely News & Safety Alerts, as well as links to state and federal government agencies which provide research in this topic area.

Perhaps the most important change in private-sector information availability for this case study is that Schwan's itself now has a corporate Web site (schwansinc.com) where communicators can find the company's history, how many employees work for the company, what types of industries it is involved in, which consumer brands it owns (and links to each brand's Web site), where its plants are located, what types of charitable giving the company is doing, a list of recent press releases, and so on. It is important to note that this change in information availability about Schwan's is not due entirely to technological developments, but also indicates a change in Schwan's highly secretive corporate culture. In addition to its corporate Web site, Schwan's customers can now order directly from Schwan's consumer Web site (schwans.com)—meaning that a list of all of the products sold on the Schwan's trucks is now available online. A communicator also could place an online order as a form of *personal observation* about how the service works, and how the food tastes. This would also be an opportunity to talk to the route driver who delivers the food about what it is like to work for Schwan's.

Additionally, industry trade associations are a rich online information resource. The foodsupplier.com Web site features links to a number of food industry trade organizations, including the American Frozen Food Institute, American School Food Service Association, and the National Frozen Food Association. These sites include useful statistics, such as the size of the U.S. frozen food industry.

Trade show information is also available online, such as the dates of the Food Marketing Institute's annual convention. Attending such a trade show would be a good way for communicators to familiarize themselves with a company's products and those of competitors, talk with company sales people and executives staffing the company booth, and speak to industry trade journalists who attend the show.

Industry trade publications also include useful industry background information on their Web sites. *Refrigerated & Frozen Food* magazine, for example, lists the annual sales of each of the top ten pizza brands in the U.S., including Schwan's-owned Red Baron, Freschetta, and Tony's brands (compiled from Information Resources Inc., and InfoScan data).

Although the *LexisNexis* database existed in 1994, many communicators now have access to this resource right at their desktops. Additionally, *LexisNexis* now includes full-text news stories from a wider range of *journalistic sources* as smaller publications increasingly make their way online.

Finally, an online search of academic institutions would turn up expert interview sources from Minnesota colleges and universities who specialize in either business or food safety disciplines. A broader search might yield a group such as the National Food Safety Educator's Network (EdNet), which is a discussion group for food safety educators working together with government agencies, industry, consumer groups and health organizations to form a network for food safety education. Although academic journal articles specifically about the Schwan's salmonella case would not have been available in time for a breaking news story, articles such as, "How safe is our food? Lessons from an outbreak of salmonellosis," that ran in the *New England Journal of Medicine* on May 16, 1996, would prove useful in a follow-up story should a similar outbreak occur in the future.

The final steps in the information strategy process would be to evaluate and synthesize the information. This is the point where information needs to be double-checked and validated, and documents and statistics need to be evaluated. If two similar bits of information were found at safetyalerts.com and foodsafety.gov, for example, the communicator's task would be to check the credibility and motivations (political or otherwise) of the organization that published the information on the Web. When synthesizing and making final decisions about what actually makes it into the message, it is important to revisit the message analysis phase and the purpose of the piece you are writing. In this particular news story, for example, the emphasis is on the company itself—finding out as much as possible about Schwan's and setting the breaking news events in context for readers. Although related, the primary emphasis of this story is *not* on salmonella, the symptoms, how it occurs, etc. Knowing this may help you further pare down information.

One major advantage to having such a wealth of information at your fingertips as a communicator is the amount of time it saves you. However, the downside of this information availability is that communicators often forget to look beyond the Internet when gathering information for a message. This case study is a clear example of the rich detail that would have been lost in writing this news story today had Kennedy been satisfied with *only* using online tools instead of making a trip to Marshall. The interviews with employees at the local pub, the radio interview Kennedy caught while eating his lunch, the town map, internal newsletters and other information provided by the public library, contact information for a former company executive, and observations about the Schwan's campus, Marshall, MN, and Marvin Schwan, all would have been missing had the reporter not taken the time to travel to Marshall. And even though interviews with the *Marshall Independent* editors could have taken place by phone or e-mail, it is likely that the effort of a personal visit yielded more insights and strengthened these professional network relationships more than a quick call or message would have.

The story as it is written demonstrates a balance of information and expression. If Kennedy were writing it today and relied solely on online sources and materials found using the Internet, the balance of information and expression would have shifted to a largely informational piece. Therefore, it is important to remember that the Internet is a rich resource, but one best used in collaboration with other sources.

The material that follows shows the full text of the original news story published in 1994, the information source that contributed to each specific paragraph in the narrative, some of the access points into that information, and additional access points that would be possible today. In many cases, there is more than one way a communicator could have found the information that appears in the story. The access strategy that Kennedy used is in bold, with other alternative access points listed where appropriate.

For strategic communications professionals, pay attention to the details in the story and the information strategies and sources that led to those details. Chapter 1 introduced the notion that the information strategy in this book applies to any type of message and any topic. The *use* that is made of that information differs, depending on the type and purpose of the message, but the information strategy is the same. Therefore, the materials outlined in this case example could easily inform the production of a public relations campaign for Schwan's in the aftermath of this type of crisis, a new advertising campaign focused on the company's dedication to food safety and purity or focused on the long and rich history of the company in its home state, or a wide variety of other sorts of persuasive messages. In other words, any communications professional might use these information strategies to locate the materials they need for their messages. What they do with the information varies, but their process is the same.

The details of the information strategy process used in this news story come from interviews with Minneapolis *Star Tribune* reporter Tony Kennedy and news librarian Sylvia Frisch.

THE NEWS STORY	THE INFORMATION SOURCES	SOME ACCESS POINTS INTO THE INFORMATION (SOURCES USED BY KENNEDY AND TEAM ARE IN BOLD)	INFORMATION FROM ACCESS POINTS NOT WIDELY AVAILABLE IN 1994
Driving a rocky road Schwan's is handling salmonella crisis in its own way—quietly by TONY KENNEDY Staff Writer MARSHALL, MINN. In the beginning, there were just chocolate and vanilla.			
Those two ice cream flavors were all Marvin Schwan sold to area farm families when he founded his home delivery service in 1952 with a truck he bought for $100. He refrigerated the vehicle with dry ice and pounded out a route. It wasn't an easy ride; the truck got 22 flat tires or blowouts in that first year.	*Schwan's News*; news articles written at the time of Marvin Schwan's death	**Files kept at the Marshall-Lyon County public library; back files of the *Marshall Independent* local newspaper; *Star Tribune* backfiles**	Slightly different details are highlighted in the version on Schwan's corporate Web site. The "truck" is described as a Dodge panel van, and a reason is given for starting the route. The government had frozen the price of milk, and Schwan was trying to keep his family's dairy operating.
Somewhere along the line, the company lost that simplicity.	Observation	**Reporter on-site visit**	Searching: truck picture on Schwans.com Web site
Though the cream-colored, swan-emblazoned route trucks still deliver ice cream door-to-door, the company that has been vexed this month by a salmonella outbreak also makes robots, dominates the school lunch pizza scene, counts the U.S. Navy as a customer and guards its own identity closer than the Kremlin did during the Cold War.	*Schwan's News*; articles in the business trade press	**Marshall-Lyon County public library file; *LexisNexis* database, Dun & Bradstreet database, Trinet America database searches**	Trade association and trade publication Web sites

Story text	Information needed	Sources	Additional sources
Faced with a potential crisis of consumer confidence from an illness that has reached at least 35 states, the company has come out of its shell to communicate forthrightly with the public. But a visit to Marshall still finds Schwan's shrouded in secrecy. While the $1.8 billion firm enjoys a sterling reputation in the food industry for high quality, it clings to privacy so intensely that its code of silence has rubbed off on the adoring citizens of Marshall.	Daily breaking news accounts of the illness	**Newsroom colleagues; paper's own stories, wire service stories**	
	Prepared Foods Magazine's list of largest public and private food companies	**Interview with editor of *Prepared Foods Magazine*;** directory of industry trade publications, such as *Ulrich's*, which would list this magazine, trade association member interviews	Trade association and trade publication Web sites
	Interviews	**Observation and interviews on site**	
"People don't speak out of line about the company, or are afraid to talk, because everyone wants to respect [its] wishes," said Tracy Veglahn, executive vice president of the Marshall Area Chamber of Commerce.	Interviews	**Chamber of Commerce office in Marshall**	
The company is so insular that it asked local artist Pam Bernard not to include Schwan's in her impressionistic map of Marshall. Ridiculously, her painting includes a business as small as Lee's Tae Kwan Do but is void of any representation of the state's second-largest private company. "They told me they like their privacy," she said.	A copy of the map	**A clerk in the Chamber of Commerce office**	
	Interview	**The map included the name of the artist, who still lived in town**	
Even when Schwan's contributes money to civic projects, it prefers anonymity, said Mike Johnson, city administrator. The company recently built a new clubhouse for the Marshall Country Club, but "they didn't seek attention for it," he said.	Interview	**City administrator's office;** city and county records for licenses, building permits, tax rolls; interviews with civic project leaders	Some charitable giving information is available on the Schwan's corporate site.

(continued)

THE NEWS STORY	THE INFORMATION SOURCES	SOME ACCESS POINTS INTO THE INFORMATION (SOURCES USED BY KENNEDY AND TEAM ARE IN BOLD)	INFORMATION FROM ACCESS POINTS NOT WIDELY AVAILABLE IN 1994
Community anchor Scott Sievers, a reporter and editor at the *Marshall Independent*, said townspeople select their words about the company as if a "Schwan's police" force were listening in. By claiming to have 872 employees—a figure that seems low—Schwan's is Marshall's largest employer. Sievers said there is no worse fear in the town of 12,000 than that something bad will happen to Schwan's.	Interview Statements made by the company Interview	Professional networking News conferences; news releases; interviews with company officials Networking	According to Schwan's corporate Web site, the company has more than 20,000 employees. The Marshall Chamber of Commerce site lists 2,500 employees—likely the number who work in Marshall itself.
The company, after all, is what has anchored Marshall to the prairie in southwestern Minnesota, with the help from employers such as Southwest State University, Heartland Food Co., and Minnesota Corn Processors.	Regional business background information	Beat reporter's knowledge; local news stories; Chamber of Commerce	
"The growth of that company [Schwan's] has paralleled the growth of Marshall," said Mayor Bob Byrnes, who noted that his town is one of the few in southwestern Minnesota experiencing economic growth.	Interview	Marshall Mayor's office; census and economic data showing growth in various parts of the state	
So it must be a nightmare for all of Marshall to think that a mother and father anywhere in the United States would think twice about feeding Schwan's ice cream to their children. Though ice cream has been overshadowed by pizza as the biggest profit center at Schwan's, the frozen dessert is the company's signature product. Any reluctance to buy it would chill truck sales of other Schwan's products—from bagel dogs to chimichangas.	Private and published financial data and business analyses	Marshall-Lyon County public library file; trade publication analysis of Schwan's; food broker interviews; Trinet America database; Dun & Bradstreet database	The Schwan's corporate site now lists all of its major products and brands.

(continued)

Could the crisis eventually be cause for layoffs in the 18 yellow-and-brown Schwan's buildings that dot Marshall?	Observation	**On-site visit**
Not a chance, judging from the supreme confidence voiced by the company's supporters and from a well-executed response to the problem.	Observation	**News releases; company statements**
"It's a dagger in their side," said Tino Leitteiri, who sold his frozen calzone business in Young America, Minn., to Schwan's. "But it's a great company. They won't get hurt. I'm sure they are going to take extra measures."	Interview	**Beat reporter's familiarity with previous source, who was also a Schwan's competitor;** news stories at the time of the sale
Said Byrnes: "There's concern, but there is not fear. There's a sense of faith that the management of Schwan's will bring it through this situation."	Interview	**Marshall Mayor's office**

Handling crises

Tom Caron, a former lieutenant of the late Marvin Schwan who recently retired from the company, said the probability is close to zero that the salmonella episode will affect long-term growth at Schwan's.	Interview	**Beat reporter's previous experience with a source;** interviews with local residents who might point a reporter to Caron
"Schwan's has gone through a series of disasters and it has been very resilient," Caron said. In 1974, for instance, Schwan's managed to increase sales even though fire destroyed the company's only manufacturing site in Marshall. Production facilities were rebuilt in the city's industrial park, and the original plant location a block off the town's main street—lined only by sidewalks, not fences—was converted to a headquarters.	Observation	**On-site visit**

295

THE NEWS STORY	THE INFORMATION SOURCES	SOME ACCESS POINTS INTO THE INFORMATION (SOURCES USED BY KENNEDY AND TEAM ARE IN BOLD)	INFORMATION FROM ACCESS POINTS NOT WIDELY AVAILABLE IN 1994
The company also was hit by a tampering incident in 1987, when children in Tennessee put razor blades in a pizza product.	Previous news stories	**Star Tribune backfiles; Marshall Independent backfiles**	LexisNexis
Caron said Schwan's response to the salmonella outbreak will resemble Johnson & Johnson's textbook handling of the deadly tampering with Tylenol. In the 1982 Tylenol case, Johnson & Johnson recalled 31 million bottles of the product and adopted tamper-proof safety seal technology to reintroduce it successfully.	Previous news stories; business publication reports	**Star Tribune print backfiles; database search in LexisNexis and Dialog for articles in business publications and other newspapers**	Johnson & Johnson Web site
No deaths have been linked to Schwan's ice cream in the salmonella case, though several thousand probable cases of the illness have been found.	Breaking news stories	**Star Tribune reporting; wire service stories**	
"When it [the ice cream] comes back, the product will be very safe and very good," Caron said. "At the end of the game you have to have more public confidence than you had in the beginning."			
On Oct. 7, Schwan's shut down its Marshall ice cream plant in cooperation with regulators. Schwan's then recalled all of its packaged ice cream and has been urging any customers who show symptoms of salmonella to be tested at the company's expense.	News stories / Schwan's	**Star Tribune and wire service stories** / **News releases, news conferences**	If such an incident occurred today, all of the recall information would no doubt be available on the Schwan's Web site.
On Thursday, U.S. Food and Drug Administration Commissioner David Kessler said that a contractor's tanker truck may have carried salmonella bacteria into Schwan's	News stories	**Star Tribune and wire service stories;** electronic and print services that distribute news releases and verbatim accounts of executive	FDA Web site

(continued)

Story	Source	Search strategy	Notes
plant. Within hours of Kessler's news conference, Schwan's announced that it would switch to a dedicated fleet of sealed tankers for all future shipments of ice cream ingredients. The company also said it will re-pasteurize every future shipment of the pasteurized ingredients and test the re-pasteurized ice cream mix for salmonella bacteria before using it.	Schwan's	branch actions and announcements; FDA bulletin board service	News releases would be posted on Schwan's Web site.
Based on comments made last week by Schwan's spokesman David Jennings, the assertiveness may be paying off.		**News releases, news conferences**	Search Schwan's corporate Web site "Press Room" for spokesperson contact info.
In a live radio interview in Marshall, Jennings said the company has received "overwhelmingly positive customer feedback."	Local radio station	**Overhearing the radio interview during the on-site visit to Marshall; request to radio station for tape or transcript interview; request to Schwan's for transcript**	Monitoring newsgroups for customer feedback, potential interview sources
"Their customers do think they are wonderful," said a source who has seen research reports on Schwan's. "I mean, you read that stuff and you think, 'I wish I owned that business.'"	Interview	**Reporter's previous experience with a food broker as a source**	
But interested investors shouldn't hold their breath for a public stock sale. According to an October 1993 report by Dun & Bradstreet, 100 percent of the capital stock is owned by the estate of Marvin Schwan and Schwan family members. Marvin's older brother, Alfred, is now president of the firm, and Marvin's wishes were for the company to stay in private hands, Caron said.	Publisher of business reference tools that list annual sales, number of employees, division names and functions, and other financial information for all American firms with net worth of more than $500,000	**News library search of D & B database through Dialog; printed reference tools published by D & B**	According to a October 27, 1999, article in the Minneapolis *Star Tribune* online archives, Lenny Pippin is now the president and CEO, while Schwan remains as chairman.

Marvin's legacy

THE NEWS STORY	THE INFORMATION SOURCES	SOME ACCESS POINTS INTO THE INFORMATION (SOURCES USED BY KENNEDY AND TEAM ARE IN BOLD)	INFORMATION FROM ACCESS POINTS NOT WIDELY AVAILABLE IN 1994
It was the enigmatic Marvin Schwan, together with longtime insiders Caron, sales veteran Gordy Molitor, and financial officers Don Miller and Adrian (A.J.) Anderson, who fostered the company's cult of privacy. Schwan led his charges with merchandise incentives and personalized, positive reinforcement.	Interview with Jim Fink, who had been retired for a number of years and was more willing to talk than when he worked for the company; he lived out of state and was no longer closely associated with Schwan's	**Reporter's previous experience with the source;** interviews with local employees or former employees who would lead reporter to Fink; articles from back copies of *Schwan's News*	
"There were lots of sales-awards banquets, and everyone looked forward to sitting at the head table with Marvin," said Jim Fink, a former executive of the company. "It caused people to go the extra mile. They did it for Marvin."			Internet search for industry trade shows, where communicators could talk to company sales people on the show floor
Schwan's fatal heart attack at age 64 rocked Marshall in May 1993, prompting widespread rumors that the company would be sold and possibly moved. Alfred Schwan responded with a newspaper ad insisting that the company was not for sale.	Interviews with local residents	**Informal discussions with residents, current and former employees; review of** *Marshall Independent* **clip files**	The corporate Web site would likely post information denying the rumors.
Marvin Schwan's invitation-only funeral was televised to a large local audience. His black gravestone at Marshall Cemetery, inscribed in the familiar company script, includes this biblical quote from Matthew: "Well done, thou good and faithful servant."	Reporter observation	**On-site visit to local cemetery**	
He was a religious man who contributed to conservative political causes, including the 1991 gubernatorial campaign of Jon	Minnesota state campaign finance records	**News stories; Minnesota State Ethical Practices Board campaign finance records**	Political contribution records are now available online for every state.

(continued)

Story text	Source	Documentation
Grunseth. In 1982, he met and spoke with President Ronald Reagan.	Photograph of Schwan and Reagan shaking hands	**Marshall-Lyon County public library file; news stories**
"In many respects, Marvin was a very, very unusual individual," said Fink, who reported directly to the founder while heading Syncom, a maker of computer disks in Mitchell, S.D., that Schwan's later sold. "A lot of it [the company] operated on the mystique of Marvin Schwan."	Interview	**Reporter's previous experience with the source**
City Assessor Cal Barnett said Schwan saw to it that the company didn't overpower the community. For instance, when a local farm co-operative proposed an industrial expansion that would result in higher public utility rates, Schwan's didn't try to block it. "Certainly Marvin was the heart of the company," Barnett said. "He gave it a tremendous sense of direction."	Interview	**City Assessor's Office;** news accounts of the proposed expansion; public expansion; public utility rate increase request records
It is a testament to Schwan's stealth that his company is five times the size of International Dairy Queen Inc., of Bloomington, but infinitely more obscure.	*Prepared Foods Magazine*'s list of public and private food companies	**Beat reporter's familiarity with state businesses; magazine list**
Strong and diverse Marvin Schwan steered the company into pizza in 1966, first with route sales and later in supermarkets. According to Information Resources Inc., Schwan's controlled 24 percent of the $1.5 billion frozen pizza business in supermarkets for the year ended Aug. 14. Its two main in-store brands are Tony's and Red Baron.	Schwan's News Business information research company	**Marshall-Lyon County public library file** **Reporter phone call to source at IRI;** full-text IRI database available through Dialog or *LexisNexis*

Additional online sources:

- The Marshall Chamber of Commerce Web site heralds Schwan's participation in developing affordable housing for the community.
- According to Schwan's corporate Web site, the company has operations in MN, KS, KY, TX, GA, CA, and UT, as well as in Europe.
- Trade association and trade publication Web sites

THE NEWS STORY	THE INFORMATION SOURCES	SOME ACCESS POINTS INTO THE INFORMATION (SOURCES USED BY KENNEDY AND TEAM ARE IN BOLD)	INFORMATION FROM ACCESS POINTS NOT WIDELY AVAILABLE IN 1994
Forbes magazine reported in 1989 that Marvin Schwan also cornered a large percentage of the school lunch frozen pizza market, then estimated at $500 million in annual revenues. He did it, Forbes said, by offering schools discounts in exchange for their government cheese allotments. He later bought competitors Sabatosso Foods and Better Baked Pizza, pushing the company's market share to a near lock of 85 percent.	*Forbes*	**News library search for article about Schwan's in *LexisNexis* and Dialog databases**	A Google search on "frozen pizza" and "schools" yields a link to the Web site of the American Frozen Food Institute, which inducted Marvin Schwan into its Frozen Food Hall of Fame in 2002. The AFFI Web site includes a biography of Schwan that outlines his successful move into the frozen pizza market.
Yet another leg of the pizza business is in convenience stores and rural grocery markets such as Hy-Vee stores, where Schwan's sells slices under the Moose Bros. and Little Charlie brands.	Business analyses of frozen pizza industry Observation of brands sold in rural stores *Schwan's News*; news accounts	**News library searches in Trinet America database, business reference tools** **Reporter's on-site visits to grocery stores** **Marshall-Lyon County public library file; news stories from Marshall and Red Wing papers;** *Star Tribune* **stories**	Hy-vee.com Web site lists specials and store products.
Schwan's investment in robotics came in 1991 with the acquisition of the Robot Aided Manufacturing in Red Wing, Minn. Among the inventions to come out of the center were four robots that palletize food at the Tony's Pizza Service plant in Salina, Kan., also owned by Schwan's. "They are kind of like the 3M of the food industry, they are so diversified," said a Minnesota food industry source who asked not to be identified.	*Schwan's News* Interview	**Marshall-Lyon County public library file** **Reporter's previous experience with a food broker as a source;** interviews with industry analysts or financial analysts	A Google search on "Robot Aided Manufacturing" indicates that the robot division has changed its name to Schwan's Technology Group and has developed a fuel injection system that allows Schwan's trucks to operate on propane fuel. The Schwan's corporate site now lists its different business units and industry segments.

But unlike 3M, Schwan's grew in relative obscurity—until this month.

"When you lose your anonymity, all of a sudden you are in the spotlight," said Caron. "There are more negatives than positives that come from the spotlight."

Source: Reprinted with permission from the *Star Tribune*, Sunday, October 23, 1994, 1A.

A quiet giant

Schwan's Food Enterprises is a private food company of national proportions that intentionally maintains a very low profile. Its span is immense; it has a direct sales force of delivery route drivers who knock on kitchen doors in every state except Alaska and Hawaii.

Schwan's *Delicious* Fine Foods

Schwan's manufacturing and distribution sites

also:
- Leyland, England
  Pizza plant
- Neepawa, Manitoba
  Ice cream plant

A Schwan's snapshot:

Headquarters: Marshall, Minn.

Founded: 1952 by the late Marvin Maynard Schwan

Employees: Total, 7,500
Minnesota, 1,500

Estimated annual sales: $1.8 billion

Estimated ice cream sales: $35 million

Grocery store frozen pizza sales: $375 million

Chairman, chief executive: Alfred Schwan

Delivery trucks in 48 states: 2,300

In Marshall: 18 buildings paying $490,000 in net property tax, about 3 percent of the Lyon County net property tax base.
- Home offices; leasing headquarters
- Beverage plant
- Training center
- Airport hangar
- Industrial campus, including ice cream plant, cold storage warehouse, ice cream pail plant, specialty foods plant, convenience foods plant, food technology center, delivery route depot, wastewater pre-treatment plant.

Products sold under these brands:

Ice cream: Schwan's

Pizza: Tony's, Red Baron, Sabatasso, Better Baked, Moose Bros., Hot Stuff, Little Charlies

Others:
Florence pasta
Tino's panzerotti
Cafe' Mexico frozen ethnic foods
Minh egg rolls
Good-N-Fast sandwiches
Vita-Sun frozen juice drink concentrates
Stirling soups

Financial services:
Lyon Financial Services
Business Credit Leasing

Source: Dun & Bradstreet, private research, Schwan's News, Trinet America database, City of Marshall, Lyon County, Marshall-Lyon County Library, Information Resources Inc.

Star Tribune Graphic

Reprinted with the permission of the *Star Tribune*.

GENERAL INDEX

A Topical Tools Index, which arranges information resources by subject disciplines and usage categories, follows this general index. The general index includes proper names, titles, and subjects.

TOPICAL TOOLS INDEX

Communicators sometimes need to gather information within and across disciplines, or from specific types of tools. To address that need, sources are arranged here according to broad subject areas or by usage categories. Of course, there are hundreds of sources that are useful in each of these categories. Only those sources covered in this text are included here.